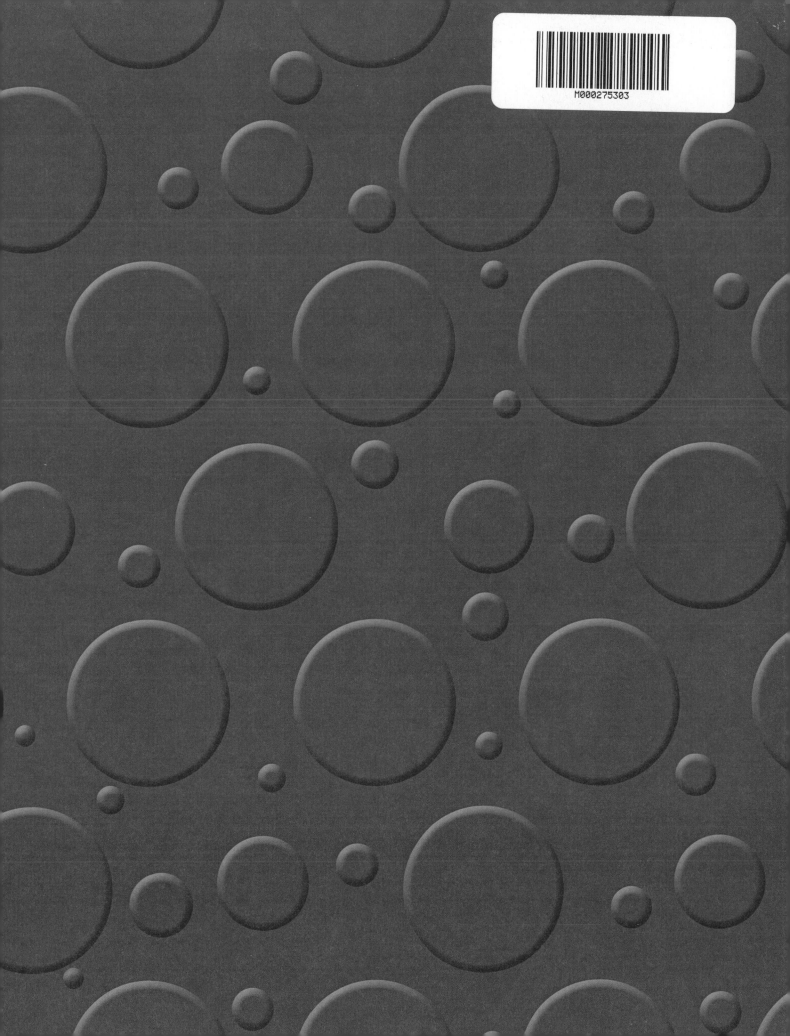

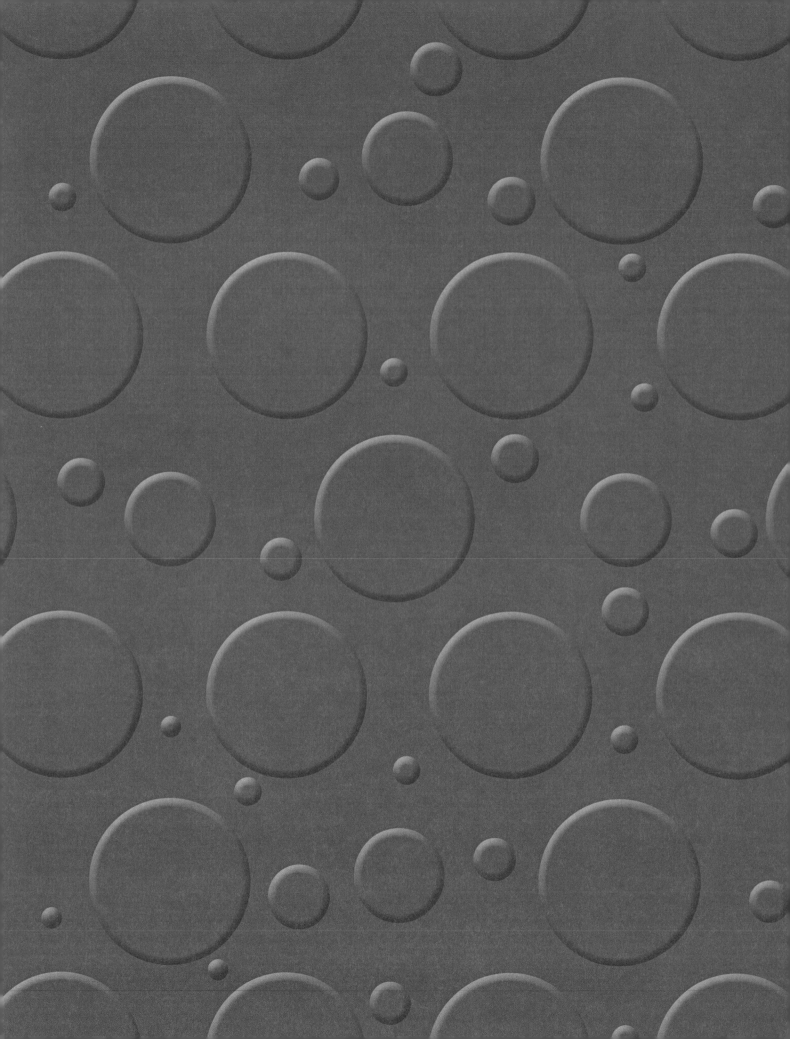

Harcourt
Health
and
Fitness

SCHOOL PUBLISHERS

Orlando • Austin • New York • San Diego • Toronto • London

Visit *The Learning Site!*
www.harcourtschool.com

CONSULTING AUTHORS

Lisa Bunting, M.Ed.
Physical Education Teacher
Katy Independent School District
Houston, Texas

Thomas M. Fleming, Ph.D.
Health and Physical Education
  Consultant
Austin, Texas

Charlie Gibbons, Ed.D.
Director, Youth and School Age
  Programs
Maxwell Air Force Base, Alabama
Former Adjunct Professor,
  Alabama State University
Health, Physical Education and
  Dance Department
Montgomery, Alabama

Jan Marie Ozias, Ph.D., R.N.
Director, Texas Diabetes Council;
  and Consultant, School Health
  Programs
Austin, Texas

Carl Anthony Stockton, Ph.D.
Dean, School of Education
The University of Texas at
  Brownsville and Texas
  Southmost College
Brownsville, Texas
Former Department Chair and
  Professor of Health Education
Department of Health and
  Applied Human Sciences
The University of North Carolina
  at Wilmington
Wilmington, North Carolina

Printed in the United States of America

ISBN 13: 978-0-15-337530-9
ISBN 10: 0-15-337530-2
12 13 14 15 0607 20 19
4500766120

Chapters

Contents

Reading in Health Handbook 400

Health and Safety Handbook 412

Glossary 432

Index 446

Why should you learn about health?

You can do many things to help yourself stay healthy and fit. Just as importantly, you can avoid doing things that will harm you. If you know ways to stay safe and healthy and do these things, you can help yourself have good health throughout your life.

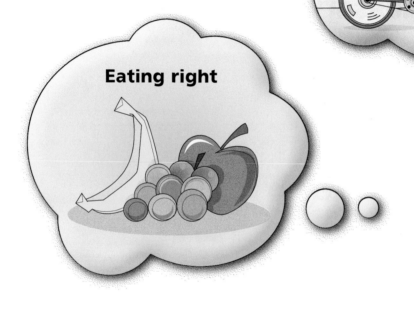

Staying active

Eating right

Getting enough rest

Keeping clean

Avoiding alcohol, tobacco, and other drugs

Having good relationships with family and friends

Dealing with emotions in positive ways

xi

Why should you learn about life skills?

Being healthy and fit doesn't come from just knowing facts. You also have to think about these facts and know how to use them every day.

These are some important life skills for you to have:

Making Responsible Decisions

Deciding the most responsible thing to do to avoid taking risks

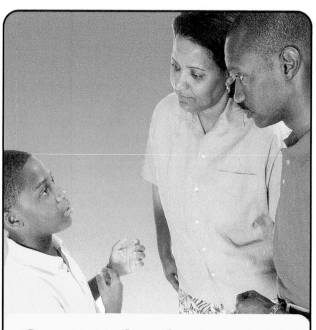

Communicating

Sharing ideas, needs, and feelings with others

Managing Stress

Finding ways to avoid and relieve negative feelings and emotions

Refusing
Saying *no* to doing things that are risky and dangerous

Resolving Conflicts
Finding solutions to problems in ways that let both sides win

Setting Goals
Deciding on specific ways to make improvements to your health and fitness

Wherever you see ![LIFE SKILLS] in this book, you can learn more about using life skills.

Building Good Character

Why should you learn about good character?

Having good character is also an important part of having good health. When you have good character, you have good relationships with others and can make responsible decisions about your health and fitness.

These are some important character traits:

Caring

Showing kindness and concern for friends, family, and others

Citizenship

Having pride in your school and community and obeying rules and laws

Fairness

Treating others equally, playing by the rules, and being a good sport

Respect

Showing consideration for yourself and others

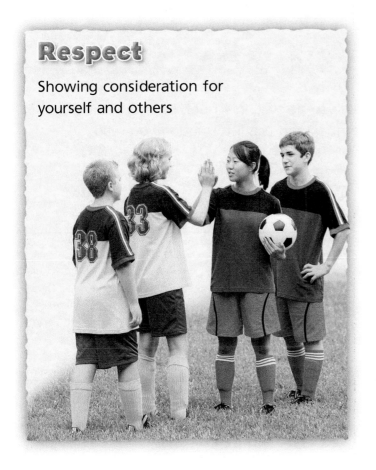

Responsibility

Doing what you are supposed to do, practicing self-control, and completing tasks

Trustworthiness

Being honest, dependable, and loyal

Wherever you see ![Building Good Character] in this book, you can learn more about building good character.

What are ways to be a successful reader?

Students need good reading skills to do well in school. Here are some tips to help you understand, remember, and use information you read.

Reading Tip

These sections can help you know what to look for as you read.

Reading Tip

Vocabulary words are listed at the beginning of the lesson so you can preview them. They are also highlighted and defined when they are first used.

LESSON 4

Your Eyes and Ears

Lesson Focus
Vision and hearing are important senses that need to be protected.

Why Learn This?
You can use what you learn to take good care of your eyes and ears.

Vocabulary
nearsighted
farsighted
conjunctivitis
sty
decibels

Common Eye Problems

You learn a lot about your world through your eyes. Although you could think of your eyes as tiny cameras, they really don't take pictures. Instead, they send electrical signals to your brain. The brain translates these signals into messages that it recognizes as pictures.

How is the light that enters your eye changed to electrical signals? The diagram below shows the path that light takes through the eye. As you read the labels, use your finger to trace the path of light.

You can see in the diagram that people with normal vision produce sharply focused images on the retina, but not everyone has normal vision. In a person who is **nearsighted**, the image does not focus on the retina

The human eye can see 10 million different colors. ▼

1. Light travels through the *cornea*, the clear covering of the eye.

2. Light enters the eye through an opening in the iris called the *pupil*.

3. The *iris*, the colored part of your eye, opens and closes to let in greater or smaller amounts of light.

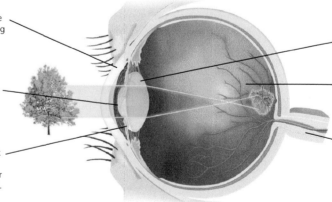

60

xvi

Check your understanding by answering these questions at the end of each section. These questions also help you practice reading skills. You will see six reading focus skills:

► Compare and Contrast

► Draw Conclusions

► Identify Cause and Effect

► Identify Main Idea and Details

► Sequence

► Summarize

Wherever you see  in this book, you can learn more about using reading skills.

Reading Tip

Use this section to summarize what you have read, review vocabulary and concepts, and practice writing skills.

Landfills may be transformed into other useful structures. If you have ever flown into John F. Kennedy Airport in New York City, your plane landed on a sealed landfill.

Sometimes trash is turned into electricity. The trash is trucked to a building in which a furnace reduces solid wastes by **incineration**, or burning. There the trash is burned to ashes. The ashes take up less than half the volume of the original trash. This saves space in the landfill to which the ashes are hauled.

Burning trash produces heat energy and some harmful gases. Devices called scrubbers remove many of the harmful gases before they reach the air. Some community incinerators have been equipped with machinery that turns the heat energy of burning trash into usable electricity.

SEQUENCE Describe in order the steps required to turn trash into a park.

A Some communities send their trash to energy plants, where the energy from burning wastes is used to produce electricity.

Lesson 3 Summary and Review

1 Summarize with Vocabulary

Use vocabulary and other terms from this lesson to complete the statements.

Many groups and organizations are required to ensure the health of the community. Food inspectors work to ensure _____. Water treatment plants help ensure _____. Solid wastes are managed by _____, or burning, and by the use of _____, or places that have been properly prepared to receive solid waste.

2 Critical Thinking Why might chemicals be added to water before it's sent through pipes to homes and businesses?

3 When installing a septic tank, what should you be careful NOT to do?

4 SEQUENCE Draw and complete this graphic organizer to show the main steps used to treat sewage.

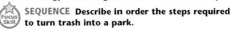

5 Write to Inform—Explanation

Do research to find out how trash is processed in your community. Write a report describing the process. Trace what happens to a piece of trash throughout the entire process.

Throughout **Harcourt Health and Fitness**, you will have many opportunities to learn new ideas and skills that will lead to good health.

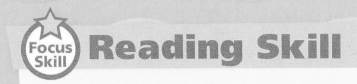
Focus Skill — Reading Skill

SEQUENCE You sequence things when you determine the order of events or steps in a process. Use the Reading in Health Handbook on pages 408–409 and this graphic organizer to help you read the health facts in this chapter.

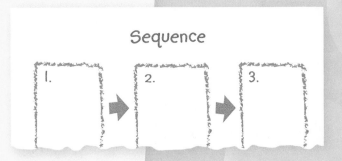

Sequence

1. → 2. → 3.

Health Graph

INTERPRET DATA Like other organs in your body, your brain increases in size and weight as you grow. Between which ages does the brain increase the most in weight? At about what age does the brain reach its adult weight?

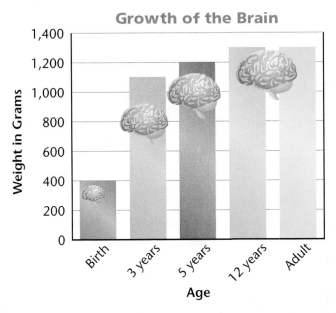

Growth of the Brain

Weight in Grams / Age

1,400
1,200
1,000
800
600
400
200
0

Birth — 3 years — 5 years — 12 years — Adult

Daily Physical Activity

Your body is composed of organ systems that work together to perform your body's functions. One way to keep your body systems healthy is to be active and exercise.

Be Active!
Use the selection, Track 1, **Saucy Salsa**, to get your whole body moving.

A Body Made Up of Systems

Lesson Focus

All body systems work together to keep the body alive and healthy.

Why Learn This?

Caring for each body system keeps all systems working together.

Vocabulary

nervous system
circulatory system
respiratory system
digestive system
excretory system
skeletal system
muscular system

The Nervous System

When you work with a group on a project, each person has a task. The entire group works together to produce a final product. In the same way, each of your body's systems plays a different role, but the systems work together to keep you alive and healthy.

Just as a leader directs a group, the **nervous system** controls the body's activities. Your nervous system is made up of the brain, spinal cord, and nerves. It controls your breathing, heart rate, and movement. Without your nervous system, you wouldn't be able to see, hear, or touch or to feel emotions.

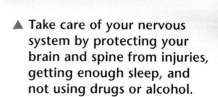
— brain

— nerves

◀ A nerve cell is called a neuron. Signals travel to and from your brain along branching fibers of one neuron to branching fibers of other neurons.

▲ Take care of your nervous system by protecting your brain and spine from injuries, getting enough sleep, and not using drugs or alcohol.

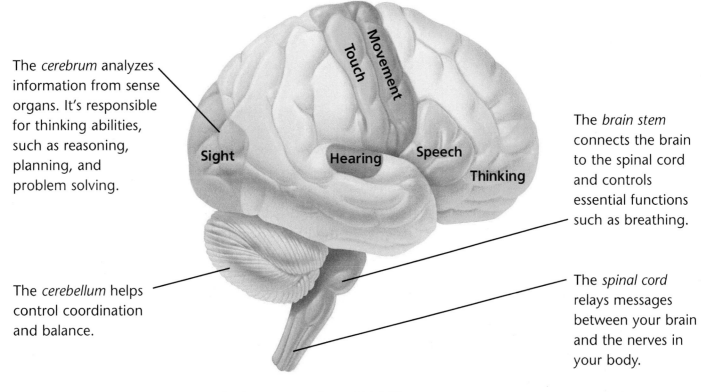

The *cerebrum* analyzes information from sense organs. It's responsible for thinking abilities, such as reasoning, planning, and problem solving.

Touch

Movement

Sight

Hearing

Speech

Thinking

The *brain stem* connects the brain to the spinal cord and controls essential functions such as breathing.

The *cerebellum* helps control coordination and balance.

The *spinal cord* relays messages between your brain and the nerves in your body.

▲ Your brain contains about 100 billion neurons. Different areas of your brain control different activities.

Every minute, your brain receives millions of signals from sensory neurons throughout your body that respond to your internal and external environment. Some of these messages travel to the brain through the spinal cord. Your brain decides how to deal with the information. Most messages from the brain travel through the spinal cord to nerves that control your body's organs.

Not all nerve messages travel to the brain. A reflex is an activity that occurs automatically, without input from the brain. Reflexes protect the body by getting you away from something that might hurt you—like a hot iron—before you have time to think about it.

 SEQUENCE Describe the events that occur when your nervous system responds to a sensory message.

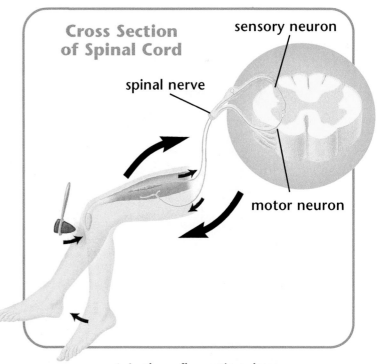

Cross Section of Spinal Cord

sensory neuron

spinal nerve

motor neuron

▲ In the reflex action shown, a sensory neuron carries a message to the spinal cord. Another neuron carries a message back to the muscle. The muscle contracts, causing the lower leg to move.

The Circulatory and Respiratory Systems

Your **circulatory system** consists of your heart, blood, and blood vessels. Three types of vessels carry blood: arteries, veins, and capillaries. Arteries carry blood away from your heart. Most arteries carry blood that is rich in oxygen and nutrients. Most veins carry blood that has picked up waste materials, such as carbon dioxide, back to the heart. Capillaries are tiny, thin-walled blood vessels that connect arteries and veins. It is in the capillaries that oxygen and nutrients in the blood pass to body tissues and that wastes enter the blood.

Take care of your circulatory system by eating healthful food, getting plenty of exercise, and avoiding tobacco use. If your circulatory system doesn't function properly, other body systems don't get the materials they need.

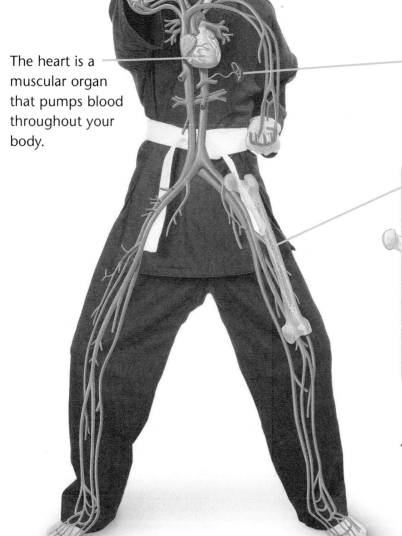

The heart is a muscular organ that pumps blood throughout your body.

The spleen destroys old and damaged red blood cells.

Various types of blood cells are made in the marrow of long bones.

red blood cells

long bone

▲ Blood is made up of red blood cells, which carry oxygen and carbon dioxide; white blood cells; platelets; and a liquid called plasma.

Your **respiratory system** moves oxygen into your body and takes carbon dioxide out of your body. Your circulatory system works with the respiratory system to complete this task. In your lungs are tiny air sacs called alveoli. Oxygen enters the blood through the capillaries that surround the alveoli. Blood vessels then carry the oxygen to all parts of the body. Also in the alveoli, carbon dioxide is removed from the blood. When you exhale, or breathe out, the carbon dioxide leaves your body.

If your respiratory system doesn't function properly, the cells that make up other body systems can't get the oxygen they need. You can take care of your respiratory system by getting plenty of physical activity and by avoiding tobacco use and air pollution.

SUMMARIZE Tell how oxygen enters the body and carbon dioxide leaves the body.

Myth and Fact

Myth: Muscles in your lungs expand and contract to move air in and out.
Fact: The lungs aren't made of muscle tissue. Air movement into and out of the lungs is controlled by the diaphragm, a broad sheet of muscle attached to your lower ribs.

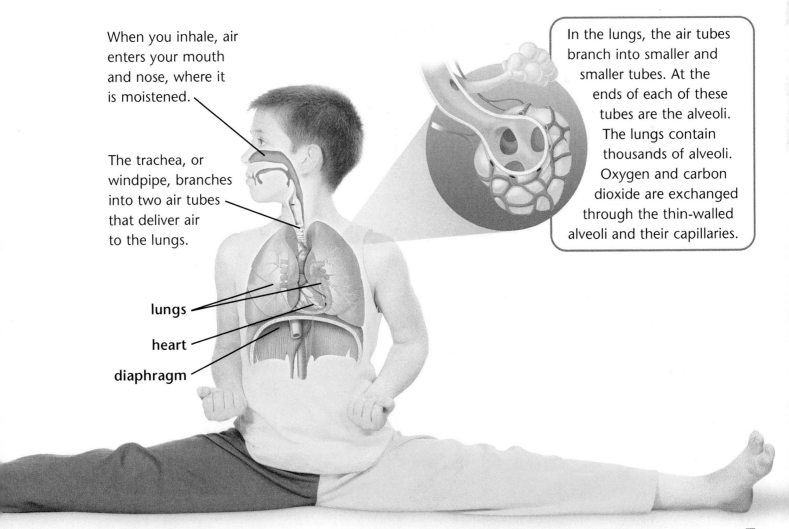

When you inhale, air enters your mouth and nose, where it is moistened.

The trachea, or windpipe, branches into two air tubes that deliver air to the lungs.

lungs

heart

diaphragm

In the lungs, the air tubes branch into smaller and smaller tubes. At the ends of each of these tubes are the alveoli. The lungs contain thousands of alveoli. Oxygen and carbon dioxide are exchanged through the thin-walled alveoli and their capillaries.

The Digestive and Excretory Systems

Just as all your body systems need oxygen, they also need nutrients for energy and for cell functions. Nutrients are found in the food you eat, but the body can't use most nutrients the way they are present in food. The **digestive system** breaks down food so that the body can use the nutrients.

Digestion begins in the mouth. Here, food is chewed and mixed with saliva, which begins digestion of some substances, and swallowed. Food is pushed from the mouth to the stomach by muscles in the esophagus. The stomach is a muscular organ that contracts and mixes food with gastric juice, a mixture of chemicals that starts breaking down protein. Partially digested food moves from the stomach into the small intestine, where most digestion takes place. There, food is churned and mixed with bile, a substance that is produced by the liver and which breaks down fats. Nutrients are absorbed through the walls of the small intestine and pass into the blood.

Blood containing newly digested nutrients flows to the liver, which stores certain vitamins and other substances. The liver breaks down wastes and some chemicals, such as medicines. The pancreas makes digestive juices that break down food. It also makes insulin, a substance that regulates the body's use of sugar.

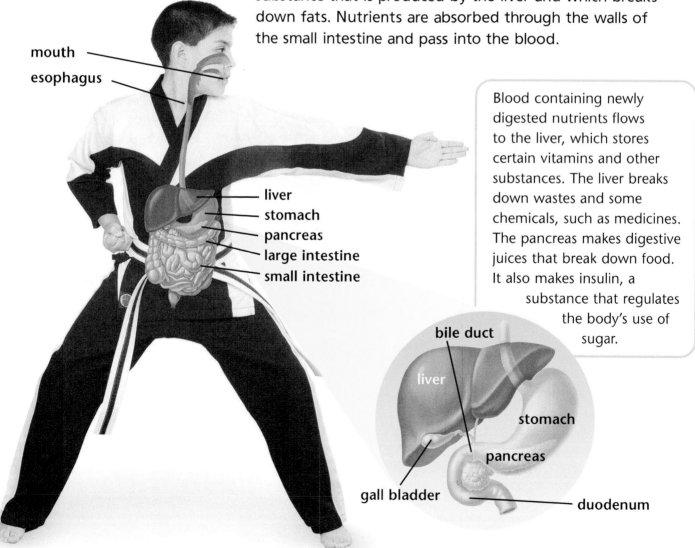

mouth

esophagus

liver

stomach

pancreas

large intestine

small intestine

bile duct

liver

stomach

pancreas

gall bladder

duodenum

Material not absorbed in the small intestine passes into the large intestine, where water and other substances are absorbed. Solid waste is stored in the large intestine until it leaves the body.

Your digestive system is just one body system that eliminates wastes. Your circulatory and respiratory systems get rid of the waste gas carbon dioxide. Your skin gets rid of some waste through perspiration. These are part of your **excretory system**, body systems and organs that remove wastes and maintain the body's balance of water and other substances.

The kidneys and bladder are also part of the excretory system. Structures in the kidneys called *nephrons* (NEF•rahnz) filter wastes from the blood. Urine formed by the kidneys moves to the bladder, where it is stored until it leaves the body.

You can take care of your digestive and excretory systems by eating healthful food, drinking plenty of water, and getting enough exercise.

MAIN IDEA AND DETAILS Tell four ways the excretory system removes wastes.

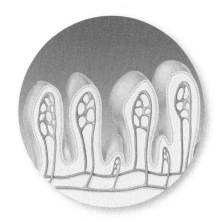

▲ The intestinal walls are lined with thousands of tiny, fingerlike projections through which nutrients are absorbed into the blood.

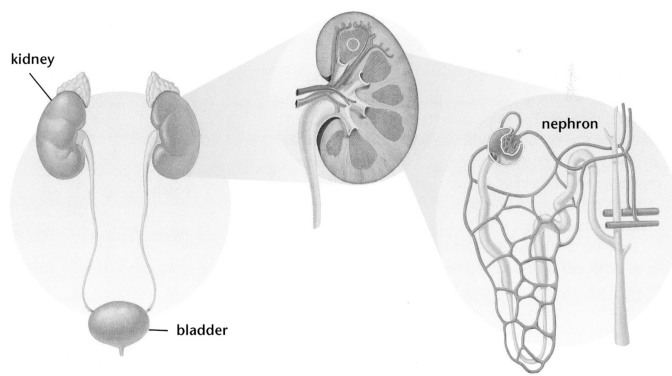

kidney

bladder

nephron

▲ Water, waste products, and other materials from blood pass into collecting tubes in the nephrons. Needed materials are returned to the blood through the many capillaries in the nephrons. Wastes and excess water remain as urine.

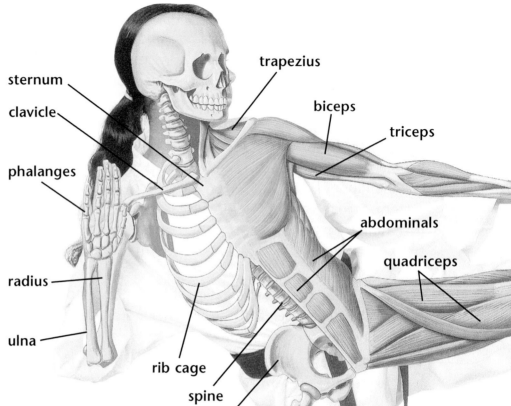

Muscles are attached to bones by strong, cordlike tendons. ▶

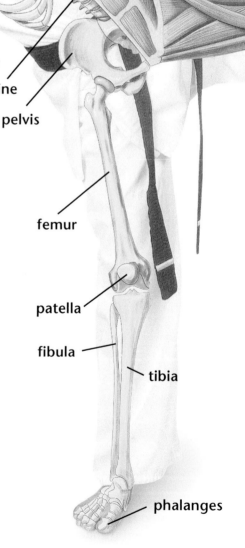

The Skeletal and Muscular Systems

A bone may look like something that isn't living, but bones are living organs that together make up your **skeletal system**. The skeletal system supports the soft tissues of the body and protects vital organs. Your skeleton also acts as the body's storage area for calcium. Some bones produce red blood cells and white blood cells. White blood cells are part of your immune system, which you will learn about in Chapter 7.

Your bones fit together at joints. Also, muscles attach to most bones across joints. Each type of joint is designed to do a certain job. Ball-and-socket joints allow rotation and movement in many directions. Hinge joints move only back and forth. Gliding joints allow side-to-side and back-and-forth movements. Some joints, such as those in your skull, permit no movement.

The muscles in your **muscular system** act on your bones to enable you to move. Muscles work in pairs to move bones. As one muscle contracts, the other relaxes.

10

▲ Skeletal muscle appears striped. It is the kind of muscle that moves bones.

▲ Smooth muscle lines the walls of blood vessels and of organs such as your esophagus and stomach.

▲ Cardiac muscle forms the walls of the heart. It contracts and relaxes to pump blood through your body.

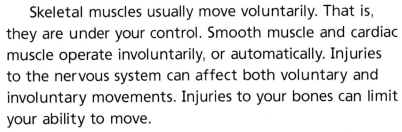

gastrocnemius

Skeletal muscles usually move voluntarily. That is, they are under your control. Smooth muscle and cardiac muscle operate involuntarily, or automatically. Injuries to the nervous system can affect both voluntary and involuntary movements. Injuries to your bones can limit your ability to move.

You can take care of your skeletal and muscular systems by getting plenty of exercise, sleep, and calcium and by protecting yourself from injuries.

COMPARE AND CONTRAST How are smooth muscle and cardiac muscle alike? How are they different?

Lesson 1 Summary and Review

❶ Summarize with Vocabulary

Use vocabulary from this lesson to complete the statements.

Your _____ and _____ systems work together to enable you to move. Your _____ and _____ systems work together to provide your body with oxygen. Your _____ system breaks down food into nutrients, and your _____ system rids your body of wastes. All systems are under the control of the _____ system.

❷ Name the three major parts of the nervous system.

❸ Critical Thinking Trace the path of oxygen from the atmosphere to a cell in the body.

❹ (Focus Skill) SEQUENCE Draw and complete this graphic organizer to show what happens during digestion.

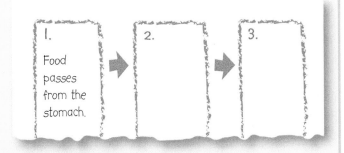

1. Food passes from the stomach.
2.
3.

❺ Write to Inform—Explanation

Write a paragraph that tells how to take care of your body systems.

11

Growth and Heredity

Lesson Focus

A person grows from a single cell containing instructions that determine the person's characteristics.

Why Learn This?

You can understand why there is no one else exactly like you.

Vocabulary

ovum
sperm
embryo
fetus
nucleus
heredity
DNA
genes
chromosome

When Growth Begins

It's hard to believe that you started out as only one cell. Your body now has billions of cells. Each cell contains information from your parents that helps determine many things about you.

Human reproduction requires one reproductive cell from each parent. The mother supplies an egg cell, or **ovum** (OH•vuhm). The father supplies a **sperm** cell. The father produces millions of sperm cells, but only one fertilizes an ovum.

An egg cell from the mother and a sperm cell from the father join to form a single cell that contains instructions from both parents. These instructions control how the developing human will grow. They also determine physical appearance, whether the baby is a boy or a girl, and some personality traits.

The new cell that forms begins to grow almost immediately. Within a few hours, it splits into two cells, then four, then eight, and so on. After about two weeks, the single cell has divided to form almost 1 million cells. Together, the dividing cells are called an **embryo** (EM•bree•oh) until around the end of the second month of development.

A sperm cell looks like a tiny tadpole. It has a head and a long, thin tail. It would take 500 sperm placed end to end to measure 1 inch.

The ovum is small—about the size of the period at the end of this sentence—but it's huge compared to the sperm cell.

12

The embryo develops in the mother's uterus, or womb. In the uterus, nutrients and oxygen pass from the mother's blood to the embryo, which grows rapidly. The embryo's cells become organized into different tissues and organs. All major organs begin to develop during the first two months of life. The embryo has arms and legs and looks distinctly human.

After the second month of development, the embryo is called a **fetus** (FEET•uhs) until birth. During the second three months of life, the fetus begins to move and can hear the sounds of the mother, such as her voice and heartbeat. During the last three months, the fetus's eyes can respond to light, the ears can hear sounds outside the uterus, and the lungs are capable of breathing air.

In all, it takes thirty-nine weeks, or about nine months, for a human to grow and develop fully inside the mother's body.

COMPARE AND CONTRAST How are an embryo and a fetus alike? How are they different?

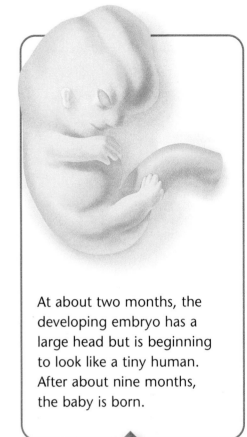

At about two months, the developing embryo has a large head but is beginning to look like a tiny human. After about nine months, the baby is born.

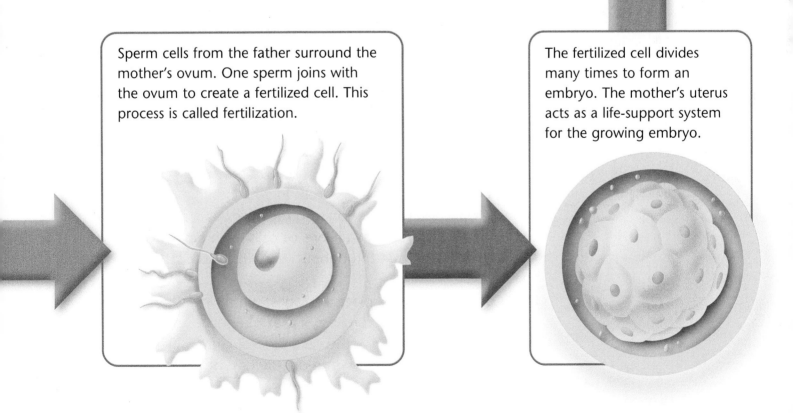

Sperm cells from the father surround the mother's ovum. One sperm joins with the ovum to create a fertilized cell. This process is called fertilization.

The fertilized cell divides many times to form an embryo. The mother's uterus acts as a life-support system for the growing embryo.

13

Cell Division

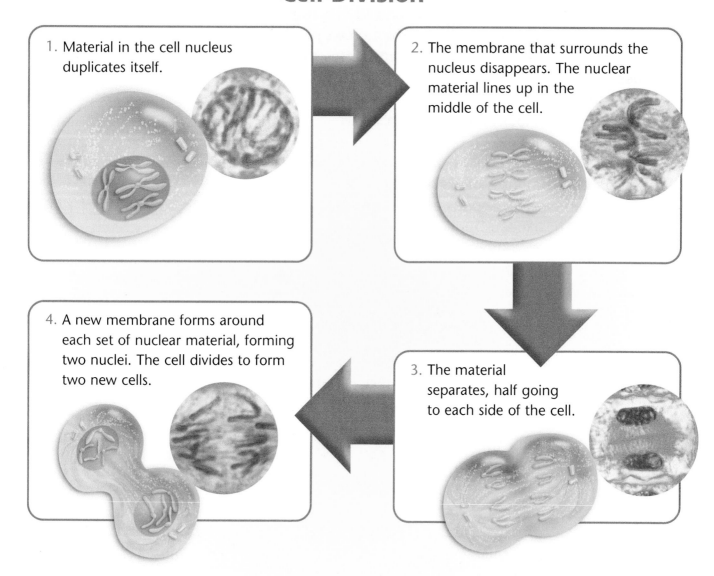

1. Material in the cell nucleus duplicates itself.

2. The membrane that surrounds the nucleus disappears. The nuclear material lines up in the middle of the cell.

3. The material separates, half going to each side of the cell.

4. A new membrane forms around each set of nuclear material, forming two nuclei. The cell divides to form two new cells.

▲ Cell division takes about thirty to forty-five minutes to complete.

How Growth Continues

You grow from the time you are born until you are eighteen or twenty years old and have reached your adult size. Growth happens as the cells in your body divide and make new cells. Cell division also replaces dead and injured cells. Your body replaces billions of cells each day. This process will continue throughout your life, even after you are grown.

Cell division takes place in stages, which are summarized above. The key to this process is that material in the **nucleus** (NOO·klee·uhs), the cell's control center, makes an exact copy of itself. When the cell divides into two cells, each of the two gets one of the copies.

Humans experience two periods of rapid growth after they are born. The first is between birth and about age two. The second period of rapid growth occurs during the teen years. Girls usually reach their adult height between the ages of fourteen and sixteen. Boys grow fastest between the ages of thirteen and seventeen, but some continue to grow until their early twenties.

Perhaps you've already started your second rapid growth period. You may be feeling awkward and clumsy as you try to get used to your new, taller body. Or you may be shorter than other people your age now. Everyone goes through the same stages of growth, but each person goes through them at his or her own pace.

CAUSE AND EFFECT **What causes you to grow?**

Did You Know?

Your body doesn't make new muscle cells. The number of muscle cells is fixed early in life. Your muscle cells grow larger through use, but they don't divide.

Body proportions change from birth to adulthood. A baby's head is one-fourth the size of the body. At six years, a child's head is one-sixth the size of the body. A teenager's head is one-seventh the size of the body, as is an adult's head.

Cells and Heredity

"Oh, he looks just like his mother!" "She has her father's eyes." Have you ever heard someone say that about a baby? The way a person looks is passed on by his or her parents. **Heredity** (huh•RED•ih•tee) is the passing of traits from parents to their children. You inherited traits from your mother and your father. They received their traits from their parents.

The nucleus of each cell of your body has exactly the same information as the nucleus of the single fertilized cell that you grew from many years ago. The nucleus contains a chemical code, called **DNA**, for all your inherited traits. DNA is a long molecule that is divided into segments called **genes**, which have the instructions that are needed to build and run your body. Each gene is part of a **chromosome** (KROH•muh•sohm), a long strand of matter composed of DNA and other chemicals.

All the cells in your body, except sperm and egg cells, have twenty-three pairs of chromosomes. Sperm and egg cells each have a single set of twenty-three chromosomes.

SUMMARIZE Explain the relationship among genes, chromosomes, and DNA.

When a sperm cell and an egg cell unite, the fertilized egg that forms has forty-six chromosomes—twenty-three from each parent. ▼

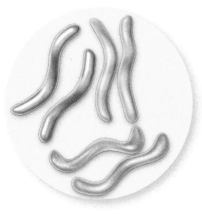

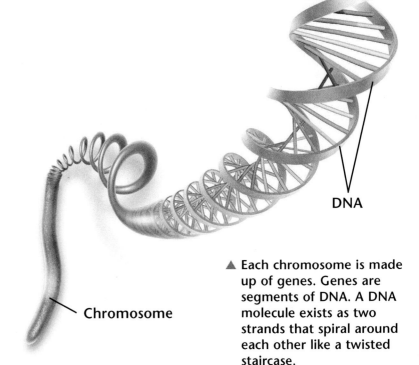

DNA

▲ Chromosomes are the nuclear material that is copied during cell division. Look again at the stages of cell division on page 14. Find the chromosomes in each picture.

Chromosome

▲ Each chromosome is made up of genes. Genes are segments of DNA. A DNA molecule exists as two strands that spiral around each other like a twisted staircase.

Some traits, such as height and weight, are inherited in a complicated way that involves many pairs of genes. Other traits are determined by just one pair of genes. When two genes determine a single trait, one member of the pair may mask, or cover, the other. The gene that causes a trait to show up is *dominant* (DAHM•uh•nuhnt). The gene that is masked is *recessive* (rih•SEHS•iv). The codes on the dominant gene keep the codes on the recessive gene from being carried out. If both genes in a pair are recessive, the recessive trait will show up.

Dominant and Recessive Traits

Dominant	Recessive
Brown hair	Blond hair
Wavy hair	Straight hair
Dimples	No dimples
Widow's peak	No widow's peak
Long eyelashes	Short eyelashes
Free earlobes	Attached earlobes

Quick Activity

Identifying Dominant Traits A widow's peak and freckles are dominant traits. Which dominant traits do you have?

Before you were born, one pair of chromosomes determined whether you are a boy or a girl. A mother's egg cell always carries an *X* chromosome. A sperm cell can carry either an *X* or a *Y* chromosome. If a sperm cell with a *Y* chromosome fertilizes an egg, the resulting chromosome pair is *XY* and the baby is a boy. If the sperm cell contains an *X* chromosome, the resulting pair is *XX* and the baby is a girl.

Recently scientists have discovered new ways to work with genes. Genetic research, or research into inherited traits, has revealed ways genes influence our health. Scientists have mapped the entire human genome, or set of genes. They know the position of each gene on human chromosomes. This research will help in gene therapy— using normal genes to replace defective genes.

DRAW CONCLUSIONS If a person is male, which two chromosomes must he have inherited?

Lesson 2 Summary and Review

❶ Summarize with Vocabulary

Use vocabulary from this lesson to complete the statements.

The reproductive cells, the _____ and _____, each contain twenty-three _____. They unite to form a cell that divides to form an _____, and after two months, a _____. The passing of traits from parents to children is called _____. The chemical code for the traits is the _____ molecule, which is located in a cell's _____. This molecule is divided into segments called _____.

❷ What is the purpose of cell division?

❸ Critical Thinking If your earlobes are attached, are your genes for that trait dominant, recessive, or both? Explain.

❹ SEQUENCE Draw and complete this graphic organizer to show how a human embryo forms and develops.

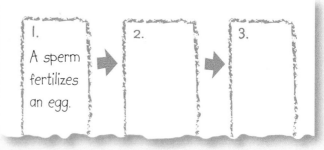

1. A sperm fertilizes an egg.
2.
3.

❺ Write to Express— Solution to a Problem

Your friend has a problem: He is upset because he is shorter than the other students in your class. Write to your friend to tell him why his height difference may be temporary.

Respect

Accepting Individual Differences

Everyone looks different and has different abilities and interests as a result of heredity and life experiences. Every person, regardless of how he or she differs from you, deserves to be treated with respect. Here are ways you can show respect to people who are different from you.

- **Treat others the way you would want to be treated.**
- **Focus on positive qualities. Say good things about people.**
- **Understand that some people have natural talents and abilities. Other people must work hard just to keep up. People who have to struggle to succeed deserve as much respect as those for whom things come easily.**
- **Don't exclude others because of the way they look or because of any disabilities they possess.**
- **Help people who are trying their best to succeed. Don't put them down.**

Activity

Think of three situations in which you can show respect to others. Work with a partner to role-play those situations. Share your ideas with your class.

One person may love to play sports, while another may prefer a less physical pastime. Respect one another's differences. ▶

19

The Endocrine System and Adolescence

Lesson Focus

Adolescence is the period in your life when you grow and develop from a child into an adult.

Why Learn This?

You will understand what is happening to your body during adolescence.

Vocabulary

puberty
adolescence
hormones
endocrine system
pituitary gland

Puberty and Adolescence

During the next few years, you will mature into an adult. Some people your age may have already begun **puberty** (PYOO•ber•tee), a physical process in which your body begins to develop reproductive cells. During puberty, girls' bodies begin to release eggs, and boys' bodies begin to produce sperm. Puberty usually starts between ages eight and thirteen in girls and between ages ten and fourteen in boys. It begins when the brain releases a chemical that starts the changes necessary to produce reproductive cells. The timing of this change is determined by a person's genes and by nutrition.

Your rate of growth will be different from that of others. Everyone changes at different times and at different rates. ▶

During puberty, your body will grow faster than it has since you were a baby. Your arms, legs, hands, and feet may grow faster than the rest of your body. You may feel clumsy until the rest of your body catches up.

Puberty takes place during **adolescence** (ad•uh•LES•uhns), the period in which you begin to grow from a child into an adult. Physical changes aren't the only changes you will undergo. You'll mature intellectually, emotionally, and socially as well. During your teen years, your ability to make plans and set long-term goals will increase. You will further develop your decision-making skills, become more independent, and show more responsibility. As you build on your experiences, you will better understand varying points of view and how to relate to others.

DRAW CONCLUSIONS Could the students shown on this page all be the same age? Explain your answer.

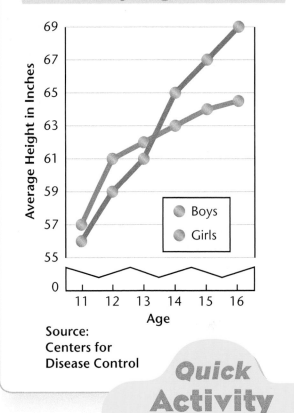

Average Heights of Girls and Boys Ages 11–16

Source: Centers for Disease Control

Quick Activity

Interpreting Graphs
Study the graph.
1. On average, at what age do boys become taller than girls?
2. Which group is growing faster at ages 11–12? At ages 15–16?

21

Hormones

The human body is like a complicated chemical factory. Glands produce chemicals called **hormones** (HAWR•mohnz) that regulate many body functions. These chemicals are released into the bloodstream, which carries them to other parts of the body, where they regulate the activities of cells and organs. Each hormone has an important job that affects how your body works. The glands that produce these hormones make up your **endocrine system** (EN•doh•krihn).

More than fifty hormones are made by the main endocrine glands. ▼

Endocrine System

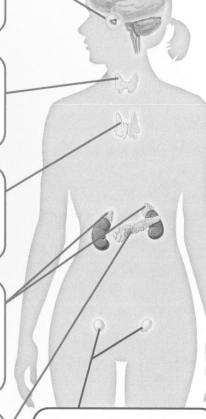

Pituitary Gland Regulates the activity of other endocrine glands; helps regulate the way nutrients are used for energy; sends out the hormones that begin puberty

Thyroid Gland Controls the speed with which nutrients are turned into energy and are used for growth and repair

Thymus Gland Causes certain cells of the immune system to mature and become able to fight infection

Adrenal Glands Help control the body's balance of salt and water; control blood pressure and blood sugar level; prepare the body to deal with stress

Testes Control the development and function of the male reproductive system

Pancreas Raises and lowers blood sugar levels

Ovaries Control the development and function of the female reproductive system

How Puberty Begins

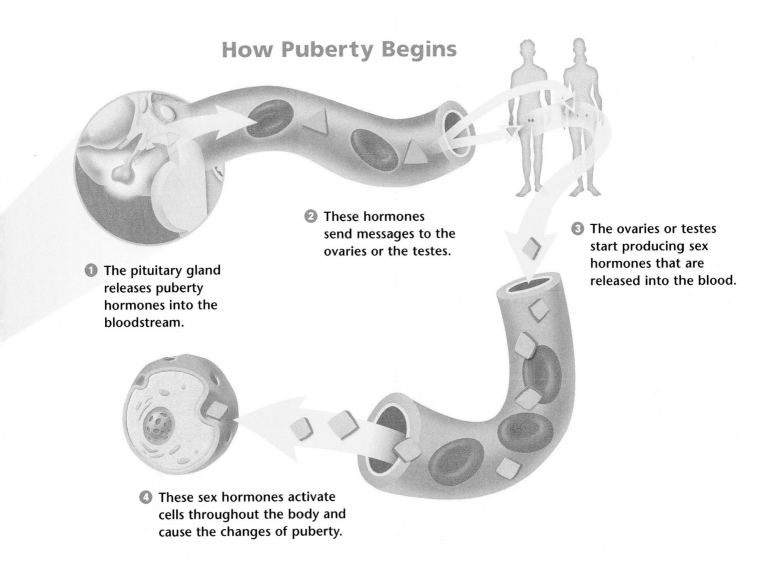

1 The pituitary gland releases puberty hormones into the bloodstream.

2 These hormones send messages to the ovaries or the testes.

3 The ovaries or testes start producing sex hormones that are released into the blood.

4 These sex hormones activate cells throughout the body and cause the changes of puberty.

The **pituitary gland** (pih·TOO·uh·tair·ee), also called the "master gland," produces hormones that control the function of other endocrine glands. One of the pituitary's most important hormones is growth hormone, which stimulates your body's overall growth. Production of growth hormone is increased during puberty.

Puberty starts when the brain greatly increases its production of a chemical that causes the pituitary to begin sending out larger amounts of two puberty hormones. In boys, the puberty hormones stimulate the testes to produce the sex hormone testosterone and sperm cells. In girls, the hormones signal the ovaries to produce the sex hormone estrogen and to begin releasing the egg cells that have existed in the ovaries since before birth.

CAUSE AND EFFECT Which endocrine gland causes the process of puberty to begin?

Physical Changes

Personal Health Plan ▶

Real-Life Situation
You will experience many changes in the next two years.

Real-Life Plan
Write down the changes you expect to see. Choose one, and describe how you can prepare yourself for the change.

The release of growth hormone and sex hormones results in many physical changes in your body. The first thing you will experience is a *growth spurt*, a period of rapid growth. You may grow four or more inches taller in one year. When the growth spurt ends, you will have reached your adult height.

The hormone testosterone causes a boy's vocal cords to become thicker, and his voice gradually gets deeper. This change may start with the boy's voice "cracking," but this will eventually stop.

Girls experience changes due to the hormone estrogen. Their hips broaden, and their bodies become curvier.

For both boys and girls, hair starts to grow on different parts of the body. Boys may have to start shaving their faces.

Boys

Increased height

Increased muscular strength

Increased weight

Body hair

Deeper voice

Sweat glands active

During puberty, both boys and girls will begin to notice body odor. This is because sweat glands under the arms become active at puberty. They produce *perspiration* (per•spuh•RAY•shuhn), or sweat. When the perspiration comes in contact with bacteria on the skin, body odor results. To help control these changes, you should continue to practice good *hygiene* (HY•jeen), or habits that keep a person clean. Bathe or shower regularly, and use a deodorant to control body odor. Brush your teeth twice a day, and also brush your tongue to help prevent bad breath.

COMPARE AND CONTRAST Tell how changes in body shape during puberty are alike and different for boys and girls.

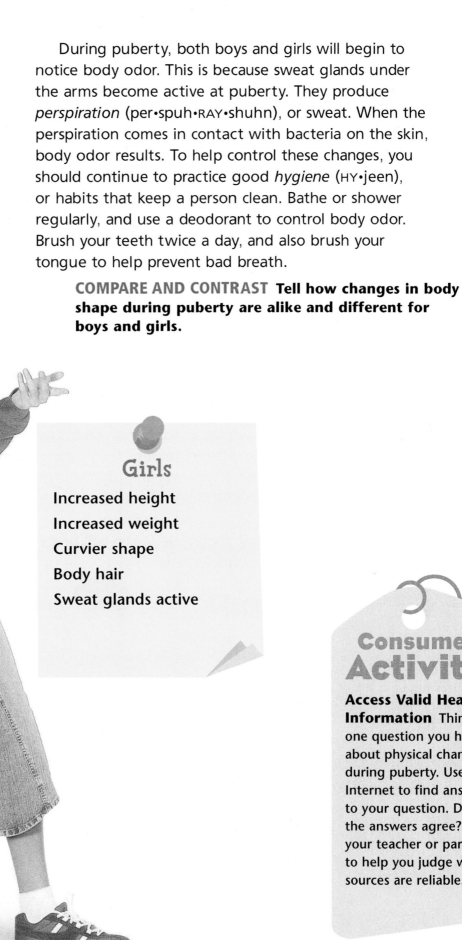

Girls

Increased height

Increased weight

Curvier shape

Body hair

Sweat glands active

Consumer Activity

Access Valid Health Information Think of one question you have about physical changes during puberty. Use the Internet to find answers to your question. Do all the answers agree? Ask your teacher or parents to help you judge which sources are reliable.

Body Image

How would you describe your appearance to someone? The way you see yourself is called your body image. As you enter puberty, you may become more concerned with your body image. Understanding the changes that affect your appearance can help you accept them and deal with them.

Acne

One change often caused by puberty is acne (AK•nee), a skin condition characterized by pimples on the face and upper body. The increase in hormones released during puberty causes the oil glands in the skin to become more active. If the amount of oil is great, the oil combines with dead skin cells in hair follicles and plugs pores. When a plugged pore becomes infected with bacteria, a pimple forms.

The best way to treat acne is to wash your face twice a day with mild soap and water. Don't scrub too hard, and don't squeeze or pick at pimples. Doing so can cause scarring. Many over-the-counter medications can help clear up acne. However, some can cause skin to become overly dry. If your acne is severe or makes you feel uncomfortable, see a physician. He or she will be familiar with the many treatments for acne.

Part of growing up is learning to accept the ways you are different from others. ▶

26

Height and Weight

As you enter your teen years, you'll need to adjust to other physical changes. You may think that you are too short, tall, thin, or heavy. Keep in mind that all people are different and that they grow and develop in their own ways.

Having a realistic body image is important. A poor body image can lead to unhealthy behaviors. For example, you might eat too little because you think you are overweight, even when you aren't. You might avoid social activities because you're self-conscious. To develop a positive body image, remember the following:

- Certain body shapes or sizes are not better or worse than others.
- Models on TV and in magazines aren't typical. Don't compare yourself to them.
- You are special and unique. Appreciate those qualities that make you different from anyone else.

SUMMARIZE Tell about the ways you should treat acne.

Lesson 3 Summary and Review

❶ Summarize with Vocabulary

Use vocabulary from this lesson to complete the statements.

Instructions coded in your genes determine when you begin _____. It starts when your _____, or master gland, releases _____ that affect the ovaries and testes. The period during which you develop into an adult is called _____.

❷ Name three ways you will change during puberty.

❸ Critical Thinking Why might a person who has a poor body image try to look like a model in a magazine?

❹ (Focus Skill) SEQUENCE Draw and complete this graphic organizer to show how pimples develop during puberty.

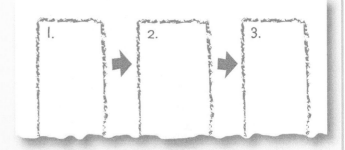

❺ Write to Inform—Explanation

Write a paragraph explaining why practicing good hygiene during puberty is important.

Dealing with Emotional Changes

Changing Feelings

When you woke up this morning, you might have felt on top of the world—full of energy and ready to have a good time with your friends. By the afternoon, your mood may have turned blue, and you just wanted to be left alone. What's happening?

Many people your age experience **mood swings**, a wide range of emotions in a short period of time. In one afternoon, you may feel bored, excited, sad, nervous, and happy. Frequent mood shifts are common during puberty and are a normal result of the emotional changes you are experiencing. Your body and your appearance are changing, and so are your relationships with your parents and friends. School is more demanding, and you have

Rapid changes in mood, or mood swings, are common during adolescence. ▼

Happy

Angry

begun to plan for your future. Some of the moodiness you feel has a physical cause, too. The increase in hormone levels during puberty is linked to mood swings.

Controlling your moods, especially when you feel angry, can be difficult. You might be surprised at the intensity of your anger. These tips can help you express and manage your anger and other feelings.

- Focus on developing your best features. Often, these aren't related to appearance. You might have a great sense of humor or a talent for music.
- Reduce stress by exercising, eating nutritious foods, and getting enough sleep.
- Work off your anger through physical activity. Then try talking calmly to the person you're angry with.
- Talk to your parents or other trusted adults. They know what you're going through. As you grow toward **maturity** (muh•TUR•uh•tee), your full development as an adult, you will find that the advice of older adults can be helpful.

CAUSE AND EFFECT What are the causes of mood swings during adolescence?

Personal Health Plan ▶

Real-Life Situation

Your changing emotions can be hard to cope with. Suppose you are feeling angry much of the time.

Real-Life Plan

Make a list of at least three adults you can talk to about dealing with the anger you are feeling.

Excited

Sad

Curious

Changing Relationships

Your attitudes about relationships are also changing. You're starting to be more independent of your parents, yet you still want their support and understanding. You're beginning to see yourself as a separate person with your own thoughts and activities. This change can lead to a desire for privacy. The need for time alone is a normal part of growing up.

Part of becoming your own person is the desire to be accepted and liked by people your own age. Adolescents care a great deal about what their peers think about them. Sometimes young people form *cliques* (KLIKS), or groups of friends who exclude others from joining. Being part of a clique can help people feel a sense of belonging and support. However, cliques can be harmful if they encourage unhealthful behavior, such as taking risks, or when they cause young people to disrespect those who are different from them.

Quick Activity

Write a Paragraph
Imagine you are the girl carrying the tray in the picture. Write a paragraph describing how you feel. In a small group, role-play various acceptable ways for the girl to gain attention and make friends.

Friendships with individuals can help make the challenging time of adolescence easier. As your interests change, you may make new friends. As you form these friendships, keep in mind that people who pressure you to do unhealthful or risky things are not your friends.

During adolescence, you may find yourself being romantically attracted to someone. This is normal. The feelings you have can be strong, but you have the responsibility to control those feelings. One way to be responsible when you begin dating is to go on group dates. When you go on a group date, you are not alone with one other person. You do not put yourself in a situation in which you might engage in risky behavior. If someone pressures you, firmly resist the person.

SUMMARIZE Tell how relationships might change during adolescence.

ACTIVITY

Building Good Character

Fairness Suppose a new girl or boy joins your class. You want to invite this person to eat lunch with you and your friends. Your friends say the new person isn't wearing the right clothes and can't join your group. Put yourself in the new person's place. How would you feel? Role-play with a partner what you would say to your friends.

Lesson 4 Summary and Review

❶ Summarize with Vocabulary

Use vocabulary and other terms from this lesson to complete the statements.

Your parents can help you deal with your changing emotions as you grow toward _____. When your emotions change rapidly over a short time, you are experiencing _____. These may be caused by changing _____ levels in the blood or by the stress of changing _____ with family and friends. Young people in a _____ can hurt others by excluding them. If someone tries to pressure you to do something risky, _____ the person.

❷ How does your relationship with your parents change as you enter puberty?

❸ Critical Thinking Why is group dating an example of responsible behavior?

❹ (Focus Skill) SEQUENCE Draw and complete this graphic organizer to show one reason why mood swings occur during puberty.

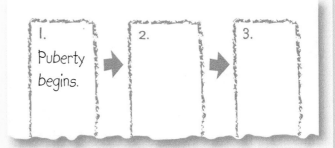

1. Puberty begins. → 2. → 3.

❺ Write to Express—Idea

Do you think cliques are a good idea? Write a paragraph that expresses and defends your point of view.

Communicate
Concerns About Changes

As you enter your teen years, you are experiencing physical, social, and emotional changes. Talking with your parents or other trusted adults can help you deal with these changes. Use the steps for **Communicating** to help you express your thoughts and feelings.

Devin is bothered because he shares a room with his little brother. Lately, he feels a need for privacy because of the way his body is changing. How can Devin explain this to his parents?

1 **Understand your audience.**

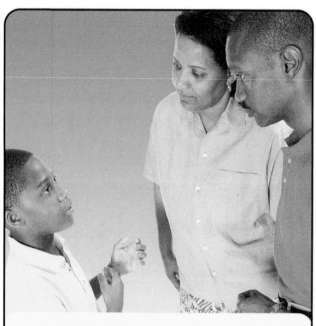

Devin realizes that he needs to talk to his parents to help establish new living arrangements. He will show his family respect, but he will also be honest.

2 **Give a clear message. Use "I" messages.**

I need privacy.

Devin clearly tells his parents why he is upset. He explains that he needs privacy because he's growing up. He respectfully asks his parents for his own room.

3 Listen carefully, and answer any questions.

Devin's parents explain that there isn't space in the house to give Devin his own room. They ask Devin if he needs more room or just more privacy. Devin says that he needs privacy. His parents tell him they can put up a divider in the boys' room.

4 Gather feedback.

Devin's brother agrees to the plan. After the divider has been up for a few days, Devin asks his family for feedback. They all agree that the arrangement is working out.

Problem Solving

A. Jamal is changing classes at school when someone accidentally bumps him. "Hey, watch it!" Jamal says angrily as he shoves the person. The other person apologizes. Jamal knows he reacted badly and that he has been feeling angry a lot lately.
   - How can Jamal use the steps for **Communicating** to talk to a trusted adult about a responsible way to deal with his anger?

B. Michi and Zoe have been best friends since first grade. Now that they are in middle school, they find themselves arguing. They can't seem to settle their differences, but they want to stay friends.
   - Who are some adults at school and outside of school who might be able to help the two girls? Role-play how the girls could show good character by respectfully communicating their concerns about their relationship.

Healthful Choices

Taking Care of Yourself

Taking good care of your body during adolescence is key to good health. If you feel good physically, you're likely to do better in all areas of your life. Taking good care of your body means choosing a lifestyle that includes getting regular physical activity, eating a healthful diet, and making sure you get enough rest and sleep. Taking care of yourself also means avoiding unhealthful behaviors. **Abstinence** is avoiding behavior that puts your health at risk. When you choose not to take illegal drugs, drink alcohol, or use tobacco, you are taking care of your physical, social, and emotional health. Abstinence from sexual activity helps you avoid certain diseases and unwanted pregnancy.

SUMMARIZE List four things you can do to take care of your body.

Quick Activity

Identify Unhealthful Behaviors List all the items and behaviors in this picture that contribute to poor health. Tell why each item is unhealthful.

COLA
CANDY
CHIPS
COLA

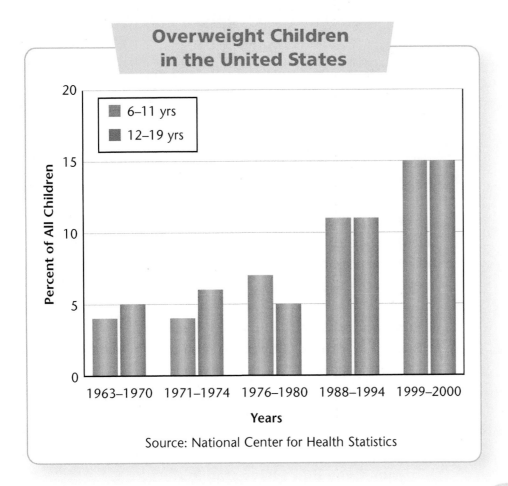

Overweight Children in the United States

Legend:
- 6–11 yrs
- 12–19 yrs

Y-axis: Percent of All Children (0 to 20)

X-axis (Years): 1963–1970, 1971–1974, 1976–1980, 1988–1994, 1999–2000

Source: National Center for Health Statistics

Healthful Habits

How your body develops during puberty depends partly on the kind and amount of food you eat. When you eat unhealthful foods, you may not get the nutrients your body needs. When you eat too much food, you become overweight.

As you can see in the graph above, the number of children and teenagers who are overweight has been increasing. The main causes are eating too much and not being active enough. Today, junk foods and fast foods are convenient and readily available, and almost half of teens watch three to five hours of TV every day. Teens spend additional time using a computer and playing video games. Both junk food (which is high in calories but low in nutrients) and inactivity contribute to children being overweight. To maintain a balanced eating plan and a healthful weight, choose nutritious foods. Avoid overeating or eating too little. Talk to your parents or your doctor if you're worried about your weight.

Did You Know?

Many overweight teens have high cholesterol levels and high blood pressure. These are risk factors for heart disease. Overweight teens also have a high risk of joint problems, liver disease, Type 2 diabetes, and breathing problems.

Both rest and physical activity are important to your health. Don't do too much of one at the expense of the other. ▶

Personal Health Plan ▶

Real-Life Situation
You have been feeling tired lately because you have been staying up late.

Real-Life Plan
Write a plan for scheduling your activities so that you can get more sleep.

Regular physical activity can help you maintain a healthful weight and have **stamina** (STAM·uh·nuh), or the ability to work or exercise for a long time without getting tired. Follow these fitness tips:

• Run, bike, or swim to improve your stamina.
• Build muscle strength by doing push-ups or pull-ups.
• Maintain your flexibility, or ability to move easily, by stretching and by swimming or doing martial arts. When you are flexible, you are less likely to hurt yourself during exercise.

DRAW CONCLUSIONS What might happen when you run if you don't have stamina?

Lesson 5 Summary and Review

1 Summarize with Vocabulary

Use vocabulary and other terms from this lesson to complete the statements.

Avoiding behavior that puts your health at risk is _____. To maintain a healthful weight, avoid _____ food and engage in physical _____. If you can exercise for a long time without getting tired, you have _____.

2 Critical Thinking How can eating too little be harmful to your health at your age?

3 Name three activities that can help you stay physically fit. Tell whether each activity builds stamina, muscular strength, or flexibility.

4 **SEQUENCE** Draw and complete this graphic organizer to show the benefits of healthful behavior.

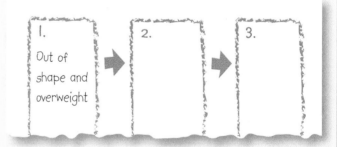

| 1. Out of shape and overweight | → | 2. | → | 3. |

5 Writing to Inform—Explanation
List three healthful behaviors you should practice and three unhealthful behaviors you should avoid. Explain why each behavior is healthful or unhealthful.

ACTIVITIES

Physical Education

Work It Off Think of physical exercises you could do to help you control the strong emotions and stress you experience during adolescence. Organize these activities in a list that you can refer to when needed.

Home & Community

Taking Responsibility Review your family's list of household chores or talk with your parents about them. Choose a job you feel you are ready to take responsibility for. Prove to your family that you can do it.

Science

Sweet Dreams A common misconception is that sleep is a period of total inactivity. Do research to find out about the different brainwave patterns that occur during sleep and how these patterns are related to dreams.

Career Link

Geneticist Geneticists can locate genes that cause some human diseases. They hope to develop gene therapies that will cure these diseases. Imagine that you are a geneticist. Which diseases will you attempt to cure? Do research at the library and on the Internet to identify genetic diseases that might be cured by gene therapy.

Technology Project

Prepare a Brochure Many dermatologists use lasers and other light-based devices to clear up acne. Find out more about this treatment by doing research on the Internet. Combine the information you find with what you already know about acne. Use a computer to prepare a brochure on the prevention and treatment of acne.

GO ONLINE For more activities, visit The Learning Site. www.harcourtschool.com/health

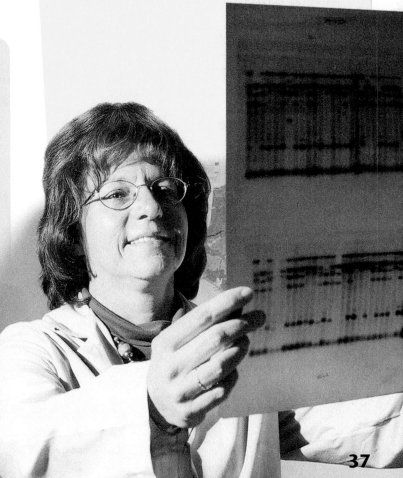

Chapter Review and Test Preparation

SEQUENCE

Draw and then use this graphic organizer to answer questions 1 and 2.

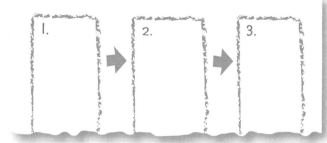

1. Describe the sequence of events that starts puberty, beginning with the brain.
2. Describe the major stages in human development, beginning with fertilization and ending with birth.

 Use Vocabulary

Match each term in Column B with its meaning in Column A.

Column A	Column B
3 Controls all of the body's activities	**A** DNA
4 Male reproductive cell	**B** maturity
5 Cell's control center	**C** nervous system
6 Chemical code for inherited information	**D** nucleus
7 The body's master gland	**E** pituitary
8 Ability to work for a long time without getting tired	**F** sperm
9 Full development as an adult	**G** stamina

Check Understanding

Choose the letter of the correct answer.

10 The circulatory and _____ systems work together to provide oxygen to the body. (pp. 6–7)
　A respiratory　　　　**C** skeletal
　B digestive　　　　　**D** excretory

11 Which is **NOT** an inherited trait? (p. 17)
　F dimples　　　　　**H** hair color
　G favorite color　　**J** height

12 You can help manage your feelings during adolescence by _____. (p. 29)
　A keeping them to yourself
　B getting plenty of exercise
　C changing your appearance
　D criticizing yourself so you try harder

organs that make digestive juices

liver　　　　　　　stomach

13 Which of the following is missing from the graphic organizer above? (pp. 8–9)
　F nephron　　　　　**H** esophagus
　G large intestine　　**J** pancreas

14 The part of the nervous system that allows you to reason is the _____. (p. 5)
　A brain stem　　　　**C** spinal cord
　B cerebrum　　　　 **D** cerebellum

15 Which change occurs in both boys and girls during puberty? (p. 24)
　F growth spurt　　　**H** curvier shape
　G wider hips　　　　**J** facial hair

16 Which is the correct sequence for blood moving **AWAY** from the heart? (p. 6)

A arteries to capillaries to veins

B arteries to veins to capillaries

C veins to capillaries to arteries

D veins to arteries to capillaries

17 Which is true of human growth? (p. 15)

F Rapid growth does not occur before puberty.

G All humans go through the same stages of growth.

H Boys grow fastest in their early twenties.

J Girls reach their adult height at a later age than do boys.

18 Which of these is **NOT** an endocrine gland? (p. 22)

A pancreas   **C** liver

B thyroid   **D** thymus

19 What is happening in the stage of cell division shown here? (p. 14)

F Half of the material moves to each side.

G The cell divides to form two new cells.

H Material in the cell is duplicated.

J Nuclear material lines up in the center.

Think Critically

20 A friend says, "I got most of my genes from my mother because I look like her." Is her statement accurate? Explain.

21 Explain how understanding the changes your body goes through during puberty can help you cope with adolescence.

22 Smoking tobacco damages alveoli. How does this explain why a person who smokes might become short of breath sooner when exercising than a person who does not smoke?

Apply Skills

23 **BUILDING GOOD CHARACTER**

Respect You have just met new friends. However, they don't want to include in any of their activities a friend you've had for many years. Apply what you know about respecting others to explain how you might handle the situation.

24 **LIFE SKILLS**

Communicate You used to spend time with your younger sister after school, but now you like to unwind for a while alone in your room. Your sister thinks that you don't love her anymore. Use communication skills to explain your feelings to her.

Write About Health

25 **Write to Inform—Explanation** Explain how having a poor body image can affect your growth and development.

Personal and Consumer Health

Reading Skill

DRAW CONCLUSIONS When you read, you draw conclusions by combining information in the text with what you already know. Use the Reading in Health Handbook on pages 402–403 and this graphic organizer to help you read the health facts in this chapter.

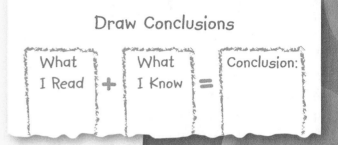

Draw Conclusions

What I Read + What I Know = Conclusion:

Health Graph

INTERPRET DATA Ultraviolet (UV) radiation is greatest when the sun is highest in the sky and rapidly lessens as the sun approaches the horizon. This graph shows the amount of skin-damaging UV radiation that reaches Earth's surface during a summer day at two different latitudes. At what time of day do you most need to protect your eyes and skin from sunlight?

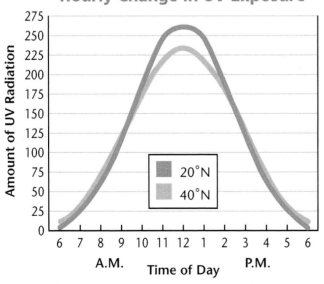

Hourly Change in UV Exposure

Amount of UV Radiation (vertical axis: 0, 25, 50, 75, 100, 125, 150, 175, 200, 225, 250, 275)

Legend:
- 20°N
- 40°N

Time of Day (horizontal axis: 6 7 8 9 10 11 12 1 2 3 4 5 6, A.M. to P.M.)

Daily Physical Activity

A seemingly endless variety of health-care products and services are available to consumers today. Using information from reliable sources can help you make healthful choices. Another way you can stay healthy is to take part in daily physical activity.

 Be Active!
Use the selection, Track 2, **Locomotion**, to take care of your muscles and bones.

Your Skin, Hair, and Nails

Your Skin at Work

After a tough sports game, you're covered with sweat. The first thing you probably do when you get home is jump into the shower. But did you know that you sweat all the time? Even as you sleep, you sweat so that your body stays at just the right temperature.

The skin is your body's largest organ, and sweating is just one of the many jobs it does to protect you—inside and out. Your skin provides a protective covering for your body. It senses temperature, texture, pain, and pressure. It protects you from disease. It produces sweat to help regulate body temperature and to help rid you of wastes. Look at the diagram below to find out more about this amazing organ.

Epidermis
Many layers of dead skin cells form the top of the epidermis. Cells in the lower part of the epidermis are always making new cells.

Dermis
The dermis is much thicker than the epidermis. It is made up of tough, flexible fibers.

Hair Follicle
Each hair follicle has a muscle that can contract and make the hair "stand on end."

Your skin has two main layers: the epidermis and the dermis. The **epidermis** (eh•puh•DER•muhs) is the outermost layer of your skin. It protects you by keeping germs outside your body and important body fluids inside.

The **dermis** (DER•muhs) is a thick layer below the epidermis. It contains many structures, including sweat glands, oil glands, and hair follicles. **Hair follicles** (FAH•lih•kuhlz) are tiny sacs from which hair grows. Oil glands are connected to the hair follicles. The oil from these glands coats the hairs and rises to the skin's surface. Sweat glands produce the sweat that helps rid your body of heat and some wastes.

Beneath the dermis is fatty tissue. This tissue helps cushion and insulate the body.

 **DRAW CONCLUSIONS** Why is taking care of your skin important?

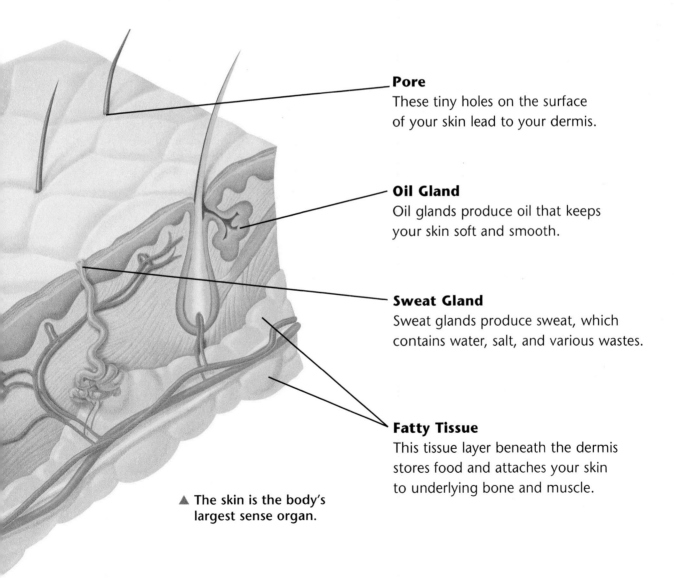

Pore
These tiny holes on the surface of your skin lead to your dermis.

Oil Gland
Oil glands produce oil that keeps your skin soft and smooth.

Sweat Gland
Sweat glands produce sweat, which contains water, salt, and various wastes.

Fatty Tissue
This tissue layer beneath the dermis stores food and attaches your skin to underlying bone and muscle.

▲ The skin is the body's largest sense organ.

Common Skin Problems

You wake up and go into the bathroom to wash your face. As you look into the mirror, you can't believe your eyes. You have a big red spot on your chin. What's going on?

As you enter adolescence, the oil glands in your skin may start working overtime. The extra oil can make your hair look and feel greasy. It can also plug the pores in your skin, causing a common skin disorder called **acne** (AK•nee). Blackheads and pimples are types of skin blemishes seen in acne. Many people have outbreaks of acne during adolescence.

Sweat glands get more active during adolescence. Sweat itself is odorless, but bacteria on the skin act on sweat and oils to produce chemicals that cause body odor.

SEQUENCE Tell how a pimple forms.

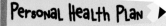

Personal Health Plan ▶

Real-Life Situation
Keeping your skin clean and healthy can help you feel good about your appearance.
Real-Life Plan
Write one daily goal for keeping your skin healthy.

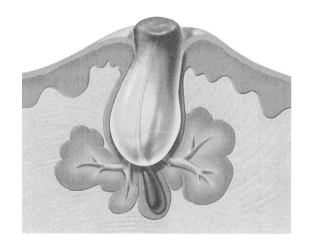

◀ A blackhead forms when an oil plug pushes to the surface of a pore, where the air turns the plug black.

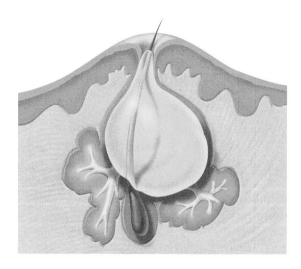

◀ A pimple forms when a plugged pore becomes infected by bacteria.

Skin, Hair, and Nail Care

If you're concerned about the changes in your skin that can come with adolescence, don't worry. There are ways to control these troublesome changes. Keeping clean is one way to help control acne, oil, and odor. The lists below give tips for keeping clean.

Because your hands come into contact with many things that contain disease-causing germs, it's important to wash your hands frequently. Remember to wash your hands with soap and water before you cook or eat, after using the toilet, after coughing or sneezing, after touching a pet, and after working outdoors.

SUMMARIZE Why should you wash your hands before eating a sandwich?

How are these students caring for their bodies? ▼

Hair

- Wash your hair with shampoo regularly to remove dirt and excess oil. Use a medicated shampoo if you have dandruff.
- To prevent dry hair and scalp, don't wash your hair too often.
- Comb or brush your hair between shampoos.

Skin

- Bathe or shower regularly to help control acne and body odor.
- Wash your skin with soap and water to remove bacteria, dirt, flaking skin cells, and excess oil.

Nails

- Use a nail brush to remove dirt from under your nails.
- Push back each **cuticle** (KYOO•tih•kuhl), the skin that grows around each nail, to keep your nails looking neat.
- Keep your nails cut. Short nails are easier to keep clean than long ones.

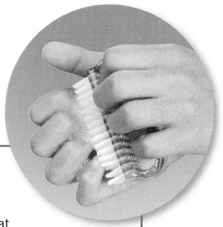

In order for a sunscreen to work properly, you should reapply it every two hours or after swimming. No sunscreen offers complete protection, so you should limit your exposure to sunlight. ▶

Protecting Your Skin from the Sun

Everyone needs to protect his or her skin from the sun's ultraviolet (UV) rays. Over time, sunlight can wrinkle and thicken the skin, making it tough and leathery. Too much sunlight can cause a sunburn now, but it also can cause skin cancer in the future.

There are many ways to help protect your skin from the harmful rays of the sun. Hats, clothes made of tightly woven fabric, and sunscreen can all protect your skin. **Sunscreen** is a cream, oil, or lotion containing chemicals that help protect you from UV rays.

Sunscreens are rated according to their ability to block UV rays. The product's SPF, or Sun Protection Factor, tells its rating. A sunscreen with SPF 30 means that you can stay in the sun 30 times longer without burning than if you weren't wearing sunscreen. You should always use a sunscreen with an SPF of 30 or more. Be sure to apply sunscreen according to the manufacturer's directions.

COMPARE AND CONTRAST How is a sunscreen with SPF 30 like a sunscreen with SPF 15? How is it different?

◀ How would each of these products protect you from UV rays?

When you are in the sun, you can feel its warmth and see its light. It's what you can't see that will harm you. The sun produces two types of rays: UVA and UVB. You can't see these rays, but when they penetrate your skin, they can damage cells and cause cancer. One way to prevent sun damage is to use a sunscreen. Today's sunscreens contain a variety of ingredients. The most common is PABA. Many people are allergic to this ingredient, so scientists continue to look—sometimes in unusual places—for newer and better ways to block the sun's harmful rays. Some scientists are studying tiny, plantlike algae. Because algae live at the water's surface, they are exposed to UV rays. However, these algae protect themselves from the sun by making substances that block UV light. Scientists are studying these substances to see how they can use them to produce sunscreens for humans.

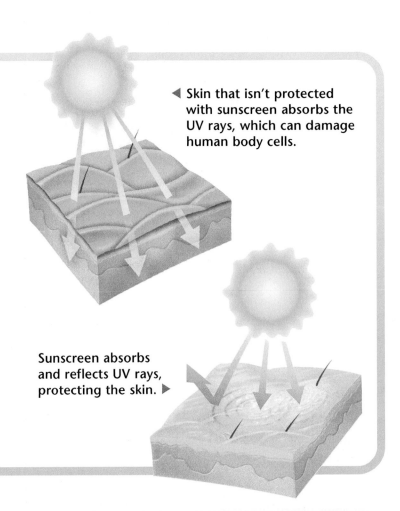

◄ Skin that isn't protected with sunscreen absorbs the UV rays, which can damage human body cells.

Sunscreen absorbs and reflects UV rays, protecting the skin. ▶

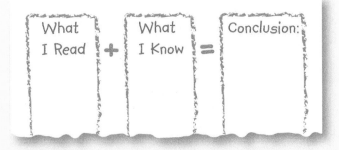

Lesson 1 Summary and Review

❶ **Summarize with Vocabulary**

Use vocabulary from this lesson to complete the statements.

The outermost layer of the skin is the _____. The _____ is the layer that contains many of the skin's structures, such as _____, which are connected to oil glands. Excess oil causes a common skin disorder called _____. To keep your nails neat, gently push back each _____. You should reapply _____ every two hours to protect your skin from UV damage.

❷ Tell how blackheads and pimples form.

❸ **Critical Thinking** Why is it important to protect your skin from the sun?

❹ (Focus Skill) **DRAW CONCLUSIONS** Why should people do more to protect their skin than apply sunscreen?

What I Read	+	What I Know	=	Conclusion:

❺ **Write to Inform—How-To**

Write a short pamphlet that tells people your age how to take care of their skin, hair, and nails and why they should do so.

Skin and Hair Products

Lesson Focus

A wise consumer selects skin and hair products consciously and carefully.

Why Learn This?

You can use what you learn to choose the skin and hair products that best meet your needs.

Vocabulary

advertising
consumer
ingredients

Companies use sports stars, singers, TV and movie stars, and other famous people to sell their products. ▼

Getting Your Attention

Each day you see products on television, in magazines and newspapers, on the Internet, and even on T-shirts. **Advertising** (AD·ver·ty·zing) is the process of giving people information and ideas that encourage them to buy something. Companies use advertising to sell their products.

You are a **consumer** (kuhn·soo·mer), someone who buys products and services. Some advertising can give you good information about products. However, some advertisers use tricks. As a consumer, be aware of the following tricks that advertisers may use to sell products.

Star Power

Some ads get your attention by featuring famous people. Companies pay famous people to say what the companies think will sell their products. Companies want you to buy their products because you like or admire the celebrities.

You, too, can have perfect skin!

We're Better!

Sometimes advertisers try to convince you that their product is cheaper than a competitor's product. Or, they might try to convince you that their product is better than someone else's. Beware of advertising that says bad things about other products but doesn't tell you anything about the advertised product.

Be Cool

Companies often show a person with a lot of friends or admirers using their products. The message they want you to get is that everyone will notice you and want to be around you if you use the product. Advertisers want to make people think that using the products will make them more popular.

 DRAW CONCLUSIONS Why might an ad focus on a product's cheap price but give no other information about the product?

▲ What information would you want to know before deciding whether buying this product is really a bargain?

Consumer Activity

Analyze Advertising Messages Most TV commercials use more than one technique to grab your attention. Carefully study two TV commercials for similar products. Write a paragraph in which you compare the techniques used in each.

◀ What message is this ad giving?

49

Analyzing Ads

Don't let advertising tricks fool you. Make sure you know what you are buying. Look at the ad below. What isn't the ad telling you that you should know?

To find out about a product, read its package label carefully. Learn about its **ingredients** (in·GREE·dee·uhnts), or the substances used in the product. Ingredients are listed by weight on the label of most products. The ingredient that makes up most of the product by weight is listed first. The one that makes up the least is listed last.

MAIN IDEA AND DETAILS **What information about a product's ingredients can you get from its label?**

Quick Activity

Interpret Label Messages Examine several labels from health-care products. What kinds of persuasive techniques does each label use?

Who says that this is America's favorite? Is there information that supports this claim?

Is this ingredient important?

Does Rachel Roxx really use the product?

What other ingredients are important in an acne product? Does this product have them? What evidence is given to prove that other products aren't as good?

How does this price compare to the prices of other acne products? Which product has more of the important ingredients?

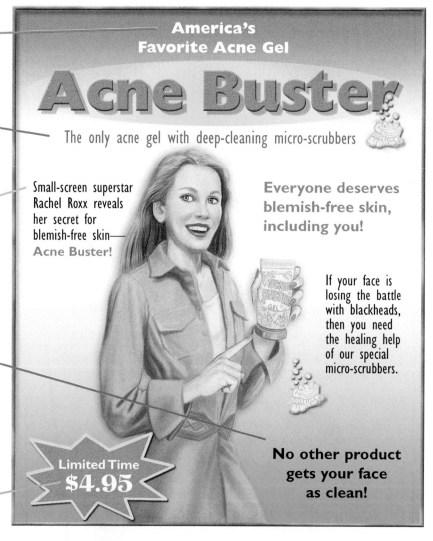

America's Favorite Acne Gel

Acne Buster

The only acne gel with deep-cleaning micro-scrubbers

Small-screen superstar Rachel Roxx reveals her secret for blemish-free skin— Acne Buster!

Everyone deserves blemish-free skin, including you!

If your face is losing the battle with blackheads, then you need the healing help of our special micro-scrubbers.

Limited Time $4.95

No other product gets your face as clean!

▲ What facts are in this ad? What inferences does the company selling the product hope you will make?

50

Evaluating Skin and Hair Products

When you decide to buy a health product, you must decide whether it has quality and is right for your needs. One way to judge the quality of a product is by finding out about its ingredients.

For many skin and hair products, small differences in ingredients are not important. Most shampoos do a fine job of cleaning hair. If your hair is oily, you can buy a shampoo that removes extra oils. People with dandruff sometimes buy shampoos with special ingredients to control it. If your hair is hard to comb after you wash it, using a conditioner might help. Some shampoos contain conditioners, or you can buy them separately.

Many people use deodorants or antiperspirants to prevent body odor. Deodorants kill some bacteria and cover up odor. Antiperspirants prevent sweating.

You might need a product that helps fight acne. There are medicated soaps, cleansers, and pads specially made for treating acne. These products remove oil from the skin's surface. There are also products that can be used on pimples and blackheads. They dry oily skin and kill bacteria. If acne is severe, a doctor can give you advice on which products or medicines would be best for your skin.

If you aren't sure which products are right for you, you can get reliable information from consumer groups. They test and compare different products. Parents and health-care professionals can also give you helpful information.

SUMMARIZE What should you consider when buying a skin or hair product?

Personal Health Plan ▶

Real-Life Situation
Carefully choosing skin and hair products can help you avoid wasting money. Suppose you need to choose a shampoo for your family.

Real-Life Plan
Write a plan for deciding which shampoo to buy.

◀ Any soap will clean your skin. Some soaps claim to make your skin soft and silky, but they don't get you any cleaner than regular soaps do.

Analyze Labels
Compare the soaps pictured on this page. Which soap label grabs your attention first? Why? Which soap costs the least per ounce? The most per ounce? Which one would you buy? Give your reasons.

Natural Deodorant Soap
Ingredients: Refined coconut oil, refined sugar, fragrance, water, propylene glycol, alcohol, lauryl ester sulfate, ionol, glycerine, neutral pigment
Weight: 4.5 oz
Price: $1.75

Liquid **HAND** Soap

Zippy
Rounds up dirt and odors and drives 'em away!
Weight: 4 oz
Price: $1.35

Moisture Rich
Leaves your skin soft and smooth.
Weight: 4.75 oz
Price: $1.75

Are Name Brands Better?

When shopping, you'll find that some products are name brands while others are store brands. A good shopping strategy is to compare the ingredients in the two products. If the ingredients are the same and listed in the same order, the products are likely the same. The store brand often costs much less and is therefore a better buy. Sometimes, products contain additional ingredients that might offer benefits in addition to the main purpose of the product. These products usually cost more than the basic product. Only you can decide whether the additional ingredients—and cost—are worth it.

MAIN IDEA AND DETAILS **How can you decide between a name-brand and a store-brand product?**

Evaluating Advertisements

❶ Read the ad carefully. Identify any tricks the ad uses to persuade you to buy the product.

❷ Look for information that can be proven true.

❸ Decide whether any information is left out.

Choosing Products

❶ Identify your needs.

❷ Examine the label to see whether the product meets your needs and has the proper ingredients.

❸ Compare products to see which offers a better value.

❹ If necessary, get information about the product from consumer groups, parents, or health-care professionals.

Lesson 2 Summary and Review

❶ Summarize with Vocabulary

Use vocabulary and other terms from this lesson to complete the statements.

A _____ is a person who buys goods or services. Companies use _____ to spread information about their products. Product labels list _____ by weight. When shopping, compare name-brand products with _____ products to see which is a better bargain. You can buy medicated soaps and cleansers to help control _____, a common skin disorder. One way to prevent body odor is to use a _____, which kills bacteria.

❷ Critical Thinking What do the various advertising tricks have in common?

❸ What are reliable sources of information about skin and hair products?

❹ DRAW CONCLUSIONS What things should you consider when buying products for your hair and skin?

| What I Read | + | What I Know | = | Conclusion: |

❺ Write to Inform—Description

Write an advertisement for a soap that makes your skin soft. Give the soap a name, and use descriptive words that might persuade people to buy the product.

Make Responsible Decisions
About Health-Care Products

Every time you buy something, you are making a decision. Often the decision is easy. But deciding which health products are best for you can sometimes be difficult. Using the steps for **Making Responsible Decisions** can help you make good choices that are right for your body.

Lin and Jerome are headed for their neighborhood pool. On their way, they zip into a store to buy some sunscreen. They are surprised to find an aisle full of choices. Which sunscreen should they buy?

1 **Find out about the choices you could make.**

2 **Eliminate choices that are against your family rules.**

Lin and Jerome check out the labels on the sunscreen bottles. The sunscreens have different SPF numbers. Some will allow skin to tan faster. Others will block more of the sun's UV rays.

Lin and Jerome's parents do not buy sunscreens with low SPF values. So, Lin and Jerome eliminate all but two products.

54

3 Ask yourself: What could happen with each choice? Does the choice show good character?

Lin has a sunscreen with SPF 30. Jerome has one with SPF 15. If used as directed, SPF 30 offers greater protection than SPF 15.

4 Make what seems to be the best choice.

Lin and Jerome decide to buy the SPF 30 sunscreen. They reason that if they use the sunscreen as directed and limit their exposure, they will reduce the harmful effects of the sun.

Problem Solving

A. Maria has run out of her face soap. Her mother gives her money to buy more. When Maria gets to the store, she discovers she has many options. There are liquid soaps and bar soaps, and each claims to be the best for cleaning your face.

- Use the steps for **Making Responsible Decisions** to help Maria make the best decision.

B. Sam sees an advertisement on television for shampoo that will keep hair clean for a week. The ad says that the consumer will save time and money because he or she will have to shampoo only once a week. Sam is impressed and considers switching shampoos.

- Explain how Sam can decide whether he should stay with his old shampoo or start using the shampoo he has seen on television.

Your Teeth and Gums

Preventing Tooth Decay

Some things, such as your hair and nails, are always growing. If you cut your hair, it will grow back. However, the teeth you have today are the teeth you'll have many years from now. If you want to keep your teeth clean and healthy, you need to take care of each and every one.

Your teeth are covered with a hard material called enamel. In fact, enamel is the hardest material in your body. Even so, enamel can be destroyed by decay. Tooth decay starts when **plaque** (PLAK), a sticky substance that coats your teeth, is allowed to build up. Hardened plaque can build up under the gums and irritate them, leading to gum disease.

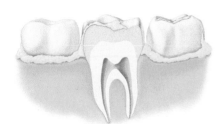

▲ If plaque is allowed to accumulate, it hardens to form a yellow substance called *tartar*.

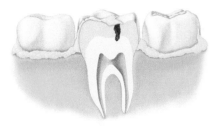

▲ When a cavity (blackened area) spreads to the pulp of a tooth, the tooth probably will become very painful and might need to be removed.

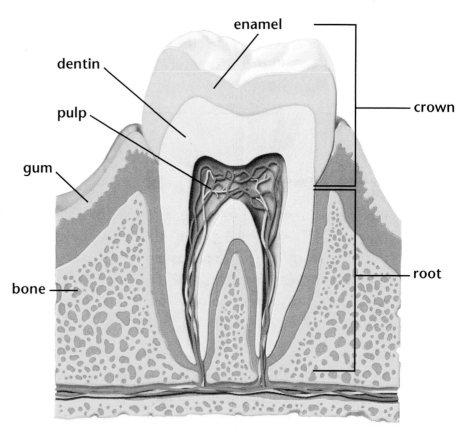

▲ Although different types of teeth have different functions, each tooth has the same parts. In what part of the tooth are blood vessels located?

56

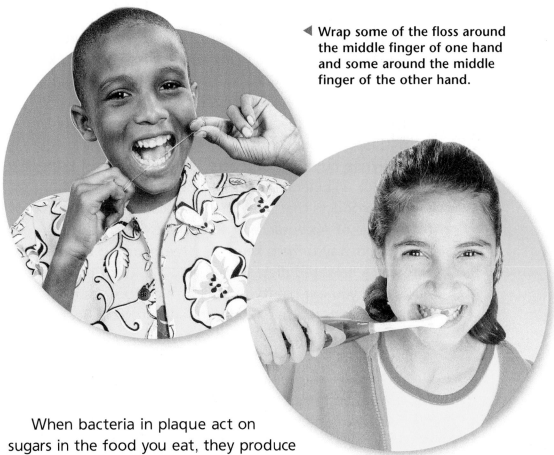

◀ Wrap some of the floss around the middle finger of one hand and some around the middle finger of the other hand.

▲ Be sure to brush all the surfaces of your teeth and along your gum line.

When bacteria in plaque act on sugars in the food you eat, they produce acids. These acids then break down the enamel on your teeth, creating small holes called cavities. If left untreated, cavities can spread to the inner parts of the tooth. The best weapons for fighting tooth decay and gum disease are dental floss and a toothbrush.

Flossing cleans places on your teeth that a toothbrush can't reach. When you floss, use a piece of floss about 18 inches long. Gently push the dental floss between two teeth. At the gum line, bend the floss around each tooth and rub gently. Then move the floss away from the gum, and move it up and down to scrape away plaque. Before going on to two more teeth, unwind a length of clean floss to use. You should floss once a day.

Brushing removes plaque and food particles. Hold your toothbrush at a 45-degree angle against your gums, and move it back and forth across your teeth. Be sure to brush at least twice each day after you eat. If you cannot brush, rinse your mouth with water.

 DRAW CONCLUSIONS **Suppose a person has a cavity in one tooth but feels no pain. What can you conclude about the tooth?**

Caring for Your Teeth

Myth and Fact

Myth: The more toothpaste you use, the cleaner your teeth get.
Fact: Putting a big glob of toothpaste on your brush is wasteful. You should use an amount equal to the size of the nail on your little finger.

A look at the dental product shelves at any store will tell you that consumers have many choices. How do you know which products to buy?

When choosing a toothbrush, choose one with soft bristles. It will clean your teeth without harming your gums. Replace your toothbrush when the bristles become worn. When buying toothpaste, choose one with fluoride (FLOHR•yd), a mineral that strengthens tooth enamel. Choose products that have the American Dental Association (ADA) Seal of Acceptance.

A good way to help keep your teeth strong and healthy is to eat a balanced diet. Teeth contain a lot of calcium, so make sure you eat plenty of calcium-rich foods, such as milk and other dairy products, spinach, and broccoli. Because sugary foods can lead to tooth decay, avoid sticky and sugary snacks.

You should also see a dentist each year. Dentists check for cavities and treat them before they become serious. Dentists also remove tartar and polish your teeth. They may coat the surfaces of your teeth with *dental sealant*, a clear coating that helps protect teeth against cavities.

CAUSE AND EFFECT What can dental sealants prevent?

Waxed or unwaxed dental floss, a manual or electric toothbrush, and gel or paste toothpaste—any of these choices is okay as long as the product has the American Dental Association (ADA) seal. ▼

Appliances for Your Teeth

Some people have teeth that are crooked. Dental appliances, such as braces and retainers, help straighten teeth and improve their appearance. Braces are dental appliances that realign the teeth. Retainers help keep teeth in position after braces are removed.

SUMMARIZE How do dental appliances help teeth?

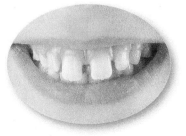

◀ Crooked teeth are more likely to get cavities than teeth that are properly aligned.

◀ Braces can take up to two years to straighten teeth, but the results can be worth it.

Many people wear braces at some point in their lives. ▶

Lesson 3 Summary and Review

❶ Summarize with Vocabulary

Use vocabulary and other terms from this lesson to complete the statements.

_____ is a sticky substance that coats teeth and can lead to cavities. Over time, it can form a hard yellow substance called _____. When you _____, you clean between your teeth. When you brush, use a toothpaste with _____ to strengthen tooth enamel. Dentists can apply a _____ to coat teeth and protect against cavities.

❷ Critical Thinking What causes tooth decay and gum disease?

❸ What kinds of foods can help you develop strong and healthy teeth?

❹ (Focus Skill) DRAW CONCLUSIONS Draw and complete this graphic organizer to show why brushing and flossing are important.

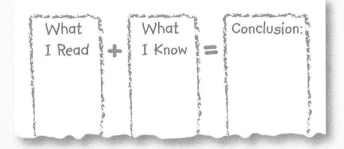

| What I Read | + | What I Know | = | Conclusion: |

❺ Write to Entertain—Poem

Write a poem about your teeth. Tell why your teeth are important. Include details that describe how to care for your teeth and gums.

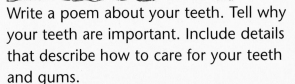

Your Eyes and Ears

Lesson Focus

Vision and hearing are important senses that need to be protected.

Why Learn This?

You can use what you learn to take good care of your eyes and ears.

Vocabulary

nearsighted
farsighted
conjunctivitis
sty
decibels

Common Eye Problems

You learn a lot about your world through your eyes. Although you could think of your eyes as tiny cameras, they really don't take pictures. Instead, they send electrical signals to your brain. The brain translates these signals into messages that it recognizes as pictures.

How is the light that enters your eye changed to electrical signals? The diagram below shows the path that light takes through the eye. As you read the labels, use your finger to trace the path of light.

You can see in the diagram that people with normal vision produce sharply focused images on the retina, but not everyone has normal vision. In a person who is **nearsighted**, the image does not focus on the retina

The human eye can see 10 million different colors. ▼

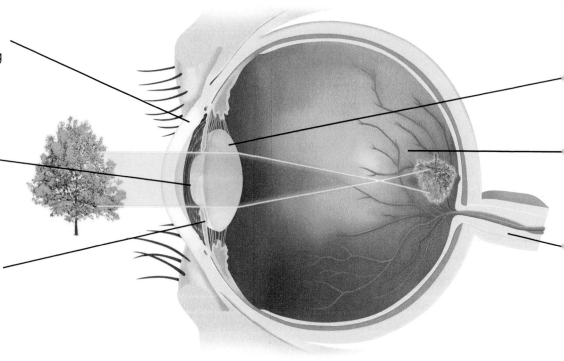

1. Light travels through the *cornea*, the clear covering of the eye.

2. Light enters the eye through an opening in the iris called the *pupil*.

3. The *iris*, the colored part of your eye, opens and closes to let in greater or smaller amounts of light.

but falls in front of it. In a person who is **farsighted**, the image is focused behind the retina. You can see in the pictures to the right how these problems affect the way a person sees.

In another common vision problem, *astigmatism* (uh·STIG·muh·tih·zuhm), the cornea or lens has an irregular shape. This causes blurred or uneven vision. Prescription eyeglasses or contact lenses can correct nearsightedness, farsightedness, and astigmatism.

Some eye problems are caused by infections. **Conjunctivitis** (kuhn·juhngk·tih·VY·tuhs), also called pinkeye, is a highly contagious infection of the tissues on the outside of the eye and under the eyelid. Symptoms include painful, red eyes and a discharge from the eye. A **sty** is an infection of an oil gland in the eyelid. It is caused by a blocked hair follicle.

Applying a clean, warm compress will help relieve the discomfort of conjunctivitis and will help sties heal. Don't squeeze sties. See a doctor for conjunctivitis and for a sty that lasts longer than one week.

 DRAW CONCLUSIONS **Why would an irregularly shaped cornea produce blurry vision?**

4. The *lens* focuses light to form an image on your retina.

5. The *retina* is made up of light-sensitive cells. When the retina receives an image, it produces electrical signals.

6. Electrical signals are sent to the brain through the *optic nerve*.

▲ A person who is nearsighted can clearly see objects that are close up. Objects that are farther away will appear blurry.

▲ A person who is farsighted can see faraway objects clearly, but close-up objects will appear blurry.

Consumer Activity

Make Buying Decisions
Not all sunglasses provide the same degree of UV protection. Use the Internet to research how sunglasses are labeled. Summarize your findings in a report that other students could use when buying sunglasses.

Protecting Your Eyes

The eye is quite an amazing organ, but it's also easily damaged. Your vision can be harmed by household chemicals, flying objects, and many other things. Even sunlight can harm your eyes. So, what can you do to protect your eyes?

Sunglasses protect your eyes from dangerous UV rays. Years of unprotected exposure to the sun can cause cataracts (KA•tuh•rakts), or clouding of the lenses. This condition can lead to blindness.

Eye Safety Rules

- Wash your hands before touching your eyes.

- Ask an adult for help if you get something in your eye.

- Keep sharp objects away from your eyes.

- Never share washcloths or towels with others.

- Wear eye protection when playing sports that require it and when working with hot liquids, chemicals, tools, and objects that could shatter and send pieces into your eyes.

- Wear sunglasses. Never look directly into the sun.

You should buy only sunglasses that meet the standards of the American National Standards Institute (ANSI). Sunglasses labeled *General Purpose* block at least 60 percent of UVA rays and at least 95 percent of UVB rays.

People with concerns about their vision or eyes should see a doctor. One type of doctor, an optometrist (ahp•TAH•muh•trist), can examine the eyes for problems and prescribe corrective lenses. An ophthalmologist (ahf•thuhl•MAH•luh•jist) can help people who have medical problems with their eyes.

CAUSE AND EFFECT How can UV rays affect vision?

Even objects as simple as rubber bands and pins can damage your eyes. Be sure to wear the correct eye protection during activities that use these objects and others like them. ▼

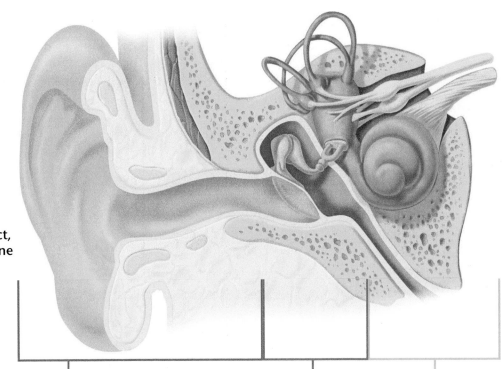

Just as your eyes can "zero in" on a particular object, your ears can hone in on particular sounds. ▶

Outer Ear

The outer ear collects sound waves. The waves move along your *ear canal* to your *eardrum*. The sound waves cause your eardrum to vibrate.

Middle Ear

Vibrations from the eardrum cause three small bones in your middle ear—the *hammer*, *anvil*, and *stirrup*—to vibrate. The vibrations pass into the inner ear.

Inner Ear

Hairlike cells in the *cochlea* pick up the vibrations and pass them on as signals to the *auditory nerve*. From there, the signals are sent to the brain, which interprets them as sounds.

Protecting Your Ears

Your ears are sensitive organs, and following a few guidelines will protect your ears and help you keep your keen sense of hearing.

- Wax in your ears helps keep foreign matter out. If the wax builds up and hardens, see a doctor.
- Never put anything—even cotton swabs—into your ears. Objects can damage your delicate eardrums.
- A blow to the ear or a serious ear infection can also damage your eardrums. See a doctor if either of these happens to you.
- Keep the volume low when you use headphones. Repeated exposure to loud sounds can cause permanent damage to your hearing.

Did You Know?

During the school year, you may be asked to participate in a health screening. A school nurse or other professional may conduct simple tests to check your vision and hearing. You may be referred to a doctor for additional testing.

Quick Activity

Calculate Damage Time Listening to noise at 90 decibels will damage your hearing after 8 hours. Every increase of 5 decibels cuts in half the time it takes for the damage to happen. How long could you listen to music through blasting headphones before you suffered hearing damage?

Effects of Sound

Sound Source	Decibels	Hearing Loss
Leaves rustling; whispering	20	none
Normal speech; bird song	60	none
Lawn mower; motorcycle; gas-powered leaf blower	90	gradual; depends on length of exposure
Loud concert; blasting headphones	110	rapid; depends on length of exposure
Jet engine, 100 feet away	130	immediate

Loud sounds can damage your hearing. The loudness of sound is measured in units called **decibels** (DEH·suh·belz). Sounds at or above 80 decibels can cause you to lose your hearing—permanently. Avoid loud sounds, including music. If you must be around loud sounds, wear ear protection, such as earplugs.

SEQUENCE Tell how sound travels from the outer ear to the brain.

Lesson 4 Summary and Review

❶ Summarize with Vocabulary

Use vocabulary and other terms from this lesson to complete the statements.

In people who are _____ or _____ , images do not focus on the retina. A person with an _____ has an irregularly shaped cornea or lens. One common eye infection is pinkeye, or _____. An infection of an oil gland in the eyelid is a _____. To protect your hearing, avoid sounds above 80 _____.

❷ Critical Thinking How can cataracts lead to blindness?

❸ What path does light take through the eye?

❹ DRAW CONCLUSIONS Why should you take steps to protect your ears and eyes?

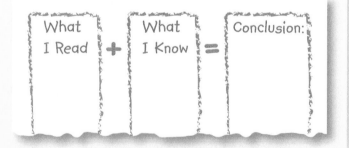

What I Read + What I Know = Conclusion:

❺ Write to Inform—Explanation

Write a paragraph that explains why it is important to cooperate in a health screening.

64

Fairness

Don't Take Advantage of Others

"That's not fair!" These are words no one wants to have to say. Fairness is important when you interact with other people. When you are fair, you look out for other people's interests. Never benefit from a weakness or physical disability someone may possess. Here are some ways that you can be fair with other people.

- **Be honest. Being honest with other people shows that you respect them.**
- **Treat other people equally. Part of being fair is not favoring one person over another.**
- **Play by the rules. When playing games, don't take advantage of the other players.**
- **Be fair to younger children. Don't use their inexperience to your advantage.**
- **If a person has a disability, consider that when you interact. Don't use the person's disability for your benefit.**
- **Take turns. Doing so gives everyone a chance, and no one feels left out.**
- **If you are participating in a group activity, find ways to adapt the activity so that everyone can participate.**

Activity

Pick a game or activity you normally play and tell how you would adapt it to include a person with a disability. For example, you could rearrange furniture to make wheelchair access possible.

65

Technology Product Safety

Preventing Computer-Related Problems

Computers have changed how we work and live. You can use computers to do research, write school reports, play games, and chat with friends. But when you spend time working on the computer, pay attention to your body. Sitting at a computer or working at a laptop for long periods can be tiring. Your arms, legs, and back can get sore from sitting. Your wrists and fingers can get tired from typing and moving the mouse.

People who spend long hours working at computers or playing electronic games sometimes develop **repetitive strain injuries**, or RSIs. These injuries result from making the same motions again and again for long periods. Typing or moving and clicking a computer mouse can cause them. Playing video games for long periods also can cause RSIs.

One RSI common to people who use computer keyboards is carpal tunnel syndrome. **Carpal tunnel syndrome**, or CTS, is a wrist injury that causes shooting pains or numbness in the hands. You can help prevent

Quick Activity

Interpret Data Today, more and more people are using computers in their homes. How has home computer use changed in the past twenty years? Write a brief paragraph that summarizes the information in the graph.

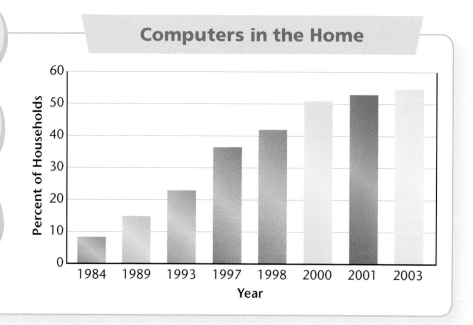

Computers in the Home

Percent of Households (y-axis: 0, 10, 20, 30, 40, 50, 60)

Year (x-axis): 1984, 1989, 1993, 1997, 1998, 2000, 2001, 2003

CTS by learning how to type properly. "Hunting and pecking" is harder on your fingers and wrists than proper typing is. Also, don't grip the mouse tightly.

If you develop good posture and typing habits now, you will be less likely to suffer injuries, such as CTS, later.

 DRAW CONCLUSIONS How does sitting with good posture while using the computer help prevent injuries?

When working at the computer, be sure to take frequent breaks during which you change position, stand up, and stretch. ▼

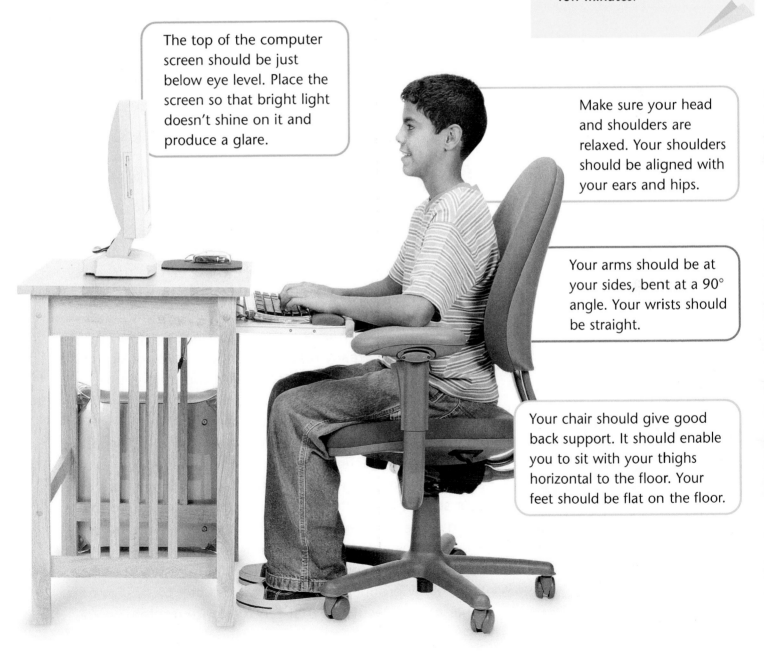

The top of the computer screen should be just below eye level. Place the screen so that bright light doesn't shine on it and produce a glare.

Make sure your head and shoulders are relaxed. Your shoulders should be aligned with your ears and hips.

Your arms should be at your sides, bent at a 90° angle. Your wrists should be straight.

Your chair should give good back support. It should enable you to sit with your thighs horizontal to the floor. Your feet should be flat on the floor.

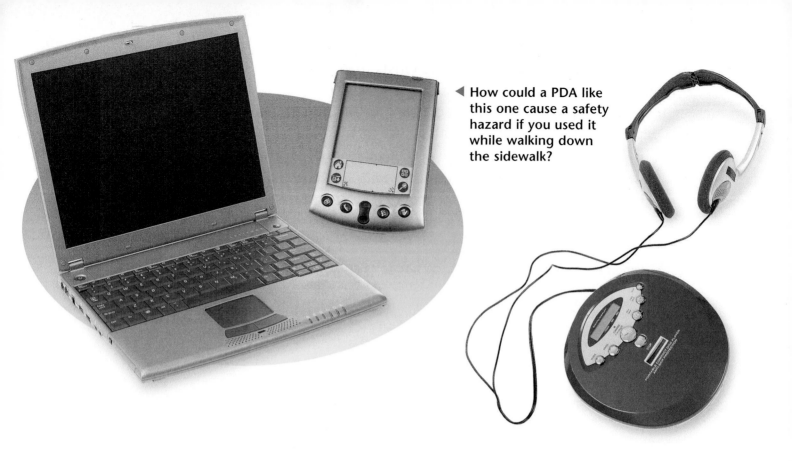

◀ How could a PDA like this one cause a safety hazard if you used it while walking down the sidewalk?

This girl is in a safe area to talk on her cell phone. ▼

Using Technology Products Wisely

Today, many kinds of technology products are at your fingertips. Cell phones, portable video games, laptop computers, personal digital assistants (PDAs), and MP3 players are just a few. Products like these can be fun and convenient to use. However, when you use technology products, you must also use common sense. Using them incorrectly can result in eyestrain, muscle fatigue, and injuries. You've already read about how to use correct posture and lighting when sitting at a computer, but there are other safety tips to keep in mind.

Some technology products are so much fun that you might forget about what's going on around you. The device becomes a **distraction**, something that takes your attention away. If you're using a technology product, stay aware of your surroundings. Remember, if your eyes are glued to a video game, you can't see important environmental cues. You may not notice safety hazards around you. This can put you in dangerous situations. For that reason, don't use technology products when you walk, skate, bicycle, or do other physical activities that require concentration.

◀ Playing computer games too often or too long can result in RSIs. ▶

Another way to avoid injuries when using some electronic devices is to keep the volume down. When the music from your portable CD player fills your ears, you can't hear important sounds around you. Also, you might damage your hearing if the sound is too loud.

Making sure that you can sense danger is an important part of staying healthy. Keep your ears and eyes in touch with the world around you as you enjoy the many technology products that are available today.

 DRAW CONCLUSIONS How might listening to music on a headset be a distraction while riding a bike?

▲ How can you use each of these technology products safely?

Lesson 5 Summary and Review

1 Summarize with Vocabulary

Use vocabulary and other terms from this lesson to complete the statements.

Part of good computer posture is to keep your arms bent at a _____ angle. To avoid _____, which causes shooting pains in the hands, learn how to type properly. Injuries that result from doing the same motion again and again are called _____. Technology products are useful and fun, but they can be a _____.

2 Critical Thinking How can you improve your own computer habits to prevent discomfort and injury?

3 What causes repetitive strain injuries?

4 DRAW CONCLUSIONS Why is it important to use technology products safely?

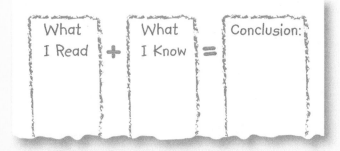

| What I Read | + | What I Know | = | Conclusion: |

5 Write to Inform—Description

Write about the last time you used a technology product. Use what you learned in this lesson to identify ways you were and weren't using the product safely.

Information About Health

Your doctor has medical training and knows your health history. When you visit a doctor, be sure to ask any questions you have. ▼

People in the Know About Health

An important skill that everyone should have is knowing how to find and use reliable health information. Today you can find health information just about anywhere—on the Internet, in books, pamphlets, newspapers, magazines, and in other printed materials. You can ask a variety of people—your parents, health-care professionals, teachers, even your friends. All these sources seem to have answers, but they don't always agree. How do you know which sources to trust? Knowing how to evaluate sources of health information will help you decide which information is reliable.

Often, the best place to start when you want health information is your parents or guardians. If they don't know the answer, they can help you find it.

Some of the best sources of health information are doctors, dentists, pharmacists, and other health-care professionals. They've spent many years learning about the human body and health products. You and your parents can talk to these professionals about health questions. Other good sources for health information are consumer groups and health organizations. Organizations such as the American Lung Association and the American Heart Association are always willing to provide answers to your questions.

One source of information you probably have considered is your friends. Getting answers from friends about most health questions isn't a good idea. Your friends probably don't know more than you do about most health topics. In addition, they don't always know what is right for you.

SUMMARIZE Why are doctors and pharmacists good sources of health information?

ACTIVITY

Life Skills
Communicate

How could a pharmacist help you choose an acne product that is right for you? What information would you give the pharmacist about yourself? What questions would you ask?

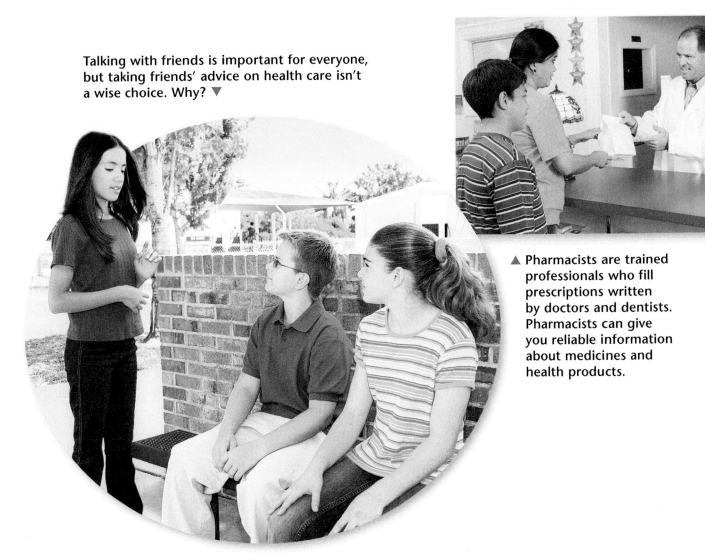

Talking with friends is important for everyone, but taking friends' advice on health care isn't a wise choice. Why? ▼

▲ Pharmacists are trained professionals who fill prescriptions written by doctors and dentists. Pharmacists can give you reliable information about medicines and health products.

Evaluating Health Websites

More and more people are turning to the Internet to find health information. You can find many websites filled with reliable health facts. However, it's important to remember that anyone can put information on the Internet. Here are some questions to help you evaluate whether a website provides solid health information.

DRAW CONCLUSIONS Why is comparing the information from several websites a good practice?

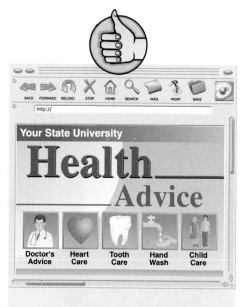

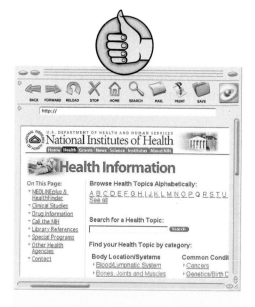

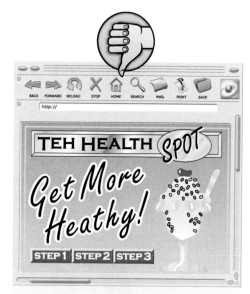

Who controls the website?

A website can be biased, or slanted, toward one viewpoint. For example, the maker of a health product may have only good things to say about the product. Look for websites that are run by a university or by the government (*.gov*). These are more reliable than websites run by individuals or by companies that make products.

Who is saying it?

Information from doctors, nurses, and other health-care professionals is usually reliable. Look for the initials of a college degree, such as M.D., R.N., Ph.D., or Pharm.D., after the writer's name. Newspaper and magazine sites usually check their facts with health professionals, so they usually are reliable, too.

Does the site look good?

Frequent spelling or grammar mistakes and poor design are warning signs. If those who made the website didn't take time to fix simple mistakes, they may not have taken time to check their health facts, either.

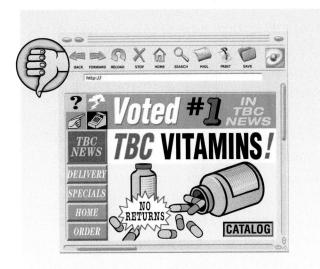

Is the website selling something?

Sites that are trying to sell products may not be reliable. Often, they tell you only what makes their products or services sound good. Nonprofit websites are usually more reliable sources of health information.

What is the evidence?

Personal stories about how a health product has changed people's lives or health can sound convincing. However, personal stories are not as reliable as scientifically tested information. Look for sites with evidence from scientific research.

Do websites agree?

Always check more than one website when looking for specific health information. You may find that the health "facts" claimed in one website are said to be false by another. If several sites agree on the facts, the information probably is reliable.

Health Facts from Other Sources

You can get health information from a variety of print materials. Reference books such as encyclopedias and dictionaries usually provide health facts that you can trust. Medical journals have information based on recent scientific research. You also can get a lot of reliable health information from the publications of health organizations.

Many magazines have health information, but be sure the information is written or approved by health professionals or consumer groups. Some magazines give information that is not supported by science. Beware of magazine articles that tell about "miracle" health products, fad diets, and weight-loss products. These articles are not reliable sources of information.

MAIN IDEA AND DETAILS **What are three reliable print sources of health information?**

Lesson 6 Summary and Review

1 Summarize with Vocabulary

Use terms from this lesson to complete the statements.

The best place to start when you want health information is at home with your _____. To learn about medicines, you could ask a _____, who is trained to fill prescriptions. Another source of information is a _____, such as the American Heart Association. Always make sure that information in a magazine is approved by a _____, such as an M.D.

2 List four people you can ask for reliable health information.

3 Critical Thinking How can health-care professionals help you make decisions about the health products you buy?

4 **DRAW CONCLUSIONS** Why is it important to evaluate sources of health information?

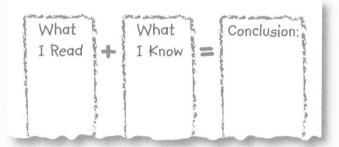

What I Read	+	What I Know	=	Conclusion:

5 Write to Express—Business Letter

Write a letter to an imaginary consumer group requesting information about a product you might buy. Be sure to tell the consumer group what information you would like and why.

ACTIVITIES

Social Studies

The History of Cleanliness Soap as we know it has not always been available or affordable. The ancient Greeks rinsed dirt and sweat off their bodies with olive oil. Do research to find out some other ways people got clean long ago.

Science

Spectrum Diagram Sunlight contains ultraviolet rays that can harm your eyes and skin. UV rays are energy waves that are part of the electromagnetic spectrum. Research the electromagnetic spectrum and write a brief report. You may use pictures, charts, and diagrams to illustrate your findings.

Technology Project

Make a chart that lists ways to tell whether a website is reliable. Post your chart in your school's computer lab or in another place where students at your school use computers.

GO ONLINE For more activities, visit The Learning Site. www.harcourtschool.com/health

Home & Community

Communicating Make a poster that explains the dangers of ultraviolet rays and the importance of wearing and reapplying sunscreen. Display your poster in your school or at a community swimming pool.

Career Link

Optometrist Optometrists test people's eyes for problems and prescribe eyeglasses and contact lenses. Suppose that you are going to visit an optometrist. Write four questions you would like to ask. Explain why you would like to know the answer to each question.

75

Chapter Review and Test Preparation

 Reading Skill

DRAW CONCLUSIONS

Draw and then use this graphic organizer to answer questions 1 and 2.

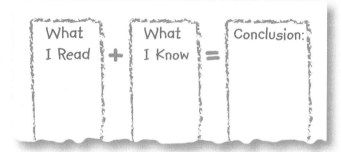

What I Read + What I Know = Conclusion:

1 Suppose Karen had pinkeye. Days later, several of her classmates had pinkeye. What can you conclude?

2 What can you conclude about the reliability of two websites, one ending in *.gov* and one ending in *.com*?

 Use Vocabulary

Match each term in Column B with its meaning in Column A.

Column A	Column B
3 Skin disorder caused by plugged pores	A consumer
	B decibel
4 Someone who buys products or services	C carpal tunnel syndrome
	D cuticle
5 Something that takes your attention away	E acne
	F distraction
6 Unit of the loudness of sound	G hair follicle
7 A common RSI	
8 Skin around the nail	
9 Tiny sac from which hair grows	

Check Understanding

Choose the letter of the correct answer.

10 Which of the following is **NOT** a long-term effect of the sun's UV rays? (pp. 46, 62)
A cancer   C sunburn
B wrinkles   D cataracts

11 The outermost layer of skin is the _____. (p. 43)
F dermis   H hair follicle
G epidermis   J cuticle

12 Which of these questions is **BEST** to ask when choosing a skin or hair product? (p. 51)
A Does a famous person advertise the product?
B Is the product the cheapest available?
C Is the product's packaging attractive?
D What are the product's ingredients?

13 Which of the following can lead to gum disease? (p. 56)
F tartar   H pulp
G calcium   J fluoride

14 Which of these does **NOT** help prevent repetitive strain injuries? (pp. 66–67)
A keeping good posture
B working without a break
C keeping your wrists straight when typing
D relaxing your head and shoulders

15 You should brush your teeth at least _____. (p. 57)
F twice a day
G once a week
H once a day
J four times a day

16 Which of the following is the least reliable source of health information? (p. 71)

A your doctor   **C** a friend

B a pharmacist   **D** a medical journal

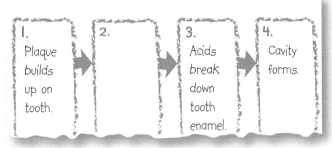

1. Plaque builds up on tooth. → 2. → 3. Acids break down tooth enamel. → 4. Cavity forms.

17 Which is the missing step in the formation of a cavity? (p. 57)

F Cavity spreads to inner part of tooth.

G Food builds up on teeth.

H Gum disease develops.

J Bacteria act on sugars in food you eat.

18 Which of these sunscreens provides the greatest protection? (p. 46)

A SPF 10   **C** SPF 20

B SPF 15   **D** SPF 30

19 Which term describes an infection of the eye? (p. 61)

F conjunctivitis

G nearsightedness

H farsightedness

J astigmatism

20 Which of the following websites would probably provide the most reliable information? (pp. 72–73)

A a university website

B a website with a personal story

C a website selling products

D a website with spelling errors

Think Critically

21 Why do you think it is important to wash your hands more often than other parts of your body?

22 Suppose you had acne and were trying to decide which skin care product to buy. What sources of information could you use to make your decision?

Apply Skills

23 **BUILDING GOOD CHARACTER**

Fairness Your friend Emily invites you to a party at her house on Friday evening. You've already promised your younger brother that you'll go to the movies with him that night. Apply what you know about fairness to help you decide what to do.

24 **LIFE SKILLS**

Make Responsible Decisions Your doctor recommended a special shampoo to help reduce the oil in your hair. Your friend tells you about a great shampoo that she bought that has helped her oily hair. Use what you know about making decisions to decide whether you should switch to the shampoo recommended by your friend.

Write About Health

25 Write to Inform—Explanation Explain why taking care of your skin, eyes, and ears now will be important to your health as you get older.

CHAPTER 3

Preparing Healthful Foods

Reading Skill

COMPARE AND CONTRAST When you compare, you tell how two or more things are alike. When you contrast, you tell how they are different. Use the Reading in Health Handbook on pages 400–401 and this graphic organizer to help you read the health facts in this chapter.

Compare and Contrast
Topic:
Alike   Different

Health Graph

INTERPRET DATA An orange and a 1-cup serving of Brussels sprouts contain almost the same amount of vitamin C. Both foods contain more than six times as much vitamin C as a banana. About how much more vitamin C is found in an orange than in an apple?

Vitamin C Content of Fruits and Vegetables

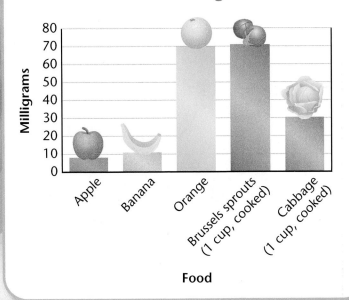

Daily Physical Activity

You should eat the right amount of healthful foods each day to provide your body with the nutrients it needs. Exercise should also be a part of each day.

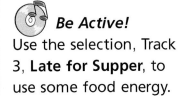 **Be Active!** Use the selection, Track 3, **Late for Supper**, to use some food energy.

The Nutrients in Foods

Lesson Focus

To stay healthy, a person needs the right amounts of six types of nutrients.

Why Learn This?

You can manage your diet to help yourself stay healthy.

Vocabulary

calories
carbohydrates
fiber
fats
cholesterol
proteins
minerals
vitamins

Nutrients as Sources of Calories

Riding a bicycle to school, laughing about a joke, breathing, and even thinking are all activities that require energy. You get energy from nutrients in the foods you eat.

Carbohydrates, fats, and proteins are nutrients that supply your body with energy and materials for growth. The amount of energy your body is able to get from food is measured in units called **calories** (KAL•uh•reez).

Carbohydrates (kar•boh•HY•drayts) are sugars and starches. There are two kinds of carbohydrates—simple and complex. Simple carbohydrates include sugars such as fructose, which is found in fruits and honey. Your body gets energy right away from simple carbohydrates. Complex carbohydrates, which include starches, are found in whole grains and in vegetables such as potatoes and corn. Complex carbohydrates are digested more slowly, so that the energy they contain is released over a longer period of time.

Nutrients
1 Sugars
2 Starches
3 Fats
4 Proteins
5 Fiber

Foods can be categorized according to the nutrients they contain. ▶

Some complex carbohydrates contain fiber. **Fiber** is the chewy or gritty material in foods such as celery and beans. Fiber is important to your health. It helps food move through your digestive system, and it may prevent certain forms of cancer.

Fats are the nutrients that yield the most calories per gram of food. However, it takes longer for your body to use the energy from fats than the energy from carbohydrates. Fats are important for normal body function, but you should limit the amount of fats—especially animal fats—that you eat. Some kinds of fat raise the level of cholesterol in the blood. **Cholesterol** (kuh·LES·ter·awl) is a substance the body needs to build cells and for other functions. However, high blood levels of some types of cholesterol are associated with heart disease.

Proteins (PROH·teenz) are nutrients that help build and repair your cells. Proteins contain the same amount of energy per gram as carbohydrates. Proteins are used mainly for building the body, but they may be broken down for energy.

⭐ **Focus Skill** **COMPARE AND CONTRAST How are fructose and starches alike? How are they different?**

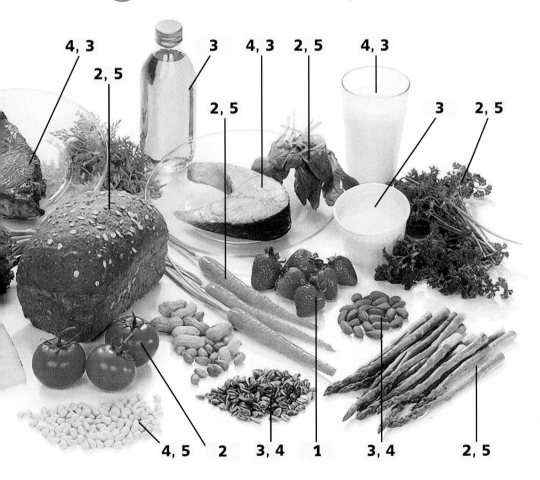

4, 3   3   4, 3   2, 5   4, 3

2, 5   2, 5   3   2, 5

4, 5   2   3, 4   1   3, 4   2, 5

Quick Activity

Minerals in Your Body Look at the diagrams on pages 4–11, and identify which parts of your body are affected by the four minerals described on this page. To which body system does each of these parts belong?

Nutrients That Control Body Processes

Some nutrients do not provide energy for your body. Even so, you need them to survive. **Minerals** (MIN·uhr·uhlz), such as calcium and iron, are nutrients that help your body grow and work. There are about twenty different minerals that are required to maintain good health.

Some minerals help your body use and store energy. Others strengthen your skeleton, heart, muscles, and nerves. Some help regulate your body's water balance, while others help move materials into and out of your cells. Minerals also help you fight diseases.

spinach

tuna

Iron is needed by red blood cells, which carry oxygen throughout your body. Sources of iron include liver, kidney, red meat, fish, beans, nuts, dried fruits, green leafy vegetables, and enriched grain products.

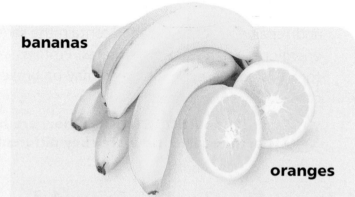

bananas

oranges

Potassium helps the muscles move, helps nerve signals travel through the body, and helps maintain the body's water balance. Potassium is found in potatoes, beans, oranges, bananas, peanut butter, and meat.

beef

pinto beans

Phosphorus helps build strong bones and teeth and helps the body store energy from food. It is found in meats, fish, eggs, dairy products, beans, and nuts.

cheeses

Calcium helps build strong bones and teeth. It is found in dairy products, sardines (with bones), and dark green, leafy vegetables.

Principal Vitamins

Vitamin	Sources	What It Does
A	Liver, fortified milk, yellow and orange vegetables, leafy vegetables, sweet potatoes or yams	Helps keep skin and eyes healthy; helps the immune system
B$_1$ (thiamine)	Whole grains, wheat germ, meat, pork, fish, pasta, navy and kidney beans	Helps keep the nervous system healthy
B$_2$ (riboflavin)	Dairy products, red meat, liver, dried fruit, enriched breads and cereals	Helps release energy from foods; helps other B vitamins
B$_{12}$	Liver, beef, eggs, milk, fish, cheese, poultry, fortified breads and cereals	Builds red blood cells; keeps nerves working
C	Citrus fruits, tomatoes, strawberries, broccoli, potatoes	Keeps gums, blood vessels, and teeth healthy; helps in absorbing iron and healing wounds
D	Fortified milk and cereals, sunlight exposure	Helps keep bones and teeth strong; helps calcium absorption
E	Unprocessed whole grains, nuts, vegetable oils, leafy vegetables, avocados	Helps build blood cells; helps nerves work
K	Green leafy vegetables, beef liver	Helps blood clot

Vitamins (VYT•uh•minz) are nutrients that help important chemical reactions take place in your body. Like minerals, they do not store energy your body can use. Your body needs only small amounts of vitamins.

Vitamins A, D, E, and K in foods cannot be absorbed by the intestine unless they are eaten with some fat. The body can store these vitamins for a long time. The B vitamins and vitamin C are absorbed through the intestinal wall along with water. The body does not store these vitamins well.

CAUSE AND EFFECT What kinds of foods might help heal a person who has unhealthy gums?

Consumer Activity

Access Valid Health Information
Manufacturers of food supplements often claim that taking a daily vitamin supplement can help prevent some chronic diseases. Use the Internet to locate information from reliable sources to help you evaluate claims that supplement manufacturers make.

The amount of water in the human body varies between about 50 percent and 75 percent. The amount depends on your body makeup. Lean muscle, for example, contains more water than fat.

All of the chemical reactions in your body take place in a watery environment. That is why you must replace water lost during exercise. ▼

The Nutrient Your Body Needs Most

Your body is mostly made of water. Although water provides no calories for energy, your body must have water to function. You need water to transport nutrients to all the cells in your body. You need it to build new cells. You need it to keep your body temperature stable. Water helps carry wastes out of your body. It helps keep your joints moving smoothly. In fact, your body needs water for almost everything. Without water, you could live only a few days.

It is a good idea to drink six to eight 8-ounce glasses of water each day—more if you are exercising or when the weather is hot. You also get water from milk and soups. Fruits and vegetables contain water too.

Some people drink bottled water because they like the taste. Other people drink it because they think it is more healthful than tap water. In some cases this is true. However, in many cases, bottled water comes from the same sources as tap water. In addition, bottled water might contain substances, like sodium, that you don't need. Bottled water sometimes lacks important minerals, like calcium and magnesium, that are often found in tap water. Most bottled water also lacks fluoride, which is often added to tap water to help prevent tooth decay.

SUMMARIZE Tell why water is a vital nutrient for your body.

Health & Technology

Water Purification In most cases, tap water that comes to your home has been cleaned with chlorine to kill harmful germs. In some places water is being cleaned instead through a process called ozonation. In this process, water is treated with a form of oxygen called ozone, which kills microorganisms that can cause illness.

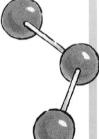

Lesson 1 Summary and Review

❶ Summarize with Vocabulary

Use vocabulary from this lesson to complete the statements.

One source of energy in food is simple and complex _____. Another source is _____, which contain the most energy per gram of food. _____ help with the body's chemical reactions. Iron and potassium are _____ that are vital to good health.

❷ Why can it be unhealthful to eat foods that increase cholesterol in the blood?

❸ Critical Thinking Why do you think your body needs extra water when you exercise or when the weather is hot?

❹ (Focus Skill) COMPARE AND CONTRAST

Draw and complete this graphic organizer to show how proteins and carbohydrates are alike and different.

Topic: Proteins and Carbohydrates
Alike   Different

❺ Write to Inform—Explanation

Write a paragraph in which you tell why water is considered a nutrient and why it's important to your health.

A Balanced Diet

Lesson Focus

Eating a balanced diet can help make you healthy.

Why Learn This?

Understanding the USDA Food Guide Pyramid can help you choose a healthful diet.

Vocabulary

balanced diet
food guide pyramid
serving
vegetarian

Information Alert!

Nutrition and Research The USDA Food Guide Pyramid is based on scientific research. As scientists discover more about nutrition, the Food Guide Pyramid may change.

For the most up-to-date information, visit The Learning Site. www.harcourtschool.com/health

Forming Healthful Eating Habits

To help your body work at its best, you need to eat a balanced diet. A **balanced diet** is a diet of a variety of foods that give the body all the nutrients it needs. A **food guide pyramid** is a tool people can use to achieve a healthful, balanced diet.

The Food Guide Pyramid developed by the United States Department of Agriculture (USDA) is based on servings. A **serving** is the measured amount of a food recommended for a meal or as a snack. For example, a serving can be any of the following.

- 1 slice whole-grain bread
- $\frac{1}{2}$ cup cooked pasta
- 1 medium-sized piece of fruit
- 1 cup salad greens
- $\frac{1}{2}$ cup fruit or vegetables (chopped, cooked, or canned)

- 4 ounces unsweetened fruit juice
- 8 ounces milk
- $1\frac{1}{2}$ ounces cheese
- 1 egg
- 2 tablespoons peanut butter
- 2–3 ounces lean meat or fish

You don't have to eat all the servings from a food group at one time. Instead, you need to eat the right number of servings from each group each day for your age and size.

One of the USDA's Dietary Guidelines for Americans is to use the USDA Food Guide Pyramid when choosing foods. Using this guide will help you make decisions that lead to good health. For a list of the Dietary Guidelines for Americans, see page 99.

COMPARE AND CONTRAST How is the Vegetable Group like the Milk, Yogurt, and Cheese Group? How are they different?

The USDA Food Guide Pyramid

The number of servings from each food group are suggested for children ages 7–12.

Fats, Oils, Sweets Group
Foods in this group provide few nutrients but many calories. Eat these foods in very small amounts.

Milk, Yogurt, Cheese Group
Many dairy products supply protein, fats, carbohydrates, and minerals such as calcium and potassium.
3 SERVINGS

Meat, Poultry, Fish, Dry Beans, Eggs, Nuts Group
Foods in this group are high in protein, and some are rich in vitamins and minerals. Some are high in fats, cholesterol, and calories.
2–3 SERVINGS

Vegetable Group
Vegetables are good sources of vitamins, minerals, fiber, and carbohydrates. Many vegetables contain small amounts of protein. They contain very little fat.
3–5 SERVINGS

Fruit Group
Fruits have little fat or cholesterol and are rich in fiber, minerals, vitamins, and carbohydrates.
2–4 SERVINGS

Bread, Cereal, Rice, Pasta Group
These foods are made from grains. They can contain complex carbohydrates, fiber, minerals, protein, and vitamins. Many are low in fats and cholesterol. 6–9 SERVINGS

Quick Activity

Analyze Meals Look at the meals on these pages. Which groups from the USDA Food Guide Pyramid are represented in each meal? How many servings are there from each group? Are both meals balanced? Explain.

Having a Nutritious Diet Without Meat

ACTIVITY

Life Skills

Make Responsible Decisions

Suzanne has two meal choices. She can have a sandwich with turkey, lettuce, and tomato, along with an apple and milk. Or she can have a slice of pepperoni pizza, a chocolate milkshake, and a cookie. Use the USDA Food Guide Pyramid to help you explain which is the more healthful meal.

A **vegetarian** (veh·juh·TAIR·ee·uhn) is a person who does not eat foods that come from animals. Some vegetarians eat milk products and eggs but do not eat meat. Other vegetarians eat no animal products at all.

A diet that is balanced must include sources of protein. Milk and eggs provide protein for some vegetarians. Vegetarians who eat no animal products must eat particular combinations of plant proteins, such as beans and rice, at each meal. Soybean products, beans, peas, lentils, corn, and brown rice are all good sources of plant protein.

Vegetarians also need to eat foods high in iron, such as beans, nuts, raisins, greens, and enriched cereals and bread. Vegetarians who do not eat animal products get the calcium they need by eating green leafy vegetables, nuts, tofu, and dried figs.

MAIN IDEA AND DETAILS How can a vegetarian eat as healthfully as someone who eats meat? Give examples of foods vegetarians substitute for meat.

▲ People can eat a nutritious diet without meat by following the vegetarian food guide pyramid.

Vegetarian Food Guide Pyramid

Fats, oils, sweets

Milk, yogurt, cheese

Dried beans, eggs, nuts, seeds, and meat substitutes

Vegetables

Fruit

Bread, cereal, pasta, and rice

Lesson 2 Summary and Review

❶ Summarize with Vocabulary

Use vocabulary and other terms from this lesson to complete the statements.

You can plan a _____ by consulting a _____, which tells you how many _____ from each food group you should eat each day. A _____, or a person who doesn't eat animal products, gets _____ from other foods, such as soybean products, lentils, and brown rice.

❷ Which food group provides the most calories for the fewest nutrients?

❸ Critical Thinking Suppose you are a scientist who discovers that large numbers of Americans eat too much. Tell how you would change the USDA Food Guide Pyramid.

❹ COMPARE AND CONTRAST Tell how the USDA Food Guide Pyramid and the vegetarian food guide pyramid are alike and different.

Topic: USDA and Vegetarian Food Guide Pyramids

Alike   Different

❺ Write to Inform—Explanation

Suppose someone says that the diet of a vegetarian is not as healthful as the diet of someone who eats meat. Write a paragraph explaining how vegetarians can achieve a balanced diet without meat.

Nutrition Around the World

Lesson Focus

Each region in the world has its own typical foods that provide good nutrition.

Why Learn This?

You can use what you learn to enjoy a wide variety of foods in a healthful diet.

Vocabulary

staple

Mexican Cooking

The rich varieties and flavors of Mexican food come from its ingredients. A platter of Mexican food is likely to include beans. Beans are a **staple**, or key food ingredient, in the Mexican diet. The platter might also include beef, pork, fish, or chicken. It may contain cheese and green guacamole (gwah•kuh•MOH•lay) as well. Guacamole is made from mashed avocado mixed with chopped onions, tomatoes, hot peppers, lemon juice, and a tangy herb called cilantro.

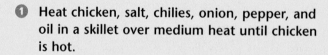

Chicken Soft Tacos

2 c cut-up cooked chicken
$\frac{1}{4}$ tsp salt
4 oz green chilies, chopped
1 onion, sliced
$1\frac{1}{2}$ tbsp vegetable oil
8 tortillas

2 peppers (red, green, or yellow), chopped
1 large tomato, chopped
$\frac{1}{2}$ c sliced black olives
1 medium avocado, chopped
Taco sauce

1 Heat chicken, salt, chilies, onion, pepper, and oil in a skillet over medium heat until chicken is hot.

2 Wrap tortillas in foil, and warm in 250°F oven for 10 minutes.

3 Spoon $\frac{1}{4}$ c chicken mixture onto each tortilla. Top with tomato, avocado, and olives. Serve with taco sauce. Serves 4 people.

Many Mexican meals are served with stacks of thin, round tortillas (tawr•TEE•uhs), or Mexican flatbread. You spoon a little of each ingredient from your platter onto a tortilla, fold the tortilla, and feast on the delicious combination of flavors. Tortillas are also an ingredient in various dishes, such as enchiladas and tacos.

Does Mexican food provide a balanced, healthful meal? Take a look at the USDA Food Guide Pyramid on page 87. Does the platter of food described at the start of this lesson have foods from each of the food groups? Tortillas belong in the Bread, Cereal, Rice, and Pasta Group. Lemons come from the Fruit Group. Tomatoes, onions, and cilantro are in the Vegetable Group, and the beef, pork, fish, chicken, and beans are in the Meat Group. Cheese belongs to the Milk, Yogurt, and Cheese Group, while avocados and the oil used to prepare the food are in the Fats, Oils, and Sweets Group.

 COMPARE AND CONTRAST How is a chicken soft taco like a cheeseburger on a wheat roll with lettuce, tomato, and onion? How are the two different?

Personal Health Plan ▶

Real-Life Situation

Suppose you go to a Mexican restaurant with your family. You want to order a balanced meal.

Real-Life Plan

Use your knowledge of the USDA Food Guide Pyramid to order a meal that is well balanced. If necessary, ask your server to describe the ingredients used in various dishes.

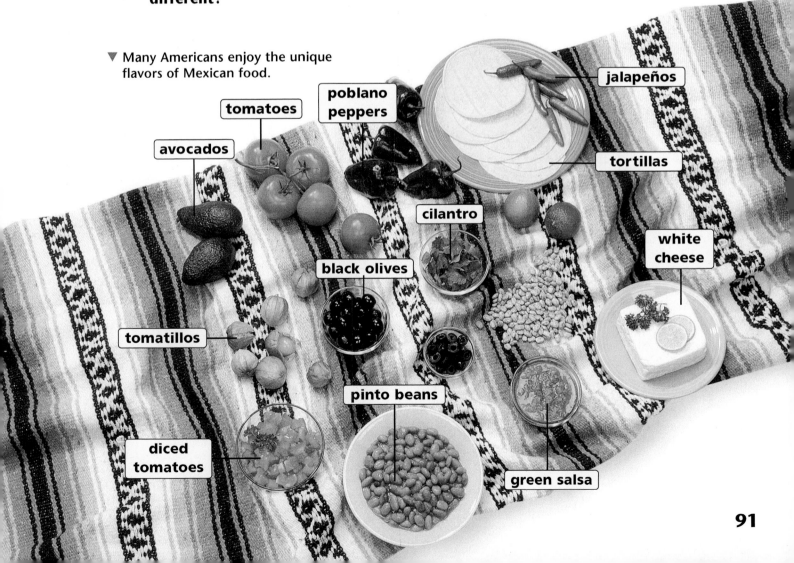

▼ Many Americans enjoy the unique flavors of Mexican food.

- jalapeños
- poblano peppers
- tomatoes
- avocados
- tortillas
- cilantro
- black olives
- white cheese
- tomatillos
- pinto beans
- diced tomatoes
- green salsa

Asian Food

The Asian continent, which consists of more than forty nations, is home to more than half of Earth's population. It is no wonder, then, that Asian foods show such variety. The Asian diet is made up of foods from all of the food groups.

Stir-Fried Tofu and Vegetables

1 block of very firm tofu
2 c each of three kinds of sliced vegetables (such as carrots, red pepper, zucchini)

1–2 tbsp stir-fry oil
Hoisin or teriyaki sauce to taste

❶ Cut tofu into cubes.

❷ Stir-fry vegetables in hot oil until tender.

❸ Stir in tofu, and cook a few minutes longer.

❹ Add sauce.

❺ Serve by itself or over hot cooked rice. Serves 4 people.

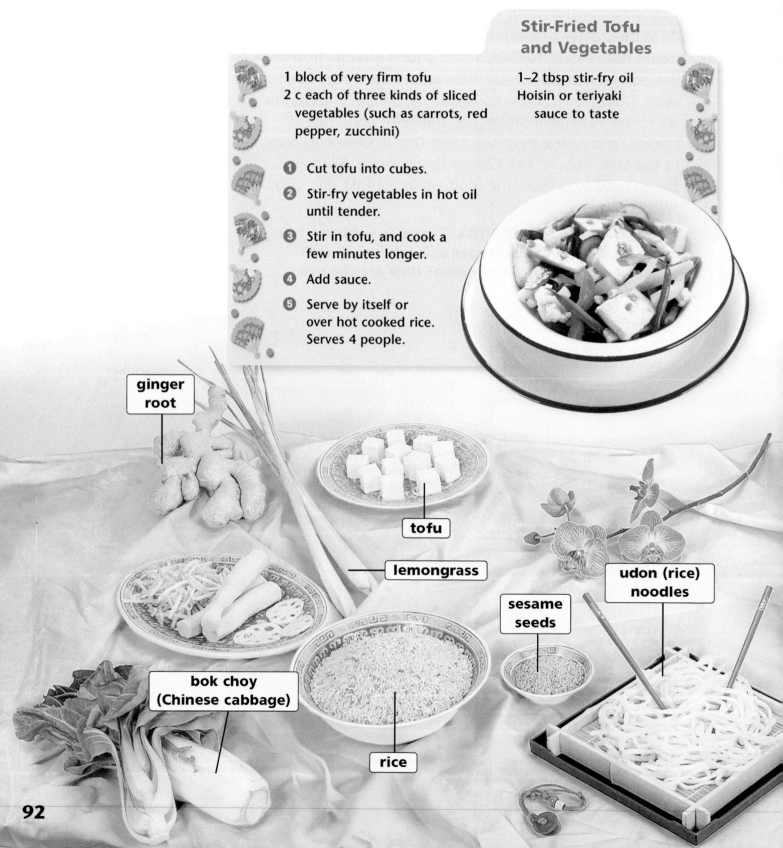

ginger root

tofu

lemongrass

bok choy (Chinese cabbage)

rice

sesame seeds

udon (rice) noodles

Spicy foods are common in India, Pakistan, and nearby countries. Many of these foods use curry powder to make a spicy curry sauce. Curry is spread over rice, meat, vegetables, and other foods. Many Asian dishes are prepared with rice, a staple of the Asian diet.

Spicy pickled cabbage is popular in Korea. Foods in Thailand are often flavored with lemongrass, lime, and peanuts. Foods from Vietnam sometimes show the influence of French cooking. A great variety of dishes come from various regions of China. Spicy foods are eaten in the Sichuan province, in southern China. Milder foods are eaten in Guangzhou (Canton), in the southeast.

Sushi is a staple in Japan. One type of sushi consists of raw fish placed atop small beds of sticky, vinegar-flavored rice and wrapped with a thin ribbon of seaweed. Sushi is served cold along with slices of pickled ginger and spicy wasabi (WAH·suh·bee) paste.

MAIN IDEA AND DETAILS Why are there many different kinds of food in Asia?

Myth and Fact

Myth: All Asian food is like Chinese food.

Fact: Asian foods are as varied as the more than forty countries that make up the Asian continent. Indian, Afghan, Thai, Malaysian, Vietnamese, Japanese, and Korean foods are other examples of Asian food.

scallops

seaweed sheets

soybeans

cashews

93

Quick Activity

Compare Foods Make a table in which you compare the three recipes in this lesson. Which food groups are represented in each recipe? Do the recipes all provide about the same number of servings per food group? How do the recipes differ?

Mediterranean Food

The Mediterranean Sea borders more than a dozen countries in Africa, Europe, and the Middle East. Foods prepared in these countries are often based on local food products, such as olives. Many recipes include olive oil.

Greeks serve a sweet dessert called baklava (bahk•luh•VAH). It is made of nuts baked inside thin pastry that is covered with honey-and-lemon syrup.

Italians who live near the sea often eat pasta dishes with different kinds of seafood. Those who live inland where tomato vines grow are likely to serve pasta with a variety of tomato-based sauces.

People in North Africa eat couscous (KOOS•koos), which is steamed coarsely ground wheat. Couscous is served with chopped bell peppers, tomato, lemon juice, peas, carrots, and poultry or meat.

CAUSE AND EFFECT Why do many Mediterranean dishes contain olive oil?

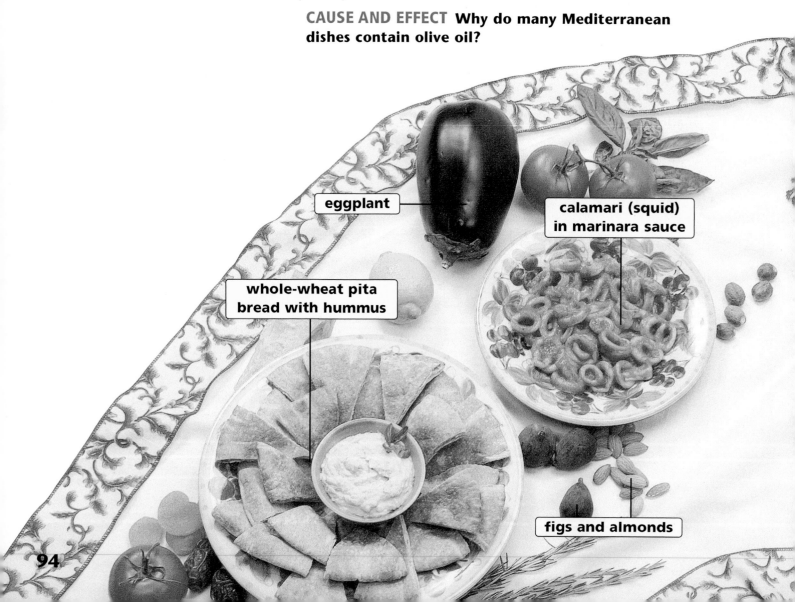

eggplant

calamari (squid) in marinara sauce

whole-wheat pita bread with hummus

figs and almonds

Kebabs

2 lb of beef, chicken, or lamb
$\frac{1}{2}$ c olive oil
Fresh lemon juice
Salt and pepper to taste
$\frac{1}{2}$ tsp dried oregano
1 tbsp minced garlic

12 cherry tomatoes
1 medium Spanish onion,
    quartered and separated
2 peppers (red, green, or
    yellow), cut into 1-in. squares
1 large zucchini, sliced

1. Cut the meat into 1-in. cubes, and place it in a large bowl.

2. Combine olive oil and lemon juice, and pour over meat.

3. Sprinkle with salt, pepper, oregano, and garlic.

4. Add tomatoes, onion, zucchini, and pepper squares.

5. Weigh down the ingredients with a heavy plate; refrigerate, covered, for a few hours or overnight.

6. Place meat, tomato, onion, zucchini, and pepper on 8 skewers.

7. Cook over charcoal or broil in an oven for 20–25 minutes until thoroughly cooked. Serves 4 people.

Lesson 3 Summary and Review

1 Summarize with Vocabulary

Use vocabulary and other terms from this lesson to complete the statements.

The food items that go into a particular dish are its _____. A key food in the diet of the people of an area is called a _____. A balanced meal should provide you with selections from all food _____. A corn tortilla, for example, provides a serving from the _____, Cereal, Rice, and Pasta Group.

2 What is a staple of the Mexican diet?

3 Critical Thinking Describe an Asian meal that provides servings from at least three food groups.

4 (Focus Skill) COMPARE AND CONTRAST

Draw and complete this graphic organizer to show how Asian and Mediterranean foods are alike and different.

Topic: Asian and Mediterranean Foods
Alike   Different

5 Write to Inform—Description

Describe a meal you have eaten from another culture. Describe how the food looked, tasted, and smelled. Then tell which food groups were represented in the meal.

95

Satisfying Your Nutritional Needs

Eating Too Few Nutrients

People grow especially quickly between the ages of ten and twenty. During these years your body needs plenty of nutrients of every kind.

Unfortunately, some young people between these ages begin to cut back on the amount of food they eat. Teenage boys hoping to build muscle mass may eat foods rich in protein but lacking in carbohydrates. Teenage girls may avoid all foods they think are fattening, including calcium-rich dairy products. The result is that they rob their bodies of needed calories and important nutrients.

Some young people, especially girls, become overly concerned about their body image and develop serious eating disorders. One such disorder, called **anorexia** (an•uh•REK•see•uh), involves dieting nearly to the point of starvation. It causes general poor health, low blood pressure, heart problems, and bone weakness.

Eating well gives you the energy you need to perform your daily activities. ▶

Problems Caused by Lack of Nutrients

Nutrient	Cause of Deficiency	Long-Term Symptoms
Carbohydrate	Not enough grains, dairy products, fruits, or starchy vegetables	Poor growth; weight loss; lack of energy
Iodine	Lack of seafood or iodized salt	Swelling of thyroid gland in throat; impaired mental and physical development
Calcium	Lack of dairy products and dark green, leafy vegetables	Weak bones and teeth; poor blood-clotting ability
Protein	Lack of animal foods, dairy products, or grains	Poor growth; diarrhea; weight loss; weakness; brittle hair and nails
Vitamin A	Lack of yellow and orange vegetables	Poor night vision; nausea; loss of appetite; low resistance to disease
Vitamin C	Lack of fruits and vegetables	Weakness; joint pain; poor tooth and gum health; bleeding gums; poor blood clotting
Vitamin D	Lack of eggs and milk; lack of sunlight	Softening or brittleness of bones; bowed legs
Vitamin K	Long-term antibiotic treatment; chronic diarrhea	Poor blood-clotting ability

Bulimia (byoo•LEE•mee•uh), another eating disorder, involves eating a great deal of food and then vomiting right away to get rid of the food. Both anorexia and bulimia can lead to death.

Other problems can be caused by not eating enough of the right kinds of food. A **nutritional deficiency** is the lack of a certain nutrient in the diet.

Many people have a deficiency of iron. This deficiency can cause anemia, in which the blood carries less oxygen than the body needs. Children, pregnant women, and those people who find it difficult to shop or cook for themselves are especially at risk. Meat, poultry, broccoli, raisins, dried beans, and whole-wheat and enriched breads are good sources of iron. In addition, people who are anemic need iron supplements. The table above lists some other nutritional deficiencies.

 COMPARE AND CONTRAST How are the symptoms of iron deficiency like those of vitamin K deficiency? How are they different?

Myth and Fact

Myth: **Most teenage girls are overweight.**
Fact: Although 35 percent of teenage girls think they are overweight, only about 15 percent actually are overweight.

Eating Too Much

When the calories in the food you eat equal the calories your body needs, your body is in *energy balance*. If you take in more calories than your body requires, the extra calories are stored as fat. Stored fat means extra weight.

Being overweight can damage your health. Overweight people are much more likely to develop high blood pressure, heart disease, and Type 2 diabetes. They also have greater chances of having strokes and developing certain cancers.

You can maintain a healthful weight by balancing the calories you take in with the calories you use. One way to do this is to be active and get plenty of exercise. You should also make healthful food choices, such as selecting foods that contain little fat. When shopping with your family, look for low-fat or extra-lean meats. Substitute skinless poultry for fatty meats, and eat fish a few times a week. Buy low-fat dairy products, such as milk that contains 1 or 2 percent fat. You should also limit sweets, sodas, juices, and other sugary foods.

Another way to maintain a healthful weight is to control the size of the portions of food you eat. When you eat out, resist the temptation to order giant-sized portions of food. This is especially important when you eat at fast-food restaurants. Giant-sized portions aren't a bargain when they contain more calories and fat than you need.

CAUSE AND EFFECT **What conditions can result from being overweight?**

Giant-sized portions are tempting, but taking in more calories than your body needs can lead to health problems. ▶

Dietary Guidelines

The USDA provides a nutritional health plan called the Dietary Guidelines for Americans. This plan suggests things people can do to eat well, make good choices, and be physically active.

Aim for Fitness

- Aim for a weight that is good for you. Ask a health professional what your recommended weight range is, or look it up in a reliable source. If you need to, set goals to reach a good weight.
- Be physically active each day. In the next chapter you will discover how the Activity Pyramid can help you plan each week's activities.

Build a Healthy Base

- Use an appropriate food guide pyramid to guide your food choices.
- Each day choose a variety of grains such as wheat, oats, rice, and corn. Choose whole grains when you can.
- Each day choose a variety of fruits and vegetables.
- Keep food safe to eat. Follow the tips in Lesson 6 for safe preparation and storage of food.

Choose Sensibly

- Choose a diet that is moderate in total fat and low in saturated fat and cholesterol.
- Choose foods and drinks that are low in sugar.
- Choose foods that are low in salt. When you prepare foods, use very little salt.

MAIN IDEA AND DETAILS List the main categories of the Dietary Guidelines. Then write two things that belong in each category.

Real-Life Situation

Three days a week, when you come home from school, you have only 30 minutes before you must leave for softball practice.

Real-Life Plan

Write a list of snacks that are low in sugar and fat and will provide the energy you need to play softball.

Snacks and Nutrition

What foods do you choose when you snack? Do you think your choices are healthful or unhealthful? Below are some guidelines for choosing healthful snacks.

- If you need quick energy for exercising, eat fruits rather than sweets.
- Carrot sticks will give you plenty of vitamin A. Broccoli also has vitamin A and is rich in vitamin C.
- You can dip pieces of carrot or broccoli in low-fat yogurt, which provides calcium for bone growth.
- You can obtain complex carbohydrates by snacking on low-sugar cereals or crackers.
- Avoid eating junk foods, which are high in calories from fat and sugar.
- Avoid beverages high in sugar (soda, juice, fruit drinks, and sports drinks).

DRAW CONCLUSIONS If you need energy quickly, what healthful snack might you choose?

Lesson 4 Summary and Review

1 Summarize with Vocabulary

Use vocabulary and other terms from this lesson to complete the statements.

Two common eating disorders are _____, which involves dieting nearly to starvation, and _____, which involves eating followed by vomiting. A _____ occurs when a person's diet is low in a certain nutrient. For example, lack of vitamin _____ can cause poor night vision.

2 How can a person who cannot eat dairy products avoid calcium deficiency?

3 Critical Thinking Suppose a person is diagnosed with a nutritional deficiency that affects the blood. Which nutrient might the person lack?

4 (Focus Skill) COMPARE AND CONTRAST Draw and complete this graphic organizer to show how anorexia and bulimia are alike and different.

Topic: Anorexia and Bulimia
Alike   Different

5 Write to Inform—Explanation

Write a paragraph in which you explain how a person who is overweight can set goals to reach a healthful weight.

Responsibility

Practicing Self-Control

Suppose you have just arrived home from school, and you are hungry for a snack. You open the refrigerator and look over your choices. Should you choose a piece of chocolate cake? Or should you choose a handful of fresh strawberries? Answering the following questions can help you act responsibly and exercise healthful self-control.

- **Is this food healthful?**
- **Can I substitute a more healthful food for this one?**
- **How will the nutrients and other substances in this food affect my body?**
- **Do I really need such a large portion of this food? Will a smaller portion satisfy me?**
- **How will I feel about myself when I'm not eating healthful foods but know I should be?**

Activity

Keep a log of the food choices you make each day. Note how many times you practice self-control. Look for a trend in your behavior. Are you making more healthful food choices? If so, you are learning to practice self-control. If not, use the log as motivation to improve your dietary habits.

Prepared Foods and the Consumer

Lesson Focus

It is important to make healthful choices when shopping for food and when eating in a restaurant.

Why Learn This?

Knowing what is in a food enables you to choose it or select a more healthful alternative.

Vocabulary

convenience foods
additives
preservatives

Packaged Foods

Cooking can be a lot of fun. Sometimes, though, people are too tired or too busy to prepare a meal. When this happens, many people use convenience foods.

Convenience foods are foods that are partly or completely prepared when you buy them. Such foods include frozen dinners, soups, and canned fruits and vegetables. Unfortunately, many convenience foods do not provide healthful amounts of some nutrients. For example, many are high in fat and salt. Many also contain **additives** (AD·uh·tivz), or substances added to foods to keep them fresh longer or improve their color or flavor. Some chemical additives, called **preservatives** (pree·ZERV·uh·tivz), help keep food from spoiling. Some food packagers add fat, salt, or sugar to foods. They might also add dyes and thickeners, neither of which are nutrients.

Many foods are processed and packaged. ▲

Another factor to consider when shopping for packaged foods is a product's unit price, or its cost per item or per unit of weight or volume. For example, to decide which of two jars of peanut butter is the more cost-effective choice, a shopper would compare their costs per ounce.

Consumer Activity

Make Buying Decisions
A box of cereal A costs $4.00 for 16 ounces, and a box of cereal B costs $3.90 for 14 ounces. Calculate the unit cost of each cereal, and tell which is the more economical choice. On your next trip to the supermarket, make a list of foods other than cereals that differ in unit cost.

How do you know what is in a packaged food? By law all packaged foods in the United States must have food labels. These labels provide nutrition information about the food, including serving size and calorie content. They also tell you, for example, how much protein, carbohydrate, sugar, fat, fiber, and salt the food contains. Nutrition labels are designed to help you compare foods so that you can make healthful food choices.

 COMPARE AND CONTRAST **How are preservatives like and different from other additives?**

Quick Activity

Analyze a Food Label
Examine the nutrition labels on three or more packaged foods you have in your home. Make a table that shows how the calories and nutrients in each package of food compare with each other.

Calories per serving: This tells you the energy content of the food, as well as how many of the calories come from fat.

Nutrient amounts: This lists the amounts of nutrients in grams. Check the Percent Daily Values to find out if the food is high in cholesterol or sodium (salt). Choose foods with high fiber content.

Vitamin and mineral amounts: This tells you what percent of the required daily amounts of vitamins and minerals the food contains. These amounts are based on a 2,000-calorie diet.

Cereal

Nutrition Facts

Serving Size	1cup (29g)
Servings Per Package	8

Amount Per Serving

Calories 140	Fat Calories 25

	% Daily Value
Total Fat 3.0g	5%
Cholesterol 0mg	0%
Sodium 110mg	5%
Total Carbohydrate 27g	9%
Dietary Fiber 1g	10%
Sugars 11g	
Protein 2g	

Vitamin A	15%	Niacin	25%
Vitamin C	0%	Vitamin B6	25%
Calcium	0%	Folate	10%
Iron	10%	Phosphorus	4%
Thiamin	25%	Magnesium	2%
Riboflavin	25%	Zinc	10%

*Percent Daily Values are based on a 2,000-Calorie diet. Your daily values may be higher or lower depending on your Calorie needs:

	Calories:	2,000	2,500
Total Fat	Less than	65g	80g
Sat. Fat	Less than	20g	25g
Cholesterol	Less than	300mg	300mg
Sodium	Less than	2,400mg	2,400mg
Total Carbohydrate		300g	375g
Dietary Fiber		25g	30g

Calories per gram
Fat 9 • Carbohydrate 4 • Protein 4

Serving size: This is a guideline on the appropriate amount to eat. It tells you how much to eat to get the number of calories and the amounts of nutrients listed.

Percent daily value: This helps you decide how a food fits into a healthful diet. For example, one serving of this food provides 5 percent of the sodium, or salt, you should eat in one day. Your remaining meals and snacks should provide no more than 95 percent of the sodium you need in one day. Percent Daily Values are based on a 2,000-calorie diet.

Daily values: This part of the label lists the amounts of major nutrients you need each day.

Sugar-free
Each serving has less than 0.5 g of sugar.

Low-fat
One serving has 3 g or less of fat.

Low-sodium
There is less than 140 mg of sodium per serving.

High-fiber
Each serving contains 5 g or more of fiber. Food must also qualify for a *low-fat* label, or number of grams of fat must appear next to fiber information.

Enriched
Vitamins and minerals have been added.

No sugar added
The food may contain sugar, but none was added.

Fortified
A vitamin or mineral has been added to reach at least 10 percent of the Daily Value of that nutrient.

Reduced or fewer calories
The number of calories in the food is not more than three-fourths of the number in the food with which it is compared.

Cholesterol-Free
Each serving has less than 2 mg of cholesterol and 2 g or less of saturated (unhealthful) fat.

Understanding Advertising Jargon

Companies usually hire advertisers to help sell their products. Advertisers conduct research to find out what words and phrases influence people the most. You have probably noticed some or all of these terms, known as *advertising jargon*, in food ads. Above are some common terms and their meanings.

SEQUENCE What do advertisers do before they produce ads for food products?

Understanding Serving Size

What is a serving size? It's a measured amount of food, such as 1 cup or 8 ounces. A serving is different from a portion, which has no standard size. A portion is the amount of food you choose to eat at one time. It may be made up of several servings.

A food label tells you the amounts of nutrients in a serving. The label also tells you exactly what size a serving is. It is useful to be able to estimate serving sizes. This table will help you.

DRAW CONCLUSIONS What is one conclusion you can draw from the fact that one serving of cooked dry beans is $\frac{1}{2}$ cup, while one serving of peanut butter is only 2 tablespoons?

Estimates of Serving Sizes

Food Group	Amount of Food in One Serving	Easy Ways to Estimate Serving Size
Bread, Cereal, Rice, and Pasta Group	$\frac{1}{2}$ c cooked pasta, rice, or cereal 1 c ready-to-eat (dry) cereal 1 slice bread, $\frac{1}{2}$ medium bagel	ice-cream scoop
Vegetable Group	1 c raw leafy vegetables $\frac{1}{2}$ c other vegetables, cooked or chopped raw $\frac{1}{2}$ c tomato sauce	about the size of a tennis ball
Fruit Group	1 medium apple, pear, or orange 1 medium banana $\frac{1}{2}$ c chopped or cooked fruit 1 c fresh fruit 4 oz fruit juice	about the size of a baseball
Milk, Yogurt, and Cheese Group	$1\frac{1}{2}$ oz cheese 8 oz yogurt 8 oz milk	about the size of three dominoes
Meat, Poultry, Fish, Dry Beans, Eggs, and Nuts Group	2–3 oz lean meat, chicken, or fish 2 tbsp peanut butter $\frac{1}{2}$ c cooked dry beans	about the size of a computer mouse
Fats, Oils, and Sweets Group	1 tsp margarine or butter	about the size of the end of your thumb

Tips for Eating Out

Restaurants generally offer an array of appetizing foods. However, meals tend to be high in fat, oil, salt, or sugar, and many dishes are prepared with heavy, high-fat sauces or creams. In addition, not all restaurant meals are balanced. For example, some choices might contain large portions of beef or pork but not enough food from the other food groups. Read a menu carefully to look for a meal that is both tasty and healthful. Some restaurant menus have symbols next to items that are low in fats and cholesterol. Although most menus don't list all the ingredients in a dish or tell how it is prepared, your server can usually provide this information. You can also use the information given below to make healthful choices.

Common Choices

1. Doughnut, sweet roll, or croissant
2. Pancakes or toast with butter, cream cheese, or syrup
3. Roast beef, salami, or bologna with mayonnaise on a white roll
4. Cheeseburger with french fries and ketchup
5. Fried fish or chicken
6. Lasagna, manicotti, or cannelloni with meat sauce
7. Broccoli-and-cheese soup
8. Fried Chinese dumplings or fried rice

Healthful Alternatives

1. Low-fat bran muffin
2. Pancakes or toast with unsweetened fruit or jam, or low-fat cottage cheese
3. Plain tuna, turkey, or chicken on whole-wheat bread with mustard, lettuce, and tomato
4. Baked or broiled chicken and a baked or mashed potato with chives and a spoonful of Parmesan cheese
5. Broiled fish or chicken with lemon juice
6. Pasta with stir-fried vegetables
7. Chicken or vegetable soup
8. Steamed Chinese dumplings or steamed rice

If you ask them to, many restaurants will leave out ingredients you don't like or don't want in your food. Some will bake or broil a food if you don't want it fried. Many will allow you to share a main dish with a friend to reduce portion size. If more people ask for healthful foods, more restaurants will make changes to provide those foods. You might ask your server the following questions:

- "Is the sauce, butter, or dressing served on top of the food?" If these are served on the side, you can use just a little and make your meal more healthful.
- "How is the food cooked?" Boiled, baked, broiled, steamed, and stir-fried dishes are more healthful than pan-fried or deep-fried foods.
- "What kinds of fats or oils are used?" Foods prepared with safflower, olive, or sesame oil are better for you than foods made with butter, cream, or lard.

ACTIVITY

Life Skills

Make Responsible Decisions

Look at the list of foods in the menu on page 106. Which foods in the right-hand column would you like to try? Tell why these foods are more healthful than the corresponding foods in the left-hand column. Use this information to help you make healthful choices when you eat out.

SUMMARIZE Describe things you can do when eating out that will help you eat healthfully.

Lesson 5 Summary and Review

1 Summarize with Vocabulary

Use vocabulary and other terms from this lesson to complete the statements.

Many _____, which can be prepared quickly, do not provide healthful amounts of some _____. Also, such foods may contain ingredients that you do not want to eat, such as _____ to improve their color and flavor and _____ to help prevent them from spoiling. You can get an idea of what is in a packaged food by reading its _____.

2 What is one question you might ask a food server in a restaurant if you want to know whether a dish is healthful?

3 Critical Thinking How does the information on a food label help you compare foods?

4 (Focus Skill) COMPARE AND CONTRAST Draw and complete this graphic organizer to show how fried rice with chicken and steamed rice with chicken are alike and different.

Topic: Fried Rice and Steamed Rice, with Chicken
Alike   Different

5 Write to Express—Business Letter

Write a letter to a restaurant manager explaining how a menu could be rewritten so that people could easily choose between healthful and less-healthful dishes.

107

Make Responsible Decisions

About Food

It is important to maintain your energy level by eating enough food during the day. Sometimes you need to eat a snack between meals. How can you make responsible decisions about what and how much you eat? You can use the steps for **Making Responsible Decisions** to help you.

Kevin has just arrived home after playing basketball with his friends, and he feels hungry. He finds a bag of potato chips on the kitchen shelf and a bowl of fruit in the refrigerator. Which should he eat?

1 **Find out about the choices you could make.**

2 **Eliminate choices that are against your family rules.**

Kevin can eat the fruit, which is rich in vitamins, or the potato chips, a food high in fat and salt.

Kevin remembers that his mother has told him to have a healthful snack when he's hungry.

108

Ask yourself: What is the possible result of each choice? Does the choice show good character?

Fruit is healthful, but potato chips belong at the top of the USDA Food Guide Pyramid. Kevin knows he should only eat small amounts of food from the top group.

4 **Make what seems to be the best choice.**

Kevin decides to choose the fruit. It contains important vitamins and carbohydrates, and it does not contain fats or salt.

Problem Solving

A. Ramona just finished playing a long game of tennis. She is thirsty and tired. There are two vending machines next to the tennis court. One machine has soda, and the other has bottled water. Which drink would be the more healthful choice?

- Use the steps for **Making Responsible Decisions** to show how Ramona can make a healthful choice.

B. Tyrel's parents send him to the supermarket to shop for snacks for his family. Tyrel enjoys sweets and has trouble controlling the amount of sweets he eats.

- Explain how Tyrel can act responsibly in choosing snacks for his family. How can Tyrel show good character by limiting the amount of sweets he purchases?

109

Safe and Tasty Preparation of Food

Lesson Focus

Foods should be handled and prepared so that they are both safe and tasty to eat.

Why Learn This?

You can use what you learn to handle and prepare foods safely.

Vocabulary

contamination

Safety Concerns for Food Preparation

Food **contamination** (kuhn•tam•uh•NAY•shuhn) is the process that occurs when food is exposed to harmful substances. These harmful substances include microorganisms, such as bacteria, that cause disease.

Food can become contaminated when it is not properly prepared. It is important to cook meat thoroughly. This will kill most microorganisms. Otherwise, the bacteria in some meat products, such as chicken and beef, can make you ill.

It is also important to prepare food on clean surfaces. Be sure to use a clean countertop or cutting board. This will keep the bacteria on one food from contaminating another food you are preparing. For the same reason, utensils that have been used to prepare uncooked chicken and other meats should be washed thoroughly with hot water and soap before being used to prepare other foods.

Thoroughly wash all fruits and vegetables. ▶

◀ Raw chicken and other meats can have harmful bacteria on them. Always wash hands, plates, cutting boards, countertops, and utensils after using them for raw poultry or meats.

Many foods should be stored in a refrigerator or freezer if they are not going to be eaten right away. This is because harmful microorganisms don't multiply as quickly at low temperatures. Refrigerate raw meat, poultry, and fish in such a way that their juices don't drip onto and contaminate other foods.

Chemicals can also contaminate foods. Factories sometimes dispose of harmful chemicals that later get into crops, livestock, and fish. Pesticides, which are used to kill insects that damage crops, can also contaminate food. The United States government tests food samples to make sure that the foods people buy do not contain unsafe amounts of these chemicals. Nevertheless, it is wise to wash fruits and vegetables before eating them, to remove traces of these chemicals.

People with certain illnesses, such as the flu, should never handle food that others will eat. As a general precaution, people who handle food should first wash their hands or put on disposable gloves.

 COMPARE AND CONTRAST How are bacteria the same as chemicals that contaminate food? How are they different?

111

Real-Life Situation

Foods tend to stay in a family's refrigerator for long periods of time.

Real-Life Plan

Develop a plan to monitor and ensure the freshness of foods in a refrigerator.

Did You Know?

Not all microorganisms spoil foods. Some are actually used to produce foods. Certain bacteria make yogurt, cheese, sour cream, and buttermilk. Other bacteria are used to make pickles, sauerkraut, and vinegar. Bacteria that live permanently in your intestines digest food and produce vitamins your body needs, such as vitamin K and folic acid.

Determining Product Freshness

Foods spoil when microorganisms grow on or in them. These microorganisms usually develop when food is not properly stored or is kept too long. For example, milk not kept in a refrigerator will spoil. Some meat will spoil in a few days even if kept in the refrigerator.

Often, you can tell that a food has spoiled because it smells and looks bad. For example, spoiled milk smells bad, and spoiled bread has mold growing on it. Never eat such foods.

Sometimes contaminated foods will look and smell fine. To be safe, you should throw away meat, poultry, fish, milk, shellfish, or eggs that have been left at room temperature for more than <u>two hours</u> or that have been kept in the refrigerator for too many days. Don't taste such foods.

When you shop for food, you can determine the freshness of many items. Look for labels on the packages that say *Sell by*, *Use by*, or *Best if used by*, followed by dates. Foods that have freshness dates include dairy products, such as milk and cottage cheese, and fresh meat, fish, and poultry products.

Do not buy food after the *Sell by* date printed on the package or container. This date is the last date a food should be sold. *Sell by* dates, however, do not tell whether a food is actually safe to eat. If milk, for example, is not properly refrigerated, it will spoil before its *Sell by* date.

BEST BY AUG8
P1691A 790

Foods stored in a refrigerator usually are safe to eat for a certain amount of time after their *Sell by* dates. However, different foods remain fresh for different amounts of time. Raw chicken is safe for only one or two days in your refrigerator. Eggs, however, will usually stay fresh for two weeks. If you aren't sure that a food has been stored safely, it is best to throw the food out.

DRAW CONCLUSIONS Suppose a carton of milk is left out overnight. Is the milk safe to drink?

Bacterial Growth

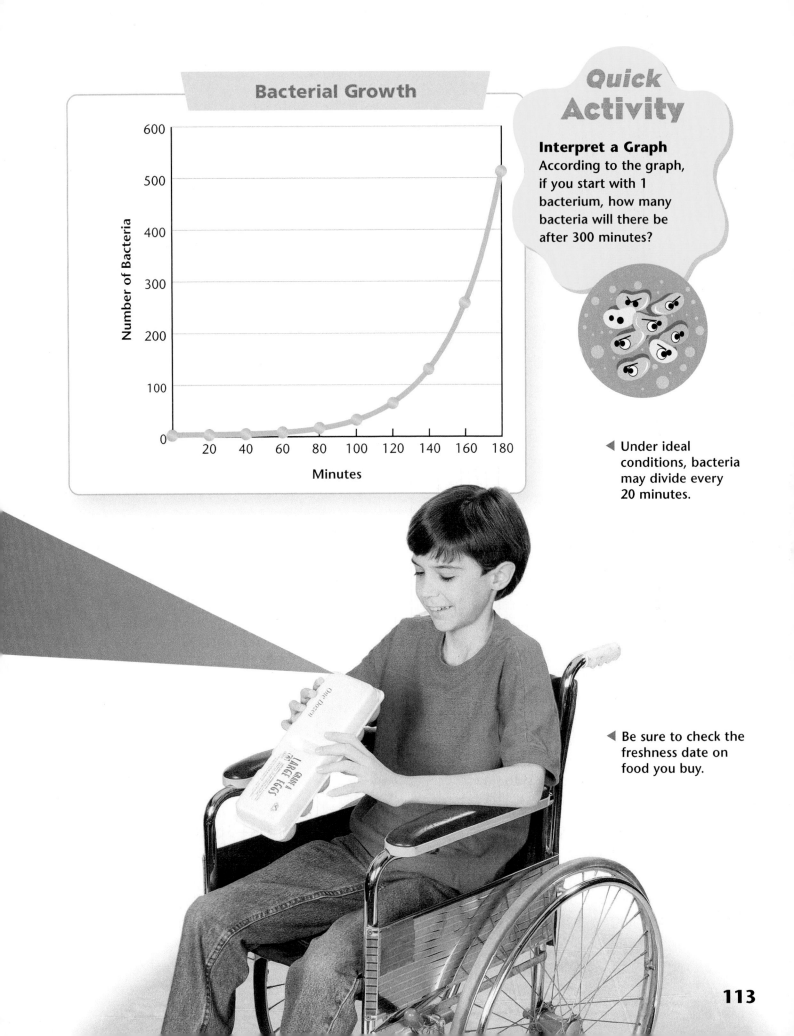

Number of Bacteria (y-axis): 0, 100, 200, 300, 400, 500, 600

Minutes (x-axis): 20, 40, 60, 80, 100, 120, 140, 160, 180

Quick Activity

Interpret a Graph
According to the graph, if you start with 1 bacterium, how many bacteria will there be after 300 minutes?

◀ Under ideal conditions, bacteria may divide every 20 minutes.

◀ Be sure to check the freshness date on food you buy.

Seasonings Used in Cooking

Salt and pepper are common seasonings used in cooking. However, too much salt can be unhealthful. To reduce the amount of salt in their diets, many people use herbs and spices to flavor their foods when they cook. For example, the herb cilantro enhances the flavor of many Mexican dishes. Italian cooks often use the herb basil. Curry is a mixture of spices used in Indian foods. Cinnamon is a spice commonly used in desserts.

Herbs are flavorful leaves of small plants. Most spices come from tropical trees, shrubs, and vines. There are many herbs and spices to choose from, so try one the next time you cook.

MAIN IDEA AND DETAILS What are seasonings used for? Give some examples.

Did You Know?

Long ago salt was so valuable and the demand for it was so high that it was as precious as gold. In addition to flavoring food, it was used to preserve meat. The Romans and other peoples around the Mediterranean Sea even used salt as money!

Lesson 6 Summary and Review

1 Summarize with Vocabulary

Use vocabulary and other terms from this lesson to complete the statements.

Foods can spoil as a result of _____ by microorganisms such as _____. You can often tell that a food has spoiled by the way it _____ and _____. Never buy food after its _____ date. If you are unsure whether a food is safe, _____ it away. _____ such as basil are used to flavor foods.

2 What is the main reason to wash raw vegetables and fruits?

3 Critical Thinking Why do you think people used to put salt on meat to keep it from spoiling?

4 (Focus Skill) **COMPARE AND CONTRAST** Draw and complete this graphic organizer to compare and contrast herbs and spices.

Topic: Herbs and Spices

Alike	Different

5 Write to Express—Solution to a Problem

Suppose that food in your refrigerator at home tends to spoil before you use it. Write a paragraph that proposes possible solutions to this problem.

114

ACTIVITIES

Math

Graph Snacks Make a list of all the snacks you eat on a particular day. Look at the nutrition information for each snack. Write down the grams of total fat, carbohydrate, and protein in each snack. Add to find the total amount of each nutrient. Calculate calories for each nutrient by multiplying fats by 9, carbohydrates by 4, and protein by 4. Make a graph to show your data.

Science

Water and Living Things
Obtain two beef bouillon cubes.
Place each of the cubes in a separate zip-top bag. Add about 1 cup of water to one bag. Do NOT add water to the other bag. Seal both bags, and leave them in a warm place. Observe the contents of each bag daily for five days. Write down your observations and conclusions. When finished, leave the bags sealed. Your teacher will dispose of them.

Technology Project

Use the Internet to find out what various government agencies, such as the Centers for Disease Control and Prevention (CDC) and the Department of Agriculture, recommend as healthful snacks. Work with a partner to make a poster that shows some of these snacks. If you don't have Internet access, use what you've learned in this chapter to make a poster that shows a variety of healthful snacks.

For more activities, visit The Learning Site.
www.harcourtschool.com/health

Home & Community

Communicating Interview people of different cultures in your community. List the seasonings they use to prepare foods. Make a chart showing how the seasonings are alike and different.

Career Link

Chef Suppose you are a chef in a restaurant. Write a speech you could deliver to people who are training to be chefs. In your speech, explain why the foods they prepare should be pleasing to look at as well as tasty and healthful to eat. Also tell why they should try recipes from other countries and cultures.

Reading Skill

COMPARE AND CONTRAST

Draw and then use this graphic organizer to answer questions 1 and 2.

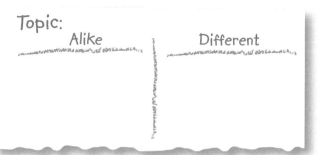

Topic:

Alike   Different

1 Write at least two ways carbohydrates and vitamins are alike and different.

2 Write at least two ways meats and vegetables are alike and different.

Use Vocabulary

Match each term in Column B with its meaning in Column A.

Column A	Column B
3 Sugars and starches	**A** fat
4 Eating disorder in which a person eats and then vomits	**B** staple
	C bulimia
	D carbohydrates
	E preservatives
5 Eating disorder that involves dieting nearly to starvation	**F** anorexia
6 Substances added to foods to prevent spoiling	
7 Nutrient that contains the most calories per gram	
8 Key ingredient in the food of a culture	

Check Understanding

Choose the letter of the correct answer.

9 High blood levels of which of these substances have been linked to heart disease? (p. 81)

A fructose   **C** fiber

B cholesterol   **D** protein

10 From which food group should you eat the greatest number of servings each day? (p. 87)

F Vegetable Group

G Fruit Group

H Fats, Oils, Sweets Group

J Bread, Cereal, Rice, Pasta Group

11 Which of the following is a source of calories for the body? (p. 80)

A water   **C** carbohydrates

B vitamins   **D** minerals

12 A nutritional deficiency of iron would likely result in _____. (p. 97)

F anemia

G soft bones

H unhealthy teeth and gums

J swelling of the thyroid gland

13 Foods spoil because of _____. (p. 112)

A refrigeration   **C** seasonings

B pesticides   **D** microorganisms

14 When you shop for healthful meats, which label should you look for? (p. 98)

F Best for Burgers   **H** Extra Lean

G Juicy   **J** Tender

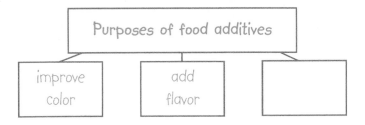

Purposes of food additives

improve color | add flavor |

15 The graphic organizer above gives information about food additives. Which of the following belongs in the empty box? (p. 102)

A add fiber **C** reduce calories
B replace nutrients **D** keep fresh

♥ **GRILLED SALMON** *with vegetable medley*

16 In the menu entry shown above, the symbol is meant to show that this dish _____. (p. 106)

F is popular with customers
G contains unhealthful chemicals
H can be eaten by vegetarians
J is low in fats and cholesterol

17 The term *high-fiber* means that the fiber content of a food serving is at least _____. (p. 104)

A 3 g **C** 7 g
B 5 g **D** 9 g

18 A measured amount of a food for a meal is called a _____. (p. 86)

F diet **H** serving
G dinner **J** portion

19 Which of the following is **NOT** an herb or spice? (p. 114)

A cinnamon **C** basil
B cilantro **D** lettuce

Think Critically

20 Suppose you took in fewer than the recommended number of servings from the Milk, Yogurt, and Cheese Group. How might doing so affect your health?

21 You just watched your favorite TV show. One of the commercials was for a sweet chocolate snack. Why do you think this commercial was shown during this show?

22 For a healthful restaurant meal, what are three things you can do when selecting foods from a menu?

Apply Skills

23 **BUILDING GOOD CHARACTER**
Responsibility You are planning a party, and you decide to invite ten friends. You remember that one of these friends has diabetes. Diabetes is a condition in which sugar can build to dangerous levels in a person's blood. What kinds of foods should you plan to serve at the party?

24 **LIFE SKILLS**
Make Responsible Decisions You are under stress because a big test is coming up at school. You know that when you are under stress, you overeat. What decisions can you make about your dietary and study habits to help reduce the stress you feel and not overeat?

Write About Health

25 **Write to Inform—Explanation** Write a paragraph in which you explain how to maintain a healthful weight by balancing calories from food with calories used by the body.

CHAPTER 4

Keeping Active

Reading Skill

★ Focus Skill

IDENTIFY CAUSE AND EFFECT Often when you read, you must understand cause-and-effect relationships. An effect is what happens. A cause is the reason that something happens. Use the Reading in Health Handbook on pages 404–405 and this graphic organizer to help you read the health facts in this chapter.

Identify Cause and Effect

Cause:		Effect:
	➡	

Health Graph

INTERPRET DATA Exercise does not always have to be vigorous. You can get health benefits from easier activities, including everyday tasks such as walking up the stairs. In the graph below, which activity uses about half the calories each minute as shooting baskets?

Energy Used by Physical Activities

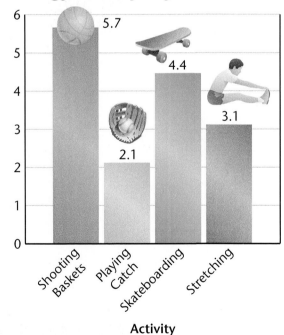

Calories Used per Minute (by a 110-pound person)

- Shooting Baskets: 5.7
- Playing Catch: 2.1
- Skateboarding: 4.4
- Stretching: 3.1

Activity

Daily Physical Activity

Physical activity has a number of benefits. It can increase your endurance, improve your cardiovascular fitness, and help you maintain a healthful weight. Daily physical activity is part of a healthful lifestyle.

🎵 **Be Active!**
Use the selection, Track 4, **Jumping Jam Jive**, to give your heart a workout.

Your Fitness and Exercise

Lesson Focus

Exercise can help you become physically fit and maintain a healthy weight.

Why Learn This?

Being physically fit enables you to do the things you need and want to do with ease.

Vocabulary

muscular strength
muscular endurance
flexibility
cardiovascular fitness
Activity Pyramid

Becoming Fit

How do you become fit? Fun activities such as biking, jogging, shooting baskets, or playing baseball can help you get fit and stay in shape. Everyday activities and chores such as raking leaves or walking your dog can help, too. Exercise is the key to physical health and fitness.

Physical fitness has four parts: muscular strength, muscular endurance, flexibility, and cardiovascular fitness. Exercises such as lifting weights, squeezing a tennis ball, and doing push-ups and sit-ups will help you build muscular strength. **Muscular strength** (MUHS·kyuh·ler STRENGKTH) enables you to use your muscles to lift, push, or pull heavy objects.

Another part of physical fitness is muscular endurance. Having **muscular endurance** (in·DUR·uhnts) means that you can use your muscles for a long time without stopping. Walking, running, swimming, and cycling can help build muscular endurance.

Kayaking and rock climbing can help build muscular strength and endurance. ▼

120

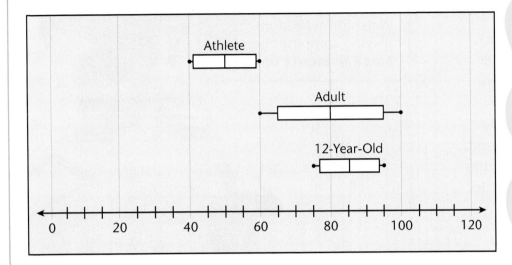

Average At-Rest Heart Rates in Beats per Minute (bpm)

Quick Activity

Interpret Graphs This box-and-whisker graph shows average resting heart rates. For each box and whiskers, look from dot to dot to find the range of heart rates. How do resting heart rates differ across the three groups?

Flexibility also contributes to physical fitness. **Flexibility** (flek•suh•BIH•luh•tee) is the ability to move your body easily from one position to another. In baseball, a shortstop needs to be flexible to field balls. Gymnasts and dancers must also be flexible. Stretching exercises help build flexibility.

Cardiovascular fitness (kar•dee•oh•VAS•kyuh•ler) means that your heart, lungs, and circulatory system work well. A healthy heart and lungs are able to deliver plenty of oxygen and nutrients to your body.

Activities such as fast walking, running, in-line skating, swimming, and soccer can improve your cardiovascular fitness. If you do these activities regularly, your heart will get stronger. A strong heart pumps more blood with each beat, which means it can pump at a slower rate even while you are resting. Having a low resting heart rate is usually a sign of good overall health.

 CAUSE AND EFFECT How might swimming laps several times each week affect your health?

Gymnasts need to be flexible as well as strong to perform well. ▼

121

Your Activity Pyramid

Regular physical activity helps you build and maintain strong bones, muscles, and joints. It helps control weight and reduce stress. When you're fit, you feel better about yourself and you can think more clearly. Exercising is also a fun activity to do with family and friends. The **Activity Pyramid** shows different types of activities and how often people should do them. Try following the Activity Pyramid guidelines to improve your physical fitness.

Sitting Still
Watching television, playing computer games
Small amounts of time

Light Exercise
Playtime, yardwork, softball
2–3 times a week

Aerobic Exercises
Biking, running, soccer, hiking
30+ minutes, 2–3 times a week

Routine Activities
Walking to school, taking the stairs, helping with housework
Every day

Use Data in Tables
Answer these questions using the table:
1. How many calories would you use if you skated for 30 minutes?
2. Choose one activity. How long would you have to do the activity to use 400 calories?

Strength and Flexibility Exercises
Weight training, dancing, pull-ups
2–3 times a week

Calories Used in One Hour by People of Different Weights

Activity	77 lb	99 lb	110 lb
Basketball	335	430	480
Bicycling	300	385	430
Climbing stairs	210	270	300
Dancing	160	200	225
Jogging (12 minutes/mile)	280	360	400
Skating	210	270	300
Skiing, cross-country	335	430	480
Soccer	300	385	430
Swimming	270	345	385
Tennis	230	300	325
Walking (20 minutes/mile)	120	155	175

Exercise alone will not make you physically fit. You also need to eat good foods in the right amounts so that you stay at the proper weight for your height. Staying at a healthy weight is important. If you weigh too much, you may have problems with your bones and joints, your heart, and your other organs. If you weigh too little, you may not have the energy and strength to be active and well.

Food energy is measured in units called calories. When you're active, you burn some of these calories. If you're inactive, you will probably consume more calories than you use. Extra calories, which are stored in the body as fat, cause you to gain weight. If you burn more calories than you take in, you lose weight.

MAIN IDEA AND DETAILS Give three examples of activities you can do every day to keep healthy.

Never bend at the waist when trying to lift a heavy object. Instead, bend your knees. Keep your head up. Then lift the object as you slowly straighten your legs. Hold the object close to your body as you lift it. ▼

Practicing Good Posture

Strong muscles help you maintain good posture. When you stand and sit up straight, you look your best and feel good about yourself. On the other hand, when you slouch or stoop, it puts pressure on your back and often causes backaches and other back problems.

Good posture is important when you are standing or sitting. Standing with good posture means that your whole body is balanced comfortably. Your head is directly over your shoulders, your shoulders are over your hips, and your hips are over your feet. Your shoulders are relaxed and level, and your knees are relaxed as well. Good sitting posture is similar to good standing posture. Your upper body is balanced and relaxed, and your feet are on the floor. Sitting often puts more stress on your back than standing does. For this reason it is important to use chairs that support your back, especially your lower back.

Good posture is also important when your body is moving. Using the correct body positions when you are lifting something helps prevent painful injuries.

SEQUENCE Give the steps that a person should follow to pick up a heavy object.

◀ Good posture is needed when you wear a backpack. Use both shoulder straps on your backpack. This will balance the weight and prevent shoulder, back, and neck problems.

▲ When loading your backpack, put the heaviest items closest to your back. Pack items so that they won't shift around and throw you off balance.

Lesson 1 Summary and Review

① Summarize with Vocabulary

Use vocabulary and other terms from this lesson to complete the statements.

The four parts of physical fitness are _____, _____, _____, and _____. Activities that build these four types of fitness are found on the middle two rows of the _____. The bottom row shows everyday activities. It is important to do all of these kinds of activities regularly. The goal is to use enough _____ through physical activity to maintain a healthful weight.

② Critical Thinking Why is a low resting heart rate usually a sign of good overall health?

③ Why is it important to maintain an appropriate weight for your height?

④ (Focus Skill) CAUSE AND EFFECT Draw and complete this graphic organizer to show how regular physical activity can produce positive effects.

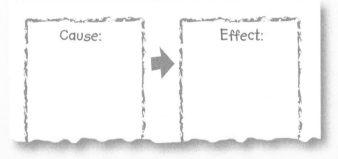

| Cause: | | Effect: |

⑤ Write to Inform—Description

Describe how to use good posture while sitting at your desk.

125

Set Goals
For Fitness

In your life, you are learning to set and work toward different goals. Do your goals include staying healthy and fit? Using the steps for **Setting Goals** can help you improve your own fitness level.

Nekoma signed up for a two-day hiking trip at a park with her class. A few weeks before the trip, she began to worry about whether she would be able to keep up with the rest of the group. Here is how Nekoma used goal setting to help prepare herself.

1 Choose a goal.

Nekoma set a goal to increase her fitness level so that she could hike up some of the steep hills at the park.

2 List and plan steps to meet the goal. Determine how long it will take.

Nekoma planned to reach her goal in three weeks by taking these steps:
- Walk to school and back each day.
- Gradually increase walking speed.
- Use stairs whenever possible.

3 Check your progress as you work toward the goal.

Nekoma recorded the number of minutes it took to get to school each day. She recorded the number of times that she used stairs.

4 Reflect on and evaluate your progress.

Nekoma was proud of her progress. She knew that when the time came, she would enjoy hiking with her class.

Problem Solving

A. Janice loves music. She sings in a choir, and she plays in the school band. She practices singing and playing for an hour every day. She also has to do her homework and help around the house. Janice often feels stressed by her busy schedule. She would like to exercise more, but there never seems to be enough time.
  • Use the steps for **Setting Goals** to help Janice find time for exercise.

B. Marco spends all of his spare time playing computer games and surfing the Web. After spending hours at his computer, he always feels tired and drained. Marco knows that he would feel better if he became more active, but he is having trouble getting started.
  • Explain how Marco can act responsibly by setting a goal to become more active.

127

Your Exercise and Fitness Program

Evaluate Your Fitness

Now is the time to start your own exercise and fitness program. Before you begin, check with a health-care professional, especially if you have questions about your health. He or she will tell you what exercises you can do safely to receive the most benefit. Next, you will need to test your level of fitness.

Curl-Up You will do curl-ups to test the strength and endurance of your stomach muscles. To do a proper curl-up, lie on your back with your knees bent. Your feet should be flat on the floor, about 12 inches from your buttocks. Cross your arms over your chest. Your hands should rest on opposite shoulders. Next, contract your stomach muscles to lift your head and upper back off the floor. Raise your body about halfway to sitting, and then lower yourself so that your shoulders touch the floor. This is one curl-up. Do as many curl-ups as you can in 1 minute.

Curl-ups test strength and endurance. ▶

National Fitness Standards for Twelve-Year-Olds

	Curl-ups (number in 1 minute)	V-Sit Reach (inches beyond the line)	1-Mile Run (minutes: seconds)
Boys	50	+4	7:11
Girls	45	+7	8:23

Source: National Physical Fitness Awards Program

Did You Know?

Nearly half of all young people between the ages of twelve and twenty-one don't get regular, vigorous exercise. Furthermore, people are less likely to exercise as they grow older. Start a regular exercise program now—and stick with it!

V-Sit Reach Test your flexibility by performing V-sit reaches. Sit down, straighten your legs, and place your heels against a line made with masking tape. Then bend at the waist and reach as far forward as possible without bending your knees. Practice three times. Then record the number of inches you reach beyond the line.

1-Mile Run To test your cardiovascular fitness, run a 1-mile course as quickly as you can. Walk part of the way if you need to. Record the time it took you to cover the distance.

Compare your scores on these tests with the national fitness standards shown in the table.

 CAUSE AND EFFECT
What activity could you do to strengthen your stomach muscles?

◄ A V-sit reach measures the flexibility of your lower back and hamstrings (the muscles in the back of your thighs).

Planning Your Exercise Program

Once you have determined which areas of fitness you need to work on, you can plan your personal exercise program.

First, set some goals. Be sure your goals are realistic. Start with activities suited to your fitness level. You can add more difficult ones later. For each activity, consider frequency (how *often* you do it), intensity (how *hard* you do it), and time (how *long* you do it). Keep track of your activities in an exercise log so you can see improvement.

What activities should you include in your program? Gear the activities toward the goals you want to achieve. For example, if you want to improve your endurance, choose activities that will help accomplish that goal. The activities you choose should also be fun. If you enjoy the activities, you are more likely to stick with your exercise program. Plan some activities with a family member, friend, or group. Sharing experiences and achievements can be fun and rewarding.

DRAW CONCLUSIONS Why is it important to choose an exercise and fitness program that is fun?

Quick Activity

Analyze Tables
Exercise can help you improve flexibility, muscular strength and endurance, and cardiovascular fitness. Which activity in the table at the right provides all these benefits? Make a list of other activities that would help you improve in all four areas of physical fitness.

Activity Table

Fun Activity	Muscular Strength	Muscular Endurance	Flexibility	Cardiovascular Fitness
Hiking		X		X
Soccer		X	X	X
Canoeing	X	X	X	X
Skating		X	X	X
Cycling	X	X		X
Tennis		X	X	X

Jumping jacks will help get your heart pumping harder. ▼

Workout Safety Rules

- Stop exercising if you have dizziness, shortness of breath, chest pain, or severe muscle pain.

- Wear comfortable shoes that have good arch support.

- Don't push yourself too hard. Gradually increase the level and duration of the activity over time.

- Maintain good posture while you exercise.

Your Workout

You are now ready to begin your **workout**, or exercise session. Just like a story, a workout has a beginning, a middle, and an ending.

The first part of a workout is the **warm-up**. The purpose of a warm-up is to prepare your body for exercise. The goal is to gradually increase your heart rate and blood flow.

The warm-up should last at least five to ten minutes. It should consist of light exercise that makes you breathe a little harder than normal. If you are going to jog, you might warm up with a short, brisk walk. If you are going to swim laps, you might warm up by swimming one length of the pool at a slow pace. After the light exercise, stretch your muscles carefully.

The middle part of a workout is the main exercise itself. This is described on the next two pages. The **cool-down** is the last part of a workout. The purpose of a cool-down is to let your breathing and heart rate slowly return to normal. You can do this by continuing your exercise activity at a slower pace for at least five to ten minutes. Then you can do some stretching exercises.

SUMMARIZE Kim likes to swim laps for exercise. Explain how she should begin and end each workout.

Personal Health Plan ▶

Real-Life Situation

Your daily life is often full of activities. Managing your time well can help you live a healthy life.

Real-Life Plan

Write a 24-hour schedule that shows how much time you will spend on different activities. Include plenty of time for exercise, relaxation, and sleep.

Quick Activity

Analyze Exercise Types Look at the pictures on this page and the next. Explain why each activity is an example of aerobic exercise or of anaerobic exercise.

Types of Exercise

There are two main types of exercise. To be healthy, you should do some of each.

Aerobic Exercise The main part of your workout should be aerobic exercise. **Aerobic exercise** (air•OH•bik) is vigorous activity that strengthens your heart and lungs. To be beneficial, aerobic activities should be done two to three times per week for at least 30 minutes at a time. Biking, jogging, walking, and swimming are examples of aerobic exercise. Sports such as handball, racquetball, in-line skating, and cross-country skiing are also good aerobic exercises. When you do these activities, your heart speeds up and pumps greater amounts of blood with each beat. In addition, you breathe more deeply. Over time, your heart and lungs become stronger. When you are at rest, your heart will beat more slowly than it did before you began your aerobic program. This is because your heart is now capable of doing more work with less effort. A lower resting heart rate is a sign that you are getting in shape.

Families can improve their cardiovascular fitness together by cross-country skiing. ▼

▲ Hand-walking across monkey bars strengthens your arms and upper body.

You need to work hard enough to benefit from aerobic activity. At the same time, don't overdo it. You can learn how hard to work by finding your **target heart rate**, which is the heart rate at which your heart and lungs become stronger.

For people under age twenty, the target heart rate is between 100 and 150 beats per minute (bpm). During your workout, check to see if you are reaching this target zone. To do this, find the pulse at your wrist. Count the number of heartbeats in 10 seconds. Then multiply that number by 6 to find your heart rate. If it is lower than the target rate, you should exercise a little harder. If it is higher than the target rate, you should slow down a bit. You should maintain your target heart rate for at least 25 minutes.

Anaerobic Exercise Your workout program should also include **anaerobic exercise** (an•air•OH•bik), which builds muscle strength. Anaerobic exercises are short, intense activities, such as lifting weights, sprinting, and doing push-ups. When doing an anaerobic exercise, you should stop if you feel a cramp or a burning sensation.

COMPARE AND CONTRAST Tell how aerobic and anaerobic exercise are alike and different.

▲ Everyone can benefit from aerobic exercise.

133

Sleep and Rest

A good balance of exercise, sleep, and rest is needed to overcome tiredness. Sleep refreshes your body and mind. When you sleep, your muscles relax. Your breathing and heart rate slow down. Try to get nine to ten hours of sleep each night. Sleep will help you be alert so that you can do your best in school. It will also give you energy for physical activities.

DRAW CONCLUSIONS Why is it important to get enough sleep?

▲ Sleep restores your energy and helps you grow. It also helps your mind and body repair themselves.

Lesson 2 Summary and Review

1 Summarize with Vocabulary

Use vocabulary from this lesson to complete the statements.

An exercise session, also known as a _____, has three parts. First comes the _____. Second comes the main activity. This may be an _____ exercise, such as running, during which you check your pulse for your _____. Or, it may be an _____ exercise, such as lifting weights. Third comes the _____. Every exercise session should include all three parts.

2 Critical Thinking Is walking at a slow pace that doesn't make you breathe hard *aerobic* exercise? Explain your answer.

3 How much sleep should you get?

4 (Focus Skill) CAUSE AND EFFECT Draw and complete this graphic organizer to show how warming up before exercise leads to three physical effects.

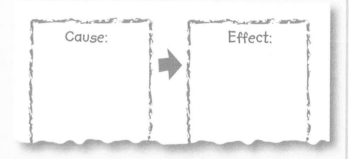

Cause: → Effect:

5 Write to Inform—How-To

Imagine that you are writing a book for physical education teachers. Pick one of the three fitness tests described in this lesson. Provide detailed instructions for giving the test to a class of sixth graders.

134

Respect

Being a Good Sport

Playing active games and sports with your friends and family is a great way to get exercise. To keep it fun, everyone needs to be a good sport. This means playing hard while behaving appropriately. It means being a team player as well as treating members of the other team with courtesy and respect. Here are some simple guidelines for being a good sport:

- **Learn and follow the rules of the game.**
- **Play fair. Cheating makes you a loser, no matter how the game turns out.**
- **Whether you win or lose, thank your opponents and tell them "Good game!"**
- **Stay calm. Don't get angry. It's just a game.**
- **Give everyone a chance to play. If you have to sit out for a while, be nice about it.**
- **Have fun. Don't get so wrapped up in winning that you forget to have a good time.**
- **Respect referees and officials.**

Activity

Pick a sport, and organize a game with your family, classmates, or friends. Have everyone agree to play by the guidelines given above. You can act as a role model by not getting angry and by showing respect for all the players.

Exercising with Safety in Mind

Safety Equipment

Sports and exercise are fun and keep you fit. However, more than 3 million young people are hurt each year in sports and other activities. One way to play safely is to use proper safety equipment.

Helmets You should wear helmets for football, baseball, biking, skateboarding, skiing, and many other activities. Helmets reduce the risk of receiving brain and head injuries. Choose a helmet that fits properly and is designed for the specific activity you want to do.

Mouth Guards You may play a contact sport or a sport, such as racquetball, in which you might be hit in the mouth. If so, you should wear a mouth guard, which will protect your teeth and help cushion blows that could break your jaw.

Other Safety Gear Special pads or guards for your elbows, knees, shins, and wrists are needed for many sports. These sports include skateboarding and in-line skating. Some sports, such as racquetball, also require protective goggles.

Consumer Activity

Analyze Media Messages Wearing sneakers can help you play safely. But can a particular brand of sneaker really make you run faster, jump higher, or win more games? Explain your answer.

The graph shows the number of injuries that occur each year in five popular sports. ▶

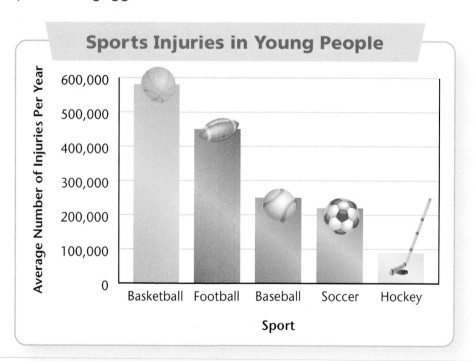

Sports Injuries in Young People

Average Number of Injuries Per Year

600,000
500,000
400,000
300,000
200,000
100,000
0

Basketball Football Baseball Soccer Hockey

Sport

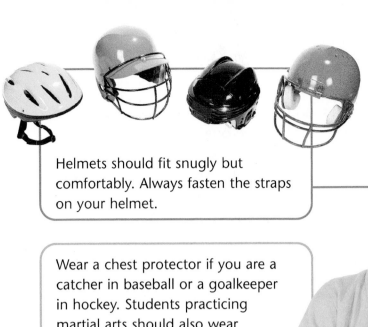

Helmets should fit snugly but comfortably. Always fasten the straps on your helmet.

If you wear glasses, you should wear goggles over them during most sports.

Wear a chest protector if you are a catcher in baseball or a goalkeeper in hockey. Students practicing martial arts should also wear chest protectors when sparring.

Mouth guards can be purchased inexpensively. Mouth guards can also be custom-made by a dentist.

wrist guards

Wrist guards and elbow pads can protect you from scrapes as well as broken bones.

elbow pads

Wear shin guards when you play soccer. Wear knee pads when you go skateboarding.

knee pads   **shin guards**

Ask your coach or another adult to help you choose the correct shoes for the sport you want to play.

 CAUSE AND EFFECT Which safety equipment prevents injuries to the face and head?

Focus Skill

Quick Activity

Compare Equipment Lists List two or three sports that you like to play. Beneath each sport, list safety equipment that might be used for that sport. Then list the safety equipment you use when you play each sport. How do the lists compare?

137

Life Skills

Make Responsible Decisions Design your own exercise program for the next week. Plan to get at least 30 minutes of exercise each day. Be sure that your program includes aerobic exercises, strength exercises, and a warm-up and a cool-down for each workout. You will need to decide which exercises to include in your plan.

Take Responsibility for Your Safety

Teachers, coaches, and parents can give you valuable safety tips. However, you are the one who is primarily responsible for your safety when you play.

Make sure equipment is safe before you use it. Before riding your bike, for example, you should check to see that the tires have enough air. Also make sure you have reflectors on the front, rear, and sides of the bike. If you see something that does not look safe, ask an adult to check it for you. Some exercise equipment, such as weight machines and treadmills, can be dangerous. You should always have an adult with you when you use these types of machines.

What safety suggestions would you give to this skater? ▼

Exercising Safely

- Exercise with a partner when needed. Also, be sure that a responsible adult knows where you will be and what you will be doing.

- Watch the weather. Avoid exercising outdoors when it's very hot or humid, very cold, or stormy. Dress appropriately for the weather. Drink plenty of water, and use sunscreen.

- Use the proper equipment. If you don't have the proper safety equipment, don't do the activity.

- Know what you can do. Don't overdo it. You can injure yourself by trying to do too much.

- Clean up the area before using it. Make sure your playing field is safe.

- Pay attention to your body. If you get hurt or become ill while exercising, stop right away! Then tell a parent or another trusted adult.

▲ Following these rules will help you prevent many types of injuries.

When you play on a team, make sure you learn and follow the rules. Learning the rules is necessary if the game is to be played properly. Following rules is also important because many of them were made to help prevent injuries.

When you play sports, things often happen quickly. This is why you must always keep your mind on the game. If you don't, you could get injured very easily.

You can prevent many injuries if you use common sense. This is especially true when choosing a place to play. You should never play a game in the street. Once you find a good place to play, check the area for possible dangers. Look for anything that might cause a problem, such as bottles, cans, broken glass, and rocks.

Although it is safe to do some activities and exercises on your own, some of them can be done more safely with a partner. Swimming, for example, should always be done with another person and should be supervised by an adult.

 CAUSE AND EFFECT Suppose someone ignores a "No Skateboarding" sign posted outside a busy store. What are the possible consequences?

Consumer Activity

Make Buying Decisions
A bicycle helmet that meets government safety standards should have a sticker that says CPSC, ASTM, or Snell B-95. What are some other things you should consider when buying a bicycle helmet?

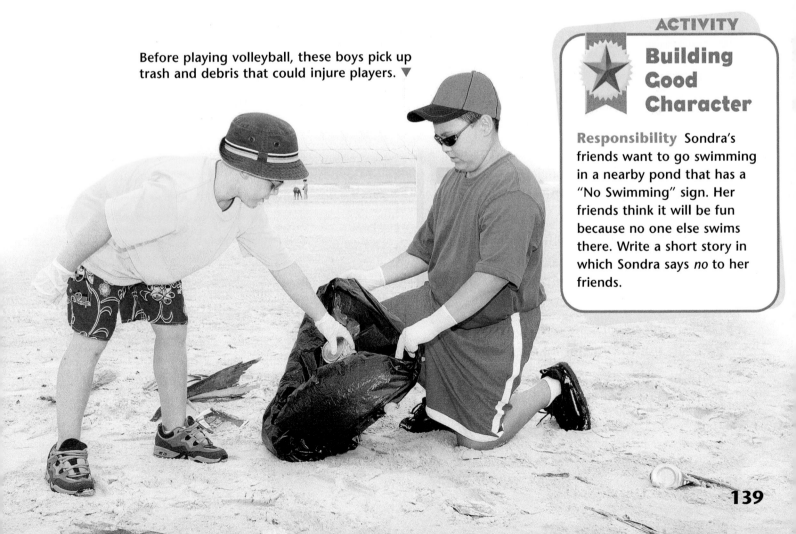

Before playing volleyball, these boys pick up trash and debris that could injure players. ▼

ACTIVITY

Building Good Character

Responsibility Sondra's friends want to go swimming in a nearby pond that has a "No Swimming" sign. Her friends think it will be fun because no one else swims there. Write a short story in which Sondra says *no* to her friends.

Exercising Outdoors

Always be aware of the environment and how it might affect you. Avoid exercising outdoors when it is very hot or cold. Extreme temperatures can make you ill.

Hyperthermia (hy•per•THER•mee•uh) is the name given to several illnesses in which the body's internal temperature becomes too high. Heat stroke is the most serious of these. Signs include hot skin, high body temperature, rapid pulse and breathing, and confusion. To prevent heat-related illnesses, drink plenty of water and wear loose, lightweight, light-colored clothes.

Hypothermia (hy•poh•THER•mee•uh) is a condition in which the body's internal temperature becomes too low. Signs include low body temperature, shivering, slurred speech, confusion, and drowsiness. To avoid hypothermia in cold weather, dress warmly and keep active.

COMPARE AND CONTRAST How are hyperthermia and hypothermia alike? How are they different?

Lesson 3 Summary and Review

1 Summarize with Vocabulary

Use vocabulary and other terms from this lesson to complete the statements.

One way to play a sport safely is to wear protective _____. Be especially cautious when exercising in extreme weather. In hot weather, people can develop _____. One of the most serious forms of this illness is _____. In cold weather, people can develop _____, in which a person's body _____ becomes too low.

2 List four pieces of safety equipment that you can use to prevent injuries.

3 Critical Thinking Why must you take personal responsibility for your safety when exercising?

4 CAUSE AND EFFECT The effect is sports-related injuries. What are four possible causes?

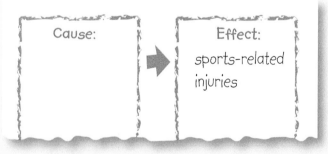

Cause:

Effect: sports-related injuries

5 Write to Express—Solution to a Problem

Pick a sport that interests you. Write a report about the kinds of injuries that can occur while playing it and the steps people can take to help prevent such injuries.

ACTIVITIES

 **Physical Education**

Plan a Workout Develop a workout program for yourself. Include a warm-up, at least 30 minutes of aerobic exercise, anaerobic exercise, and a cool-down. Show your program to your physical education teacher. Be sure to follow safety rules during these activities.

Science

Pulse-Rate Experiment

1. Take your pulse for 10 seconds. Multiply that number by 6, and record it.
2. Run in place for 1 minute.
3. Again, take your pulse for 10 seconds. Multiply that number by 6, and record it.
4. Continue to take your pulse every 2 minutes for 10 minutes. Record each rate.

How does exercise affect your pulse rate?

Technology Project

List six tips for increasing the amount of physical activity in your daily life. For example, you might walk to school instead of taking the bus. Use a computer to create a slide show of the tips. If no computer is available, make a colorful poster instead.

GO ONLINE For more activities, visit The Learning Site. www.harcourtschool.com/health

 **Home & Community**

Physical Fitness Poster Make a poster about the four parts of physical fitness. Illustrate each part of physical fitness with three to five pictures of activities that help build it.

Career Link

Softball Coach Imagine that you are a softball coach. Prepare a handout for players, listing appropriate safety rules. Include at least five rules. Explain why each rule is important.

Reading Skill

CAUSE AND EFFECT

Draw and then use this graphic organizer to answer questions 1 and 2.

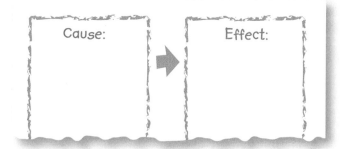

1 You do aerobic exercise 3 days a week for 6 weeks. What are possible effects?

2 You don't wear safety gear while skateboarding. What injuries might occur?

 Use Vocabulary

Match each term in Column B with its meaning in Column A.

Column A	Column B
3 The ability of a muscle to exert force	**A** cardiovascular fitness
4 The ability to bend, twist, and stretch	**B** muscular endurance
5 A workout that benefits the heart and lungs	**C** aerobic exercise
6 A short, intense physical activity	**D** muscular strength
7 Having a strong heart, lungs, and circulatory system	**E** anaerobic exercise
8 The ability to use muscles for a long time	**F** flexibility

Check Understanding

Choose the letter of the correct answer.

9 If you wanted to test the strength and endurance of your stomach muscles, what should you do? (p. 128)
A V-sit reaches   **C** curl-ups
B push-ups   **D** 1-mile runs

10 Which activity lets your breathing and heart rate slowly return to normal? (p. 131)
F warm-up   **H** cool-down
G workout   **J** stretching

11 For people under age twenty, a typical target heart rate is _____. (p. 133)
A 40–80 bpm   **C** 80–150 bpm
B 50–100 bpm   **D** 100–150 bpm

12 Cardiovascular fitness means that a person's heart _____. (pp. 121, 132)
F beats rapidly at rest
G does more work with less effort
H pumps less blood with each beat
J needs fewer nutrients from food

13 Which of these activities is the **BEST** way to build flexibility? (p. 121)
A lifting weights
B stretching
C doing pull-ups
D running

14 Which of the following belongs at the very top of the Activity Pyramid? (p. 122)
F bicycling
G playing basketball
H watching TV
J stretching

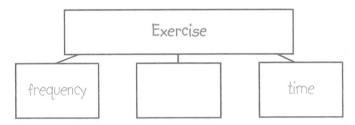

Exercise

frequency

time

15 What aspect of exercise is missing from the graphic organizer above? (p. 130)
A strength
B flexibility
C intensity
D balance

16 Which is **NOT** an effect of long-term exercise? (p. 122–123)
F strong bones
G strong muscles
H lower body fat
J decreased endurance

17 Energy from food is measured in units called _____. (p. 123)
A pounds
B beats per minute
C heart rates
D calories

18 How many hours of sleep should you try to get each night? (p. 134)
F six to seven
G seven to eight
H eight to nine
J nine to ten

19 When lifting a heavy object, what is one thing you should **NOT** do? (p. 124)
A Bend at the waist to pick it up.
B Bend your knees to pick it up.
C Hold it close to your body.
D Stand up slowly as you lift.

Think Critically

20 How can you tell the difference between normal soreness after exercise and an injury?

21 You want to take up in-line skating. What safety rules should you follow?

22 Look at the weekly exercise plan below. How could you improve it?

Apply Skills

23 **BUILDING GOOD CHARACTER**
Respect Your soccer team has made it to the championship game. During the game, an official makes a call that you disagree with. As a result, the other team wins. Use what you know about being a good sport to describe how you would act after the game.

24 **LIFE SKILLS**
Set Goals You have signed up for a three-mile fun run that will be held six months from now. Right now, you can run only about half a mile before you have to slow down and walk. How will you get into shape for the run?

Write About Health

25 **Write to Inform—Explanation**
Explain how getting into the habit of regular exercise can help you both now and in the future.

Staying Safe Every Day

IDENTIFY MAIN IDEA AND DETAILS

The main idea is the most important thought in a passage. Details tell about the main idea. They tell who, what, when, where, why, and how. Use the Reading in Health Handbook on pages 406–407 and this graphic organizer to help you read the health facts in this chapter.

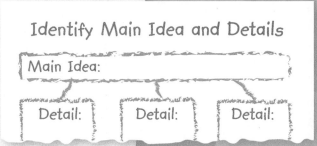

Identify Main Idea and Details

Main Idea:

Detail: | Detail: | Detail:

Health Graph

INTERPRET DATA Every year many people in the United States die from unintentional injuries. According to the graph, which three sources of injury are the leading causes of accidental death?

Causes of Death from Unintentional Injuries

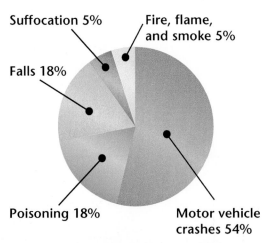

Suffocation 5%
Fire, flame, and smoke 5%
Falls 18%
Poisoning 18%
Motor vehicle crashes 54%

Daily Physical Activity

Being physically fit may help you avoid or more easily recover from unintentional injuries.

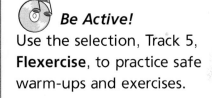

Be Active!
Use the selection, Track 5, **Flexercise**, to practice safe warm-ups and exercises.

Safety at Home

Prevent Injuries from Electricity

Lesson Focus
People need to prevent and avoid hazards to be safe in their homes.

Why Learn This?
You can use what you learn to prevent injuries at home.

Vocabulary
electric shock
flammable
fire hazard

You walk into a dark room, and at the flip of a switch, you can have light. Touch another switch, and music fills the air. Electricity is a great benefit. However, if electricity isn't used safely, it can injure or even kill you.

The wires within a building's walls and the outer parts of electric outlets have plastic or rubber coverings. Cords, plugs, and appliances also have protective coverings. These coverings keep you safe because electricity doesn't flow through plastic or rubber. When a person touches any part of an electric circuit that doesn't have this kind of covering, the person becomes part of the circuit. Electricity flows through the person, causing a painful jolt called an **electric shock**. If the electricity is strong enough, the electric shock can burn body tissues, disturb or stop a person's heartbeat or breathing, and in some cases, kill a person.

DON'T pull on a cord to unplug it. You may break the wires inside the cord or damage the protective covering. ▶

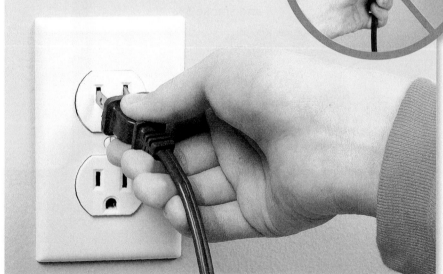

▲ **DO** cover unused outlets to prevent young children from poking things into them.

▲ **DO** safely unplug a cord by pulling on the plug itself. When inserting a plug, keep fingers away from the metal prongs.

Using an electric appliance near water can be dangerous. Under normal, dry conditions, your skin provides some protection against the flow of electricity, but electricity can pass very easily through water. When your skin is wet or damp, you have little or no protection against an electric current. In fact, just touching wires in a wall socket with a wet hand can cause the current to flow through your body.

MAIN IDEA AND DETAILS **Give three details to support this statement: Following safety measures will prevent injury from electricity.**

▲ **DO** check cords before using them to make sure that the protective covering is in good condition.

▲ **DON'T** use cords with cracked or worn coverings, and don't use tape to repair a cord.

▼ **DON'T** overload a socket. It may start a fire.

DON'T use appliances in or next to water or while standing on a damp surface. ▶

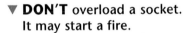

▲ **DO** keep appliances away from water. If you must use them near a sink, tub, shower, or toilet, make sure the appliances don't touch water and can't fall into the water.

▲ **DO** use only one plug in each socket. Use a power strip to plug in more than two cords.

Preventing Fires

In your home or classroom you'll see many different kinds of materials. Some materials can't be set on fire easily, but others can. Materials that burn easily are said to be **flammable** (FLAM·uh·buhl). Oil, rubbing alcohol, and nail polish remover are examples of flammable materials. A fire can start when a flammable material comes into contact with a heat source. Flammable materials should never be stored near a water heater, a stove, or an open flame.

Most flammable materials give off smoke before flames appear. Smoke detectors emit alarms when smoke is detected inside a building, allowing people to escape.

Burning candles, space heaters, careless smoking, and overloaded outlets are each a **fire hazard**, a dangerous situation that might result in a fire. It's important to keep curtains, furniture, bedding, and clothing away from hot or burning materials. Never hide an electric cord under a rug because the rug can cause a cord's insulation (protective covering) to wear away.

Quick Activity

Analyze a Graph
According to the graph, which are the two most common causes of house fires? Write at least one way each cause could be avoided.

Causes of House Fires

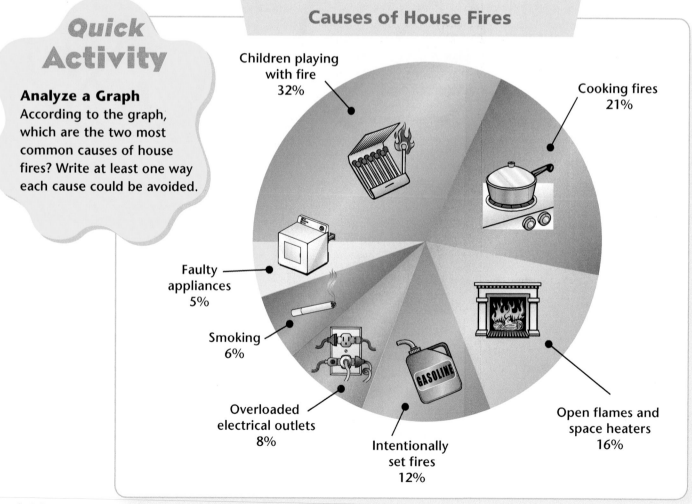

Children playing with fire 32%

Cooking fires 21%

Faulty appliances 5%

Smoking 6%

Overloaded electrical outlets 8%

Intentionally set fires 12%

Open flames and space heaters 16%

Grill

Keep grill at least 20 feet away from buildings, plants, and play areas.

Decorative Lights

Don't nail down wires or place them across metal doorways or downspouts. Don't overload outlets with lights.

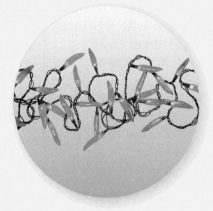

Trash and Oily Rags

Trash piles and oily rags can easily ignite when heat builds up. Keep rags in tightly closed metal cans. Discard trash frequently.

Fireworks

Don't use them—leave them to professionals. Fireworks, even sparklers, burn very hot. They can set clothing on fire. Fireworks are illegal in many areas.

Flammable Liquids

Store only in approved containers, never in glass. Keep the containers away from matches and open flames.

Campfires

Keep campfires in a fire ring. Don't start a fire when it is windy or dry. Do not wear loose clothing around a fire. Keep a bucket of water nearby to put out the campfire.

Fire hazards occur outdoors, too. To prevent fires during outdoor activities, follow the safety rules shown above.

CAUSE AND EFFECT **What might happen if you start a campfire on a windy day?**

Myth and Fact

Myth: **Wiping kitchen surfaces with a dishcloth keeps them clean.**

Fact: You could be using a cloth that is full of germs. Start each day with a fresh, clean cloth. Using paper towels also helps reduce the spread of germs.

Kitchen Safety

If you aren't careful, the kitchen can be a dangerous place. Knowing and practicing safety rules in the kitchen can help you avoid injuries. When working in the kitchen, be sure an adult knows what you plan to cook and which kitchen tools you will use.

Ovens and Stoves

Ask for permission from a responsible adult before using an oven or a stove. Here are some other things to keep in mind:

- Never add water to a pan that contains hot oil. The oil will spatter and could burn someone.
- Don't leave a pot on a hot burner unattended.
- Make sure you turn off the oven or stove when you finish using it.
- If something you are cooking catches fire, do not put water on the fire. It could make the fire bigger. Use baking soda instead.

When possible, use a microwave oven instead of a stove. When used according to instructions, the microwave oven is safer.

Make sure you have a firm grip before lifting a lid or container. When lifting a lid from a pot, be careful. Escaping steam can burn.

Keep utensils near, but not on, the stove top. Keep paper towels, dishcloths, and potholders away from the burners.

To handle hot trays or metal pot handles, use an oven mitt that covers your whole hand.

Keep pot handles turned toward the center of the stove.

Keep clothing away from burners. Sleeves should be short or rolled up, and long hair should be tied back.

Microwave Ovens

Foods cook quickly in a microwave oven. Follow these safety guidelines:

- Remove foods from the microwave oven carefully. Steam from hot food can burn you.
- Never use aluminum foil or metal containers in a microwave oven. They may spark or cause a fire.

Kitchen Appliances

Always ask permission before using kitchen appliances. Keep these tips in mind:

- Keep all electric appliances away from water.
- Don't turn an appliance on or off with wet hands.
- Be careful if you use a food processor or blender. The blades are sharp.

DRAW CONCLUSIONS What types of accidents do the guidelines for using microwaves, ovens, and stoves seek to prevent?

Health & Technology

Ground-Fault Circuit Interrupter

A ground-fault circuit interrupter (GFCI) is a fast-acting circuit breaker that quickly cuts off current to prevent a person from receiving an electric shock. One type of GFCI is used in place of a standard electrical outlet. This GFCI monitors the current going through an appliance that is plugged into it. If the GFCI senses a problem, it shuts off the current. GFCIs are often installed in areas near water, such as in a bathroom or around a swimming pool.

Lesson 1 Summary and Review

❶ Summarize with Vocabulary

Use vocabulary and other terms from this lesson to complete the statements.

If you touch a damaged power cord, you could receive a jolt called an _____. To prevent a fire, use a _____ instead of overloading a wall socket. Placing paper towels on a stove top is a _____ because paper is a _____ material. If possible, use a _____ instead of a stove.

❷ Critical Thinking
At the swimming pool, a friend gets a CD player, plugs it in, and takes it to the edge of the pool. What should you do?

❸ List four ways that you can prevent fires inside or outside the home.

❹ (Focus Skill) MAIN IDEA AND DETAILS Draw and complete this graphic organizer to tell how you can prevent kitchen accidents.

Main Idea:

Detail: | Detail: | Detail:

❺ Write to Inform—Explanation

Your friend James likes to use fireworks to celebrate the Fourth of July. James doesn't understand why you won't join him. Write what you would say to James to explain why you don't want to use fireworks.

Personal Safety

Lesson Focus

You need to be aware of hazards so that you can take precautions against them.

Why Learn This?

You will learn how to stay safe and protect others from injury.

Vocabulary

poison
weapon

Poisons

Cleaning products, medicines, vitamins, and paints are safe when used correctly. If used incorrectly, they can be harmful. A **poison** is a substance that can harm a person if it is inhaled, swallowed, or absorbed by the skin. Most household cleaners and chemicals are poisonous if swallowed. Medicines and vitamins can cause harm if they are used incorrectly. You must carefully follow all the directions printed on product labels.

Take extra care to protect young children, who may eat or drink harmful things by mistake. Keep all products in their original containers so they aren't mistaken for food or drink. Keep all products locked up or in a high cabinet where young children can't reach them. Put the number for your local Poison Control Center or physician near the phone in case of an emergency.

SUMMARIZE Tell how to protect young children from harmful substances in the home.

Quick Activity

Analyze Product Labels Read the labels of these common household products. Which are harmful to eyes? Which are harmful to skin? Which are poisonous when swallowed?

KEEP OUT OF REACH OF CHILDREN

AVOID PROLONGED BREATHING OF VAPOR

WARNING: Eye and skin irritant. Use only in well-ventilated area. Wear protective gloves. To avoid harmful fumes, do not mix with ammonia or other cleaning products.

FIRST AID:
Eyes: Flush with water for 15 minutes.
Skin: Rinse skin with water.
If Swallowed: Drink large amounts of water.
DO NOT induce vomiting.

KEEP OUT OF REACH OF CHILDREN

CAUTION: Wash hands after use. If you have sensitive skin, use rubber gloves. Avoid contact with eyes. If irritation persists, or if swallowed, seek medical advice.

DO NOT reuse container.
Discard after use.

Weapons Safety

Some adults keep weapons in their homes for hunting or protection. A **weapon** is an object, such as a gun or knife, that can be used to injure or kill an animal or a person. All weapons can be dangerous if they are used inappropriately.

Everyone should treat a gun as if it were loaded. Guns can fire accidentally, so they should never be pointed at anyone. The most important rule about guns that you should follow is this: Never handle a gun without a responsible adult present.

If you find a gun or if someone shows you a gun, follow these steps:

1. Stop! Don't touch the gun.
2. Leave the area.
3. Tell an adult as quickly as possible.

SEQUENCE What steps should you follow if a friend your age shows you a gun?

Did You Know?

Most schools have zero-tolerance policies for weapons, including toy guns and toy knives. Anyone caught with a weapon at school is in serious trouble. **DO NOT take weapons of any kind, or objects that look like weapons, to school.**

▲ Knives, including hunting knives, are considered weapons.

▲ Guns should be kept in a locked case.

POISON
WARNING: Harmful or fatal if swallowed. Causes severe burns to eyes and skin. Can cause blindness.
FIRST AID:
   Eyes: Flush with water for 20 minutes.
   Skin: Rinse skin with water for 15 minutes, and then wash with soap and water.
   If Swallowed: Drink 1 to 2 glasses of water or milk.
DO NOT drink vinegar, citrus juice, or other acidic fluids.
DO NOT INDUCE VOMITING.
CALL POISON CONTROL OR SEEK MEDICAL ATTENTION IMMEDIATELY!

Responsibility Mattie baby-sits her neighbor's toddlers every Wednesday night. Her friend Emily calls and wants to talk while Mattie is baby-sitting. What should Mattie do to show responsible behavior?

Baby-Sitting

When you baby-sit, you are responsible for the safety of others. Arrive early to discuss important safety information with the parents or guardians. Find out what foods the children are allowed to eat and what activities they may do. Find out if the children have any allergies, and ask what to do if they have an allergic reaction. Take your baby-sitting responsibilities seriously so that you and the children will have a safe and enjoyable time.

DRAW CONCLUSIONS How are you like a parent when you are baby-sitting?

Baby-Sitting Safety

When you arrive, find out

1. phone numbers at which you can reach the parents.

2. emergency phone numbers, including those of relatives, doctors, neighbors, and the Poison Control Center.

3. where first-aid supplies are kept.

4. the locations of any hazards, such as matches, electric cords, plastic bags, and medicines.

After the parents leave

1. don't allow anyone in the house without permission from the parents.

2. don't give children medicine unless directed to do so by the parents or a doctor.

3. don't leave the children alone. Check on them every fifteen minutes while they sleep.

Safety in and near Vehicles

Because cars and trucks are large and powerful, accidents involving them can cause serious injuries or death. Always be careful when you are in or around a vehicle. These guidelines can help you.

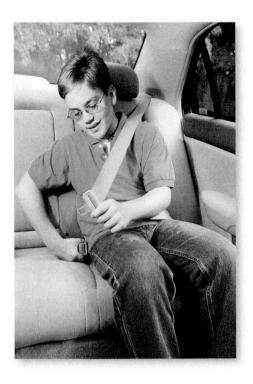

Pedestrians

Pedestrians, or people who are walking, must be especially careful near traffic.
- When you are walking along a road where there is no sidewalk, walk facing the oncoming traffic. Avoid walking on roads after dark.
- Watch for vehicles that are backing up, turning, or pulling out of driveways.

Passengers

What you do as a passenger affects the safety of everyone in the car.
- Always wear a safety belt. If the car doesn't have a safety belt for everyone, avoid riding in it.
- Don't distract the driver by making sudden, loud noises.
- Keep your hands and feet in the car at all times.

Drivers

If you are driving a motorized vehicle, such as a motorized scooter, you are responsible for the safety of everyone near you on the road.
- Always wear a helmet, kneepads and elbow pads, and sturdy shoes.
- Do not ride after dark.
- Children under the age of twelve should not drive motorized scooters.

DRAW CONCLUSIONS Why should you watch for vehicles that are backing up or turning?

Myth and Fact

Myth: **It is safe to ride in the back seat without wearing a safety belt.**
Fact: Always wear a safety belt when riding in a vehicle. During an accident, passengers who aren't wearing safety belts may be thrown against something hard, or they may be thrown out of the vehicle.

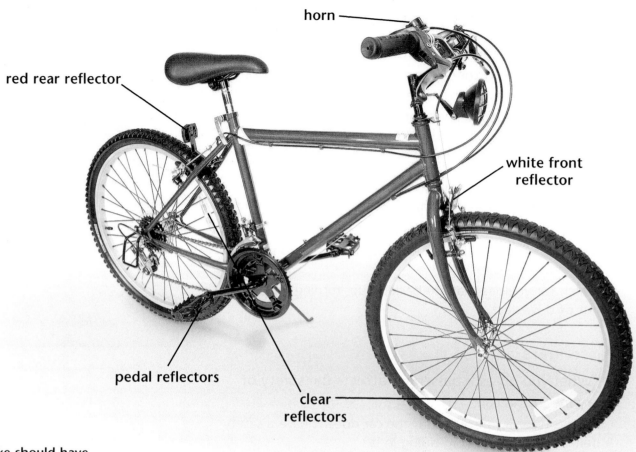

horn

red rear reflector

white front reflector

pedal reflectors

clear reflectors

▲ A bike should have reflectors and a horn. Why are these features important?

Bicycle Safety

You may not think of a bicycle as a hazard, but you can be injured riding one. Make sure that the bicycle is the right size for you and is properly adjusted. When you sit on the bike with the pedal in the lowest position, you should be able to rest your heel on the pedal. Adjust your bike seat so that your knee is slightly bent when your foot is resting on the pedal.

Follow these tips for safe bicycle riding:

- Check your bike each time you ride it to make sure all parts, such as handlebars, seat, brakes, tires, chain, and wheels, are working and properly adjusted.
- Ride single file in the same direction as traffic. Don't weave in and out between parked cars.
- Never ride while wearing a backpack. Attach a basket to your handlebars or a rack over your rear tire.
- Before you enter a street, stop. Look left, then right, and then left again. Listen for any traffic. Think before you go.
- Walk your bike across an intersection. Look left, then right, and then left again. Wait for traffic to pass.
- Obey all traffic signals.

Thousands of children are involved in bike-related crashes every year. That's why you should always wear a helmet when riding your bike. Buy a helmet that sits flat on your head. Be sure that it straps snugly under your chin so that it will stay in place if you fall.

SUMMARIZE **Tell the important features to look for when buying a bike helmet.**

Consumer Activity

Make Buying Decisions
How much does a good bike helmet cost? Find out about the features and prices of several bike helmets. Do the more expensive helmets offer better protection?

The hard outer shell holds the inner foam and helps the helmet skid easily on rough pavement if you fall. This helps prevent neck injuries.

The padding absorbs blows to the head. If you fall and strike your helmet on the ground, you should replace it, even if it doesn't look damaged, because the hard foam padding inside may be crushed.

Look for an approval sticker to make sure the helmet meets safety standards set by the Consumer Product Safety Commission (CPSC).

Air vents allow perspiration to evaporate, which will help keep you cool.

The helmet should have a quick-release strap.

Internet Safety

The Internet is a helpful tool that you can use for education, research, and chatting with family and friends. The Internet has drawbacks, too. Some websites, and some people you "meet" there, are unsafe. Talk to a family member to set up rules like these before you go online.

- Don't give out personal information, such as your address, your telephone number, or the name or location of your school.
- If you find information or receive messages that make you feel uncomfortable, tell a trusted adult right away.
- Never agree to meet anyone or send a picture of yourself to a person whom you meet online.

SEQUENCE **What should you do immediately if you receive an online message that makes you feel uncomfortable?**

Information Alert!

New Trends in Internet Safety The computer industry changes at a rapid pace. As technology improves, trends in Internet safety will also change.

GO ONLINE **For the most up-to-date information, visit The Learning Site. www.harcourtschool.com/health**

Lesson 2 Summary and Review

1 Summarize with Vocabulary

Use vocabulary and other terms from this lesson to complete the statements.

A _____ is a substance that can harm a person if it is swallowed, inhaled, or absorbed by the skin. If used incorrectly, _____ prescribed by a doctor can do harm. A _____, such as a gun, should not be mishandled. When _____, never leave children alone. You should always wear a _____ to protect your head when riding a bicycle. Also, always wear a _____ when you ride in a motor vehicle.

2 Critical Thinking How can medicine, which helps treat medical conditions, be dangerous?

3 What steps should you follow if you find a gun or if someone at school shows you a gun?

4 MAIN IDEA AND DETAILS Draw and complete this graphic organizer to tell about ways to be safe in or around motor vehicles as a driver, pedestrian, or passenger. Give two safety tips for each detail box.

Main Idea: _____

Detail: _____ Detail: _____ Detail: _____

5 Write to Express—Idea

Do you think everyone should be required by law to wear a helmet when riding a bike? Write a paragraph in which you give your opinion about this idea. Be sure to include reasons to support your opinion.

Fairness

Play Fairly and by the Rules

Games have rules that perform two functions: they tell you how to play, and they help keep you safe. When you play fairly and by the rules, you show both common sense and good character. When you play games with others, remember these tips:

- **Before beginning a game, make sure everyone knows and understands the rules.**
- **Enforce the rules fairly during the game.**
- **Rotate players. Everyone has fun if everyone gets to play.**
- **Remember that rules are made for your safety. For example, to help prevent injuries during a basketball game, players are not allowed to charge, hold, or unfairly block an opponent. To prevent eye and face injuries during a hockey game, players are penalized for carrying their sticks too high.**
- **Don't blame others for your mistakes. Instead, learn from them. In this way you avoid conflict and show good character.**

Activity

Play a group sport with your friends. Discuss the rules before the game begins. Play the game fairly. Enforce the rules equally so that both teams are treated fairly and everyone stays safe. If a disagreement occurs, work together to find a solution.

Water Safety

Safety While Swimming

Knowing how to swim is the key to being safe in the water. In addition, it helps to know some water-safety tips. For safe swimming, always follow these rules when at a pool, beach, or water park.

- Follow the posted pool or beach rules.
- To avoid choking, don't chew gum or eat while swimming.
- Use extra care when swimming in an ocean, a lake, or a river. The bottom may be hard to see and may have drop-offs, or rocks or other debris.
- Stop swimming and get away from the water as soon as you see lightning or hear thunder.
- At an ocean, a lake, or a river, swim only in supervised areas.
- Never run or push others on wet patios or decks; these surfaces can be slippery.
- Don't dunk others or play roughly.
- Listen to the lifeguard. It's his or her job to make sure you are safe.

Check for signs that warn of unusual water conditions. ▼

Never swim alone. If something happens, one of you can go for help. ▼

DANGER
HIGH SURF

危険 高波

DANGER!
RIP CURRENT

Diving can be fun, but make sure you are doing it safely. Diving into water that is too shallow can result in neck or spinal injuries, which may cause paralysis. Before diving, always find out how deep the water is. Before diving off a board, make sure the water is more than nine feet deep. Never dive off the side of a pool or in a place where you can't see the bottom. And even if you can see the bottom, remember this rule: "Feet First, First Time."

SEQUENCE What should you do before you dive into water?

ACTIVITY

Life Skills

Refuse You are with a group of friends at a lake that has a "No Swimming" sign. Your friends want to go swimming anyway. They say that no one will know and that with all of you there, no one could drown. How can you tell your friends that you don't want to swim?

Read the signs and follow the rules at water parks. Go down slides feet first to avoid head and neck injuries. ▶

Responding to Water Emergencies

There are two words to remember when responding to a water emergency—*reach* and *throw*. **Reach and throw** are lifesaving techniques used to help people who are at risk of drowning. Don't try to swim to a person who is struggling in the water unless you are trained in lifesaving. The person may pull you under in his or her struggle, and both of you may drown.

Reach

Find something you can hold out for the person to grab. It could be a sturdy branch, a stick, or an oar. Before reaching out, brace your feet and your free hand securely. If possible, have someone hold onto the back of your belt or pants. Then reach out for the person.

Throw

If the person is too far away to reach, throw something that will float to him or her. You might use a life jacket, an empty plastic jug, or a lifesaving ring. Tie one end of a rope to whatever you throw. Tie the other end to something secure, such as a pier support, so that if you miss, you can try again.

Steps in Survival Floating

1. Rest Lie on the surface of the water. Hold your breath, put your face down, and let your arms and legs dangle.

2. Surface When you need to breathe, slowly raise your arms in front of you to shoulder height. At the same time, move one leg forward and the other back.

3. Breathe Push down with your arms, and bring your legs together. This should enable you to bring your nose and mouth out of the water. Breathe. If your mouth doesn't come out of the water, move your arms and legs more quickly.

4. Sink As your body sinks again, hold your breath and return to resting position. Repeat the steps as needed.

Survival floating is a technique to increase your chances of survival if you are caught without a life jacket in deep, warm water. This kind of floating will help you conserve your energy and allow you to breathe. But remember, the safest thing to do is to always wear a life jacket when you are boating or around water.

SUMMARIZE Use your own words to describe the steps of survival floating.

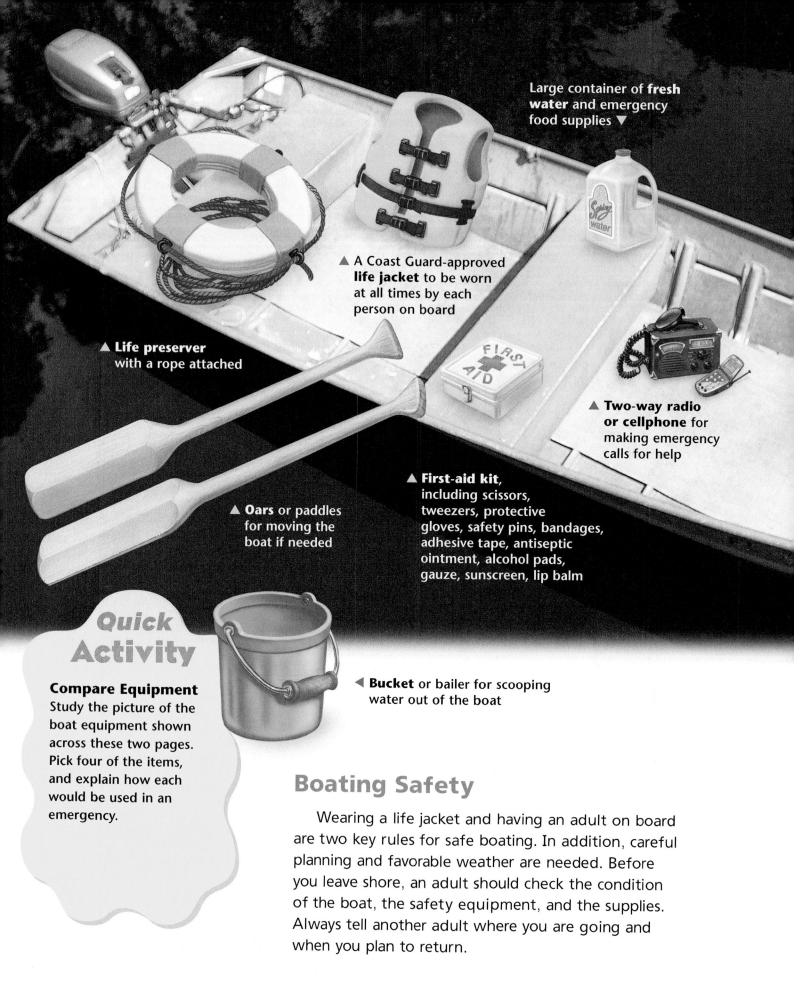

Large container of **fresh water** and emergency food supplies ▼

▲ A Coast Guard-approved **life jacket** to be worn at all times by each person on board

▲ **Life preserver** with a rope attached

▲ **Two-way radio or cellphone** for making emergency calls for help

▲ **First-aid kit**, including scissors, tweezers, protective gloves, safety pins, bandages, adhesive tape, antiseptic ointment, alcohol pads, gauze, sunscreen, lip balm

▲ **Oars** or paddles for moving the boat if needed

◄ **Bucket** or bailer for scooping water out of the boat

Quick Activity

Compare Equipment Study the picture of the boat equipment shown across these two pages. Pick four of the items, and explain how each would be used in an emergency.

Boating Safety

Wearing a life jacket and having an adult on board are two key rules for safe boating. In addition, careful planning and favorable weather are needed. Before you leave shore, an adult should check the condition of the boat, the safety equipment, and the supplies. Always tell another adult where you are going and when you plan to return.

Safety supply kit, including knife, whistle or horn, flashlight, flares, smoke canister, mirror for signaling, blanket, and waterproof matches ▼

Cold Water Safety

Cold water causes body temperature to drop suddenly, which increases the risk of drowning. That's why it's important to conserve body heat if you are caught in cold water. Here's what to do until help arrives. Leave your clothes on. Trapped air will help maintain body heat and help you float. Do not tread water. Instead, float to conserve energy. Pull your knees up to your chest, and put your arms around them. Clasp your hands. Your life jacket will keep your head above water.

CAUSE AND EFFECT **What is the effect of air's being trapped in your clothes if you are caught in cold water?**

Lesson 3 Summary and Review

1 Summarize with Vocabulary

Use vocabulary and other terms from this lesson to complete the statements.

One water safety tip is to never _____ headfirst into shallow water. Also, always listen to the _____, whose job is to keep you safe. To save someone from drowning, remember the words _____. A type of floating that conserves energy and helps you breathe is _____. When boating, always wear a Coast Guard-approved

_____.

2 Name three pieces of safety equipment that should be on all boats, and explain the purpose of each piece.

3 Critical Thinking Why is it important to rest during survival floating?

4 (Focus Skill) MAIN IDEA AND DETAILS Draw and complete this graphic organizer to give details about water safety and survival. Label each detail box with one of these labels: *Swimming, Boating, Surviving*. Write two details in each of these boxes.

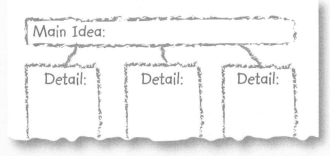

Main Idea:

Detail: | Detail: | Detail:

5 Write to Inform—Narrative

Suppose your best friend invites you on an outing to a nearby lake. Your friend accidentally falls from a boat pier into the water. Write a story that tells how you and your friend's parents save your friend.

Resolve Conflicts
That Can Lead to Violence

Sometimes we face situations that can lead to violence. We need to know how to handle these situations. Using the steps to **Resolve Conflicts** can help you avoid violence.

Betty and Wendy are seated at the same table in the library. Both girls have an assignment that requires them to use a CD. As Betty prepares to leave, she picks up the CD that is on the table. Wendy jumps up and tries to take the CD from Betty. Both girls become angry.

1 Use "I" messages to tell how you feel.

2 Listen to each other. Consider the other person's point of view.

"This is my CD," Wendy says. "Do you think it's yours?" "Yes, I do," Betty says.

"I need this CD to do the assignment, but you are trying to take it," Betty says. Wendy replies, "This is my CD. I checked it out a few minutes ago. You must have lost yours."

3 **Negotiate.**

I'll give you the CD tomorrow morning.

Our assignment isn't due for two days.

The girls decide to share the CD. Wendy will use the CD first and then give it to Betty.

4 **Compromise on a solution.**

"That's a good idea," Betty says. "We'll both have plenty of time to finish the assignment. See you tomorrow."

Problem Solving

A. Malcolm and Raymond collect baseball cards. Malcolm takes his card collection to Raymond's house. The boys spread both collections across Raymond's bed so they can admire all the cards. Later, as Malcolm gathers his cards, he picks up a card that Raymond says belongs to him. Malcolm replies that the card was a birthday present from his father. The boys start to argue.

- Use the steps to **Resolve Conflicts** to help Raymond and Malcolm agree on a way to find out who actually owns the card.

B. Natalie is playing a game with her big sister, Kate. Kate is cheating so that she can win every time. Explain how Natalie might resolve this conflict in a way that shows good character.

167

LESSON 4

Preventing and Surviving Violence

Lesson Focus

Learning how to avoid or resolve conflicts and violent situations will help you avoid injury.

Why Learn This?

Learning how to respond to confrontations and violence will help keep you safe.

Vocabulary

gang
terrorism

Gangs

A **gang** is a group of people who have an informal but close relationship, often with strict rules. Gang members spend time together and back each other up if a conflict arises. The problem is that gangs typically engage in crimes and violence. These activities often include the use of drugs and weapons.

People join gangs because it gives them a sense of belonging. Being part of a gang also makes them feel powerful and protected. Gang members can identify one another because they

- wear a particular color of clothing, item of jewelry, or symbol, and wear the item in a particular way.
- use certain hand signals.
- draw gang symbols and use gang handwriting.

Myth

In a gang, you get respect.

Fact

When you join a gang, you may be beaten up or forced to commit a crime. If you try to quit, you or your family may be threatened.

Myth

You can have lots of money and excitement from selling drugs and committing other crimes.

Fact

You can be killed by rival gangs or go to prison as a criminal. Many gang members become drug addicts.

Myth

You are protected by the members of your gang.

Fact

All gang members are highly likely to be injured or killed.

Myth

You have to join a gang to survive in a tough neighborhood.

Fact

Many communities and schools have programs that provide healthful ways to build a sense of personal power and belonging.

▲ The best way to avoid gangs is to participate in alternative activities. Think of five alternative activities available in your community or school.

Learn to recognize gang members in your area, and avoid the people and places that are associated with violence. Don't wear the same clothing or symbols that gang members use to identify one another. Do not confront gang members—leave that to law enforcement.

If gang members confront you, avoid violence. Don't let your anger or fear control you. Keep things light, and go slowly. Convince the other person that the problem isn't worth fighting about. Don't provoke gang members by cornering or crowding them.

If a gang member confronts you, tell your parents or guardians, school officials, and police what happened. Don't be afraid to talk.

COMPARE AND CONTRAST How is an ordinary group of friends like a gang? How is it different from a gang?

Personal Health Plan

Real-Life Situation
A gang member pressures you to join a gang.

Real-Life Plan
Write a step-by-step plan explaining what you might do in this situation.

169

Working to Prevent Violence

People can work together to learn how to communicate to resolve conflicts. The following activities show how people can work together in ways that provide support and help for each person.

SUMMARIZE List four ways that will help you learn how to resolve conflicts by working with other people.

Make a Booklet

Work with others to make a booklet about ways to avoid violence and resolve conflicts. Include "super-hero" stories of real people who have successfully dealt with potentially violent situations.

Make a Video

Role-play how to make difficult choices when confronted with dangerous situations. Videotape your role-play, and show it to others. Use it to help people think about how to avoid or resolve conflicts and how to stay safe in violent situations.

Debate

Debate the pros and cons of a situation. This helps you learn to accept differing viewpoints without having to use violent words or actions to defend your opinion. Debating an issue also helps you learn the reasons for others' opinions and may lead you to reassess your own.

Volunteer

Participate in a service project in your community. For example, you can collect food and clothing for charity or participate in campaigns to reduce violence. When you volunteer, you broaden your understanding of people and of society.

Violence in Public Places

In recent years many nations, including the United States, have experienced terrorist attacks. **Terrorism** is the use of violence to promote a social or political cause. Violent acts have even occurred in schools. As a result, schools have developed emergency procedures that include locking students in their classrooms to protect them from violence.

Terrorist attacks and school violence are rare. However, should they occur, follow these guidelines:

- Stay calm.
- Follow your family's or school's emergency plan; obey instructions given by your parent or teacher.
- Be alert. Report anything suspicious to a parent or school official.

SUMMARIZE How should you respond to a violent act at school?

◄ The threat of terrorism has resulted in heightened security, such as the careful screening of passengers and baggage at airports.

Consumer Activity

Analyze Media Messages Many songs released today have lyrics that portray violent or hurtful acts. Write a paragraph describing some effects these lyrics may have on listeners. In your opinion, are these types of lyrics harmful to those who listen to them regularly?

Violence and the Media

Does watching violence create more violence among young people? Some experts think so. The average child in the United States is said to have watched 8,000 murders and 100,000 acts of violence on television and in movies before finishing the sixth grade. Behavior experts say that when people constantly see violent acts, they start to accept violence as normal. Moreover, television, movies, and other media often do not fully explore the negative side of violence—the great emotional and physical pain it causes.

To help parents and guardians decide what their children should and should not see, most television programs, movies, music, and video games have ratings or warning labels that tell whether they contain violent language or show violent acts.

DRAW CONCLUSIONS **How can violence in the media influence a person's behavior?**

Lesson 4 Summary and Review

❶ Summarize with Vocabulary

Use vocabulary and other terms from this lesson to complete the statements.

The members of a _____ may feel protected, but they often die violently. The use of violence to promote a social or political cause is called _____. Watching _____ on television may change your idea of acceptable behavior. If you are exposed to violence, it is important to stay _____ and relaxed.

❷ What are four activities you can do with other people to learn how to resolve conflicts?

❸ Critical Thinking Explain what you should do if another student threatens to bring a gun to school.

❹ **MAIN IDEA AND DETAILS** Draw and complete this graphic organizer to tell facts about gang life.

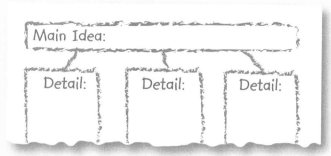

Main Idea:

Detail: Detail: Detail:

❺ Write to Express—Solution to a Problem

Suppose your friend knows that a gang member is going to confront him. Write to tell your friend what he can do to avoid a violent conflict.

ACTIVITIES

Science

Electrical Safety If too much current flows through the wires in a circuit, the wires may overheat and cause a fire. Circuit breakers and fuses are safety devices that cut off current if it becomes dangerously high. Research circuit breakers and fuses. Find out if there are unsafe ways to use either kind of device. Present your findings in a report that includes diagrams and other illustrations.

Physical Education

Swimming Strokes There are four strokes commonly used in swimming: crawl, butterfly, breaststroke, and sidestroke. Find out how each stroke is done. Decide which stroke would be best for a person to use if he or she is stranded for long hours in the water. Present your findings in an oral report to the class, using pictures and demonstrations to illustrate your findings.

Technology Project

Poison Bearers Research poisonous plants and venomous animals. Then make a poster, pamphlet, or computer slide presentation that shows what each plant or animal looks like, what the effects and signs of its poison or venom are, and how to treat it.

GO ONLINE For more activities, visit The Learning Site. www.harcourtschool.com/health

Home & Community

Perform a Home Inspection Make a checklist of possible safety hazards that could occur in a home. Then tour your home with your family, using your checklist to look for possible hazards. Correct or repair the hazards. Be sure to check your smoke detectors, carbon monoxide detectors, and fire extinguishers.

Career Link

Lifeguard Suppose you are a lifeguard at a beach. A group of school children has come to the ocean for the first time to swim. What will you tell the group about water safety?

173

Reading Skill

MAIN IDEA AND DETAILS

Draw and then use this graphic organizer to answer questions 1 and 2.

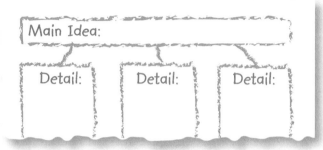

Main Idea:

Detail: Detail: Detail:

1 Give details that support the idea that you can avoid an electric shock.

2 Give details to support the idea that you can prevent fires inside and outside the home.

 Use Vocabulary

Match each term in Column B with its meaning in Column A.

Column A	Column B
3 A burning candle	**A** reach and throw
4 Describes materials that burn easily	**B** gang
5 Informal group of people with strict rules	**C** electric shock
	D flammable
	E poison
6 Use of violence to promote a cause	**F** weapon
	G fire hazard
7 A knife or a gun	**H** terrorism
8 Ways to rescue people in danger of drowning	
9 A painful jolt	
10 Causes harm if swallowed	

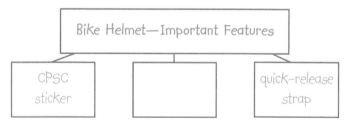 **Check Understanding**

Choose the letter of the correct answer.

11 Which is the leading cause of house fires? (p. 148)
A smoking
B intentionally set fires
C children playing with fire
D overloaded electrical outlets

12 Which of these is the **BEST** conductor of electricity? (pp. 146–147)
F water
G electrical tape
H dry skin
J plastic

13 You should put out a cooking fire with _____. (p. 150)
A oil
B household chemicals
C baking soda
D water

14 What should you do if a person you have met online wants to meet you after school? (p. 158)
F Ask a friend to go with you.
G Insist that you meet in a public place.
H Send a picture so the person will know you.
J Tell a parent or guardian immediately.

Bike Helmet—Important Features

CPSC sticker

quick-release strap

15 Which of these belongs in the graphic organizer? (p. 157)
A fit
B price
C style
D color

16 Survival floating enables a person to _____. (p. 163)

  F survive an ocean undertow

  G conserve energy between breaths

  H survive indefinitely in icy water

  J rescue others in danger of drowning

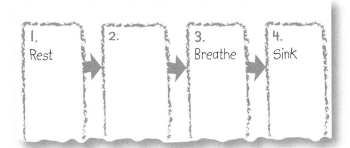

| 1. Rest | 2. | 3. Breathe | 4. Sink |

17 Which of the following belongs in this graphic organizer about survival floating? (p. 163)

  A Float   **C** Relax

  B Surface   **D** Swim

18 Every person aboard a boat should have a _____. (p. 164)

  F cell phone   **H** radio

  G water bottle   **J** life jacket

19 If a person is confronted by a gang member, the person should _____. (p. 169)

  A laugh at the gang member

  B stay calm and keep the mood light

  C threaten the gang member

  D tell no one about the encounter

20 Which of the following is an appropriate way to respond to school violence? (p. 171)

  F Leave school immediately.

  G Call your parents to report the situation.

  H Follow your teacher's directions.

  J Attempt to reason with the attackers.

Think Critically

21 Suppose you are baby-sitting and one of the children insists that he takes a prescription medication every night at bedtime. The parents did not mention this in their instructions to you. What should you do?

22 A friend's older brother has offered to give several students a ride home from school. As you get in the car, you notice that there are not enough safety belts for everyone. You live only a short distance from school, so the ride would be brief. What should you do?

Apply Skills

23 **BUILDING GOOD CHARACTER**

Fairness You are playing a game with a group of friends. In the middle of the game, one friend makes a move that doesn't appear fair. Apply what you know about fairness to work out a solution to the problem. Explain your solution.

24 **LIFE SKILLS**

Resolve Conflicts Joey loaned his favorite music CD to his friend Paul. It has been three months, and Paul has not returned the CD. Joey has asked for his CD twice, and Paul still has not returned it. Use what you know about resolving conflicts to help these boys arrive at a solution.

Write About Health

25 **Write to Inform—Explanation**

Write a paragraph explaining why everyone should know safety rules that apply to being at home and that apply to being away from home.

Emergencies and First Aid

Bandages

Adhesive Bandages

SUMMARIZE When you summarize, you give the main idea and most important details of a passage. You also tell how the main idea and its details are connected. Use the Reading in Health Handbook on pages 410–411 and this graphic organizer to help you read the health facts in this chapter.

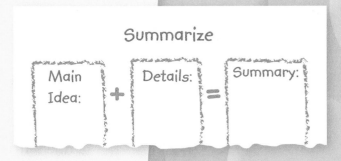

Summarize

| Main Idea: | + | Details: | = | Summary: |

Health Graph

INTERPRET DATA Each year hundreds of people in the United States are injured or killed by severe weather. Which of the weather events shown in the graph is the greatest threat to people? How many people are injured or killed by this kind of event during a typical year?

Deaths and Injuries from Severe Weather in One Year

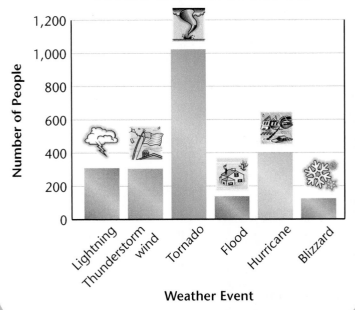

Number of People (y-axis): 0, 200, 400, 600, 800, 1,000, 1,200

Weather Event (x-axis): Lightning, Thunderstorm wind, Tornado, Flood, Hurricane, Blizzard

Daily Physical Activity

Obeying sports rules and wearing protective equipment are ways you can avoid injury during physical activities.

Be Active!
Use the selection, Track 6, **Muscle Mambo**, to move your heart and muscles toward good health.

Responding to Emergencies

Preparing for Emergencies

Although many harmful situations can be avoided, some are unexpected and call for quick action to protect you or others from harm. Such situations are called emergencies.

If you are in an emergency, you need to be prepared and able to act quickly. To be prepared, know the immediate actions you should take. Have a list of people you may need to contact. Keep necessary supplies readily available and located in a convenient spot.

Emergency Supply Kit

Ryan Clark's family members are working together to plan for emergencies. Each family member has a job to do. Ryan's father gathers supplies for an emergency such as a severe storm or a power outage. Here's what he gathers:

- drinking water in jugs, 3 gallons (12 liters) per person; water-purifying tablets
- canned or packaged foods that don't need to be refrigerated or cooked—enough for several days
- soap, hygiene supplies, and a first-aid kit
- blankets and sleeping gear; large plastic bags
- flashlights, lanterns, candles, and matches in a waterproof container
- battery-powered radio and extra batteries
- nonelectric can opener; eating utensils

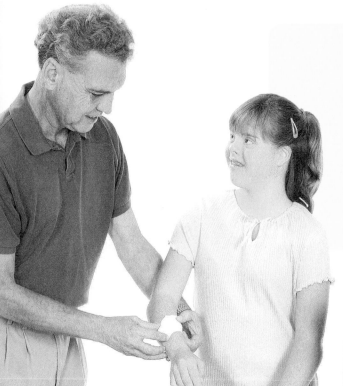

◀ It is important to check a first-aid kit every three months or so to see if anything needs to be replaced.

A contact list for your family may be similar to this one. Each family member should be familiar with this information.

First-Aid Kit

Ryan's mother collects the items listed below for a first-aid kit. She will check the kit every three months and replace old medicines and materials that have been used.

- hand cleaner
- antiseptic wipes
- scissors and tweezers
- cold packs
- medicines needed by family members

- disposable gloves
- bandages and tape
- cotton swabs and gauze
- triangular bandages

Emergency Telephone Information

Ryan gathers emergency information to keep by the phone. Although many 911 systems automatically report the telephone number and location from which calls are placed, Ryan should be prepared to give the exact address of the emergency and the telephone number from which he is calling. Ryan must also be prepared to describe the nature of the emergency, how many people need help, and what first aid has already been given. Ryan should stay on the line until the 911 operator tells him to hang up.

 SUMMARIZE What materials and information should a family gather for use in an emergency?

Consumer Activity

Make Buying Decisions
First-aid kits can be purchased. Visit a store that sells first-aid kits, and compare the contents and prices of two kits. Write a paragraph that describes each kit and explains which kit is the better buy.

179

Responding to Fire

Because fires need oxygen to burn, you can easily smother a small fire with a blanket or a fire extinguisher. Larger fires can't be easily put out. To be safe, you need an escape plan. You and your family should plan at least two escape routes from each room of your home. You should also identify a place outside to meet. The map on page 181 shows the escape map Ryan's sister prepared for her family after they had met and discussed their options.

If you are trapped by a fire and can't get out, open a window to shout for help. Avoid breaking the window. You may need to close it if smoke starts to come in from outdoors. If your clothes catch fire, *stop*, *drop*, and *roll*. Rolling on the ground will help smother the flames. Never run, because the rush of air will fan the flames.

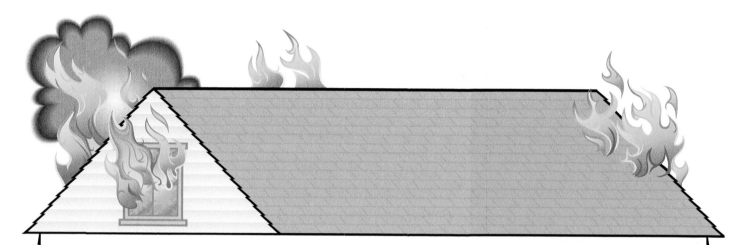

What to Do in a Fire Emergency

1 Stay close to the floor, under the smoke.

2 Yell "Fire!" to alert everyone in the home. Blow a whistle or bang on the walls, if necessary.

3 Feel a door with the back of your hand before opening it. If the door is hot or warm, keep it closed. If it's cool, open it slowly and look around. Slam the door shut if you see heavy smoke or fire. Then try another escape route.

4 Leave the building. Close any open doors. Continue to yell to other family members.

5 Meet your family at the place outside that you have agreed upon.

6 From a neighbor's home, call 911.

7 If you're trapped, stuff clothing around the edges of the door, hang a sheet out the window, and call for help.

8 Never go into a burning building.

9 If you live in an apartment building, set off the fire alarm by following the instructions on it. To alert others, yell "Fire!" in the hallway before leaving the building.

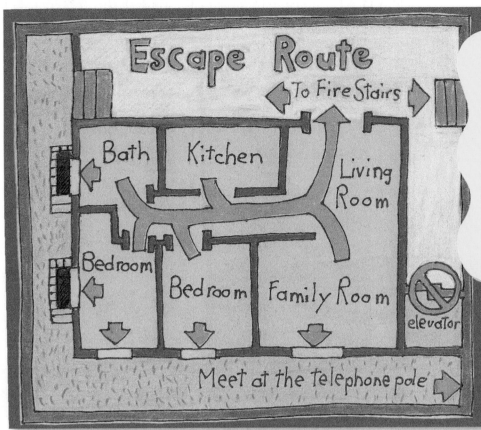

Quick Activity

Make an Escape Plan
Look at the floor plan of the Clarks' apartment. Using your finger, trace the escape routes from each room. With your family, draw a plan that shows two routes of escape for each room in your home.

In the Clark family, Ryan and his dad have the job of checking the smoke alarms monthly and changing the alarms' batteries every six months. Choosing dates will make these chores easy to remember. For example, they check the alarms on the first day of each month and replace batteries on the first day of fall and spring.

Ryan's dad also checks the family's "ABC-rated" fire extinguisher each month to make certain it's fully charged. A fire extinguisher is a metal tank filled with water or chemicals for putting out a fire. An ABC-rated fire extinguisher contains a chemical foam that can smother three types of fires. *A* is for wood, paper, trash, plastic, cloth, and cardboard fires. *B* is for burning grease, oil, gas, lighter fluid, and other flammable liquids. *C* is for electrical fires, which can't be put out by water due to the danger of electric shock. At least one ABC-rated fire extinguisher and one smoke alarm should be placed on each floor of a building or home.

DRAW CONCLUSIONS **Why should the fire extinguisher in your home be ABC-rated?**

Health & Technology

Fire Extinguishers The gas *halon* is used to extinguish fires in the electronics industry and in museums and libraries where water would damage sensitive materials and equipment. Halon is colorless and odorless, and it leaves no residue. It extinguishes fires by interrupting the chemical reaction that occurs when fuels burn. Production of halon was stopped in 1994 because scientists found that it harms the environment. However, existing supplies continue to be used. Other gases are being used as alternatives to halon.

Natural Disasters

Tornado
Stay away from all windows. Go to one of these places: below ground, under stairs, under a heavy table, in a basement corner, in a bathroom, or in a closet.

Earthquake
Stay indoors. Take cover under a heavy desk or table, or crouch against an interior wall. Stay away from glass doors, windows, and furniture that may topple over.

Severe Thunderstorm
Quickly get inside a building or an automobile. Avoid open ground, trees, and tall structures. Crouch down. Make yourself as small as possible, but do not lie down flat.

Reduce Disaster Risks

A **disaster** (dih·ZAS·ter) is a dangerous situation that affects many people. Disasters can be caused by natural forces, such as severe storms or floods. Many disasters occur each year throughout the country.

A *blizzard* is a dangerous snowstorm with strong winds and heavy snowfall. The temperatures during a blizzard can be very cold. A *severe thunderstorm* is a storm with strong winds, heavy rain, lightning, and possibly hail. A *hurricane* is a violent storm with strong winds and heavy rain that forms over a warm ocean. A *tornado* is an extremely strong windstorm that forms a funnel shape. Tornadoes and flooding are often associated with severe thunderstorms and hurricanes. An *earthquake* is a strong rolling, shaking, or sliding of the ground.

COMPARE AND CONTRAST How are a blizzard, a thunderstorm, a hurricane, and a tornado alike? How are they different?

Blizzard

Stock up on packaged and canned foods before the winter season. Dress warmly in several thin layers of wool or silk, a warm hat, and mittens. If caught in a car, don't leave it. Tie something bright to the car antenna so that the car can be easily located.

Hurricane

Move all toys, bicycles, lawn furniture, and trash cans indoors. Cover windows with boards. Close drapes. Fill the car's gas tank. Move inland if advised.

Lesson 1 Summary and Review

❶ Summarize with Vocabulary

Use vocabulary and other terms from this lesson to complete the statements.

When faced with an _____, you need to act quickly. Having a _____ kit handy can help you treat minor injuries in a hurry. A _____ may be useful in putting out a small household fire. A _____, or funnel-shaped windstorm, is one type of _____. Another is a _____, which forms over water. Supplies from an _____ kit can help you get through such an event.

❷ Critical Thinking
To prepare for a flood, people are instructed to fill containers with fresh water. Why?

❸
What types of fires can an ABC-rated fire extinguisher put out?

❹ (Focus Skill) SUMMARIZE
Draw and complete this graphic organizer to summarize this main idea: You can reduce your risk of injury during a natural disaster.

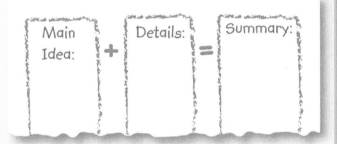

| Main Idea: | + | Details: | = | Summary: |

❺ Write to Entertain—Short Story

Write a short story in which the main character uses appropriate actions to save his or her sleeping family members from a fire.

Communicate
During an Emergency

Emergencies happen every day. Would you know what to do if you were the first person to recognize an emergency? Using the steps for **Effective Communication** can enable you to get help quickly.

Mark has been listening to the sound of his neighbor's lawn mower. When the sound stops, Mark looks out the window. He sees his neighbor lying motionless by the mower. How can using communication skills help Mark get help for his neighbor?

1 **Understand your audience.**

Mark knows that he must call 911. He knows that the 911 operator will need facts about the emergency.

2 **Give a clear message. Express ideas in a clear, organized way.**

Mark dials 911. He is prepared to give the exact location, his name and telephone number, and the type of emergency—the neighbor is lying motionless in her yard.

184

3 Listen carefully, and answer any questions.

Mark listens to questions the operator asks. He answers all questions about the emergency. He doesn't hang up until the operator tells him to.

4 Follow directions.

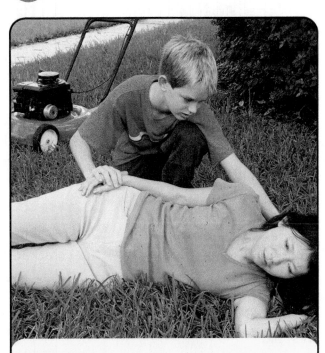

Mark follows the operator's directions and waits with his neighbor until the emergency medical personnel arrive.

Problem Solving

A. Jillian and her mother are camping. Jillian's mother gets stung by a bee and has an allergic reaction. A ranger station is nearby.
  • Tell how Jillian could use the steps for **Effective Communication** to get help for her mother.

B. You are watching your baby brother at home while your dad shops at the hardware store. A friend calls to talk about a school project. After you finish talking, you find your little brother lying face-down on the floor next to an empty cough syrup bottle.
  • Explain how you could act responsibly to get appropriate help for your brother.

185

First Aid for Common Injuries

Lesson Focus

First aid can be used to help an injured person before medical help arrives.

Why Learn This?

You can use what you learn to get adult help quickly for an injured person, to help prevent further injuries, and to help the injured person be more comfortable.

Vocabulary

first aid
fracture
sprain
seizure
hyperthermia
hypothermia
frostbite

Broken Bones and Sprains

When a person is injured, he or she may need **first aid**, immediate care that is given to someone who is injured or suddenly becomes ill. First aid doesn't take the place of a doctor, but it can help protect someone or prevent further harm. Always call for an adult to help. If the illness or injury is serious or life threatening, call 911 for medical help.

Fractures

One serious injury is a **fracture**, which is a broken or cracked bone. The skin in the area of the fracture may or may not be broken. Look for these signs of a fracture:

- pain or tenderness, swelling, and bruising
- a strange angle or bend in a bone or joint
- inability of the injured person to move a bone

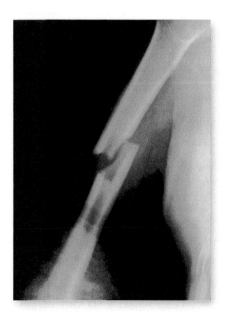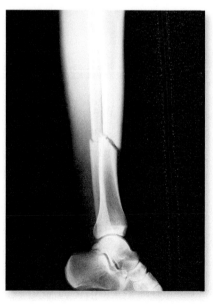

▲ Fractures of the upper arm and lower leg, like these, are serious injuries. If not properly treated, fractures can heal improperly and cause other health problems.

To provide first aid for a fracture, keep the injured person as still as possible until medical help arrives. To prevent further injury, keep the bone and its surrounding joints completely still. If an adult is present, he or she may place a padded splint on the area. A *splint* is something straight and stiff, such as a board, that is used to hold a bone or joint in place. If the skin is broken, the adult should stop any bleeding and then cover the open area with a clean cloth.

Sprains

A **sprain** is an injury caused by twisting a joint. Some signs of a sprain are

- pain, especially when the joint is moved.
- bruising.
- tenderness.
- rapid swelling.

A bad sprain must be treated as if it were a fracture. The bandage on the splint should not be too tight, because sprains swell. To treat a minor sprain, remember the letters *R-I-C-E*, for *Rest*, *Ice*, *Compress*, and *Elevate*. The photographs at the right show the four steps of the RICE treatment.

 SUMMARIZE Tell how to treat a fracture.

Sprains

Rest helps reduce bleeding inside the injury, prevents further injury, and speeds healing.

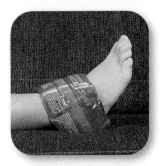

Ice can limit swelling and pain. (Do not apply ice directly to the skin.) Apply an ice pack or a cold pack for twenty minutes every two to three hours for one to two days.

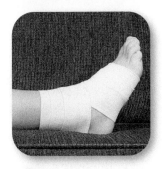

Compress the injured area by wrapping it with an elastic bandage for about two days. Loosen the bandage if it gets too tight.

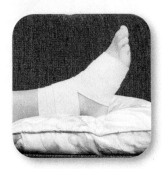

Elevate the injured area, or keep it raised above heart level, several times a day for one to two days. This will reduce swelling and bleeding.

Sports Injuries

Sports injuries can be divided into two groups—those that happen suddenly and those that happen over time. Sudden injuries result from a sudden force, such as a fall or a collision with another person or an object. Injuries that occur over time result from overuse of muscles or from doing a motion incorrectly, such as swinging a bat the wrong way. Most sports injuries are minor.

You can reduce the risk of a sports injury by staying in good physical condition, wearing proper safety equipment, and doing warm-up and cool-down exercises. Some sports, such as skateboarding and in-line skating, require a variety of safety equipment.

First aid for most minor sports injuries includes the RICE treatment. Injuries can sometimes remain minor if you stop an activity when you first feel pain. Continuing the activity can cause more damage and delay healing.

MAIN IDEA AND DETAILS Give details that explain the two types of sports injuries.

Quick Activity

Analyze Graphs The graph shows percents for the types of injuries treated in the United States in one year. Explain which injuries could have been caused by sports. What safety precautions might have reduced the number of sports injuries?

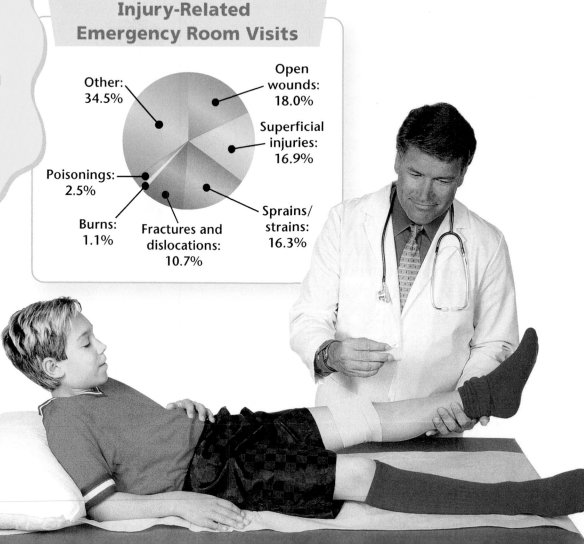

Injury-Related Emergency Room Visits

Other: 34.5%
Open wounds: 18.0%
Superficial injuries: 16.9%
Sprains/strains: 16.3%
Fractures and dislocations: 10.7%
Burns: 1.1%
Poisonings: 2.5%

First Aid for Burns

Some burns are minor, but others are medical emergencies. First-degree burns affect only the top layer of the skin, causing redness, mild swelling, and pain. Second-degree burns affect both outer and inner layers of skin, causing blisters, redness, pain, and swelling. Third-degree burns destroy all layers of the skin and sometimes the underlying tissues as well. The surface of a third-degree burn is grayish white and charred.

Seek immediate medical attention for third-degree burns. You can provide first aid for a minor burn, such as the burn you receive when you briefly touch a hot object. The pictures below show how to treat a minor burn.

SEQUENCE What steps should you follow to provide first aid for a minor burn?

What to Do for . . .

Burns

❶ Cool the burn. Use large amounts of *cool* water, except on small first-degree burns. Do not use ice or ice water.

❷ Cover the burn. Use dry, sterile dressings or a clean cloth. Don't use lotions, creams, or ointments.

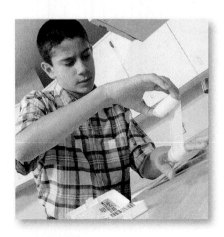

❸ Inform a parent or another trusted adult that you were burned. Always seek medical attention for serious burns.

First Aid for a Seizure

A **seizure** (SEE•zher) is a sudden, uncontrollable loss of consciousness caused by unusual nerve activity in the brain. A seizure may include muscle spasms and jerky or stiff movements. Seizures can come from many different medical conditions, including epilepsy, high blood pressure, heat stroke, poisoning, electric shock, low blood sugar, and brain injury.

If you see a person experiencing a seizure, you should **NEVER**

- hold the person down.
- put anything between the person's teeth.
- give the person anything to eat or drink.
- throw water in the person's face.

CAUSE AND EFFECT **What might cause a person to have a seizure?**

Did You Know?

There's nothing you can do to stop a seizure. The purpose of first aid is to keep the person from being injured. Seek medical help if needed.

What to Do for . . .

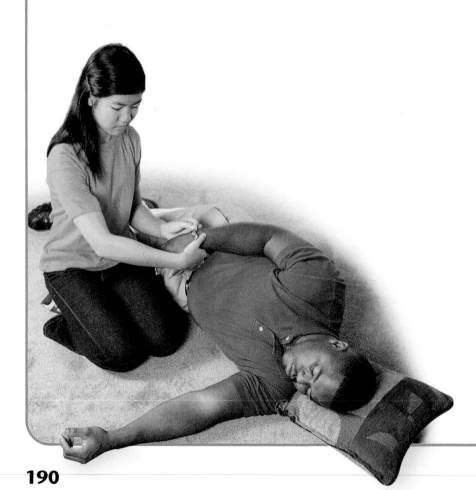

Seizures

DO call 911 if the person does not regain consciousness.

DO loosen the person's collar.

DO turn the person on his or her side.

DO look for a medical information bracelet or tag.

DO cushion the person's head with something soft.

DO offer help when the seizure ends. Let the person sleep.

Exposure to Heat and Cold

Health problems can occur in both hot and cold weather. The conditions that result can be life threatening.

Hyperthermia

A person who spends too much time in the sun or in a hot place can develop **hyperthermia** (hy·per·THER·mee·uh), a condition in which the body's internal temperature becomes too high. A person in this situation may first develop heat cramps as his or her muscles tighten. If the person doesn't cool off, he or she could develop heat exhaustion. In this condition, the skin is still moist from sweat. If the person remains in the heat and stops sweating, the condition progresses to heat stroke. Signs of heat stroke include hot skin, high body temperature, rapid pulse, rapid breathing, and confusion. Below are actions you should take for hyperthermia.

What to Do for . . .

Hyperthermia

1. Call 911. Hyperthermia is a life-threatening condition.

2. Move the person to a cooler place. Elevate the feet 8 to 12 inches. Loosen any tight clothing.

3. Cool the person quickly. Apply moist, cool towels. Fan the person or spray the skin with cold water.

Hypothermia and Frostbite

Hypothermia (hy•poh•THER•mee•uh) is a condition in which the body's internal temperature becomes too low. The condition may begin with shivering, slurred speech, and confusion. As the condition worsens, signs may include stiffness, slow and shallow breathing, bluish skin, and unconsciousness. **Frostbite** is a condition in which body tissues freeze. The lists below tell how to treat hypothermia and frostbite.

Consumer Activity

Access Valid Health Information Search the Internet and other sources for additional information about hypothermia and frostbite. Look for ways to both avoid and treat these conditions. Be sure to use reliable sources.

What to Do for . . .

Hypothermia	Frostbite
• Call 911. Keep the person lying flat.	• Call 911 immediately. Get the person indoors or into a sheltered spot.
• Stop the heat loss. Get the person out of the cold and into a warm room as quickly as possible. Remove wet clothing, and wrap the person in dry blankets.	• Loosen tight clothing and remove jewelry.
	• Do not rub the frozen skin. Place the frozen part next to a warm body part.

SEQUENCE **What stages might a person go through as he or she develops hyperthermia?**

Lesson 2 Summary and Review

❶ Summarize with Vocabulary

Use vocabulary from this lesson to complete the statements.

One injury that requires _____ is a _____, or break, in a bone. Immediate care is also needed for a person having a _____, caused by unusual brain activity. To treat a person with _____, apply cool, moist towels.

❷ Explain the differences between first-, second-, and third-degree burns.

❸ Critical Thinking When treating a sprained ankle, why does elevating a person's feet reduce swelling and bleeding?

❹ SUMMARIZE Draw and complete this graphic organizer to summarize the RICE treatment.

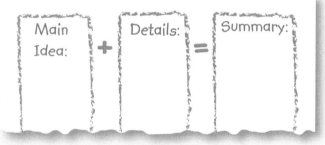

❺ Informative Writing—How-To

Suppose you were with a classmate who was having a seizure. Write a paragraph to explain how you would provide first aid.

192

Responsibility

Following Safety Rules

You have a responsibility to take appropriate action when you are confronted with an emergency situation. To act responsibly, you must learn about and follow safety rules and guidelines that protect both rescuers and victims. The guidelines below will help you respond in an appropriate manner.

- **First, call 911.**
- **Approach a victim only after you have quickly surveyed the scene to be sure it's safe.**
- **If possible, get permission from a victim before helping.**
- **Don't move a person until you have made sure that no neck or back injury has occurred.**
- **Wear disposable gloves when treating a wound. This universal precaution helps prevent the spread of disease. Properly dispose of gloves. If gloves aren't available, use the victim's hand and multiple layers of cloth to apply pressure to the wound to reduce blood loss.**

Activity

With a partner or in a small group, role-play various emergency situations to illustrate each of the safety considerations given above. Then discuss why it is important for each person to take responsibility for knowing how to act in an emergency.

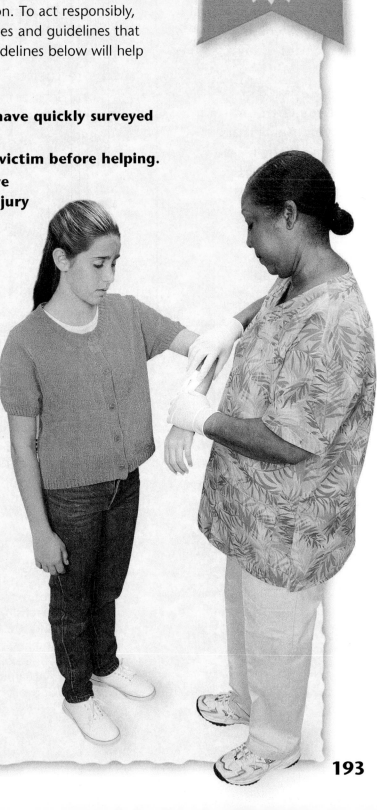

193

First Aid That Saves Lives

Lesson Focus

After calling for help, a person can provide first aid in life-threatening emergencies.

Why Learn This?

What you learn can help you give first aid and possibly help save someone's life during a medical emergency.

Vocabulary

abdominal thrusts
rescue breathing
shock

Quick Activity

Identify a Muscle Look at the diagram of the respiratory system on page 7. What muscle is affected when you perform an abdominal thrust?

First Aid for Choking

A life-threatening medical emergency is one in which a person could die. Calling 911 for help is the first thing to do in a life-threatening situation. First aid performed by a rescuer can sometimes save a life. In some situations, you can perform simple first aid while you wait for medically trained help to arrive.

Choking is a life-threatening emergency in which a person's airway becomes blocked.

Causes

- trying to swallow pieces of food
- swallowing a nonfood item such as a balloon or gum
- eating too fast; eating while talking or laughing
- playing or running with objects in the mouth

Signs

- inability to breathe, cough, or talk (The airway is completely blocked.)
- clutching the throat with both hands

Clutching both hands at the throat with fingers and thumbs extended is the universal sign for choking. Do this if you are choking. If you see someone doing this, ask, "Are you choking?" ▶

Choking

If the choking person can breathe, cough, or speak, encourage him or her to cough up the object that is blocking the airway. Do not slap the person on the back. If the person can't speak, perform one or more **abdominal thrusts** (ab•DAHM•uh•nuhl THRUSTS). Do so using these steps.

1 Get behind the person, and put your arms around his or her waist. Make a fist, and place it above his or her navel, with the thumb joint against the abdomen. Grasp the fist with your other hand. Do not squeeze.

2 Give up to five quick, hard upward thrusts by strongly pulling your two hands toward you.

▲ Place your hands in this position, well below the person's rib cage, during an abdominal thrust.

During abdominal thrusts, the force of air moving upward out of the lungs is powerful. It is often strong enough to pop the object that's blocking the airway out of the throat. ▶

 SUMMARIZE Explain the procedure for performing abdominal thrusts.

Personal Health Plan ▶

Real-Life Situation
You want to improve your first-aid skills by attending a training class.
Real-Life Plan
Make a list of places or groups that might offer first-aid training.

First Aid for Stopped Breathing

A person who has stopped breathing even for a short time can be in serious trouble.

Causes

- airway blockage
- suffocation
- electric shock
- head or chest injuries
- poisoning
- drug overdose
- allergic reaction
- drowning

Signs

- unconsciousness or not responding
- no sign of breathing

First aid for stopped breathing is **rescue breathing**, or giving your breath to another person.

What to Do for . . .

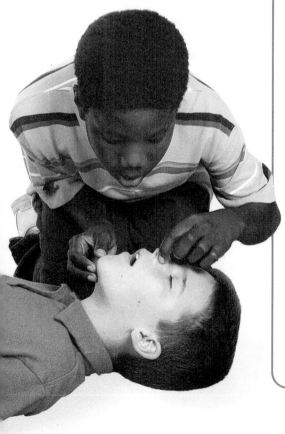

Stopped Breathing

1. Open the airway by gently tilting the head back until the chin points straight up. Check the mouth to make sure it's clear.

2. Give two rescue breaths. Pinch the nose closed, take a deep breath, and place your mouth over the person's mouth, making a tight seal. Breathe out until you see the person's chest rise. Remove your mouth between breaths.

3. Check the pulse. Place two fingers on the person's neck on the side nearest you, in the groove next to the windpipe. Press gently. Don't rush; take from five to ten seconds to find a pulse.

4. If you feel a pulse but the person still isn't breathing, continue. Give the person one breath every five seconds.

5. Recheck the pulse and breathing about every minute. Continue until help arrives or the person begins to breathe on his or her own.

6. If you can't feel a pulse, have someone call 911, and try to find a person qualified to start CPR (cardiopulmonary resuscitation).

CAUSE AND EFFECT **What are three situations that can cause a person to stop breathing?**

196

First Aid for Severe Bleeding

Severe bleeding results from breaks or tears in blood vessels. Severe bleeding requires immediate treatment.

Causes

- a cut, gash, scrape, or puncture wound
- a knife slash or gunshot wound

Signs

- blood spurting, flowing, or oozing out of a wound

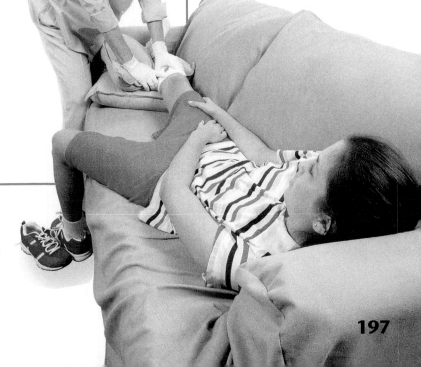

Myth and Fact

Myth: A wound needs fresh air to heal.
Fact: Research shows that a wound that is covered will have less scarring and will heal faster.

What to Do for . . .

Severe Bleeding

1. Protect your hands from blood by wearing disposable gloves.

2. Expose the wound to see where the blood is coming from.

3. If an object is embedded in the wound, do not remove the object.

4. Apply pressure. Place a clean gauze pad or cloth over the wound, and press firmly for ten minutes.

5. Elevate the wound. Make sure the wound rests above heart level, unless a broken bone keeps you from moving that part of the body.

6. If the bleeding doesn't stop in ten minutes, press harder over a wider area for another ten minutes.

7. If the pressure pads get soaked with blood, don't remove them. Place another set of pads on top.

Never touch another person's blood. Protect yourself from blood by wearing disposable gloves. If necessary, use a hand of the bleeding person to apply pressure. ▼

DRAW CONCLUSIONS Under what circumstance would you NOT raise a badly cut arm above the heart?

197

First Aid for Shock

Shock is a condition in which the circulatory system slows down. During shock, blood pressure falls. The person's pulse then speeds up to try to send blood to the body's organs and tissues. However, the blood pressure is too weak to force enough blood to all parts of the body. Shock is a life-threatening condition.

Causes

- heart attack
- severe burn
- severe bleeding or injury
- severe diarrhea or vomiting
- serious allergic reaction

Signs

- restlessness, anxiousness, and weakness
- rapid pulse and breathing that is rapid, shallow, or too little
- moist, clammy skin
- bluish skin around the lips and fingernails
- sleepiness
- thirst
- vomiting
- unconsciousness

Personal Health Plan ▶

Real-Life Situation

Some people are severely allergic to certain foods. Suppose you are allergic to peanuts.

Real-Life Plan

Tell what you should do when you eat away from home to make sure you don't eat foods with peanuts.

For some people, certain foods, insect bites and stings, and materials like latex—used to make some disposable gloves—can cause an allergic reaction and result in shock. ▶

Shock

1. Call 911.

2. Keep the person lying down. Make sure that his or her airway is clear. If possible, treat the injury or problem that is causing the shock.

3. Elevate the feet and legs, unless a fracture or a possible spine injury prevents it. If the person has head injuries or has trouble breathing, elevate the head instead.

4. Loosen any tight clothing. Cover the person with a blanket to keep the body temperature normal. If needed, put a blanket under the person as well.

5. Don't give the person anything to eat or drink because the person may vomit or need surgery later.

6. Stay with and reassure the person until help arrives. Check the person's pulse and breathing often. If necessary, perform rescue breathing.

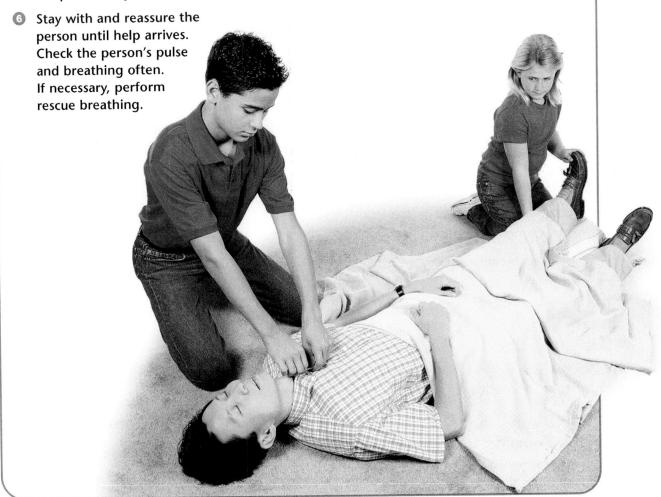

MAIN IDEA AND DETAILS **List the main things you should do for someone who is in shock.**

What to Do for . . .

Poisoning

1. Find out the age and weight of the person, and identify the poison; if poison was swallowed, find out how much was swallowed and how long ago it was swallowed.

2. Call 911 if the person is unconscious. Otherwise, call the Poison Control Center.

3. Check the person's airway and pulse.

4. Keep the person lying on his or her side. This position will keep the lungs clear in the event the person vomits.

First Aid for Poisoning

Poison can be swallowed, inhaled, absorbed through the skin, or injected.

Causes

- drug or medicine overdose
- household chemicals
- poisonous plants
- insect bites or stings

Signs

- burns or stains around and in the mouth; nausea or abdominal pain
- drowsiness or unconsciousness
- difficult or painful breathing

 SUMMARIZE **List four ways poisons can enter the body.**

Lesson 3 Summary and Review

1 Summarize with Vocabulary

Use vocabulary and other terms from this lesson to complete the statements.

First aid is especially important for _____ emergencies. Performing _____ can save the life of a person who is choking. _____ is necessary to help a person who has stopped breathing. Pressure on a wound can stop _____. Elevating feet and legs is important in treating _____.

2 Describe the universal sign for choking.

3 Critical Thinking Why is it important to protect your hands from blood when treating someone who is bleeding?

4 SUMMARIZE Draw and complete this graphic organizer to tell how you can help a person in a life-threatening situation.

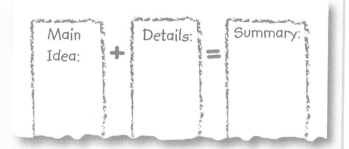

| Main Idea: | + | Details: | = | Summary: |

5 Write to Express—Solution to a Problem

Suppose you saw a person who was unconscious. Write to tell what you would do.

ACTIVITIES

Language Arts

Be Prepared Find out what natural disaster is most likely to occur in the area where you live. Then write a script for a public service message that tells people how to be prepared for this type of disaster. Record or videotape your message, and present it to your class.

Home & Community

Communicating Make a display to help people become aware of the causes and signs of choking and to show how to treat a choking victim. Post your display at home or in your school cafeteria.

Science

Demonstrate Abdominal Thrusts Fit the top of an empty two-liter plastic bottle with a plug made of cloth. Tie the plug to the neck of the bottle with a short piece of string. Insert the plug into the top of the bottle, making sure it is snug. Hold the bottle in front of you, and position your hands as you would for an abdominal thrust. Pull your hands toward you to demonstrate how abdominal thrusts dislodge materials from the airway.

Career Link

911 Operator A 911 operator performs two basic services. One service is to dispatch the police. The other is to send fire units, which include firefighters and medical technicians, to help people in emergency situations. Make a list of emergencies. Beside the name of each emergency, indicate whether it would require one or both of the 911 services.

Technology Project

First Aid Booklet Make your own first-aid booklet for minor medical emergencies. Use a computer to format your pages.

GO ONLINE For more activities, visit The Learning Site. www.harcourtschool.com/health

Reading Skill

SUMMARIZE

Draw and then use this graphic organizer to answer questions 1 and 2.

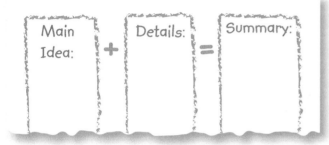

Main Idea: + Details: = Summary:

1 Tell how to treat a sprain.
2 Tell how to treat severe bleeding.

Use Vocabulary

Match each term in Column B with its meaning in Column A.

Column A	Column B
3 Condition in which body tissue freezes	A hypothermia
	B sprain
4 Treatment for choking	C shock
	D fracture
5 Condition caused by unusual nerve activity in the brain	E abdominal thrusts
6 Condition caused by twisting a joint	F frostbite
	G seizure
	H first aid
7 Condition in which the circulatory system slows down	
8 Condition in which the body temperature becomes too low	
9 Broken bone	
10 Immediate care given to an injured person	

Check Understanding

Choose the letter of the correct answer.

11 Which of the following should be located on each floor of a home? (p. 181)
  A phone list   C weather radio
  B smoke alarm   D fresh water

12 If you are trapped in your room by a fire, you should _____. (p. 180)
  F stuff clothing around the door
  G barricade the door with furniture
  H break the glass in each window
  J attempt to escape through the flames

13 Which of the following is true of both hurricanes and tornadoes? (pp. 182–183)
  A They form over the ocean.
  B They produce flooding.
  C They have destructive winds.
  D They cause the ground to shake.

14 To treat a person having a seizure, you should _____. (p. 190)
  F hold the person down
  G elevate the person's legs
  H give the person a drink of water
  J cushion the person's head

15 When giving rescue breaths, you tilt a person's head back in order to _____. (p. 196)
  A feel a pulse
  B protect the skull
  C open an airway
  D stimulate the brain

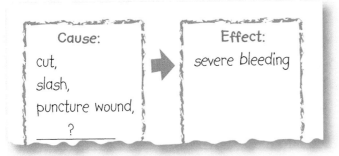

Cause:
cut,
slash,
puncture wound,
_____?_____

Effect:
severe bleeding

16 Which of the following belongs in this graphic organizer? (p. 197)

F sprain   H suffocation

G gash   J poison

17 One sign of heat stroke is _____. (p. 191)

A sweating   C no pulse

B hot skin   D no breathing

18 Which of the following happens to a person in shock? (p. 198)

F The blood pressure drops.

G Body tissue freezes.

H Heat cramps occur.

J Bones break.

19 During a thunderstorm, you should _____. (p. 182)

A stay away from all windows

B fill containers with fresh water

C avoid open ground and trees

D take cover under a heavy desk

20 Which type of fire could **NOT** be put out with an AB-rated fire extinguisher? (p. 181)

F paper

G grease

H plastic

J electrical

Think Critically

21 Why should everyone know how to perform simple first aid?

22 How does elevating a wound above the level of the heart help in cases of severe bleeding?

Apply Skills

23 **BUILDING GOOD CHARACTER**
Responsibility While walking your dog, you find a jogger who has fallen and is sitting in the middle of the path. She has broken her ankle. Apply what you know about safety rules and guidelines to respond to this situation.

24 **LIFE SKILLS**
Communicate Suppose you need to call 911 to report that a family member has been injured by a fall. Tell what information the 911 operator will need you to give.

Write About Health

25 **Write to Inform—Explanation** Suppose you have been assigned to write an article for your school newspaper about first aid for burns. In your article, explain the types of burns and the actions a rescuer should take in response to a minor burn and a serious burn.

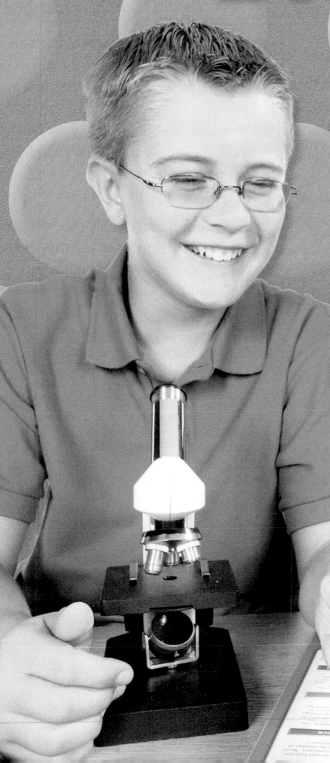

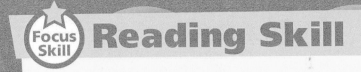
COMPARE AND CONTRAST When you compare, you tell how two or more things are alike. When you contrast, you tell how they are different. Use the Reading in Health Handbook on pages 400–401 and this graphic organizer to help you read the health facts in this chapter.

Compare and Contrast

Topic:

Alike	Different

Health Graph

INTERPRET DATA Diseases that in the past killed hundreds of thousands of people can be cured today with medicines. Yet people still die of diseases. About how many people died of acute respiratory infections in 1998? Which communicable disease caused the fewest deaths? Why do you think this is so?

Deaths Due to Communicable Diseases:
Millions of Deaths Worldwide in 1998

Tuberculosis (TB):
1.5 million
12%

Diarrheal diseases:
2.2 million
17%

Malaria:
1.1 million
9%

Measles:
0.9 million
7%

AIDS:
2.3 million
18%

Others:
1.25 million
10%

Acute respiratory infections (including pneumonia and influenza): 3.5 million
27%

Daily Physical Activity

Staying active helps you stay healthy and helps you avoid many different diseases. Exercise should be part of your daily health plan.

 Be Active!
Use the selection, Track 7, **Movin' and Groovin'**, to beef up your body's protection.

Conditions That Contribute to Disease

Lesson Focus

Three factors—heredity, environment, and behavior—can increase or decrease your chances of becoming ill.

Why Learn This?

What you learn can help you stay well.

Vocabulary

health risk factor
pathogen

Heredity and Environment

David is rarely sick. His friend Larry is sick much of the time. Why? Perhaps Larry has more health risk factors. A **health risk factor** is a condition that increases a person's chances of becoming ill. There are three types of health risk factors: hereditary, environmental, and behavioral.

Hereditary Factors

Heredity (huh·RED·ih·tee) is the passing of traits from parents to their children. Your eye color, for instance, is a trait you received by heredity. Many other traits are only partly affected by heredity.

Hereditary (huh·RED·ih·ter·ee) *risk factors* are inherited traits that increase a person's chances of becoming ill. A hereditary risk factor can cause a person to have an inherited disease or can increase his or her chances of getting a disease. For example, some forms of heart disease affect several members of the same family. You cannot change what you have inherited.

Many traits are passed from parents to their children. What traits do Frank, Dianne, David, and Trisha share? ▼

Dianne and her parents (David and Trisha's grandparents)

Frank and his parents (David and Trisha's grandparents)

▲ This man wears a breathing mask as he releases insecticide, which pollutes the air. Chemicals used on farms and lawns can end up in drinking water.

Environmental Factors

Environmental risk factors are harmful conditions in the environment that increase people's chances of becoming sick. Polluted air and water are major environmental risk factors.

Polluted air can cause lung cancer. It often harms people with allergies, asthma, and other respiratory illnesses. Exhaust from cars and trucks produces much of the outdoor air pollution in the United States. Indoor air can also be polluted. For example, tobacco smoke pollutes indoor air.

Like the air we breathe, the water we drink may contain harmful substances. Water can be polluted with chemicals such as fertilizers and with pathogens. A **pathogen** (PATH•uh•juhn) is an organism or a virus that can make people sick.

 COMPARE AND CONTRAST How are hereditary risk factors and environmental risk factors alike? How are they different?

Quick Activity

List Rules for Health
Many of the rules you were taught as a small child are meant to lower your health risks and help prevent illness. Think of one such rule, such as "Wash your hands before eating." Draw your rule in a comic strip.

207

▲ At water treatment plants, pathogens are killed and pollutants are removed. This makes the water safe to drink.

▲ Water that drains from sinks, toilets, and washing machines may contain pathogens and pollutants. This water is unsafe to use.

Avoiding Risk Factors

You can avoid many environmental risk factors. For example, on days when the air pollution is greater than normal, don't play outside. Wear sunscreen when you're outdoors, to reduce your risk of developing skin cancer.

If you must stay in a building that has indoor pollution, keep the air inside fresh by opening windows. If someone is painting, or installing wallpaper or carpeting, remind parents to open the windows and use fans to blow out the fumes. Try to stay somewhere else until the work is finished.

If your family's water comes from a well instead of a city water supply, the water should be tested to make sure it's free of pathogens and other pollutants. In some areas, well water must be tested for pathogens before a home can be sold.

DRAW CONCLUSIONS Why is it important to be aware of environmental risk factors?

Choosing Good Health

You cannot change your heredity. You can change only part of your environment. But you have a great deal of control over your own behaviors. You can choose ways of living that promote good health.

One way to stay in good health is to control *behavioral risk factors*. These are harmful behaviors that increase a person's chances of becoming ill. Using drugs, drinking alcoholic beverages, and using tobacco products are all behavioral risk factors. Other factors include eating a high-fat diet, not exercising, and acting in dangerous ways.

You can reduce your risk of lung cancer, for example, by refusing to smoke cigarettes or to use drugs such as marijuana. Exercising regularly and eating a balanced, low-fat diet will help you avoid cancer and heart disease. Following a healthful lifestyle even includes getting enough sleep so that you are at your best every day.

SUMMARIZE How does your behavior affect your health?

ACTIVITY

Life Skills
Make Decisions

Dale has skin that sunburns easily. His mom has told him to use sunscreen every time he goes outside, but his friends are at the door and he's late for a bike ride. Use decision-making steps to help you decide what Dale should do.

Using sunscreen properly when you go outside can reduce your chances of developing skin cancer. ▼

Seeing Inside the Body

Magnetic resonance imaging, or MRI, is a powerful way of "seeing" inside the body without surgery. MRIs use radio waves and a strong magnetic field to give a clear, detailed picture of soft tissues and internal organs. Doctors use the images to detect problems such as spinal injuries, reproductive system disorders, and even heart diseases.

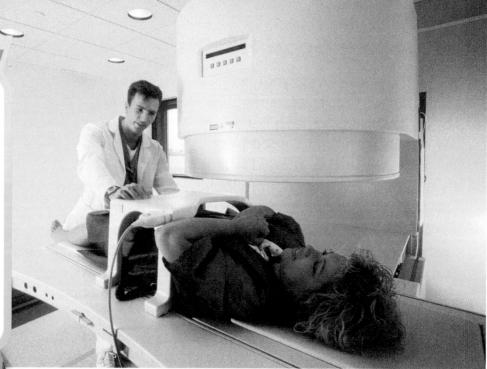

▲ Many patients who need MRIs prefer the newer open MRI units, like this one. Why do you think this is so?

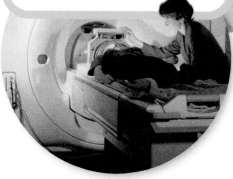

▲ The traditional MRI unit is a very large magnet in the shape of a tube. The patient must lie completely still inside it.

Kinds of Health Care

Choosing a healthful lifestyle will help you stay well. However, everyone becomes ill from time to time. Suppose you become ill. What kinds of health-care resources are available to you?

If you sprain an ankle at school, you may have a school nurse to turn to. If you develop a fever at home, a parent will likely take you to a doctor. There are many kinds of doctors. Some are family physicians who have general knowledge about the whole body. Others are specialists who focus on certain parts of the body or certain kinds of diseases.

Some doctors practice medicine in private offices, while others work in clinics. Some clinics receive money from state or local governments. There, families who have little money can get health care.

If you need major surgery, if you have an illness that requires a lot of care, or if you need tests that cannot be done at a doctor's office or clinic, you will probably go to a hospital.

MAIN IDEA AND DETAILS Name four health-care resources that might be available to you if you get sick.

Disability

Unless you or someone you know has a long-lasting illness or disability, you might not realize how disabilities affect people's lives. When someone becomes disabled, he or she might have to avoid or give up favorite activities or foods. A person may have to change daily routines. Some disabilities can keep people who like to be active from taking part in organized sports.

Many people with serious illnesses or disabilities suffer because of the reactions of other people. If their classmates are uncomfortable around them, they might feel left out and lonely as a result. How could you help someone with a serious illness or disability feel accepted?

 COMPARE AND CONTRAST Think about the problems faced by students who are disabled and by students who are not disabled. How do you think the problems are alike? Different?

Lesson 1 Summary and Review

1 Summarize with Vocabulary

Use vocabulary and other terms from this lesson to complete the statements.

Anything that increases your chances of becoming ill is a _____. Three examples of these factors are _____, _____, and _____. Some diseases, such as water-borne diseases, are spread by _____.

2 Critical Thinking How might the risk of heart disease or cancer be affected by heredity?

3 Name two environmental risk factors.

4 COMPARE AND CONTRAST Draw and complete this graphic organizer to show similarities and differences in the three types of health risk factors.

Topic: Health Risk Factors

Alike	Different

5 Write to Inform—Explanation

Make a list of five behaviors that affect health negatively. Next to each item, list something a person could do to change the behavior to improve his or her health.

211

LIFE SKILLS

Manage Stress
To Prevent Disease

Everyone experiences stress from time to time. However, too much stress in your life can make sleeping difficult, upset your stomach, and give you headaches. It also lowers your natural resistance to disease, so you may get colds and other communicable diseases more easily. Using the steps for **Managing Stress** can help you stay healthy.

Darla's grandmother has just had an operation, and she is still very ill. Darla loves her grandmother and is very worried that she might die. How can Darla manage her stress in this situation?

1 **Know what stress feels like.**

Darla isn't sleeping well, and her stomach hurts. She's also having trouble concentrating at school. She thinks she might be feeling stress.

2 **Try to determine the cause of your stress.**

Darla knows that she is feeling stress about her grandmother's illness.

3 Talk to someone about the way you're feeling.

Darla talks to her parents about her grandmother's illness and about the way she's feeling. They help her think of ways to manage her stress.

4 Do something to help relieve your stress.

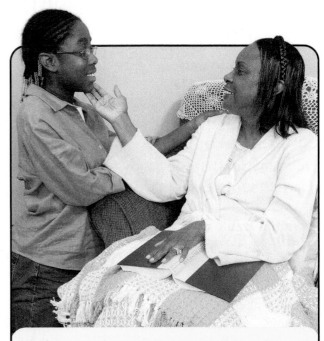

Darla spends as much time with her grandmother as she can. To relax, she takes long rides on her bike in the park and plays soccer with her friends.

Problem Solving

A. Philip has band practice, trumpet lessons, and basketball practice, and a science project is due. Now he's been asked to be in the school play. Philip is so tense that he's having trouble sleeping. Use the steps for **Managing Stress** to help Philip make a responsible decision about how to handle the situation.

B. Jen, Maria, and Ann were best friends. Maria is angry at Ann for breaking Maria's watch and wants Ann to replace it. Ann says she won't replace it because it wasn't her fault. Jen feels caught in the middle. She's upset and can't eat. Identify what parts of this situation Jen can and can't control. Then tell how this information would help Jen manage her stress.

Communicable Diseases

Lesson Focus

Pathogens that spread from person to person cause communicable diseases.

Why Learn This?

You can use what you learn to protect yourself as well as others from communicable diseases.

Vocabulary

communicable disease
infection
toxins
symptoms
sexually transmitted
  disease (STD)
abstinence

How Pathogens Spread

A disease is a condition that damages or weakens the body. A disease like influenza, or flu, which can spread from one person to another, is called a **communicable disease**. Until the early 1900s communicable diseases were the major causes of death. In 1918 influenza killed more than 20 million people worldwide. Communicable diseases are still very common, but modern medicines can be used to prevent and treat many of them.

In Lesson 1 you read that pathogens can pollute water and cause water-borne illnesses. In fact, pathogens cause all kinds of communicable diseases. Pathogens include viruses, bacteria, fungi, and protozoa.

Some pathogens are spread by indirect contact, or by just being near a person with the disease. The picture below gives an example. Other pathogens are spread only by direct contact, such as by shaking hands or sharing food. If a pathogen multiplies in your body, you develop an **infection** (in•FEK•shuhn).

Some pathogens can be passed to others simply by being next to an infected person. How could the girl help prevent her cold from spreading to others? ▶

Types of Pathogens

Fungi

Some fungi are normally present in the body, where they usually do no harm. However, sometimes these normal fungi grow out of control and cause disease. The fungus shown here, called *Trichophyton*, causes athlete's foot, an infection of the skin on the feet.

Trichophyton

Protozoa

Some protozoa cause serious diseases. The protozoan shown here, *Plasmodium vivax*, is one of four different protozoa that cause malaria. *Plasmodium vivax* travels through the bloodstream to the liver—where it multiplies, clogging blood vessels and bursting blood cells.

Plasmodium vivax

Viruses

Viruses are very small pathogens that cannot live on their own. Many are carried through the air and can be breathed in. The virus shown here, *Variola*, causes smallpox. Worldwide vaccinations have wiped out this serious, often deadly disease.

Variola

Bacteria

Bacteria are single-celled organisms that are bigger than viruses but are still too small to be seen without a microscope. These pictures show three types of bacteria. This species of *Streptococcus*, a bacteria that forms round chains, causes strep throat. The rod-shaped bacteria in the middle, called *Escherichia coli*, can cause food poisoning. The spiral-shaped bacteria on the right, called *Treponema*, cause syphilis.

Streptococcus

Escherichia coli

Treponema

Bacteria live just about everywhere, including in and on your body. Most bacteria are harmless, but some can make you ill if they enter your body—in food or through a cut, for example. These harmful bacteria produce wastes called **toxins** (TAHK•suhnz) that damage your body's cells.

Fungi are organisms similar to plants. Unlike plants, fungi can't make their own food. Instead, they absorb food from their surroundings. Most common fungal diseases are not very serious.

COMPARE AND CONTRAST How are bacteria and fungi alike and different?

215

Catching Common Communicable Diseases

Colds and influenza are communicable diseases caused by viruses. These two common diseases have similar **symptoms** (SIMP·tuhmz), or the signs of a disease. Typical cold symptoms include runny nose, sneezing, watery eyes, sore throat, and coughing. Some people with colds also have headaches or slight fevers.

Colds are spread by direct contact. Suppose Thom has a cold. If you shake hands with him—and then rub your eyes or scratch your nose without washing your hands—you can get a cold, too. Colds are also spread indirectly. If Thom coughs and sneezes without covering his mouth and nose, he will spray viruses into the air. You could breathe the virus in if you're standing nearby.

To keep from catching colds, wash your hands often. Stay away from people who have colds. If you do get a cold, stay home for at least one day. Rest, and drink plenty of liquids. Some medicines can help you feel better.

Quick Activity

Interpret Graphs
There are about 280 million people living in the United States. Use the bar graph to calculate the percentage of Americans who get the flu every year. What percentage contract pneumonia?

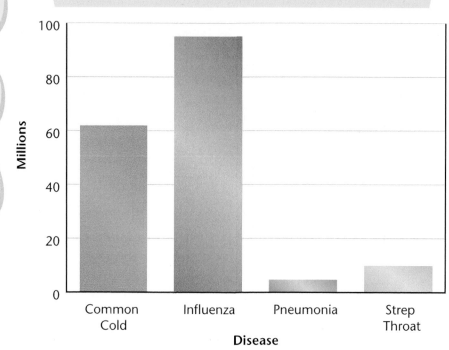

Number of Cases Reported Annually

Millions

Disease: Common Cold, Influenza, Pneumonia, Strep Throat

Influenza symptoms are similar to cold symptoms—but much worse. You generally feel very bad with the flu. Your muscles and head ache. You run a high fever. You might be very congested or have a dry cough and a sore throat. Some people even get nauseated. In addition, the flu may leave you feeling weak for days or weeks after you recover.

Flu viruses are spread in the same ways as cold viruses—through direct and indirect contact. You can protect yourself from the flu in the same way as you do from a cold: wash your hands often, and avoid people who have the disease. Many adults and some children get a flu shot every year for extra protection.

If you get the flu, treat it as you would a cold—with rest and plenty of liquids. Medicines won't cure the flu, but they can relieve your aches and pains. Be sure to cooperate with your parents and with health-care providers so that you can make a quick recovery.

COMPARE AND CONTRAST How does the flu differ from the common cold?

Consumer Activity

Make Buying Decisions
Suppose you are shopping with your parents for an over-the-counter cold medication. You find two different brands. One costs $1.50 less than the other. What other information should you look for before you decide which one to buy?

Luis is following his doctor's and mom's guidance by resting and drinking plenty of fluids. ▼

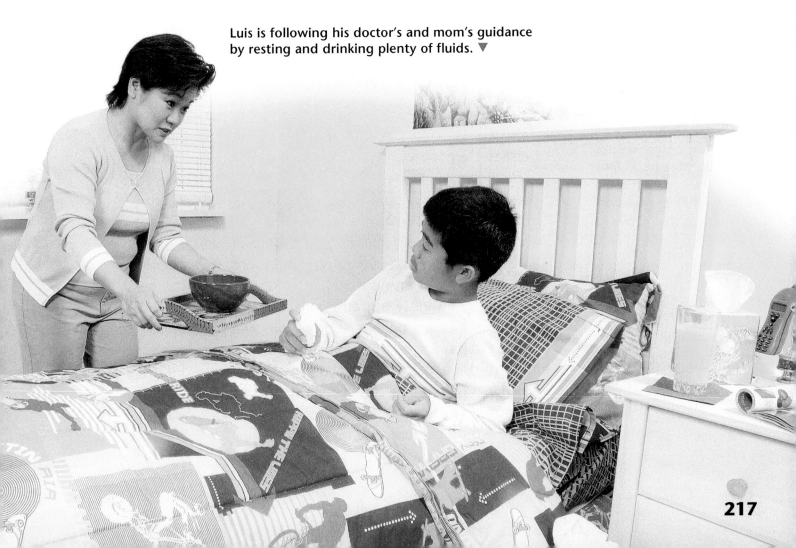

Some Serious Communicable Diseases

Disease	Type of Pathogen	Symptoms
measles	virus	fever, runny nose, cough, swollen glands, rash, coughing and sneezing
German measles (rubella)	virus	slight fever, swollen glands, rash, coughing and sneezing
chickenpox	virus	slight fever, blistery rash, coughing and sneezing
mumps	virus	fever, very swollen glands, coughing and sneezing
strep throat	bacteria	sore throat, fever, nausea
influenza	virus	fever, headache, muscle aches, coughing, chills, runny nose, sneezing
hepatitis B	virus	vomiting, abdominal pain, loss of appetite, yellow tint to eyes and skin

Quick Activity

Prevent the Spread of Disease Consider how the diseases listed in the table are transmitted. List steps you could take to protect yourself and others from the spread of these communicable diseases.

Serious Communicable Diseases

Most people recover quickly from communicable diseases like colds and the flu. Other communicable diseases are more serious and have longer recovery times. Some communicable diseases are even deadly. Three serious but fairly common communicable diseases are *pneumonia* (noo•MOHN•yuh), *hepatitis* (hep•uh•TYT•is), and *mononucleosis* (mahn•oh•noo•klee•OH•sis).

Pneumonia is an infection of the lungs. It can begin with other, less serious infections, like the flu. It can be caused by a variety of pathogens, including viruses and bacteria. Healthy people recover from viral pneumonia in as little as a week. Other people, including elderly people or people who are already sick, can die from it. Bacterial pneumonia is more serious. However, unlike viral pneumonia, it can be treated with antibiotics, which kill the harmful bacteria.

▲ Chickenpox is caused by a virus.

▲ The symptoms of chickenpox include fever and an itchy rash.

Symptoms of pneumonia include fever, cough, chills, chest pain, and rapid breathing or shortness of breath. If you develop these symptoms, see a doctor. Treatment includes resting in bed, plenty of liquids, and medicines to relieve symptoms and kill pathogens.

Hepatitis is an infection of the liver, an organ that filters the blood. Symptoms of hepatitis include fever, yellowing of the whites of the eyes, and loss of appetite and energy. Several different viruses cause hepatitis. The three most common ones are known as hepatitis A virus (HVA), hepatitis B virus (HVB), and hepatitis C virus (HVC). The three viruses are transmitted from person to person in different ways.

The mildest hepatitis, HVA, is transmitted by consuming food or water that contains the virus. HVB and HVC are transmitted by contact with infected blood or by direct sexual contact. These forms of hepatitis can be much more serious than hepatitis A. Unlike HVA, they can affect the liver for many years.

Mononucleosis, which is often called mono, is another communicable disease caused by a virus. Symptoms include fever, headache, sore throat, swollen glands, weakness, extreme tiredness, and sometimes a rash. The most common treatment is bed rest, fluids, and medicine for fever. People who have had mono can still feel weak months after they have recovered from the virus.

CAUSE AND EFFECT A teenager is diagnosed with hepatitis A. What is a likely cause?

ACTIVITY

Life Skills

Communicate

Lori is sick. Her dad has taken her to the doctor. For the doctor to figure out exactly what is wrong, Lori needs to communicate her symptoms clearly. What are some questions the doctor might ask? Practice asking and answering appropriate questions with a partner.

STDs—Practice Prevention!

A **sexually transmitted disease**, or STD, is a communicable disease spread by sexual contact. You can't get an STD by hugging or kissing. Common STDs include *syphilis* (SIF•uh•lis), *gonorrhea* (gahn•uh•REE•uh), and *chlamydia* (kluh•MID•ee•uh). Although most STDs can be cured with medicine, prevention is the best strategy. The only sure way to prevent STDs is through **abstinence** (AB•stuh•nuhns)—avoiding behavior that puts your health at risk.

Syphilis and gonorrhea are caused by bacteria. Women with gonorrhea often have no symptoms, but men have pain when they urinate. Untreated gonorrhea can prevent a woman from having children. Chlamydia is caused by bacteria, too. Its symptoms are sores and swollen glands.

AIDS AIDS (Acquired Immune Deficiency Syndrome) is a disease caused by a virus known as HIV. These letters are short for another long name: Human Immunodeficiency Virus. HIV is a virus that attacks certain white blood cells and weakens the immune system.

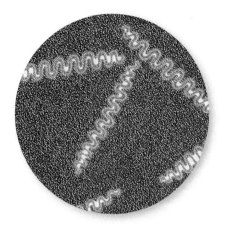

▲ Syphilis is caused by bacteria that cause small sores. If the disease is not treated, the bacteria can infect the brain and other organs and cause death.

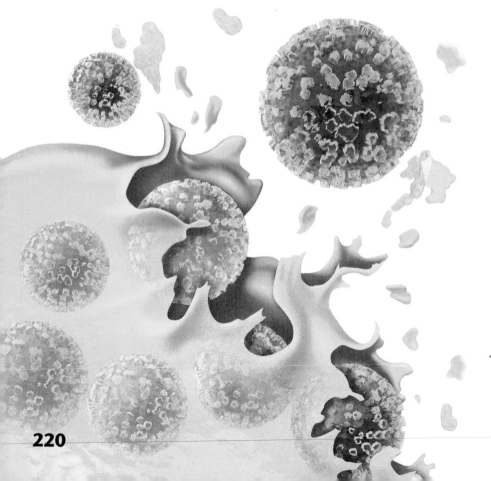

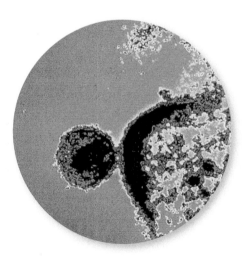

◀ HIV, shown here, attacks a person's helper T-cells so that they cannot help fight invading pathogens.

White blood cells detect pathogens entering the body and signal other blood cells to kill them. A type of white blood cell called a helper T-cell plays an especially important role.

HIV destroys helper T-cells, weakening the body's ability to fight infections. Because they have weakened immune systems, people with AIDS get communicable diseases that people with strong immune systems rarely get.

HIV can't be spread by casual contact. People most commonly contract the virus through sexual contact with an infected person or by injecting drugs with a needle that an infected person has used. An unborn baby can contract HIV through the mother's blood supply if she has HIV. Preventing HIV infection is the only way to survive it. There is no cure.

DRAW CONCLUSIONS **What are two ways that people can prevent HIV from spreading?**

Myth and Fact

Myth: **An insect such as a mosquito can transmit HIV if it bites you.**
Fact: There are no known cases of HIV being transmitted by the bite of a mosquito or any other insect.

Lesson 2 Summary and Review

1 Summarize with Vocabulary

Use vocabulary and other terms from this lesson to complete the statements.

_____ diseases are caused by pathogens, which are easily _____ from person to person. An _____ develops when pathogens multiply in the body. _____ are spread by sexual contact. _____ is the best way to keep from getting STDs.

2 Give examples to show that viruses can cause both mild and serious diseases.

3 Critical Thinking How is AIDS different from other STDs? How is it similar?

4 COMPARE AND CONTRAST Draw and complete this graphic organizer to show how viruses are similar to and different from bacteria.

Topic: Viruses and Bacteria
Alike   Different

5 Write to Explain—Description

Describe how colds and the flu are transmitted from one person to another. Then describe some ways to prevent getting these diseases.

The Immune System

Fighting Communicable Diseases

Pathogens are in the air you breathe and the food you eat. They are on almost everything you touch and everyone you get close to. So why aren't you sick all the time?

Your body has a natural ability to fight pathogens. This ability is called **resistance** (rih•ZIS•tuhnts). Think of resistance as a series of defenses meant to keep pathogens out. Some defenses keep pathogens from entering your body. When those defenses fail, other defenses find and kill pathogens that do get in. However, when your own resistance is not enough and you become sick, medical science works to cure you.

Your body's first line of defense is the skin—and the mucous membranes lining your mouth, throat, and other surfaces inside your body. Your skin and your mucous membranes form a barrier that helps keep pathogens out. Some of the substances produced by the skin and mucous membranes, including sweat, tears, and saliva, contain chemicals that kill pathogens.

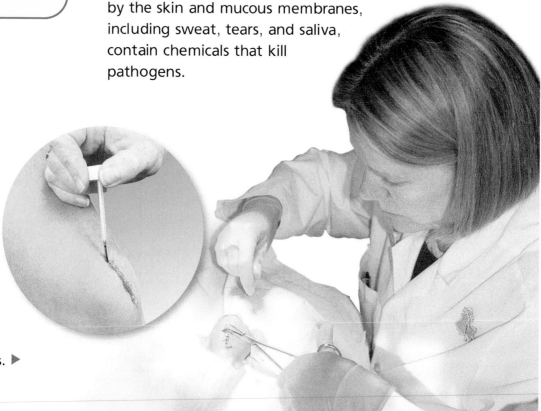

This liquid skin adhesive ("skin glue") can quickly and gently close cuts that might otherwise need stitches. ▶

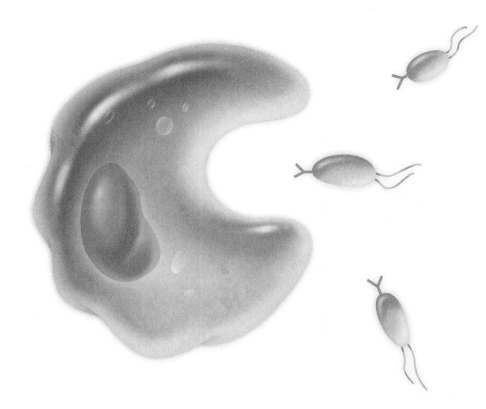

There are millions of different pathogens, and your body makes millions of different antibodies to fight them. Antibodies target specific pathogens, either killing them or marking them. Marked pathogens can be destroyed by a kind of white blood cell that surrounds and destroys them.

If pathogens push past the barrier formed by the skin and mucous membranes, a second line of defense goes into action. This is the **immune system** (ih·MYOON), the body system that recognizes and destroys invading pathogens. White blood cells are a key part of your immune system. One kind of white blood cell makes **antibodies** (AN·tih·bahd·eez) that help fight disease by attaching to specific pathogens.

Your immune system "learns" how to fight specific pathogens each time you become ill. The next time the pathogen enters your body, your immune system rapidly produces antibodies to fight it. This ability of the body to "remember" how to make antibodies to a specific pathogen is called **immunity** (ih·MYOON·uh·tee).

Often when you have an infection, you may run a fever—a body temperature higher than 100°F (37.8°C). The fever helps fight the infection by speeding your body's defensive response.

 COMPARE AND CONTRAST Compare and contrast the ways your skin and immune system keep you from getting sick.

Myth and Fact

Myth: All fevers are bad for you.

Fact: A fever does make you feel uncomfortable, but it also helps your body fight an infection. In some cases, taking a fever reducer can make you worse. It can make you feel well enough to get out of bed and do your normal activities. However, because you are actually still sick, what you need is more rest to recover.

223

Your Body's Defenses

Mucous membranes produce mucus, a sticky substance that traps pathogens as they enter your body. Some mucous membranes are lined with tiny hairlike structures that move with a wavelike motion. These sweep pathogens toward the outside of the body.

Fever helps your body produce the kinds of cells that fight invading pathogens. Fever also slows the growth of some bacteria and speeds cell repair. Look at the temperature shown by the thermometer. What does it mean?

thymus

spleen

The thymus and spleen produce white blood cells called lymphocytes. One type of lymphocyte produces antibodies. Antibodies attach themselves to pathogens.

Blood platelets are fragments of cells that live in your bone marrow. When you get cut and puncture a blood vessel, platelets rush to the wound. The platelets release chemicals that start a clotting process. Your blood forms a clot—called a scab—on the surface of your skin. Your punctured blood vessel is repaired.

If you feel particularly sick, your doctor might test your blood to find out how many white cells it contains—and the percentage of each kind of white blood cell. This test can help your doctor understand how sick you are and may help identify the specific pathogen causing the problem.

Skin blocks many pathogens from entering the body.

The cells inside long bones produce phagocytes. Phagocytes surround and destroy pathogens.

DRAW CONCLUSIONS How are platelets important to your immune system?

Boosting Your Body's Defenses

Some communicable diseases can cause death if they are left untreated. Others can be dangerous for people whose immune systems are weak, including the very old, the very young, and people with AIDS. You can boost your body's defenses with vaccines and antibiotics.

A **vaccine** (vak•SEEN) is a medicine that contains dead or weakened pathogens. These dead or weakened pathogens cause the immune system to form antibodies. In turn, the antibodies produce immunity to the disease without having the pathogens cause the disease. Vaccines are given either by mouth or by injection—that is, in a shot.

You can be vaccinated against many viral diseases, including measles, rubella (German measles), mumps, and chickenpox. A few vaccines for diseases caused by bacteria, including tetanus and whooping cough, are also available.

An **immunization** (ih•myuh•nuh•ZAY•shuhn) is a dose of vaccine that makes you immune to a disease. To remain immune, you sometimes must be vaccinated more than once. For some diseases, including tetanus, you need **boosters**, or later doses of vaccine, to stay immune.

SUMMARIZE Use the words *vaccine, injection*, and *booster* to explain what immunization is.

Consumer Activity

Accessing Valid Health Information Search the Internet to find out whether the benefits of getting a flu shot are worth the costs for young, healthy adults and for adults over 65 years old. Make sure to use reliable sources, such as the Food and Drug Administration.

Many adults get a flu shot to keep from getting the flu. The virus that causes the flu can be different each year. What does this fact tell you about how often people must get flu shots? ▶

225

Miracle Medicines

Vaccines have saved millions of lives, but the real miracle medicines are antibiotics. An **antibiotic** (an•ty•by•AHT•ik) is a medicine that kills pathogens such as bacteria. Antibiotics can quickly and completely cure many communicable diseases that once were deadly. For example, today an antibiotic called streptomycin helps control bubonic plague. In the 1300s this plague killed about one-third of Europe's population. Antibiotics can also kill pathogens that cause less serious diseases, including ear infections and acne.

Most antibiotics cure infections caused by bacteria. Others fight harmful fungi and protozoa. Antibiotics do not kill viruses, so they cannot be used to cure colds, the flu, AIDS, or other viral diseases. However, some antiviral medicines do help control viral infections.

One of the first antibiotics was discovered by accident. In 1928 English scientist Sir Alexander Fleming was growing *Staphylococcus* bacteria in a lab dish. The dish was contaminated by a mold called *Penicillium*. The mold oozed a fluid that killed *Staphylococcus*. Fleming called the fluid penicillin. Today many types of penicillin are used to treat many kinds of bacterial infections.

Fleming observed that some molds killed bacteria. He had discovered an antibiotic. ▼

In 1945 Sir Alexander Fleming—along with Howard Florey and Ernst Chain, who also did work on penicillin—received the Nobel Prize in medicine. ▼

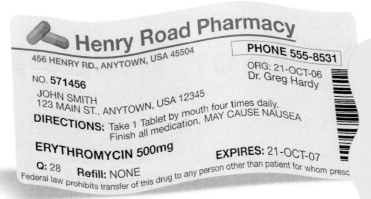

Henry Road Pharmacy
456 HENRY RD., ANYTOWN, USA 45504

PHONE 555-8531

ORG: 21-OCT-06
Dr. Greg Hardy

NO. 571456

JOHN SMITH
123 MAIN ST., ANYTOWN, USA 12345
DIRECTIONS: Take 1 Tablet by mouth four times daily.
Finish all medication. MAY CAUSE NAUSEA

ERYTHROMYCIN 500mg

EXPIRES: 21-OCT-07

Q: 28   Refill: NONE
Federal law prohibits transfer of this drug to any person other than patient for whom presc

Quick Activity

Read a Prescription Medicine Label Read the prescription label on this page. What is the name of the medication? Who should take it? When does it expire? What is a side effect? What additional information does the label provide?

When a large number of people have been using an antibiotic for a long time and for many minor infections, pathogens can develop resistance to the drugs. If this happens, the antibiotic can no longer kill the pathogen. Almost all the important human pathogens that can be treated with antibiotics have developed some resistance to them.

You can avoid making a bad problem worse. Take only antibiotics that your doctor has prescribed. Finish your whole prescription, even if you feel better before it is gone.

MAIN IDEA AND DETAILS **Explain the importance of antibiotics. Include one supporting detail.**

Lesson 3 Summary and Review

❶ Summarize with Vocabulary

Use vocabulary from this lesson to complete the statements.

Your body has a natural _____ to disease. Your skin and mucous membranes and your _____ make up your first and second lines of defense. You can get _____ to diseases by having the disease or, in some cases, by receiving a _____. Many bacterial diseases can be cured with _____.

❷ Critical Thinking Some vaccines are made by exposing an animal to a disease and harvesting the antibodies. How might this vaccine work in the human body?

❸ Name one benefit of vaccines.

❹ COMPARE AND CONTRAST Draw and complete this graphic organizer to show similarities and differences between antibiotics and vaccines.

Topic: Antibiotics and Vaccines
Alike   Different

❺ Write to Inform—Explanation

Write about the last time you had a cold. Use the information in this lesson to describe how your body fought the cold.

Other Diseases

Diseases You Cannot Catch

Heart disease is the leading cause of death in the United States. However, you cannot "catch" heart disease. It is a noncommunicable disease. **Noncommunicable diseases** are illnesses that are not caused by pathogens and do not spread from person to person. Instead, they are caused by hereditary, environmental, or behavioral risk factors or by a combination of the three.

One group of noncommunicable diseases is cardiovascular diseases. **Cardiovascular diseases** (kar•dee•oh•VAS•kyuh•ler) are diseases of the heart and blood vessels. They include atherosclerosis (ath•uhr•oh•skluh•ROH•suhs) and hypertension.

EKGs, stress tests, and other tests are used to test for cardiovascular diseases. An image from a stress test tells how a patient's heart responds to physical activity. ▼

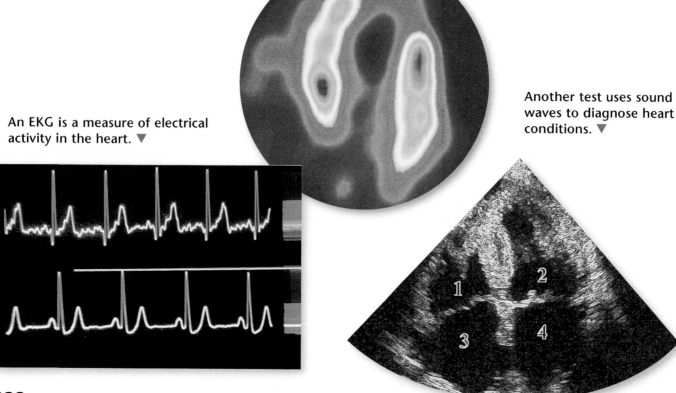

An EKG is a measure of electrical activity in the heart. ▼

Another test uses sound waves to diagnose heart conditions. ▼

Some Common Heart Problems

Heart Rhythms
A harmless extra beat can occur in the atria of the heart. If irregular beats occur in the ventricles, they can be quite dangerous.

Pacemaker
The sinus node, or pacemaker, controls the heartbeat. If the sinus node malfunctions, a surgeon can implant an electronic pacemaker to control the irregular heartbeat.

Valves
Four flaps, called valves, control blood flow through the heart. One kind of heart disease develops when a valve does not operate properly—for example, when a valve narrows or doesn't close all the way.

Heart Murmurs
A heart murmur is an extra sound in the heartbeat. Nearly two-thirds of heart murmurs are harmless. They are common in children.

Atherosclerosis is a disease that clogs the arteries, which are the blood vessels that carry oxygen and nutrients to cells. Think about what happens when an artery that carries oxygen to the heart becomes clogged. The flow of oxygen to the heart is reduced or cut off altogether. The heart becomes starved for oxygen, and a heart attack occurs.

In addition to causing a heart attack, atherosclerosis can also lead to high blood pressure, or hypertension. This condition puts stress on the entire circulatory system. Because high blood pressure rarely produces symptoms, it is important to have your blood pressure checked regularly.

CAUSE AND EFFECT **What can happen if the sinus node of the heart does not work properly?**

▲ Healthy arteries are hollow inside. In a patient with atherosclerosis, the arteries are lined with fatty matter and calcium. This decreases the amount of blood the arteries can carry.

229

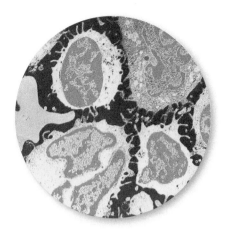

▲ Notice the hairlike projections on these white blood cells. They show that the patient has hairy cell leukemia.

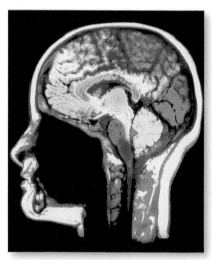

▲ Since the 1970s, new ways have been found to detect cancer. MRIs help doctors find tumors by giving clear, detailed pictures of the brain or other body parts.

Cancer

Cancer is caused by a change in the way body cells grow. With most kinds of cancer, body cells multiply rapidly and form a *tumor* (TOO•mer), an abnormal mass of cells. Some tumors spread when cancer cells are carried through the blood vessels to other parts of the body. It can take years for the original tumor to grow large enough to cause symptoms. By then, other tumors might already be growing. Once cancer has spread in this way, it usually cannot be cured.

Symptoms of cancer vary, depending on the kind of cancer. The most common cancer in children is *leukemia* (loo•KEE•mee•uh). Its symptoms include feeling extremely tired and running a slight fever for a long time.

Substances that cause cancer are known as **carcinogens** (kar•SIN•uh•juhnz). Some carcinogens are chemicals. The chemical carcinogens in tobacco smoke are the leading cause of lung cancer. Sunlight is also a carcinogen because UV rays can cause skin cancer.

Some people can be exposed to carcinogens and not develop cancer. A person's heredity and the health of his or her immune system affect the person's chances of getting cancer.

CAUSE AND EFFECT Describe the relationship between carcinogens and cancer.

Eight Warning Signs of Possible Childhood Cancer

❶ Continued and unexplained weight loss

❷ Headaches, with vomiting in the morning

❸ Increased swelling or persistent pain in bones or joints, sometimes accompanied by limping

❹ Lump or mass in the abdomen, neck, or elsewhere

❺ Development of a whitish appearance in the pupil of the eye, or sudden change in vision

❻ Recurrent fevers not due to infections

❼ Excessive bruising or bleeding (often sudden)

❽ Noticeable paleness or prolonged tiredness

Dealing with Diabetes

Diabetes is a common noncommunicable disease that occurs when the body stops making insulin or using it properly. **Insulin** (IN·suh·luhn) is a substance that helps move blood sugar into the cells. It is produced in an organ called the pancreas. Without insulin, your body cannot store or use the energy that comes in food. You feel weak and tired. Diabetes is a very serious condition. If left untreated, diabetes can cause death.

There are two main types of diabetes. Type 1 diabetes, also called juvenile diabetes, usually begins in a person's childhood or teenage years. In Type 1 diabetes, the pancreas makes too little insulin or none at all, and the person must take insulin. In Type 2 diabetes, the body makes some insulin but cannot use it properly. Anyone of any age can develop Type 2 diabetes, but obesity and lack of exercise are its chief causes. Type 2 diabetes can usually be controlled with diet and exercise. Diabetes often occurs in families, so heredity is an added risk factor.

DRAW CONCLUSIONS How can people help protect themselves from developing Type 2 diabetes?

Insulin Therapy For insulin to get into the blood, it must be injected into the fat under the skin. People who need insulin inject it using a needle and syringe. A newer means of delivery is the insulin pump. Insulin flows from the pump through a very thin needle injected into the abdomen. Researchers are seeking ways to deliver insulin to the blood without using a needle. Some promising new techniques include a skin patch, pill, oral spray, and nasal spray.

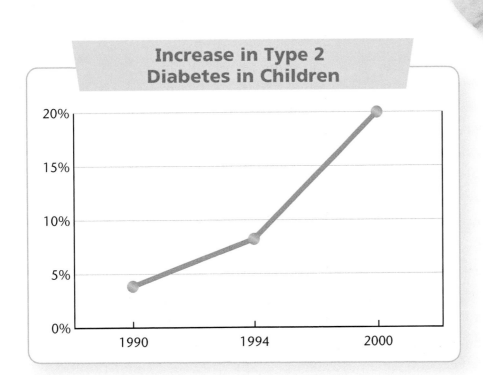

◀ Type 2 diabetes has been rising steadily in children.

Increase in Type 2 Diabetes in Children

	1990	1994	2000
20%			
15%			
10%			
5%			
0%			

Narrow, unhealthy
air passages ▼

Clear, healthy
air passages ▶

▲ Asthma narrows air passages in the lungs, making it hard to breathe. Inhaled medicine works quickly to open air passages so breathing can return to normal.

Respiratory Diseases

Your respiratory system takes oxygen into your body and gets rid of carbon dioxide, a waste gas. The respiratory system includes your nose, throat, and trachea, which carry air into your body. It also includes the lungs, where oxygen is taken into the blood and carbon dioxide is released.

Substances such as mold or dust often enter the lungs during breathing. For most people, these substances are harmless. However, in some people the immune system attacks these substances. These people may develop a respiratory disease, such as asthma or respiratory allergies.

Asthma is a controllable disease of the lungs that makes breathing difficult. Asthma attacks, or episodes can be triggered by substances, such as pollen in the air, or by stress, cold air, or exercise.

The good news for asthma patients is that the coughing and difficult breathing can be reduced or prevented. The first step in treatment is to avoid things that cause asthma episodes. This can be challenging when the cause is something enjoyable, like playing soccer (exercise). Some people who have asthma take medicine through an inhaler to relax the muscles around the lungs. Students who experience an asthma episode should seek care from the school nurse.

Respiratory allergies, often called hay fever, produce symptoms such as runny nose and sneezing. Heredity is the main risk factor in this noncommunicable disease. If one or both of your parents have respiratory allergies, you are likely to develop them, too.

Finding out exactly what a person is allergic to usually requires being tested by a doctor. Once the person knows what causes the allergy, he or she can try to avoid the cause. Medicines that help control the symptoms can make the person more comfortable.

One way doctors treat allergies is to give the patient injections of tiny amounts of the substances they are allergic to. This helps their bodies get used to the substances and learn not to react to them. Unfortunately, it can take months of regular injections to control allergies in this way.

MAIN IDEA AND DETAILS **Name two chronic noncommunicable diseases that affect the respiratory system.**

Consumer Activity

Access Valid Health Information One way to deal with the stress of having a disease is to learn about the disease and know what to expect. Suppose a family member has been diagnosed with asthma. List four sources for reliable information about the disease and its treatment.

◀ Many people are allergic to pollen, a powdery substance given off by some plants and carried in the air.

Controlling Noncommunicable Diseases

Modern medical practices enable doctors to detect and treat a number of noncommunicable diseases. If you have one of these diseases, you can—and should—become an active partner in your own health care. Here are some ways that modern medicine can help you:

- By seeing a doctor each year, you can be tested for hypertension, diabetes, and some kinds of cancer.
- Improved medicines have been developed to treat cancer. These cause fewer side effects than older medicines.
- New kinds of radiation equipment focus radiation on cancer cells so less damage occurs to other cells in the body.
- New medicines can dissolve blood clots, which can cause heart attacks and damage the heart.
- Mammograms help doctors find breast tumors that are too small to be found in any other way. Early detection and treatment means a better chance of a complete cure.

SUMMARIZE How can noncommunicable diseases be controlled?

Lesson 4 Summary and Review

❶ Summarize with Vocabulary

Use vocabulary and other terms from this lesson to complete the statements.

Most _____ diseases, such as cancer, show up during a person's adult years. Being around _____ can cause people to get cancer. The major causes of Type 2 diabetes are _____ and lack of exercise. People with serious diabetes must control it with _____. _____ is a respiratory disease in which the air passages in the lungs become narrow.

❷ What are cardiovascular diseases? Give two examples.

❸ Critical Thinking What can you do to avoid carcinogens?

❹ COMPARE AND CONTRAST Draw and complete this graphic organizer to show similarities and differences in Type 1 and Type 2 diabetes.

Topic: Type 1 and Type 2 Diabetes

Alike	Different

❺ Write to Inform—Description

Suppose you are a doctor who has detected cardiovascular disease in a patient. Write a brief description of your findings. Classify the disease.

Caring

Showing Concern for Those Who Are Ill

It can be very hard to know how to show your concern for someone who is sick, especially when that person is a close friend or family member. Here are some tips to help you, even when you feel sad or nervous.

- **Imagine how you would want people to act around you if you were sick.**

- **Simply spending time with the person is a good way to show that you care.**

- **If you can't visit, call or send letters or e-mail.**

- **Offer to help the person with tasks that might be difficult, such as grocery shopping.**

- **If you don't know what to do when you visit, ask questions such as, "How can I make you feel better?" and "Would you like me to stay, or would you rather rest?"**

- **Remember that a person with a serious illness is experiencing a lot of stress. He or she may also be in pain. Don't take it personally if the person acts grouchy or doesn't want to see you.**

Activity

With a partner, role-play a visit to a family member who is in the hospital. One of you will play the visitor, and the other will play the person who is sick. Then switch roles. Afterward, discuss how it felt to be the visitor and how it felt to be the patient.

Certified volunteer teams of people and dogs visit patients in many hospitals and nursing homes. Some hospitals also allow family pets to visit. Visits by pets can help sick people cope with stress. ▶

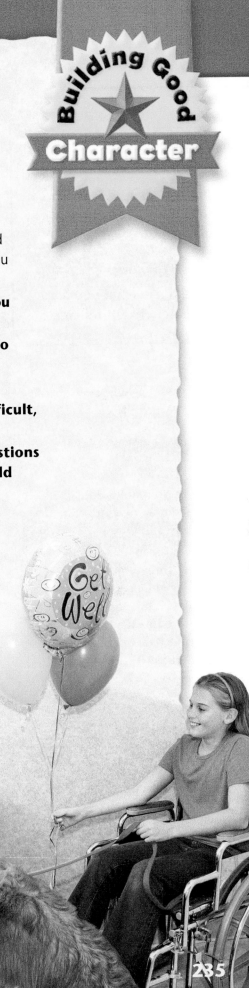

LESSON 5

Living a Healthy Life

Lesson Focus

Your habits and lifestyle play important roles in your health.

Why Learn This?

You can use what you learn to create a healthful life.

Personal Health Plan ▶

Real-Life Situation

You can do many things to prevent some kinds of diseases.

Real-Life Plan

Identify three enjoyable activities you can take part in to make your body stronger and more flexible and to give your heart and lungs a workout.

Reduce Your Risk

Living a healthy life means forming habits that decrease your chances of catching communicable diseases. It also means making lifestyle choices that reduce your risk of developing chronic diseases. You can reduce your risk of getting communicable diseases. The best way to do this is easy—keep clean. Bathe or shower every day. Wash your hands with soap and warm water after going to the bathroom, before fixing food, and after touching anyone who is sick. Don't rub your eyes or put your fingers in your mouth or nose.

Not all of the illnesses that are caused by pathogens are communicable. For example, it's impossible to catch food poisoning from someone who has it. Instead, you get it by eating foods that contain pathogens. To keep bacteria from growing in foods, keep hot foods hot and cold foods cold. Eat meat only after it has been cooked thoroughly.

COMPARE AND CONTRAST How are food poisoning and colds alike? How are they different?

Animals are a possible source of pathogens. To lower your risk of infection, avoid animals that appear sick or act unusual. Some animals, including bats, foxes, and raccoons, can carry rabies, a deadly viral disease. ▶

236

Living Well

Exercising regularly, eating a balanced diet, getting enough sleep, and participating in health screenings are important ways to stay healthy. Exercise helps protect you from cardiovascular diseases. Exercise burns body fat and helps control weight.

By eating a healthful diet, you can enhance your overall health. You can also guard against high blood pressure, diabetes, and some kinds of cancer. Eat plenty of vegetables, fruits, and grains. Limit foods high in fat, salt, and sugar. Eat only when you are hungry, and eat just enough to feel satisfied.

Your body needs sleep to rest and repair itself. Avoid stimulating activities, such as action-packed movies, right before bed. Keep a regular sleeping and waking schedule.

To safeguard your health, you should take part in health screenings. These include vision and hearing tests, dental checkups, and general medical exams. Cooperating in health screenings allows health-care professionals to screen for and treat problems before they become serious.

CAUSE AND EFFECT What are three ways of living that you can choose to keep yourself healthy?

▲ Regular exercise has many health benefits. A balanced diet supplies everything your body needs for growth and good health.

Hamburger must be cooked to at least 160°F to kill pathogens in the meat. ▼

Coping with Stress

Anything new or different in your life—bad or good—can cause stress. Moving to a new city or changing schools is stressful. Schoolwork and sports can also be stressful. Everyone feels stress at the death of a loved one or the divorce of parents. Even a happy change, such as the arrival of a baby in your family, can cause stress.

Sometimes stress can be a good thing in your life. For example, the stress that comes with working on a big science fair project can bring out strengths you didn't know you had. Some people actually work better under stress.

However, too much stress can be overwhelming. As the stresses in your life add up, you become more likely to become sick or get injured. Stress can keep you from sleeping well or can give you headaches. It may cause your heart to race, your stomach to be upset, or your allergies or asthma to get worse.

Stress lowers your natural resistance, so you may get colds and other communicable diseases more easily. It can also lead to noncommunicable diseases such as ulcers and heart disease.

Quick Activity

Cope with Stress Look over the tips on page 239 for handling stress. Decide which tips can be most helpful to you. Then write one to three more ways that you can improve how you handle stressful situations in your life.

◄ Enjoying a game or an activity or learning a new skill can help you deal with stress. ▼

Stress also affects people's emotions. You might feel angry and lose your temper over little things. You might have trouble concentrating. You might forget important things or make careless mistakes.

You can't always avoid stress, so it's important to recognize and deal with the symptoms. Do you know how *your* body reacts to stress? Maybe you get a pain in your shoulders or a knot in your stomach. When you feel your body reacting in these ways, take steps to cope with the stress you're feeling.

Some people respond to stress by overeating, drinking alcohol, or using tobacco. These are unhealthy ways of handling stress. These behavioral factors increase your risk of getting diseases of all sorts.

How *can* you deal healthfully with stress? Try to think about one problem at a time. Instead of worrying about what might go wrong, make a decision to take positive action. Use the additional tips in the list to the right to help reduce the harm stress does to your body.

SEQUENCE Suppose a friend says something that annoys you a great deal. You get a nagging ache in your neck. Name two things that could happen next, depending on how you handle stress.

Tips to Handle Stress

1 Relax by taking deep breaths, thinking about something pleasant, or listening to quiet music.

2 Talk to someone about how you're feeling.

3 Get exercise. Run, ride your bike, or swim a few laps.

4 Make sure you're getting enough sleep.

5 Cry if you need to.

Spending time with people you enjoy being with is one good way to help reduce stress. ▼

239

Myth and Fact

Myth: Using smokeless tobacco, such as chewing tobacco or snuff, is safer than smoking cigarettes.
Fact: Smokeless tobacco is just as dangerous as cigarettes. It has many poisons that cause serious diseases, including cancer of the mouth.

Makers of tobacco products are required by law to print warnings that tell users how dangerous the products are. ▶

Say *No!* to Tobacco

Tobacco smoke contains about 4,000 different substances, of which at least 200 are poisonous to people. These poisons cause many serious diseases in smokers and in people who don't smoke but who breathe in cigarette smoke. These diseases include cardiovascular diseases, lung cancer, and respiratory diseases like asthma and emphysema. There is no safe way of using tobacco.

DRAW CONCLUSIONS How does smoking affect health?

Surgeon General's Warning: Quitting Smoking Now Greatly Reduces Serious Risks To Your Health.

Surgeon General's Warning: Smoking By Pregnant Women May Result In Fetal Injury, Premature Birth, And Low Birth Weight.

Surgeon General's Warning: Smoking Causes Lung Cancer, Heart Disease, Emphysema, And May Complicate Pregnancy.

Lesson 5 Summary and Review

❶ Summarize with Vocabulary
Use terms from this chapter to complete the statements.

By making healthful choices, such as _____ regularly and eating a _____ diet, you can lower your risk of disease. The emotional upsets caused by _____ can weaken your resistance to disease. Chewing or smoking _____ can cause many serious diseases, including lung _____.

❷ What types of health screenings should you participate in?

❸ Critical Thinking What foods should be included in a healthful diet? What foods should be avoided?

❹ **COMPARE AND CONTRAST** Draw and complete this graphic organizer to show similarities and differences in how you can avoid disease and manage stress.

Topic: Avoiding Disease and Managing Stress
Alike   Different

❺ Write to Inform—Explanation
Write an essay explaining ways you and your peers could change your behavior to make your lives more healthful.

ACTIVITIES

Science

Research Medical Advances Find out how smallpox was wiped out or how a vaccine was developed for polio. Then write a short television movie script that tells the story of this public health achievement. Make the events in your script both factual and interesting.

Language Arts

Conduct an Interview Interview someone who has a disability or a serious long-term illness. Find out how the disability or illness affects the person's everyday life. After the interview, write a description of ways you think your own life would change if you had the same disability or illness.

Technology Project

Use a computer to make a flowchart showing how communicable diseases are spread. You may choose to present a particular disease or a type of disease. If a computer isn't available, use colored markers and paper.

GO ONLINE For more activities, visit The Learning Site. www.harcourtschool.com/health

Home & Community

Promoting Health Make a funny sign for other students in your school to promote good hygiene as a way to prevent disease. With your teacher's permission, post the sign in your classroom or in a display area in your school.

Career Link

Immunologist Suppose you are an immunologist, a scientist who studies the immune system. Your job is to develop new vaccines. Write a statement in which you identify and describe the disease for which you would most like to develop a vaccine. Explain your choice.

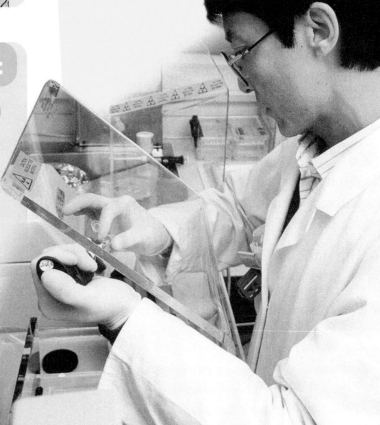

Reading Skill

COMPARE AND CONTRAST

Draw and then use this graphic organizer to answer questions 1 and 2.

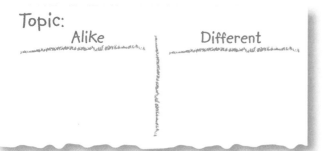

Topic:
Alike   Different

1 Write two ways communicable and noncommunicable diseases are alike and different.

2 Write two ways Type 1 and Type 2 diabetes are alike and different.

Use Vocabulary

Match each term in Column B with its meaning in Column A.

Column A	Column B
3 An organism or virus that can make people sick	**A** abstinence
	B antibodies
	C infection
4 Avoiding unhealthful behavior	**D** pathogen
	E symptoms
5 What occurs when a pathogen multiplies in the body	**F** toxins
6 The signs and feelings of a disease	
7 Harmful wastes that can damage the body's cells	
8 Substances that help fight disease	

Check Understanding

Choose the letter of the correct answer.

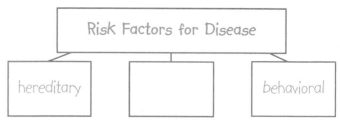

Risk Factors for Disease

hereditary   behavioral

9 Which risk factor is missing from the graphic organizer? (p. 206)
A cardiovascular   **C** chronic
B environmental   **D** pathogenic

10 _____ is a substance that helps move the sugar in blood into the body's cells. (p. 231)
F An antibody   **H** A pathogen
G Insulin   **J** Resistance

11 The body's natural ability to fight pathogens is called _____. (p. 222)
A systemic   **C** immunity
B inherited   **D** resistance

12 How is insulin being delivered to the bloodstream of the child shown below? (p. 231)
F injection
G skin patch
H vaccine
J pump

13 Which medicine can kill bacterial pathogens but can't kill viruses? (p. 226)
A decongestant   **C** antibiotic
B antihistamine   **D** aspirin

14 Which type of disease is spread by sexual contact? (p. 220)

   F noncommunicable disease

   G hepatitis A

   H cardiovascular disease

   J STD

15 Which of these medicines can give you immunity to measles? (p. 225)

   A insulin   **C** antibiotic

   B vaccine   **D** injection

16 The first line of defense your body has against pathogens is its _____. (p. 222)

   F antibodies

   G immune system

   H skin and mucous membranes

   J high temperature

17 If someone in your family has diabetes, which of the following risk factors for the disease do you have? (p. 206)

   A environmental

   B hereditary

   C behavioral

   D communicable

18 What are substances called that can cause cancer? (p. 230)

   F carcinogens

   G T-cells

   H hereditary risk factors

   J stress

Think Critically

19 Imagine that your family has a history of heart disease. What can you do to decrease your chances of having heart problems?

20 List health risk factors for the common cold and for hypertension. Which factors do you think would be easier to control? Why?

21 The chickenpox virus can survive for weeks outside the human body. Explain how this makes the chickenpox virus easy to transmit.

22 Describe how tobacco smoke could be an environmental health risk to people who do not smoke. How can you avoid this environmental risk?

Apply Skills

23 **LIFE SKILLS**

Manage Stress Your best friend is under a lot of stress because her sister is seriously ill. What things can you do to help your friend cope with stress in healthful ways?

24 **BUILDING GOOD CHARACTER**

Caring Your family doctor wants to screen your younger brother for a disease. Your brother is afraid to have the test. What can you say or do that might help?

Write About Health

25 **Write to Inform—Explanation** Write three lifestyle choices you can make now to lower your risk of getting sick both in the near future and when you're an adult. Explain why these choices work.

Drugs and Health

SUMMARIZE When you summarize, you give the main idea and most important details of a passage. You also tell how the main idea and its details are connected. Use the Reading in Health Handbook on pages 410–411 and this graphic organizer to help you read the health facts in this chapter.

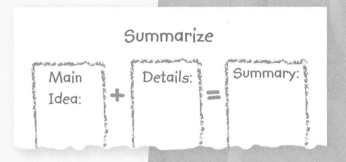

Summarize

| Main Idea: | + | Details: | = | Summary: |

Health Graph

INTERPRET DATA According to the graph, more people age 12–17 made drug-related visits to the emergency room in 2000 than in 1999 or in 2001. Summarize the pattern you see for all but the youngest age group.

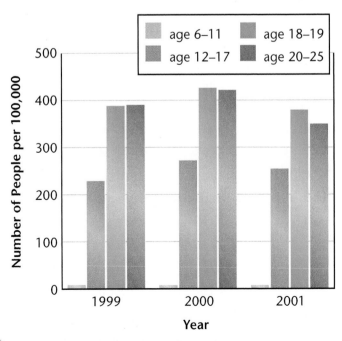

Drug-Related Emergency Room Visits in the United States

age 6–11 age 18–19
age 12–17 age 20–25

Number of People per 100,000

500
400
300
200
100
0

1999   2000   2001

Year

Daily Physical Activity

One way to stay healthy is to always follow your doctor's or your parents' advice when taking medicines. Another way to stay healthy is to be physically active.

Be Active!
Use the selection, Track 8, **Jumping and Pumping**, to make your body feel better.

Medicines Can Help People Stay Healthy

Lesson Focus

Medicines are drugs that can help you stay healthy, but they can be harmful if used improperly.

Why Learn This?

To get the greatest benefits from medicines, you must learn to use them safely.

Vocabulary

drug
medicines
side effects
prescription medicines
dosage
over-the-counter medicines
expiration date

Medicines and Drugs

What comes to mind when you think of the word *drug*? You may think of a medicine that you take when you are ill. Or you may think of an illegal drug, such as marijuana. Actually, a **drug** is any substance, other than food, that causes changes in the way the body or mind works.

Drugs that prevent, treat, or cure health problems are called **medicines**. There are thousands of different medicines. Vaccines are medicines that prevent diseases such as measles, polio, and smallpox. Some medicines, like aspirin, reduce fever and relieve pain. Antibiotics fight infections by killing disease-causing bacteria. There are a number of medicines that treat serious diseases, such as cancer and heart disease.

▲ Notice the empty areas around some of the disks. In these areas the antibiotic has killed the bacteria.

Think of the different medicines you have used in the past. How did they help you?

SUMMARIZE Why are medicines important?

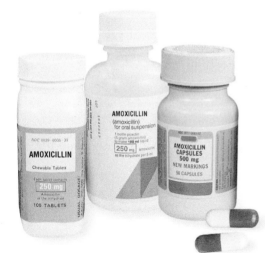

▲ Antibiotics such as those shown here fight infection.

Where Medicines Come From

Many of the medicines we use today are made in a laboratory. But about half of the medicines we use originally came from plants. The pictures below show some plants that have given us important medicines. Scientists think there are many other plants that could also be sources of useful medicines.

One kind of scientist, called a bioprospector, collects plants from all over the world and brings them back for researchers to study. These bioprospectors are looking for the medicines of the future.

 SUMMARIZE Why are plants important for medicines?

The rosy periwinkle is used to make strong cancer-fighting medicines. After being treated with these medicines, four out of five children with leukemia recover. ▼

Medicines made from the belladonna plant help people with stomach problems. ▼

The bark of the cinchona tree is boiled to make the medicine *quinine*. This medicine is used to treat malaria. ▼

Cinchona tree

Jane N. Ewan
Drug: Amoxil 400MG/5ML SUSP
Rx#: 0000   Date: 09/24
Dr. Karen Smythe

Contact Our Pharmacy Information Hotline

Directions: Give 3/4 teaspoonful 2 times a day for 10 days

COMMON NAME: AMOXICILLIN (a-mox-i-SILL-in)

COMMON USES: This medicine is a penicillin antibiotic used to treat bacterial infections.

BEFORE USING THIS MEDICINE: Some medicines or medical conditions may interact with this medicine. INFORM YOUR DOCTOR OR PHARMACIST of all prescription and over-the-counter medicine that you are taking. DO NOT TAKE THIS MEDICINE if you are also taking tetracycline antibiotics. ADDITIONAL MONITORING OF YOUR DOSE OR CONDITION may be needed if you are taking anticoagulants or methotrexate. Inform your doctor of any other medical conditions or allergies. Contact your doctor or pharmacist if you have any questions or concerns about taking this medicine.

HOW TO USE THIS MEDICINE: Follow the directions for using this medicine provided by your doctor. SHAKE WELL before taking a dose. Use a measuring device marked for medicine dosing. Ask your pharmacist for help if you are unsure of how to measure this dose. You may mix this medicine with milk or formula before taking it. If you mix this medicine with milk or formula, use it immediately after mixing. THIS MEDICINE MAY BE TAKEN on an empty stomach or with food. STORE THIS MEDICINE at room temperature or in the refrigerator. Refrigeration may improve the taste of this medicine. Check the bottle of this medicine or with your pharmacist to see if your brand needs to be refrigerated after opening. TO CLEAR UP YOUR INFECTION COMPLETELY, continue taking this medicine for the full course of treatment even if you feel better in a few days. Do not miss any doses. IF YOU MISS A DOSE OF THIS MEDICINE, take it as soon as possible. If it is almost time for your next dose, skip the missed dose and go back to your regular dosing schedule. Do NOT take 2 doses at once.

CAUTIONS: DO NOT TAKE THIS MEDICINE IF YOU HAVE HAD A SEVERE ALLERGIC REACTION to a penicillin antibiotic (such as amoxicillin, ampicillin) or a cephalosporin antibiotic (such as Ceclor, Keflex, Ceftin, Duricef). A severe reaction includes a seve rash, hives, breathing difficulties, or dizziness. If you have a question about whether you are allergic to this medicine, conta doctor or pharmacist. IF MODERATE TO SEVERE DIARRHEA OCCURS during or after treatment with this medicine, co your doctor or pharmacist. Do not treat it with non-prescription (over-the-counter) medicines. IF YOU EXPERIEN breathing or tightness of chest; swelling of eyelids, face, or lips; or develop a rash or hives, tell your doctor i any more of this medicine unless your doctor tells you to do so. IF YOU HAVE DIABETES, this med results with some urine glucose tests. Check with your doctor before you adjust the dose of diet.

...IBLE SIDE EFFECTS: SIDE EFFECTS, that m

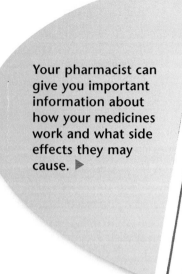

Your pharmacist can give you important information about how your medicines work and what side effects they may cause. ▶

Side Effects of Medicines

Medicines come in many forms. Skin ointments are put on the surface of the skin. Some medicines to treat asthma are breathed in. Some drugs, such as insulin, are injected.

Most medicines are taken by mouth. They are absorbed into the blood through the stomach and intestines. The blood carries medicines throughout the body.

Because most medicines cause changes throughout the body, a medicine that treats a problem in one part of the body may affect other parts as well. For example, doctors sometimes give their patients medicine to treat cancer. The medicine kills cancer cells. But it also alters the activities of other body cells. As a result, the medicine may cause vomiting, hair loss, and other unwanted reactions.

The unwanted reactions to a medicine are called **side effects**. Almost every medicine causes side effects, but most aren't serious. Some disappear as you get used to a medicine. It's important to know a medicine's side effects before you take it. Your doctor or pharmacist can tell you what they are. If you feel strange after taking a medicine, tell a parent, teacher, or other trusted adult right away.

DRAW CONCLUSIONS Why do researchers try to develop new drugs that affect only one body part?

Two Types of Medicines

People must visit a doctor to get some medicines. Adults can buy others without seeing a doctor first. What's the difference between these two kinds of medicines?

Prescription medicines are medicines that can be bought only after a doctor has written an order, or a prescription, for them. A prescription shows the name of the patient, the name of the medicine, and how frequently the medicine should be taken. It also shows the amount of medicine the patient should take each time, or the **dosage**. A pharmacist uses this information to give the correct medicine to the patient.

Over-the-counter medicines, or OTC medicines, are medicines that can be bought without a prescription. OTC medicines treat minor health problems. They include pain relievers, cough medicines, and allergy medicines.

OTC medicines can be harmful if they are used too often, in incorrect amounts, or for the wrong reasons. The most important thing to remember is always to check with a parent first. Be sure to read labels carefully. Also check expiration dates. The **expiration date** is the date after which the medicine should not be used.

SUMMARIZE **What are the differences between prescription and OTC medicines?**

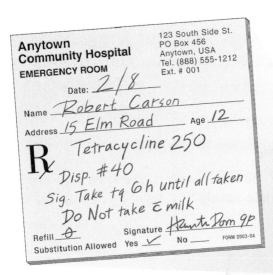

Anytown
Community Hospital
EMERGENCY ROOM

123 South Side St.
PO Box 456
Anytown, USA
Tel. (888) 555-1212
Ext. # 001

Date: 2/8

Name Robert Carson

Address 15 Elm Road   Age 12

R Tetracycline 250
Disp. #40
Sig. Take tq 6h until all taken
Do Not take c̄ milk

Refill 0   Signature Kenth Dom 9P
Substitution Allowed Yes ✓ No ___   FORM 2003-04

A doctor must write a prescription for some kinds of medicines. ▶

Safety First! Know these safety guidelines before taking any medicines.

Using Medicines Safely

If taken improperly, medicine can harm you. When taking any medicine, keep these guidelines in mind:

- Do not take any medicine on your own—always cooperate with your parents when taking medicine.
- Always follow the directions on the medicine.
- Never use someone else's prescription medicine, and never share yours with others.
- Report any side effects to a parent or other trusted adult.
- Do not take two or more medicines at the same time unless your doctor tells you to do so.
- Do not use new OTC medicines if their tamper-resistant packaging is missing or damaged.
- Do not take a medicine after its expiration date.
- Cooperate with your doctor by taking a medicine as long as directed.
- Ask your pharmacist if a medicine should be taken with or without food and if there are foods you shouldn't eat when taking it.
- Do not break, chew, crush, or dissolve pills, tablets, or capsules unless a doctor or a pharmacist tells you to do so.
- Keep all medicines in a safe place out of the reach of young children.
- Measure dosages carefully.
- Store medicines as directed on the label.

 SUMMARIZE How can you make sure you are using medicines safely?

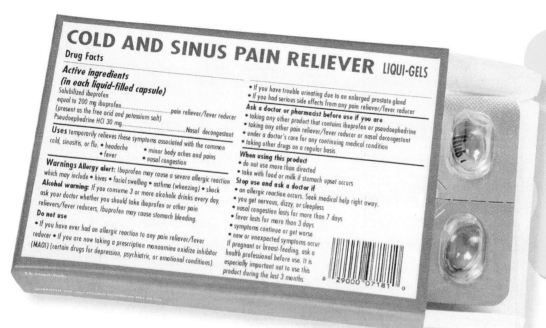

COLD AND SINUS PAIN RELIEVER LIQUI-GELS

Drug Facts

Active ingredients
(in each liquid-filled capsule)
Solubilized ibuprofen
equal to 200 mg ibuprofen..........................pain reliever/fever reducer
(present as the free acid and potassium salt)
Pseudoephedrine HCl 30 mg...........................Nasal decongestant

Uses temporarily relieves these symptoms associated with the common
cold, sinusitis, or flu. • headache • minor body aches and pains
• fever • nasal congestion

Warnings Allergy alert: Ibuprofen may cause a severe allergic reaction
which may include • hives • facial swelling • asthma (wheezing) • shock
Alcohol warning: If you consume 3 or more alcoholic drinks every day,
ask your doctor whether you should take ibuprofen or other pain
relievers/fever reducers. Ibuprofen may cause stomach bleeding.
Do not use
• If you have ever had an allergic reaction to any pain reliever/fever
reducer • If you are now taking a prescription monoamine oxidize inhibitor
(MAOI) (certain drugs for depression, psychiatric, or emotional conditions).

• If you have trouble urinating due to an enlarged prostate gland
• If you had serious side effects from any pain reliever/fever reducer
Ask a doctor or pharmacist before use if you are
• taking any other product that contains ibuprofen or pseudoephedrine
• taking any other pain reliever/fever reducer or nasal decongestant
• under a doctor's care for any continuing medical condition
• taking other drugs on a regular basis
When using this product
• do not use more than directed
• take with food or milk if stomach upset occurs
Stop use and ask a doctor if
• an allergic reaction occurs. Seek medical help right away.
• you get nervous, dizzy, or sleepless
• nasal congestion lasts for more than 7 days
• fever lasts for more than 3 days
• symptoms continue or get worse
• new or unexpected symptoms occur
If pregnant or breast-feeding, ask a
health professional before use. It is
especially important not to use this
product during the last 3 months

0 29000 07181 0

Quick Activity

Read a Medicine Label Check the label at the left and answer these questions. What symptoms does the medicine relieve? What are the medicine's possible side effects? For what reasons should you stop taking this medication?

Lesson 1 Summary and Review

1 Summarize with Vocabulary

Use vocabulary from this lesson to complete the statements.

Drugs that prevent, treat, or cure health problems are called _____. Medicines that require a doctor's order are called _____. The doctor's order specifies the kind of medicine and its _____, or how much to take. Other medicines, called _____, can be bought from the shelves at the store.

2 Where did about half of today's medicines originally come from?

3 Critical Thinking Why do you need to use the same precautions with OTC medicines as you do with prescription medicines?

4 ★Focus Skill SUMMARIZE Draw and complete this graphic organizer to answer this question: What are the most important things to remember about taking medicines?

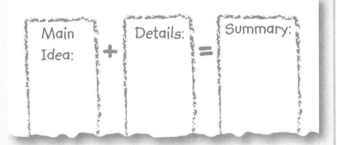

Main Idea: + Details: = Summary:

5 Write to Inform—Description

Describe the steps you would follow when deciding whether to take an OTC medicine for cold symptoms.

251

Effects of Drug Abuse

Lesson Focus

Drug abuse is harmful to the drug user and to others.

Why Learn This?

It is important to know about the negative effects that drug use can have on you, your family, your friends, and your community.

Vocabulary

drug abuse
dependence
addiction
withdrawal
tolerance
peer pressure

The Dangers of Drug Abuse

Drug abuse is the use of any illegal drug or the improper use of any medicine. Abusing drugs can put you on a dangerous path. Look at the consequences of abusing drugs shown on these pages to find out where drug abusers may be headed.

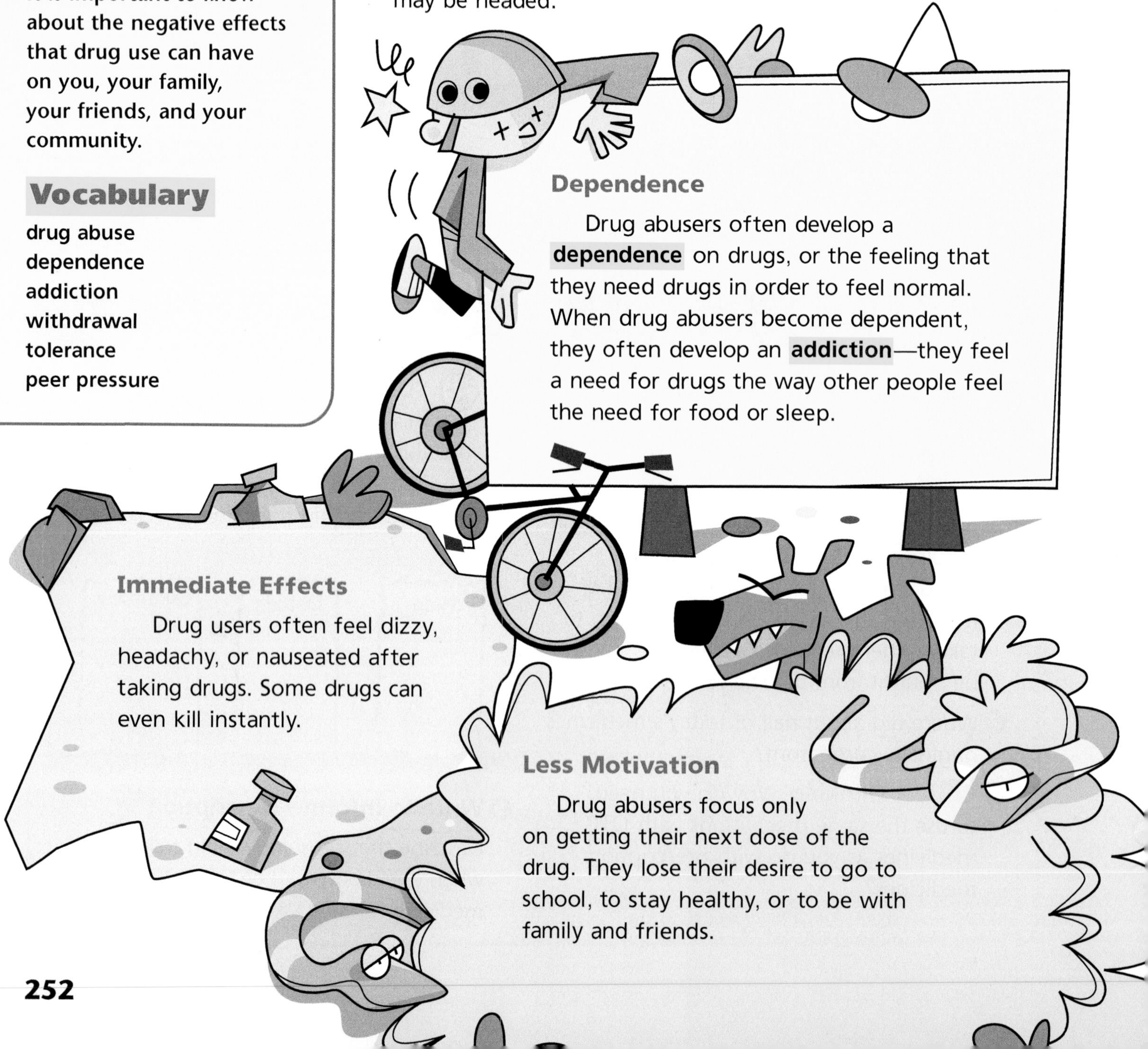

Dependence

Drug abusers often develop a **dependence** on drugs, or the feeling that they need drugs in order to feel normal. When drug abusers become dependent, they often develop an **addiction**—they feel a need for drugs the way other people feel the need for food or sleep.

Immediate Effects

Drug users often feel dizzy, headachy, or nauseated after taking drugs. Some drugs can even kill instantly.

Less Motivation

Drug abusers focus only on getting their next dose of the drug. They lose their desire to go to school, to stay healthy, or to be with family and friends.

Health Effects

Drug abusers may stop eating and may sleep very little. They may lose their ability to say *no* to unsafe activities. As a result, they may get into accidents or get sexually transmitted diseases, such as HIV.

Withdrawal Symptoms

When drug abusers try to stop, they often go through withdrawal. **Withdrawal** is the body's physical reaction to not getting a drug. Withdrawal symptoms can include chills, fever, nausea, depression, and severe pain.

Tolerance

Drug abusers often develop **tolerance**. This means they need to take larger or more frequent doses of the drug to get the same effect as when the drug was first taken.

Social and Emotional Problems

Drug abusers often become depressed and isolated because of the effects drugs have on the mind and body.

Overdose

An overdose is a drug dosage that is more than the body can handle. People who develop tolerance to a drug are more likely to take an overdose. A drug overdose causes a severe physical reaction or death.

Focus Skill

SUMMARIZE What are some of the possible dangers of drug abuse?

253

Reasons Some People Abuse Drugs

People say they use drugs for many different reasons. Some of their reasons may sound good, but they are based on myths. What's the real story about drugs?

"Nothing will happen to me."

Many young people injure themselves and others while they are using drugs. Some people even die.

"It makes me feel grown up."

Does acting silly or doing embarrassing and dangerous things make you feel grown up? Most people who abuse drugs do things they regret later.

"Everybody's doing it."

No, everyone isn't. In fact, most kids don't use drugs. **Peer pressure** is the influence that other people your age have on your decisions. Don't give in to peer pressure and use drugs just because some of your peers do. Use your own judgment. Choose friends who respect and share your choice not to use drugs.

"It makes me feel good."

Drug users feel terrible when the effects of the drugs wear off. They get sick and want more drugs.

ACTIVITY

Life Skills

Refuse Keely has lots of older friends. Some of them are experimenting with drugs. Keely is worried that she will be asked to try drugs. List at least five consequences of drug abuse. Then list at least five different ways Keely can refuse if she is ever in that situation. Practice these refusals with another person. Write a list of ideas for other ways to refuse drugs.

Some drugs make you feel powerful. But when the effect wears off, you feel depressed and anxious.

"I feel more confident."

"It helps me forget my problem."

The drugs will not make the problem go away. The drug user still has to face the problem when the effects of the drugs wear off.

SUMMARIZE Reread the thoughts here. What real-life facts show that these beliefs are based on myths?

Focus Skill

The Effects on Others

Drug abusers don't just ruin their own lives. They injure others in many different ways.

Drugs distort the way people see, hear, and feel things. They also affect coordination. Imagine what happens when someone on drugs drives a car or pilots an airplane!

Drug abusers often withdraw from family members and friends. They may steal to get the money they need for drugs. Sometimes they become violent.

Drug abuse is expensive. The cost affects everyone in the country. Law enforcement, medical expenses, property damage, and time lost from work because of drug use cost Americans almost $300 billion each year.

Injuries and property damage are just two of the many problems that are caused by people under the influence of drugs. ▼

 SUMMARIZE **What are some of the consequences of drug abuse?**

Lesson 2 Summary and Review

1 Summarize with Vocabulary

Use vocabulary and other terms from this lesson to complete the statements.

Using a drug in an inappropriate way is called _____. It can lead to _____, or a need to take more of the drug to get the same effect. It can also result in taking a greater amount than the body can handle, or _____. Finally, users may become _____ and rely on the drug completely.

2 Explain how drug tolerance makes an overdose more likely.

3 Critical Thinking Analyze the use of prescription and OTC medicines. Are they always safe? How can you tell the difference between helpful and harmful substances?

4 **SUMMARIZE** Draw and complete this graphic organizer to answer these questions: How can peer pressure influence a person's decision-making? When might peer pressure be positive?

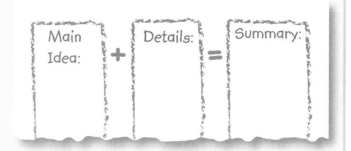

Main Idea: + Details: = Summary:

5 Write to Inform—Explanation

Compare and contrast drug dependence and drug addiction. How are their consequences the same? How are their consequences different?

Citizenship

Respecting Authority and the Law

Following laws is part of good citizenship. It helps maintain order and keep the entire community safe. When you respect the authorities in your community and the laws about the use of drugs, you are making a safer community for everyone.

Here are some ways to show respect for authority and the law:

- **Follow your family's rules about using medicines.**
- **Be aware of school rules about drugs and medicines, and follow those rules. If you need a medicine at school, make certain your parents arrange with the school for you to get your medicine.**
- **Refuse to use other people's medicines. That includes both prescription and OTC medicines.**
- **Be aware of drug use around you. If you are offered drugs, report it immediately to a parent or other trusted adult.**
- **If you find drugs or other dangerous substances, don't touch them. Leave the area, and return with a parent or other trusted adult.**
- **Help inform others about the dangers of using drugs.**

Activity

You can show good citizenship by giving people information about the help that is available to them. Make a poster that guides drug abusers to resources for helping them with their problems.

Abuse of Medicines

Stimulants and Depressants

Many people start each morning with a boost they get from a cup of coffee. Coffee, along with tea and chocolate, often contains caffeine, a mild stimulant. A **stimulant** is a drug that speeds up the way the brain works. Stimulants make a person feel more awake and alert. A little bit of caffeine isn't harmful, but heavy use of caffeine can cause sleeplessness and other problems.

◀ Many products, including coffee, tea, chocolate, and some soft drinks, contain caffeine.

Amphetamines (am·FET·uh·meenz) are powerful stimulants that greatly increase the brain's activity. Doctors prescribe amphetamines for patients with certain health problems.

Some people who want an extra jolt of energy abuse amphetamines. This is very risky. Tolerance to stimulants develops quickly. The larger doses needed by an abuser can make the heart work so hard that the heart muscle can be damaged.

The diagram on page 259 shows some short-term effects of amphetamine use. As you can see, stimulants speed up the body in many ways, causing a temporary feeling of increased energy. But depression and a desire for more of the drug soon follow.

A **depressant** is a drug that slows the activity of the brain. Depressants also slow the heart and relax the muscles. This makes a user feel sleepy and less alert. Depressants include tranquilizers, sedatives, and alcohol.

Tranquilizers calm people by acting on the part of the brain that causes anxiety. Doctors prescribe them to treat severe nervousness and to relax patients before surgery.

Sedatives, like tranquilizers, have a calming effect. But they also cause sleepiness. Doctors sometimes prescribe sedatives for patients who have trouble sleeping. One group of sedatives, barbiturates, used to be prescribed often. But they are habit-forming and are often abused. Doctors now prescribe newer, less addictive sedatives.

Sedatives and tranquilizers are dangerous and addictive when they are abused. Depressants can disrupt messages from the brain that control movement, thought, and speech. An overdose can shut down the brain completely and stop the messages that control breathing, leading to death.

COMPARE AND CONTRAST **How are depressants like stimulants? How are they different?**

Consumer Activity

Make Buying Decisions
Caffeine is often added to OTC pain relievers because it boosts their effects. Read the labels of several aspirin-free OTC pain relievers. List the ones that contain caffeine. Tell which aspirin-free pain-reliever you would choose for a simple headache. Explain why.

Effects of Stimulants

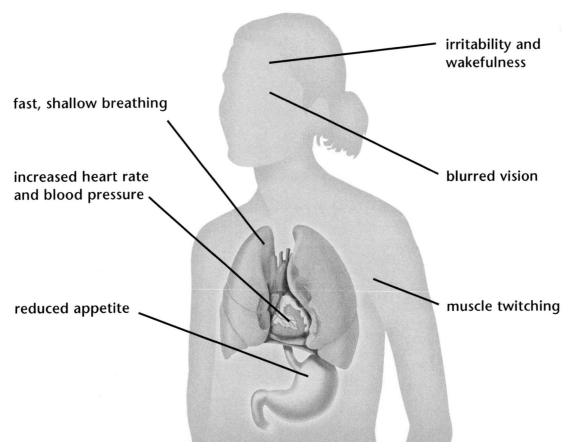

irritability and wakefulness

fast, shallow breathing

blurred vision

increased heart rate and blood pressure

muscle twitching

reduced appetite

259

Doctors are always on the lookout for new ways to relieve pain without the use of medicines. **Transcutaneous** (trans•kyoo•TAY•nee•uhs) **E**lectrical **N**erve **S**timulation, or TENS, is one way to conquer pain without using any drugs. Mild electrical impulses are sent through wires to places on a patient's skin, interfering with the sense of pain.

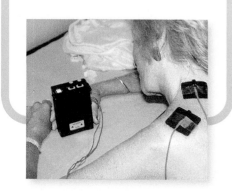

Narcotics

Narcotics (nar•KAH•tiks) are powerful depressant drugs that slow a person down and relieve pain. Narcotics include medicines made from the opium poppy plant. These drugs are called opiates. They include morphine, codeine, and oxycodone.

Morphine is a strong narcotic that interferes with the brain's ability to sense pain. It is a very effective pain reliever. Doctors use it to stop severe pain in people who have surgery or serious illnesses.

It is illegal and extremely dangerous to take morphine without a prescription. Dependence on morphine and tolerance for it develop quickly.

Codeine is a milder opiate. It relieves mild pain and stops coughs.

Oxycodone is another powerful narcotic drug. It is prescribed to treat severe pain. Some people abuse this drug to get a feeling of pleasure. Oxycodone has many side effects, including nausea, depression, and difficulty in sleeping. People who abuse oxycodone can quickly become addicted.

Focus Skill

SUMMARIZE What are narcotics, and what are they commonly used for?

Codeine is a narcotic found in some prescription cough medicines and pain relievers. ▶

PHARMACY   #181

Rx:**4104270** Dr. SCHEF   T
GRAHAM   Jan 05,200
TAKE TWO TEASPOONFULS BY MOUTH
EVERY FOUR HOURS AS NEEDED FOR
COUGH

GUAIFENESIN/CODEINE ML (BARR)

Qty:240 ML   Refills: 0
Discard After: ST4
Caution: Federal law prohibits the transfer of this drug to any person other than the patient for whom it was pre

MAY CAUSE DROWSINESS.
ALCOHOL MAY INTENSIFY THIS EFFECT.
USE CARE WHEN OPERATING A CAR
OR DANGEROUS MACHINERY.

TAKE WITH
FOOD OR MILK

Do not take alcohol or non
prescription drugs without
consulting your doctor

Steroids

Steroids are hormone drugs that doctors prescribe to treat many diseases. Some steroids, like prednisone, are used to decrease swelling. Prednisone is also often a treatment for asthma. Steroids are powerful and useful, but because they have serious side effects, most are not abused.

One group of steroids, however, is abused. These drugs are called anabolic (an•uh•BAHL•ik) steroids. They are prescribed for patients whose bodies do not produce enough of the hormones that promote normal muscle growth. Some people think that they will become stronger if they take anabolic steroids. But anabolic steroid abuse is very dangerous.

Tolerance to steroids develops quickly, and side effects can be deadly. Teenagers who abuse steroids stop growing. They develop acne and may lose hair or grow too much hair. Worse, they may develop tumors on their liver. Steroids can have harmful effects on the male and female reproductive systems. And they may cause heart attacks and strokes.

DRAW CONCLUSIONS Under what circumstances should steroids be used?

Quick Activity

Effects of Steroids
Use the diagram on page 259 as a guide, and draw a diagram that shows the effects of steroids on the body.

Lesson 3 Summary and Review

1 Summarize with Vocabulary
Use vocabulary and other terms from this lesson to complete the statements.

Drugs that speed up the way the brain works are called _____. Depressants affect the nervous system by _____ the way the brain works. They include _____, strong pain-relieving medicines that come from the poppy plant. These are also called _____.

2 Critical Thinking How does tolerance to amphetamines increase the risks associated with using them?

3 Why are barbiturates rarely prescribed now?

4 **SUMMARIZE** Draw and complete this graphic organizer to answer this question: What are the benefits and risks of each of the four groups of drugs discussed in this lesson?

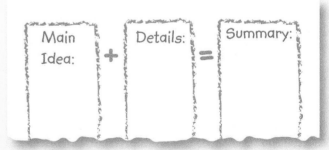

Main Idea: + Details: = Summary:

5 Write to Inform—Description
Describe for an audience of third-grade students the dangers of abusing prescription medicines.

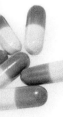

261

Illegal Drugs

Dangers of Marijuana Use

Marijuana (mair•uh•WAH•nuh) is a drug that comes from a type of hemp plant. The leaves and flowers of the plants contain a potent drug that affects the brain and changes the way people see, hear, and feel. Marijuana is usually smoked, but sometimes it is eaten. The figure on page 263 shows how marijuana affects the body.

Marijuana often makes users of the drug feel anxious. It distorts the senses, interferes with the ability to concentrate, and slows the reflexes. It is hard for someone using marijuana to play sports, swim, ride a bike, or do schoolwork.

Lesson Focus

Marijuana, narcotics, and hallucinogens are powerful and dangerous drugs. Inhalants are common household substances that are harmful when used.

Why Learn This?

Knowing the harmful effects of these substances can help you decide to avoid them.

Vocabulary

marijuana
inhalants
cocaine
crack
hallucinogens

▲ Marijuana comes from a type of hemp plant. Other plants of this family give fibers that are made into rope.

People who use marijuana become less interested in achievement. They may begin to skip school, and their grades may drop.

The use of marijuana has many negative effects on the user's health. Many of the more than 400 substances found in marijuana are poisons. Some of the poisons are the same cancer-causing substances found in tobacco smoke. Someone who smokes five marijuana cigarettes, or joints, each week takes in the same amount of cancer-causing chemicals as someone who smokes a pack of cigarettes each day. Therefore, long-term marijuana use can cause cancer and lung diseases. Long-term use also causes damage to the brain and damage to reproductive cells.

 SUMMARIZE How does marijuana affect the body?

Effects of Marijuana

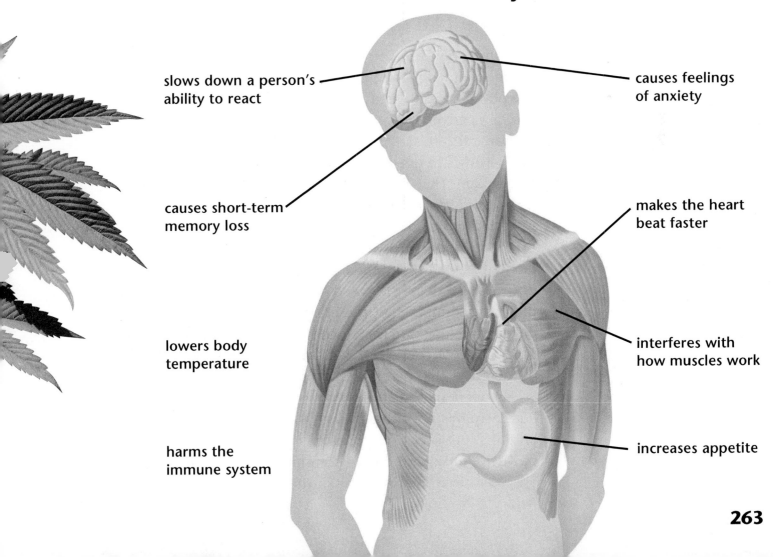

slows down a person's ability to react

causes feelings of anxiety

causes short-term memory loss

makes the heart beat faster

lowers body temperature

interferes with how muscles work

harms the immune system

increases appetite

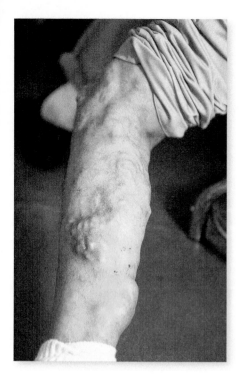

▲ This man's veins are scarred because he has injected heroin into them many times.

▲ Heroin is made from the sticky sap that comes from the seedpods of the opium poppy. Heroin is an addictive drug that is illegal in the United States.

Illegal Narcotics

Remember that narcotics, which are made from the opium poppy plant, include the powerful pain-relievers morphine, codeine, and oxycodone. The illegal drug heroin is also a narcotic.

Narcotics abusers use the medicines inappropriately. They use narcotics to get a feeling of pleasure rather than to relieve pain. They develop dependence and tolerance quickly. Users need larger and larger doses of narcotics to get the same feelings of pleasure. But narcotics have severe side effects, including sick stomach, severe emotional and mental problems, and the inability to sleep. Very large doses can be deadly because narcotics slow down a person's breathing so much that the brain does not receive enough oxygen. Breathing may stop completely, causing death. Taking narcotic drugs without a prescription is illegal and dangerous. Using heroin is always illegal.

Heroin is an addictive narcotic that has no medical use. Pure heroin is a white powder, but heroin sold illegally on the street is not pure. Dealers mix heroin with sugar, powdered milk, and other—sometimes deadly—substances. The user never knows what's in the mix.

264

Heroin users begin to need more and more heroin. When heroin addicts can't get the drug, they go through painful withdrawal. Users who inject heroin face other dangers too. Those who share needles can get painful skin sores, as well as HIV infections and hepatitis.

CAUSE AND EFFECT **Explain how narcotics use can lead to unsafe situations such as HIV infection.**

Quick Activity

Analyze Effects The people in these pictures all have important responsibilities. Explain how using drugs might interfere with those responsibilities.

tutor

bus driver

student

doctor

Inhalants

Inhalants are products that some people use by breathing in their fumes. Most of the chemicals in inhalants are poisons and can be dangerous if inhaled. Products that give off fumes should be used only in areas with a lot of air flowing through and only for the purposes for which they were intended.

Sniffing inhalants is dangerous. It causes the lungs to fill with poisonous fumes. This leaves little room in the lungs for oxygen and, therefore, less oxygen in the brain. Sniffing inhalants also forces the heart to beat faster and unevenly, which can cause sudden death.

Short-term use of inhalants causes increased heartbeat, breathing problems, dizziness, and headaches. Long-term use can damage the kidneys, the liver, the blood, and the nervous system. Inhalant users can also develop tolerance. As they sniff more and more poison, the risk of permanent harm and death increases.

SEQUENCE Describe the sequence of effects on the body as a person sniffs inhalants.

Using inhalants is a dead end!

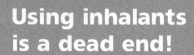

BRAIN
Destroys brain cells, causes nerve damage

HEART
Can cause heart attack

LIVER and KIDNEYS
Can cause long-term damage

BLOOD
Destroys blood cells, weakens immunity

LUNGS
Damages lung tissues, can stop breathing

MUSCLE and BONE
Weakens muscles, stops bone marrow from functioning

Other Illegal Drugs

Cocaine (koh·KAYN) is a strong stimulant made from the leaves of the coca plant. Cocaine is a powder. **Crack** is a rocklike, highly addictive form of cocaine.

Tolerance to cocaine develops quickly. It develops even more rapidly in crack users, who may become addicted after trying it only once. And cocaine use can be deadly. Taking it can lead to stroke, heart attack, or other deadly medical conditions.

Hallucinogens (huh·LOO·sih·nuh·jenz) are illegal drugs that affect the brain and distort the senses. They change the way a person sees, hears, and feels things.

LSD and PCP are hallucinogens. Both cause users to lose touch with reality in dangerous ways. LSD is colorless and odorless. The hallucinations, or false sensations, it produces may be very frightening. PCP often causes violent behavior, and using it can lead to heart and lung failure, and death.

DRAW CONCLUSIONS Why are hallucinogen users likely to have accidents?

Lesson 4 Summary and Review

① Summarize with Vocabulary
Use vocabulary and other terms from this lesson to complete the statements.

Many illegal drugs come from plants. _____ comes from a type of hemp plant. _____ is an illegal narcotic that comes from the poppy plant. Both _____ and _____ come from the leaves of the coca plant. Drugs that you breathe in are called _____. Those that cause hallucinations are called _____.

② Name two narcotics, and explain why they are dangerous.

③ Critical Thinking How can common, legal products be as harmful as illegal drugs?

④ (Focus Skill) SUMMARIZE Draw and complete this graphic organizer to answer these questions: How does heroin affect the body? What are the consequences of using heroin?

Main Idea: + Details: = Summary:

⑤ Write to Express—Business Letter

Write a letter to a newspaper telling about the harm that drug abuse causes to those not using the drugs.

Refuse
To Use Drugs

There are many reasons that people start to use drugs. One reason is peer pressure, which is hard to resist. For example, you may be offered drugs by someone you like. Or a friend may try to convince you that drugs will make you feel better or make you more popular. How can you stay drug-free when you are feeling pressured?

Remember the consequences of drug use. Keep in mind that drugs are harmful to your health. Practice refusal skills to help you say *no* and stay healthy.

1 **Say *no* firmly. State your reasons for saying *no*.**

If someone offers you drugs, say that you will not use them. Tell the person that drugs are harmful to your health and are illegal.

2 **Avoid possible problem situations.**

Get away from troublemakers. You don't need to become involved in harmful, illegal activities in order to be popular.

3 Stay with people who also refuse to take part in harmful activities.

Choose something fun to do instead. Remember, activities involving drugs are not cool—but many other activities are!

4 Ignore the person.

One way to get your message across clearly is to ignore an invitation to use drugs.

Problem Solving

A. Rama is visiting her friend Tracy. Tracy tells Rama she has found a great way to get high without using drugs. She shows Rama a bottle of something and asks her to sniff it. How can Rama say *no* to inhalant abuse?
  • Describe how Rama can show responsible behavior by using refusal skills to say *no* to Tracy.

B. Salvador is a good football player, but he is smaller than most of his teammates. His older cousin, who plays high school football, tells Salvador that he uses anabolic steroids to make his muscles larger and stronger. He offers Salvador some pills.
  • Describe how Salvador can say *no* to his cousin.

Avoiding Drug Use

Why You Should Refuse Drugs

Most people *never* use drugs. There are many reasons to avoid taking drugs and good ways to refuse to take them. And there are many people and organizations that can help you say *no* to drugs.

The first reason to refuse drugs is that drug use is deadly. Each year, drugs cause thousands of deaths in the United States. In some cases, people die from drug overdoses. In others, they die because poisonous substances are mixed in with the drugs. And in still others, drug use causes car crashes. Even when drugs don't kill, they can make a person very sick.

Another important reason to refuse drugs is that they are illegal. People who are caught buying, selling, or using illegal drugs usually go to jail.

Using drugs keeps people from fulfilling their responsibilities. It also affects their relationships. Once people are addicted, getting drugs becomes the most important thing in their lives. They neglect their families, friends, schoolwork, and other interests. They may break the law to get drugs or to get money to buy drugs. Drug users do things that are harmful, illegal, or embarrassing.

 (Focus Skill) **SUMMARIZE** **What consequences of drug use make refusing drugs important?**

Most people have fun without drugs. ▼

Drugs and Their Effects

Drugs	Examples	Some Possible Short-Term Effects	Some Possible Long-Term Effects
Stimulants	amphetamine cocaine crack cocaine MDMA (ecstasy) methamphetamine	increased respiration, heart rate, and blood pressure; dizziness; sleeplessness; chest pain; convulsions	jumpiness, tremors, violent behavior, eating disorders, heart problems, addiction
Depressants	barbiturates GHB (liquid ecstasy) Rohypnol® (R2, roofies) quaalude	decreased respiration, heart rate, and blood pressure; nausea; slow reactions; depression; confusion; seizures	anxiety, depression, dependence, addiction
Marijuana	marijuana hashish	poor concentration and coordination, increased heart rate and appetite	lung damage and cancer if smoked; brain damage
Narcotics	oxycodone morphine codeine opium heroin	lack of concentration, slow reactions, sleep changes, depressed breathing, blood pressure changes, convulsions	mood swings; heart, lung, and liver damage; skin sores, vein damage, and HIV infection if injected; addiction
Inhalants	solvents, aerosol propellants	nosebleed, nausea, loss of muscle control, memory loss, loss of consciousness, heart attack, stroke	lung congestion; violent behavior; hallucinations; brain, kidney, and liver damage
Hallucinogens	MDMA (ecstasy) ketamine (K) LSD PCP	seizures, mood swings, hallucinations, trancelike state, panic, "bad trip" that could last for several days, rush	mental disorders, brain damage, dependence, addiction
Anabolic Steroids	steroids	cramps, dehydration, nausea	acne, liver disease, high blood pressure, mental and emotional problems, stunted growth

How to Refuse Drugs

You have a right and a responsibility to refuse drugs. You don't have to give explanations or get into arguments to refuse them. You don't have to feel guilty, stupid, or uncool. Remember, most people don't abuse drugs.

Know as much about drugs as you can. Know what they are, how they work, and what their dangers are. Think about the harmful effects that drugs can have on your health and future. Remember that drugs can kill you.

Identify strategies for avoiding drugs. One strategy is to get involved in other things. Check out school clubs, sports teams, school or community plays, religious groups, and other groups in your community. Volunteer to help with community projects. There are hundreds of things you can do *instead* of using drugs.

Practice ways to refuse drugs if they are offered. You can simply say, "No, thank you." You can tell the person you have something else to do, or you can suggest something else to do. Or just walk away. No matter how you refuse drugs, you are making the right choice.

 **SUMMARIZE Identify ways to avoid drug use.**

ACTIVITY

Life Skills

Make Decisions

Jacob is new at school, and he wants to fit in with the other kids. He doesn't, however, want to use drugs. Write a skit that gives Jacob the information he needs to make a responsible decision.

Where to Get Help in Refusing Drugs

Sometimes life can be very confusing. You might feel pressure from friends to try drugs. You might want to use drugs to forget problems at home or at school. You might think you have no one to turn to for help with your problems. There are many people who can help you find solutions to your problems. Drugs will only make your problems worse.

At home, talk to parents, guardians, or older brothers and sisters about problems you may be having. At school, talk to a favorite teacher or a school counselor. You might be surprised at how helpful they can be.

There are people in your community who can help you, too. You can talk to a trusted adult such as a doctor, a member of the clergy, or a coach. They can all help you refuse drugs.

ACTIVITY

Building Good Character

Caring Mark's friend Shane refuses drugs by finding other things to do instead. Mark prefers to just say *no* and walk away. How can Mark show support for Shane's way of refusing drugs? Write a short skit about a conversation that Mark and Shane have that shows support for Shane's refusal strategy.

If you have a problem, don't turn to drugs. The problem will still be there when the effects of the drug wear off. Find someone such as a parent or another trusted adult you can talk to. ▼

▲ More and more young people are turning away from drugs.

Ask the reference librarian at your school or town library for the names of national organizations that can help you learn ways to refuse drugs. These organizations include the National Clearinghouse for Alcohol and Drug Information, the National Center on Alcoholism and Drug Dependence, and Narcotics Anonymous.

 SUMMARIZE Explain ways of maintaining healthy relationships and resisting peer pressure.

Lesson 5 Summary and Review

❶ Summarize with Vocabulary

Use terms from this lesson to complete the statements.

Drug use is deadly and illegal. It can lead to _____, or the need to have a drug to feel normal. The responsible decision is always to _____ to abuse drugs. You can get help in refusing from organizations such as _____.

❷ Demonstrate the use of refusal skills by listing three reasons to refuse drugs.

❸ Critical Thinking Why is it important to practice the way you would refuse drugs?

❹ (Focus Skill) **SUMMARIZE** Draw and complete this graphic organizer to answer this question: Why do you have a right as well as a responsibility to refuse drugs?

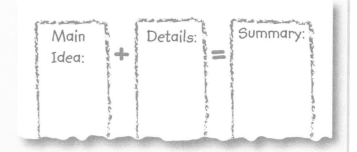

| Main Idea: | + | Details: | = | Summary: |

❺ Write to Inform—Description ✏

Choose one method of refusing to use drugs. Describe ways to use this method. What might you say or do?

274

ACTIVITIES

Physical Education

Plan Alternative Activities One good way to avoid drugs is to plan safe activities that you enjoy. Make a list of your favorite games, sports, and other physical activities. Choose one, and describe it to a friend.

Science

Research Caffeine Many common foods and medicines contain caffeine. Read the labels on several of these products. Make a list of the ones that contain caffeine. You may notice that caffeine isn't listed on the labels of coffee and tea. This is because caffeine occurs naturally in these products and isn't an added ingredient.

Technology Project

Make a Video Make a list of at least ten *dos* and *don'ts* about medicines. Write a script and produce a video that tells people how to use medicines safely. If a video camera is not available, perform a skit for your class.

GO ONLINE For more activities, visit The Learning Site.
www.harcourtschool.com/health

Home & Community

Communicating Write a song that tells other students some different ways to refuse or avoid drugs. Be sure to include the ways given on pages 268–269 as well as any other ways you can think of to refuse or avoid drug use. Perform your song for your class or for another class and have sheets with the lyrics on them to hand out to everyone after the performance.

Career Link

Research Pharmacologist Imagine that you are a research pharmacologist, a person who does research to find new medicines. Write a research plan about how you might investigate plants as a source of possible medicines for cancer. Explain why you think plants might be a good source for medicines.

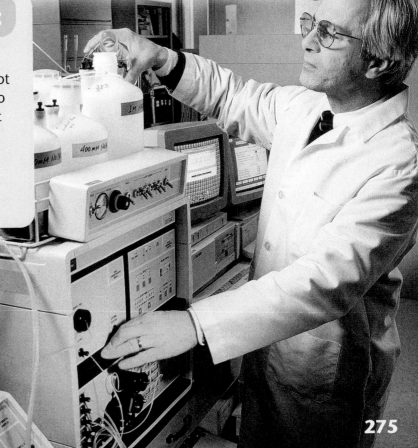

Reading Skill

SUMMARIZE

Draw and then use this graphic organizer to answer questions 1 and 2.

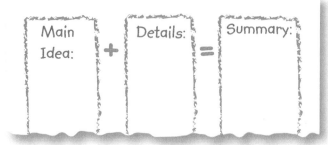

Main Idea: + Details: = Summary:

1 Why should a person refuse to abuse drugs?

2 Why is it important to practice the way you would refuse drugs?

Use Vocabulary

Match each term in Column B with its meaning in Column A.

Column A	Column B
3 Powerful stimulant	**A** inhalant
4 Need for larger or more frequent doses of a drug to get the same effect	**B** amphetamine
	C dependence
	D tolerance
5 Product that gives off harmful fumes	**E** marijuana
6 Illegal drug that comes from a hemp plant	
7 Feeling that drugs are needed in order to feel normal	

Check Understanding

Choose the letter of the correct answer.

8 Drugs that prevent, treat, or cure health problems are called _____. (p. 246)
  A antibiotics   **C** depressants
  B narcotics   **D** medicines

9 Which are strategies for refusing drugs? (pp. 268–269)
  F saying *no* and stating your reasons
  G finding alternative activities
  H avoiding unsafe situations
  J all of the above

10 What is withdrawal? (p. 253)
  A the need for more and more drugs
  B the feeling that you need drugs to feel normal
  C the body's reaction to not getting drugs
  D a side effect of OTC medicines

11 Why do drugs often have side effects? (p. 248)
  F because they do not work
  G because they circulate throughout the body
  H because they affect only their target body part
  J because the body changes temperature

12 What information is **NOT** found on a prescription for medicine? (p. 249)
  A the patient's name
  B the recommended dosage
  C the medicine's side effects
  D how often the medicine should be taken

13 People who inject drugs are at increased risk of _____. (p. 265)
  F blood infections   **H** heart attack
  G withdrawal   **J** stroke

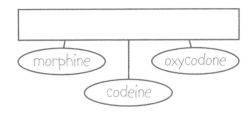

14 Which of these goes in the empty box? (p. 260)

A narcotics   C stimulants

B hallucinogens   D sedatives

15 Why do some people use illegal drugs? (pp. 254–255)

F They think no one else uses drugs.

G They recognize the dangers of drugs.

H They are confident.

J They think drugs will help them.

16 Over-the-counter drugs _____. (p. 249)

A are better than prescription drugs

B are more dangerous than prescription drugs

C do not require a prescription

D should always be recommended by a doctor

17 All drugs, including medicines, _____. (p. 250)

F are dangerous if used improperly

G are safe to use

H must be prescribed by a doctor

J come from plants

18 Hallucinogens _____. (p. 267)

A include cocaine   C are opiates

B strengthen muscles D include LSD

19 Steroids can _____. (p. 261)

F damage your liver

G cause hallucinations

H change the pattern of blood flow

J be OTC medicines

20 Aspirin and quinine are _____. (p. 247)

A prescription medicines

B used for treating asthma

C medicines that came from plants

D medicines used to treat plants

Think Critically

21 Before a drug company can sell a new medicine, the U.S. Food and Drug Administration (FDA) must study the medicine and its effects on people who take it. Why is this an important step?

22 Why is it unwise to try an illegal drug just to see what it's like?

Apply Skills

23 **BUILDING GOOD CHARACTER**

Citizenship How might you exercise good citizenship if you become aware of a family friend who is abusing drugs?

24 **LIFE SKILLS**

Refuse Imagine that you have a headache at school. A friend tells you that she has an OTC medicine that would make you feel better. She offers you a pill. Describe strategies for refusing the drug.

Write About Health

25 **Write to Inform—Explanation** Explain the impact of peer pressure on decision-making. How can practicing and using refusal skills as a teenager help you as an adult?

IDENTIFY CAUSE AND EFFECT Often when you read, you must understand cause-and-effect relationships. An effect is what happens. A cause is the reason that something happens. Use the Reading in Health Handbook on pages 404–405 and this graphic organizer to help you read the health facts in this chapter.

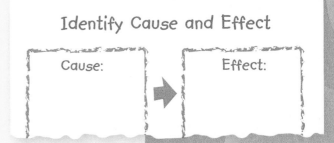

Identify Cause and Effect

Cause:		Effect:

Health Graph

INTERPRET DATA Using alcohol and tobacco leads to more than 500,000 deaths in the United States every year. Look at the graph below. About how many more deaths are caused by using alcohol and tobacco than are caused by AIDS, car crashes, murder, and using illegal drugs combined?

Some Causes of Death in the United States

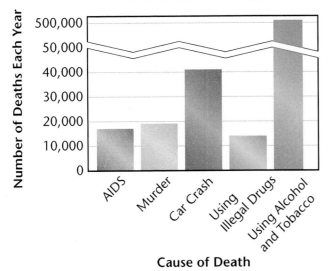

Number of Deaths Each Year

500,000
50,000
40,000
30,000
20,000
10,000
0

AIDS · Murder · Car Crash · Using Illegal Drugs · Using Alcohol and Tobacco

Cause of Death

Daily Physical Activity

Avoiding alcohol and tobacco is essential to good health. You can have fun in ways that are good for your body by exercising daily and doing activities you like.

 Be Active!
Use the selection, Track 9, **Hop to It**, to practice some healthful activity choices.

Dangers of Smoking Tobacco

Toxins from Cigarette Smoke

Cigarette smoke makes you cough and causes your eyes to water. But did you know that tobacco smoke also contains toxins, or poisons? Tobacco smoke has many harmful effects on your body. It is so dangerous that it's against the law for young people in the United States to buy tobacco products.

Tobacco (tuh·BAK·oh) is a substance made from the dried leaves of a plant. It is smoked or chewed by some people. Many people think that tobacco is not really unhealthful. That's because most of tobacco's harmful effects cannot be seen until later in a user's life. But tobacco use kills more people in the United States than alcohol, car crashes, murder, drug use, and fires combined!

Tobacco smoke contains more than 4,000 substances. Many of these substances are poisons. **Nicotine** (NIK·uh·teen) is an addictive poison found in tobacco.

Carbon monoxide, an odorless gas, makes up a large percentage of cigarette smoke. Furnaces and cars also release this gas. People can die from inhaling too much carbon monoxide. ▼

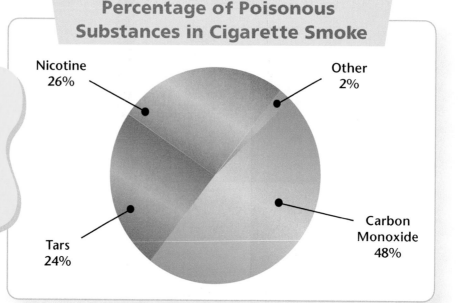

Percentage of Poisonous Substances in Cigarette Smoke

Nicotine 26%
Other 2%
Carbon Monoxide 48%
Tars 24%

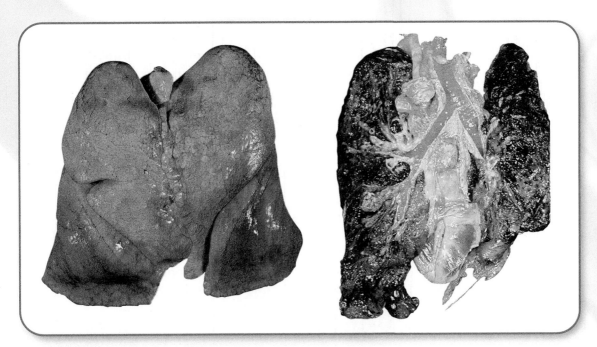

▲ The nonsmoker's lungs, on the left, are pink and healthy. The smoker's lungs, on the right, are gray and clogged with tar. Smoking causes 80 percent of all lung cancer cases.

When a person uses tobacco, nicotine enters the bloodstream and travels through the body. It stimulates the pleasure centers of the brain. However, it also stimulates the nervous and cardiovascular systems. This makes these systems work harder and leads to problems such as high blood pressure.

Tobacco smoke also contains **carbon monoxide** (KAR•buhn muh•NAHKS•yd), a poisonous gas that fills the spaces in red blood cells that normally carry oxygen. Each blood cell is able to carry less oxygen. This makes your heart and lungs work harder. Carbon monoxide also makes you cough and wheeze when you do things like run, play sports, and climb stairs.

Have you ever noticed the black, sticky grime left on a barbecue grill? That grime is caused by **tars** left by the smoke from burning substances. Tobacco smoke also contains tars. When you breathe in tobacco smoke, these tars are trapped in your lungs. The tars form a thick layer in your lungs. You can probably guess how this would affect your ability to breathe and get oxygen to your bloodstream. You can see the results of smoking in the photograph of the smoker's lungs on this page.

 CAUSE AND EFFECT What are some of the effects of nicotine on the body?

Did You Know?

Nicotine is a strong poison. Even a small amount of pure nicotine can cause vomiting, weakness, rapid and weak pulse, and even death. Because it is so poisonous, it is sometimes used as an insecticide on plants.

How Smoking Can Harm You

Inhaling smoke affects smokers and nonsmokers. People with asthma or allergies have trouble breathing if they are around tobacco smoke. Smokers get more nose, throat, and lung infections because the smoke makes it harder for those body parts to heal.

Effects of Tobacco on the Body

Face and Skin Smokers develop wrinkles at a younger age.

Mouth Smokers are more likely to get cancer of the mouth than nonsmokers are. Tobacco juice damages gums and teeth. Smokers' teeth also become stained.

Throat Tobacco smoke irritates the throat and can cause throat cancer. Smoking can make the voice thick and gravelly. It can also increase the likelihood of larynx cancer.

Brain Nicotine reaches the brain ten seconds after being inhaled. After repeated use, the brain and body become physically dependent on this drug.

Esophagus Of the number of people who get cancer of the esophagus, 80 percent are smokers.

Heart Smokers are more likely than nonsmokers to develop heart disease. Smoking also leads to high blood pressure.

Lungs Tars from smoke clog the lungs, causing coughing. Smoking damages the air sacs in the lungs, causing **emphysema** (em•fuh•SEE•muh), a disease that makes breathing difficult. Of those who die from this disease, 87 percent are smokers.

Quick Activity

Analyze Diagrams
Which body systems and organs are affected by tobacco use? Is there any system that is not affected by tobacco?

Stomach Nicotine increases the production of stomach acid, which may contribute to ulcers. Smoking is also thought to double the risk of cancer of the digestive system.

Pancreas Chemicals in tobacco have been linked to cancer of the pancreas.

Many smokers have bad breath. The smoke also makes their hair and clothing smell bad. Since smoking affects the ability to smell and taste, a smoker probably doesn't even notice how bad he or she smells. But other people do.

You already know that nutrition is important to overall health. Heavy smokers often do not feel hungry, and they often fail to eat the proper foods they need to stay healthy. A smoker's body also is less able to absorb some vitamins and other nutrients from foods. Because of this, smoking can lead to malnutrition. Some people think smoking will help them lose weight or stay slim. The truth is that the malnutrition and lack of exercise most smokers experience are just as likely to lead to weight gain as they are to weight loss.

DRAW CONCLUSIONS Why do you think tobacco use kills many people?

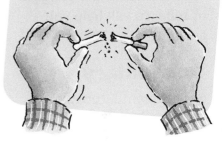

Did You Know?

In 1990, about 30 million adults died worldwide. Of these deaths, 10 percent, or 3 million, were caused by tobacco use. Researchers project that by the year 2030, worldwide deaths caused by tobacco use will jump to almost 20 percent. The percent will continue to rise unless users give up tobacco.

Lesson 1 Summary and Review

1 Summarize with Vocabulary

Use vocabulary from this lesson to complete the statements.

Cigarettes are made from the _____ plant. It contains the addictive substance _____. When smoked, tobacco releases _____, an odorless gas. Tobacco smoke also contains sticky, black _____. Smoking damages the air sacs in the lungs, causing _____, a disease that makes breathing difficult.

2 Describe how tobacco is addictive.

3 Critical Thinking What are two reasons to avoid tobacco?

4 **CAUSE AND EFFECT** Draw and complete this graphic organizer to show the harmful effects of smoking.

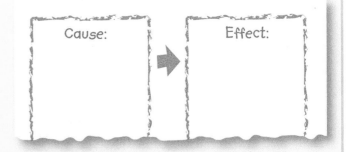

Cause:		Effect:

5 Write to Inform—Explanation

You read in the lesson that nicotine stimulates the pleasure centers in the brain. For this reason, many people smoke cigarettes to relax. Write a paragraph explaining why smoking is not a healthful way to manage stress.

Other Dangers of Tobacco Use

Lesson Focus

Tobacco can harm you even if you don't smoke.

Why Learn This?

Understanding the dangers of tobacco will help you avoid it.

Vocabulary

environmental tobacco smoke (ETS)
smokeless tobacco

Danger to Nonsmokers

Have you noticed more "No Smoking" signs lately? In many states and cities, it is illegal to smoke in public places. That's because people who smoke harm not only their own bodies but also the bodies of nonsmokers. Nonsmokers can be harmed by **environmental tobacco smoke (ETS)**—smoke in the air they breathe. ETS causes watery eyes, a burning feeling in the nose, and asthma attacks. People who are around ETS for a long time can have all of the same health problems that smokers can have.

ETS is dangerous because it has the same harmful substances in it that a smoker inhales. Scientists have linked ETS with lung cancer, heart disease, and other health problems in adults. But the people who are most harmed by ETS are children. Children who breathe ETS every day are more likely to get pneumonia, bronchitis, and other serious respiratory diseases.

SUMMARIZE Why is ETS dangerous?

People who don't smoke can be affected by smoke from those who do. ▶

Personal Health Plan ▶

Real-Life Situation

Suppose you walk into a room filled with ETS.

Real-Life Plan

List five ways you can protect yourself from ETS.

284

◀ The rate of mouth cancer is 50 times higher among people who use smokeless tobacco than among nonusers. Mouth cancer can disfigure the face and lead to death.

WARNING: This product may cause mouth cancer.

Smokeless Tobacco

More and more people are deciding not to begin smoking cigarettes because of the health risks to themselves and to others. Still, many people think that it is only tobacco smoke that is harmful. They believe they can safely enjoy nicotine if they use smokeless tobacco. **Smokeless tobacco** is tobacco that is chewed or sucked rather than smoked. This type of tobacco includes snuff and chewing tobacco. Smokeless tobacco is not safer than smoking tobacco. In fact, it may be even more harmful.

Smokeless tobacco can cause sores in the user's mouth, throat, and stomach. These sores sometimes become cancerous. One-third of the people who get mouth cancer die from it.

The risks of using smokeless tobacco are as bad as or worse than the dangers of using cigarettes. One usage of smokeless tobacco has as much nicotine as two cigarettes. The nicotine in smokeless tobacco raises blood pressure and heart rate, and the sugar in smokeless tobacco causes gum disease and tooth decay. Also, using smokeless tobacco for a long time can cause a person to lose his or her teeth.

COMPARE AND CONTRAST **Compare and contrast smoking tobacco with smokeless tobacco. Tell some reasons why people would choose to use either product.**

Myth and Fact

Myth: **Smokeless tobacco is less addictive than smoking tobacco.**
Fact: Chewing or sucking on tobacco causes more nicotine to enter the body than smoking tobacco does. This means that smokeless tobacco can be more addictive than smoking tobacco. More than two-thirds of the smokeless tobacco users who try to quit fail.

Life Skills

Manage Stress

Wade's mother has decided to quit smoking. Wade wants to help his mom. He knows she smokes more when she is feeling stressed. What are some things Wade can do to help her? Think about some activities that help a person who is feeling stressed.

How to Quit

In order to quit using tobacco, a person must first make the decision to quit. Being addicted to nicotine means that the brain and body become uncomfortable when the use of tobacco stops. When a person first stops using tobacco, the nicotine level in the body falls. As a result, he or she might feel nervous, irritated, hungry, and tired. Before too long, though, the body gets used to not having nicotine. Once the body stops needing the nicotine, the person feels better.

Tobacco users can quit using tobacco quickly or slowly. Some people find it easier to give up tobacco a little at a time. Nicotine gum or a nicotine skin patch might help. These are best used with the help of a doctor. It can also be helpful to be part of a support group. Hospitals, schools, the American Cancer Society, and the American Lung Association can help find counselors and support groups.

MAIN IDEA AND DETAILS Where can you find stop-smoking programs and resources in your community?

Lesson 2 Summary and Review

❶ Summarize with Vocabulary

Use vocabulary and other terms from this lesson to complete the statements.

Nonsmokers can get sick from _____. Another dangerous form of tobacco is _____, such as _____ and _____. Chewing or sucking on tobacco causes more _____ to enter the body than smoking tobacco does.

❷ Suppose a friend of yours tells you that he plans to use smokeless tobacco. What reasons could you give him not to do it?

❸ Critical Thinking What advice would you give a smoker who wants to quit?

❹ **CAUSE AND EFFECT** Draw and complete this graphic organizer to show some of the effects of ETS.

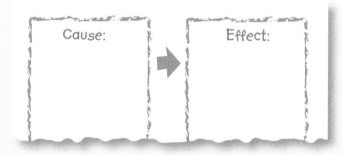

Cause: → Effect:

❺ Write to Express—Idea

Write an article for a local newspaper to discuss how you feel about smoking being allowed at public places such as restaurants and video game arcades.

Trustworthiness

Tell the Truth About Problems

Being trustworthy means being honest, telling the truth, and keeping your promises so that people trust you. Discussing problems with trusted adults, such as your parents, is part of being trustworthy. Telling the truth about a problem will make it easier to solve the problem. You will also feel better after talking about the problem. Always tell the truth about situations such as these:

- **Seeing a friend use tobacco or alcohol**
- **Having someone try to persuade you to use tobacco or alcohol**
- **Being somewhere without your parents where tobacco or alcohol was used**
- **Seeing someone using or selling illegal drugs**
- **Seeing someone being physically hurt by another person**

Activity

Write a story about a young person whose friends try to get him or her to try tobacco. The young person should decide to talk with his or her parents about the problem. Include the dialogue the young person has with them.

Dangers of Alcohol Use

What Happens When a Person Drinks

People in movies who have been drinking alcohol often make us laugh. But there are many real-life stories that aren't funny at all about people who use alcohol. Alcohol can cause serious problems—and even death. Alcohol is so dangerous that it is illegal for young people in the United States to buy it or use it.

Alcohol (AL·kuh·hawl) is a drug found in drinks such as beer, wine, and liquor. Once it reaches the stomach and small intestine, alcohol moves into the bloodstream. Once in the blood, alcohol travels quickly to the brain.

The more alcohol a person drinks, the more he or she will be affected by it. The amount of alcohol in a person's body is called the **blood alcohol level (BAL)**. In most states it is against the law to drive with a BAL of more than 0.08 or 0.10. With a BAL this high, the driver is four to seven times more likely to be involved in a car crash than a driver who has not been drinking.

Intoxicated drivers cause many deadly car crashes. Never get into a car with somebody who has been drinking alcohol! ▶

BAL Effects

BAL	Effects
0.30	vomiting alternating with unconsciousness, death a possible result
0.20	difficulty walking or standing, possible loss of bladder control
0.10	greatly slowed reaction time, likelihood of auto crash seven times greater, legally drunk in most states
0.05	changes in behavior, slower reaction time, some loss of self-control and judgment

WARNING: Women should not drink alcoholic beverages while they are pregnant because alcohol may cause birth defects. Do not drive a car or operate machinery while under the ... are linked to certain health problems.

▲ The more alcohol a person drinks, the higher his or her blood alcohol level becomes.

Quick Activity

Analyze Data Do you think it is safe for a person with a BAL of 0.05 to drive a car? Explain your answer.

WARNING: Consumption of alcoholic beverages impairs your ability to drive a car or operate machinery, and may cause health problems.

Different people can drink the same number of drinks and have different BALs. Small, light people reach illegal BALs sooner than large, heavy people. As a result, many young people are affected more strongly than adults.

Alcohol is a depressant. A depressant slows down the speed at which messages travel along nerve cells to and from the brain. Alcohol lowers body functions such as breathing rate, balance, and body temperature. The parts of the brain that control speech, judgment, memory, and attention are also affected by alcohol.

Alcohol affects people's actions in different ways. As the level of alcohol rises in the body, people become **intoxicated** (in·TAHK·sih·kay·tuhd), or drunk. Some intoxicated people are rude and loud. Others get depressed or silly.

People who are drunk may vomit. This could be the body's way of protecting itself from alcohol's harmful effects. Other people might fall asleep. At a high enough BAL, alcohol can make people pass out or even die.

 CAUSE AND EFFECT How can the effects of alcohol on the way a person acts be dangerous?

Myth and Fact

Myth: **Drinking alcohol makes a person fun to be around.**
Fact: Intoxicated people can be noisy, smell bad, vomit, and say mean things. Nobody wants to be around somebody like that!

Health & Technology

Drunken-Driving Simulator There are special cars that enable the driver to see what it is like to drive while intoxicated. The cars are taken to schools, where students can try to drive the cars through obstacle courses. The students learn firsthand why it is so dangerous to drink and drive!

Alcohol and Safety

People who drink too much alcohol feel dizzy, lose their balance, and have trouble walking. They also have trouble making wise judgments about safe and unsafe actions. People who have had too much alcohol can get injured because they fall or bump into things. Also, some people who are drunk become violent. As a result, people who drink alcohol sometimes hurt others.

People who drink alcohol can be injured or even killed by making bad decisions. For example, a person who drinks too much may swim too far from shore and not have the strength to swim back.

Drinking and driving not only is against the law but also costs lives. More than 40 percent of deaths in car crashes are alcohol-related. Many of the people who are killed in such crashes have not been drinking at all. They are victims because someone else chose to drink and drive.

SUMMARIZE How are alcohol and car crashes connected?

Alcoholism

Just as there are some people who would like to quit using tobacco but can't, there are people who want to stop drinking but can't. A person who is dependent on alcohol needs to drink it to feel normal. The person is an **alcoholic** (al·kuh·HAWL·ik). You may think of alcoholics as people who wear rags and live on the streets. However, many alcoholics appear to lead normal lives. Their dependency on alcohol may not be visible to you, but it causes problems in their lives. These problems usually get worse with time.

Alcoholics suffer from a disease called **alcoholism** (AL·kuh·hawl·ihz·uhm). People who suffer from alcoholism cannot control their use of alcohol. Even though they know that drinking is only going to make things worse, they keep drinking.

Anyone who drinks too much and too often has a drinking problem. A drinking problem can lead to other problems in the person's life. It is illegal for young people to drink alcohol. Those who drink may get in trouble with the law and at school and home. Many people with a drinking problem become alcoholics. Usually, people who have a drinking problem don't even realize they are becoming alcoholics. They tend to drink more and more alcohol without realizing it. Why does this happen? In addition to being dependent on alcohol, their bodies develop a tolerance for it.

SEQUENCE Describe the steps a person goes through while becoming an alcoholic.

PersoNal HeaLth PlaN ▶

Real-Life Situation

Imagine that your friend's older brother is supposed to give you a ride home from school, but you see some empty beer cans in his car.

Real-Life Plan

Find another way home. Discuss the situation with your parents, and come up with at least three options to stay safe in the future.

More than 17,000 people die every year in alcohol-related car crashes. ▼

291

How Alcohol Can Harm You

People who drink too much can't avoid the long-term effects of alcohol. Over time, alcohol harms the body in many ways. One of the most serious harmful effects is the destruction of brain cells. This causes people to lose their memory and their ability to think clearly.

Effects of Alcohol on the Body

Mouth and Esophagus Alcohol numbs and irritates the drinker's mouth and esophagus.

Heart, Arteries, and Veins Alcohol abuse can cause hypertension, a condition of constant high blood pressure.

Liver Long-term alcohol abuse damages the liver. As a result, the liver is unable to keep the blood free of toxins.

Brain Alcohol numbs nerve centers that control speech and motor skills needed for driving, walking, and other activities. It blurs vision. Alcohol makes the blood vessels in the brain expand, resulting in increased pressure that produces a headache.

Stomach Alcohol irritates the stomach lining and causes the stomach to make more of the acids that digest food. Small holes called ulcers may form in the stomach lining.

Small Intestine Alcohol can destroy special enzymes in the small intestine, making it harder for the body to digest food.

Quick Activity

Analyze Diagrams
Identify the body systems and major organs affected by alcohol. Is there any system that is not affected by alcohol?

Drinking too much over a long time harms other vital organs. For example, the liver of a heavy drinker can develop scar tissue. This condition is called *cirrhosis* (suh•ROH•sis). Sometimes this scar tissue gets so thick that the liver stops working and the person can die.

Long-term drinking also damages the pancreas. The pancreas is a small organ that makes substances called hormones. These hormones help keep the amount of sugar in the blood at the right level. In the stomach, alcohol can create small holes, or ulcers.

People who drink too much alcohol are more likely to develop certain kinds of cancer. In a healthy body, specialized agents help keep cancer cells from growing. But when there is too much alcohol in the body for too long, this changes. The ability to fight off cancer is weakened. The diagram on the previous page shows some other effects of alcohol on the body.

MAIN IDEA AND DETAILS List five long-term effects of alcohol use.

▲ The liver on the top is healthy. The liver on the bottom has been affected by alcohol and has developed cirrhosis.

Lesson 3 Summary and Review

1 Summarize with Vocabulary

Use vocabulary and other terms from this lesson to complete the statements.

Beer, wine, and liquor all contain _____. When a person drinks a lot of alcohol, he or she becomes _____ and has a high _____. People who are addicted to alcohol are _____. They have a disease known as _____. Drinking too much alcohol over a long time damages vital organs such as the liver, which can develop _____.

2 Why is drinking alcohol a safety issue?

3 Critical Thinking Why would a child feel the effects of alcohol faster than an adult?

4 **CAUSE AND EFFECT** Draw and complete this graphic organizer to show some of the long-term effects of alcohol on the body.

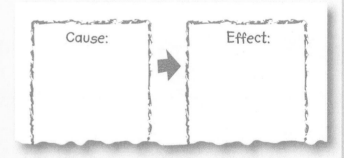
Cause: Effect:

5 Write to Inform—Report

Write a report that describes the connection between alcohol addiction and deadly diseases. You may want to research death statistics to include in your report.

Choose Not to Use Alcohol or Tobacco

Peer Pressure

"Oh, come on, everyone else is doing it." This statement is an example of negative peer pressure. Negative peer pressure can influence people to do things they otherwise would not do. Positive peer pressure can help people do the right things. People can exert peer pressure without even saying anything. For example, you might be with a group of friends when someone starts passing around a bottle of alcohol. If everyone else takes a sip, you may feel pressure to do the same.

Negative peer pressure causes many young people to start drinking. You don't have to give in to negative peer pressure. You have learned how dangerous alcohol and tobacco are. You can plan ahead and resist peer pressure. And when you say *no*, you will exert positive peer pressure on others.

There are many fun things that you can do with your friends—and none of them involve alcohol or tobacco! ▼

294

There are many ways to refuse alcohol and tobacco. You can simply say *no* and start talking about something else. You can suggest doing something else. Or you can just walk away. Refusing alcohol and tobacco is a sign of confidence. Even if others don't admit it at the time, they'll respect you for your confidence. Saying *no* to alcohol and tobacco also shows that you have self-respect. **Self-respect** is valuing yourself as a person. It includes liking yourself, taking care of your body, and making good health choices.

Of course, the best way to avoid alcohol and tobacco is to avoid places where they might be used. For example, going to parties with no adults present can often lead to problems. Instead, go with friends to places or events where you know alcohol or tobacco won't be used.

 CAUSE AND EFFECT What might be one effect of refusing to use alcohol or tobacco?

People do not need alcohol or tobacco to have fun and enjoy life. ▼

Media Influence

Many companies make a lot of money from the sale of alcohol and tobacco. They do this by spending a lot of money on advertising. In fact, the tobacco industry is the second-largest advertiser in magazines and newspapers. Each year, tobacco companies spend more than $8 billion on advertisements. That's more than $23 million a day to persuade you to use tobacco!

Why is so much money used for advertising? These companies want to get people to start using alcohol and tobacco. Young people are targeted because they are twice as likely to be influenced by ads as they are by peer pressure. Some people who start using these products at a young age will keep spending money on them for years and years.

Ads make young people think that smoking and drinking will make them attractive, popular, successful, glamorous, and energetic. This is because many alcohol and tobacco ads show good-looking models having fun, driving fast sports cars, and wearing stylish clothes.

▲ Two views of alcohol use are shown here. Which do you think is more accurate?

296

In reality, alcohol and tobacco ads don't tell the whole story. They don't show the effects of alcohol and tobacco on people's lives and health. They don't show the damage done to the body and the mind. People who use these products for a long time are not energetic, and they don't have much fun. They may smell bad and suffer from serious health problems. These advertisements also never show how hard it is to quit using these products.

Scientists predict that more than 1 million young people will start smoking this year. Almost half of them will die from the effects of their addiction. Ads for alcohol and tobacco never show the millions of people who have gotten ill, have been injured, or have died from using these products.

Many state and local governments have become more aware of the harmful effects of alcohol and tobacco. As a result, many laws now limit the advertising of these products on public property and in publicly owned stadiums.

COMPARE AND CONTRAST Describe at least one way you have seen alcohol use portrayed on TV. Compare and contrast that portrayal with the facts you have learned about alcohol.

Two views of smoking are shown in these pictures. Which do you think is more accurate? ▼

Smokees
ADD EXCITEMENT
TO YOUR LIFE

▲ Young people who get together with those who choose not to use alcohol or tobacco find it easier to avoid these drugs. This positive peer pressure can influence others to avoid these drugs or to quit using them.

Personal Health Plan ▶

Real-Life Situation
You are curious about what alcohol or tobacco tastes like.
Real-Life Plan
Talk with your parents about your curiosity. Work with them to make a list of reasons why you should avoid alcohol and tobacco products.

Choose Not to Use

Millions of people have chosen not to use alcohol or tobacco. Some may try these products, quit, and decide to never use them again. Why do people make these decisions? Some people decide not to use alcohol because of the health risks. Others find that drinking makes them tense, depressed, or anxious. They enjoy life more without the alcohol.

Many people are allergic to ingredients in wine, beer, or liquor. Drinking alcohol makes them ill and can even cause death. For them, the decision not to drink is an easy one!

People refuse alcohol for other reasons as well. Family or religious rules may forbid it. A desire to succeed in school, sports, or work doesn't leave room for alcohol or tobacco. Many people simply wish to be in control of their own behavior.

Many of these same reasons help people decide not to use tobacco. People who want to stay healthy stay away from tobacco. People whose families or religions forbid tobacco use often choose not to smoke. Bad breath, bad-smelling clothes, and stained teeth keep others from smoking. Finally, smoking is not cheap. Many people simply don't want to be addicted to something that costs so much money.

The best choice for all young people is not to use alcohol and tobacco at all. A young person's body is still growing. This makes the effects of alcohol and tobacco much greater. Many young people prefer to get involved in programs at their school or in their community that help prevent others from using alcohol and tobacco.

DRAW CONCLUSIONS **How can your family and friends influence your choice not to use tobacco or alcohol?**

ACTIVITY

Life Skills

Refuse Arturo has finally had his big chance to be a ball boy for the high school tennis team. After the game, the school's star tennis player offers him a beer. Choose a refusal strategy, and describe a way Arturo can say *no*.

Lesson 4 Summary and Review

❶ Summarize with Vocabulary

Use vocabulary and other terms from this lesson to complete the statements.

Negative _____ and _____ messages on TV and in magazines can encourage a person to use alcohol and tobacco. Positive _____ and _____ help people refuse alcohol and tobacco.

❷ List five different fun and satisfying activities you can do that do not involve alcohol or tobacco.

❸ Critical Thinking Why do companies that make and sell tobacco and alcohol products have an interest in getting young people to use their products?

❹ CAUSE AND EFFECT Draw and complete this graphic organizer to show some additional effects of having little or no self-respect.

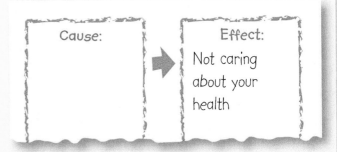

Cause:

Effect:
Not caring about your health

❺ Write to Express—Idea

Some people can become addicted to tobacco and alcohol more easily than others. Write a paragraph describing your opinion of what characteristics and behaviors can lead a person to addiction.

Refuse
Alcohol and Tobacco

At some time you may be asked to try alcohol and tobacco. It is important to have a plan made ahead of time so that you will know what to do. Use these refusal skills to help you make your plan for refusing alcohol and tobacco.

Michael and James are talking during lunch. Michael invites James to join him at his house after school. "Are your parents going to be home?" James asks. "No," Michael replies. "And my mom has some wine coolers in the refrigerator we can try." James wonders how he can get out of this one. He considers several options.

1  **Say *no*.**

James knows that Michael's mom would notice missing wine coolers. Also, it's against James's family rules to drink alcohol.

2 **Suggest something else to do.**

James thinks of his new guitar. The boys could jam instead of drinking.

3 Reverse the peer pressure.

That's really lame.

James gives his opinion of Michael's idea.

4 Leave the situation.

James just shakes his head and turns to leave.

Problem Solving

A. Maria is at the mall. She sees a group of popular girls from her class. They call her over to talk. One of the girls pulls a cigarette out of her purse and offers it to Maria.

   • Choose a refusal strategy that can help Maria make a responsible decision and say *no* in this situation.

B. Li is spending the weekend at his uncle's ranch. His uncle chews tobacco, and he offers Li a pinch just to see what it is like.

   • Choose a refusal strategy that can help Li make a responsible decision and say *no* in this situation.

Getting Help for Alcohol Problems

Where to Get Help

Everyone needs help at one time or another. You might need help with something small, such as getting a school project done on time. You might need help with something big, such as running for a school office. Overcoming a problem with alcohol is something big. It's also difficult. Anyone attempting to quit using alcohol needs as much help as he or she can get. If you think you know somebody with an alcohol problem, talk to your parents, a teacher, or another trusted adult. They will help you. Just ask.

How do you know if somebody has a problem with alcohol? Some alcoholics might not wash their hair or their clothes. They might look tired or smell of alcohol. Many alcoholics may look normal, but they may not act normal. For example, alcoholics may miss school or work often. Or they may have trouble controlling their moods and become very angry.

Personal Health Plan ▶

Real-Life Situation

Suppose a friend has admitted that he has a problem with alcohol, but he refuses to get help.

Real-Life Plan

Write down three things you would say to persuade your friend to seek help.

Finding Help

❶ Talk to a trusted adult, such as a parent or teacher.

❷ Ask your school counselor for advice.

❸ Discuss the problem with a doctor.

❹ Contact a community agency such as a mental health center or hospital.

❺ Contact a national group such as Alcoholics Anonymous or the National Clearinghouse for Alcohol and Drug Information.

▲ Peer support groups can help people deal with problems such as alcoholism.

People who show signs of alcoholism do not always ask for help. Admitting there is a problem and asking for help are the hardest steps in giving up alcohol. Alcoholics often fear that others will think they are weak or bad. Instead, a person who has the courage to admit to the problem gains respect and support.

A good way for alcohol abusers to begin to get help is to go to someone they know and trust. For a teenager, this might be a parent, teacher, school nurse, school counselor, doctor, or family friend. Other good choices include a coach or religious leader. These people often have helped others who have problems with alcohol. They might also know or be able to find out the names of counselors, groups, or others who can help.

MAIN IDEA AND DETAILS Identify ways to seek assistance for an alcoholic.

ACTIVITY

Building Good Character

Caring Marie has noticed that her uncle Ron often smells of alcohol. He is always tired and in a bad mood. Marie cares about her uncle and wants to help him. How can Marie show her uncle Ron that she cares?

Alcoholism affects more than the alcoholic and his or her family—it affects the entire community. Almost every community has a group that helps people deal with alcoholism. ▼

Community Groups

Alcohol-abuse counselors are trained to work with alcoholics and their families. They help alcoholics face their problems and challenges. One of these challenges is low self-respect. Counselors help people find ways to feel better about themselves. They also show them how to develop a plan to rebuild their lives.

There are many ways to find alcohol-abuse counselors. Doctors can provide the names of trained counselors. Also, local agencies such as mental health centers and hospitals may have counselors on staff.

Several well-known organizations offer free information about alcohol and alcoholism. These include the National Clearinghouse for Alcohol and Drug Information and the National Council on Alcoholism and Drug Dependence.

Two community groups, Mothers Against Drunk Driving (MADD) and Students Against Destructive Decisions (SADD), have state and local chapters that help teach people about alcohol. SADD sponsors parties and other social events that do not include alcohol.

SUMMARIZE Where could you find an alcohol-abuse counselor?

◄ When one person in a family is an alcoholic, everybody in the family is affected. The whole family may benefit from counseling.

Recovery

Recovery programs are available to help people who are learning to live without alcohol. They also help families and friends of alcohol abusers.

Some people enter *hospital recovery programs* or *treatment centers* for a certain period of time. Abusers attend counseling sessions by themselves or in groups. Families of abusers also attend special sessions. The counseling helps people learn new behaviors and ways of coping with their problems.

In *residential programs*, or *halfway houses*, people live away from home in a living space that does not allow drinking. These programs can last from many months to a year. They provide individual and group counseling.

Day-treatment programs allow people to continue their normal lives at home. They provide treatment for several hours a week while the person continues going to school or work.

Many people in the United States go through recovery by going to meetings run by alcoholics who have quit drinking. The people in these *support groups* share their successes and failures with each other. They have all faced the problems caused by alcoholism.

Information Alert!

Treatment for Alcoholics
New methods are always being found to help alcoholics.

GO ONLINE
For the most up-to-date information, visit The Learning Site.
www.harcourtschool.com/health

Alcoholism and Epilepsy Drugs Recent research suggests that the epilepsy drug topiramate may help alcoholics say *no* to alcohol. Researchers found that alcoholics who took the drug drank three fewer drinks a day. They also had 26 percent more days in which they did not drink alcohol at all.

The best-known support group for alcoholics is Alcoholics Anonymous (AA). Members of AA attend meetings at least once a week. People can go to meetings as often as they like. Some people attend as many as two or three meetings a day.

Some people prefer programs other than AA. Other support groups include Rational Recovery and Women for Sobriety.

The type of treatment in different recovery programs varies. No one program works best for everyone. Finding the best program for a particular person might take some research. However, it is worth the effort!

Friends and family members need help, too. It is not always easy to know how to help a friend or relative who is an alcoholic. Support groups such as Al-Anon, Alateen, and the National Association for Children of Alcoholics do what they can to help families of alcoholics.

DRAW CONCLUSIONS Name one kind of recovery program, and tell what you think the advantage is of joining such a program.

Lesson 5 Summary and Review

❶ Summarize with Vocabulary

Use vocabulary and other terms from this lesson to complete the statements.

Alcoholics who want to quit drinking can go through _____ to get support. Some recovery programs, such as _____ or _____, require a person to live away from home. Others, such as _____, allow the person to stay home and continue working or going to school.

❷ List four people or groups that can help an alcoholic who wants to quit drinking.

❸ Critical Thinking Why is getting help important for a person who is trying to stop drinking?

❹ (Focus Skill) CAUSE AND EFFECT How does alcoholism affect a person's life?

Cause: Alcoholism → Effect: Alcoholics deny their problem.

❺ Write to Explain—Explanation

Think of a habit that you would like to change. It could be something like eating too much candy or biting your nails. Write a paragraph explaining whether you think joining a support group would help you break the habit.

ACTIVITIES

Physical Education

Effects of Smoking Write a report for a person who is interested in participating in sports about how smoking affects the body. Explain how smoking might affect his or her performance in the chosen sport.

Science

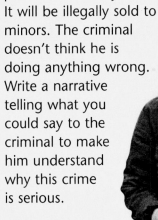

Reaction Time and Alcohol Find statistics on the effects of alcohol on reaction time, and write a hypothesis about how drinking alcohol might affect the ability to drive a car. Look at published statistics or scientific studies for evidence to support your hypothesis. Summarize your conclusions in a short science fair project or poster.

Technology Project

Graph Driving Statistics Collect statistics on alcohol-related auto crashes. You can get data from state or federal government agencies. Use a computer graphing program to make a graph illustrating your statistics.

GO ONLINE For more activities, visit The Learning Site.
www.harcourtschool.com/health

Home & Community

Make a Poster Find out about the Great American Smokeout or a similar program that raises awareness about the dangers of tobacco or alcohol use. Create a poster to publicize the event, letting people know how they can participate. Ask permission to put the poster up somewhere in your community.

Career Link

ATF Officer Suppose you are an officer with the ATF (Bureau of Alcohol, Tobacco, Firearms and Explosives). You have caught a criminal trying to smuggle alcohol into the United States. The alcohol is especially powerful and may contain toxic substances. It will be illegally sold to minors. The criminal doesn't think he is doing anything wrong. Write a narrative telling what you could say to the criminal to make him understand why this crime is serious.

Reading Skill

CAUSE AND EFFECT

Draw and then use this graphic organizer to answer questions 1 and 2.

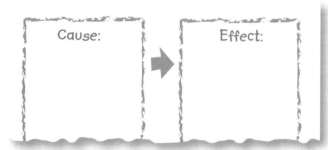

Cause: → Effect:

1 Write about the social, physical, and legal effects of tobacco.
2 Write about the social, physical, and legal effects of alcohol.

 Use Vocabulary

Match each term in Column B with its meaning in Column A.

Column A	Column B
3 The amount of alcohol in a person's body	A nicotine
4 Grimy substances left by smoke	B carbon monoxide
5 Disease characterized by a scarred liver	C tars
6 Disease characterized by an addiction to alcohol	D recovery program
7 A poisonous gas	E blood alcohol level
8 An addictive poison	F alcoholism
9 Support for people learning to live without alcohol	G cirrhosis

Check Understanding

Choose the letter of the correct answer.

10 Environmental tobacco smoke is smoke
_____. (p. 284)
A in the air people breathe
B around a tobacco factory
C that is good for Earth
D a person inhales when smoking a cigarette

11 Alcohol is a _____. (p. 289)
F stimulant
G narcotic
H nutrient
J depressant

12 Long-term alcohol use can destroy cells in a drinker's _____. (p. 292)
A kidneys
B heart
C brain
D leg muscles

13 People who want to quit drinking should
_____. (p. 302)
F take up smoking
G eat only protein
H seek help
J buy only beer

14 Which of the following warning labels would be suitable for a package of snuff? (p. 285)

A
WARNING: Using this substance may lead to emphysema.

B
WARNING: Do not use this substance while operating heavy machinery.

C
WARNING: Using this substance may lead to mouth cancer.

D
WARNING: Using this substance may lead to cirrhosis.

15 Tobacco that is chewed or sucked is _____. (p. 285)

   F intoxicating   **H** smokeless

   G safe   **J** less addictive

16 Which of the following belongs in the graphic organizer? (p. 292)

   A ulcers   **C** hypertension

   B headaches   **D** scar tissue

17 A long-term treatment program that provides a place to live for people trying to recover from alcohol problems is a _____. (p. 305)

   F residential recovery program

   G hospital recovery program

   H day-treatment program

   J support group

18 A plant whose large leaves are used for smoking and chewing is _____. (p. 280)

   A whiskey   **C** tar

   B menthol   **D** tobacco

19 When a person drinks too much at one time and alcohol accumulates in the body, he or she becomes _____. (p. 289)

   F a drunk driver

   G intoxicated

   H an alcoholic

   J fun to be around

Think Critically

20 A friend has decided to start using alcohol. You are trying to change her mind. List the evidence you would use to persuade her not to drink alcohol.

21 Look at the advertisement for tobacco. What message does the ad seem to be giving? Is it accurate? Explain.

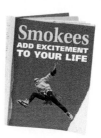

22 Why is it important not to drive after drinking alcohol?

Apply Skills

23 **BUILDING GOOD CHARACTER**
Trustworthiness Suppose you arrive at a party and find that everyone there is drinking alcohol. Explain what you could do to show your trustworthiness.

24 **LIFE SKILLS**
Refuse You have decided not to attend parties where alcohol is being served. List three ways you could say *no* to a friend who has invited you to a party where people your age will be drinking alcohol.

Write About Health

25 **Write to Inform—Description**
Describe some things adolescents and teens can do to avoid peer pressure to smoke or drink alcohol.

10 Setting Goals

IDENTIFY MAIN IDEA AND DETAILS The main idea is the most important thought in a passage. Details tell about the main idea. They tell who, what, when, where, why, and how. Use pages 406–407 in the Reading in Health Handbook and this graphic organizer to help you identify the main ideas in this chapter.

Identify Main Idea and Details

Main Idea:

| Detail: | Detail: | Detail: |

Health Graph

INTERPRET DATA The graph shows the hobbies of a group of 100 sixth graders. Which hobby is as popular as dance? Which hobby attracts the most students?

Hobbies of Sixth Graders

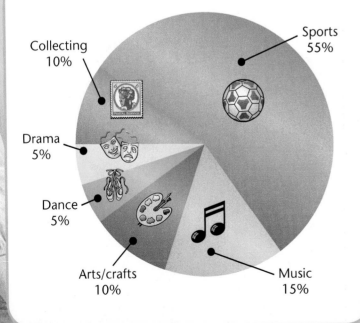

- Collecting 10%
- Sports 55%
- Drama 5%
- Dance 5%
- Arts/crafts 10%
- Music 15%

Daily Physical Activity

Everyone has different interests and hobbies. Another important part of having a healthful lifestyle is getting plenty of physical activity.

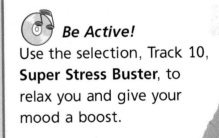 **Be Active!**
Use the selection, Track 10, **Super Stress Buster**, to relax you and give your mood a boost.

Your Self-Concept

Lesson Focus

How you feel about yourself affects how you make decisions and set goals, and helps you identify your strengths and weaknesses.

Why Learn This?

Knowing your strengths helps you feel good about yourself and improve your weaker areas.

Vocabulary

self-concept
self-respect
body image

Getting to Know Yourself

Your body is starting to change, and so are some of your feelings and ideas. The way you think about yourself is your **self-concept**. Your self-concept develops as a result of many things, such as these:

- how you think of yourself, both alone and with other people.
- how you think other people think of you.
- how you would like other people to think of you.
- how well you understand your own feelings and ideas.

Your self-concept affects every part of your life. It affects how you relate to other people. If you feel good about yourself, you have a positive self-concept. You also have self-respect. **Self-respect** is valuing yourself as a person.

Your self-concept is influenced by your skills and interests. It's also influenced by the people around you. ▼

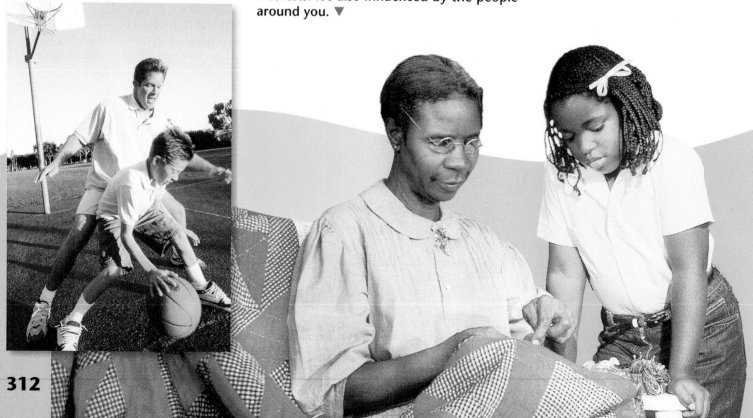

What you think of yourself and what others think of you may be different in different situations. For example, you may feel confident in your neighborhood but shy in your classroom.

Whether you are shy or outgoing, you can still have a positive self-concept. You can feel good about being you. This self-respect gives you the confidence to make your own decisions. You can say *no* to things you know are wrong. You have the courage to take healthful risks. You are not afraid to make mistakes because you know they are part of learning new skills and ideas.

Think of yourself as a "work in progress." You can improve your self-concept by continuing to do things you do well and by learning new skills. Self-respect gives you the confidence to make any needed changes in your life. In this way, you are taking more and more responsibility for yourself.

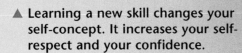 **MAIN IDEA AND DETAILS Your self-concept is shaped by many things. Name three of them.**

Did You Know?

Taking healthful risks increases your self-respect. Examples of healthful risks include learning a new skill, entering a contest, and performing in front of an audience. Having the courage to try something new helps you feel proud of yourself.

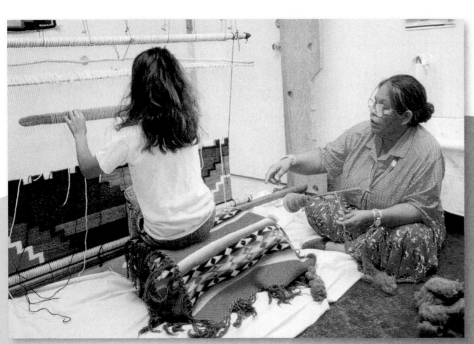

▲ Learning a new skill changes your self-concept. It increases your self-respect and your confidence.

Real-Life Situation

Suppose softball is your favorite sport, but you don't play as well as some of your friends do.

Real-Life Plan

Write a plan that will help you identify how to improve your softball skills.

Taking a Reality Check

Do you ever worry that you are not tall enough or attractive enough? Is your hair too curly—or too straight? Do you wish your muscles were bigger?

Everyone wonders about himself or herself at times. That's normal. However, many people your age are too hard on themselves. They tend to be the most negative about their body image. Your **body image** is your opinion about your physical appearance.

Are you comfortable with the way you look? If so, you have a positive body image. If you do not like the way you look, you may be judging yourself unfairly. Many young people are too critical of themselves. They do not see themselves as they really are.

For example, one girl might be certain that she is overweight. In fact, she may be healthier than the pencil-thin fashion models that she sees in many magazines.

To know yourself, you must be able to identify your strengths and your weaknesses. Then you can plan how to change anything that really does need changing.

Before you start worrying about your body, make sure you see yourself clearly and truthfully. ▼

314

Make a careful survey of yourself. Look at yourself as a scientist would—decide on the facts without adding your feelings. For example, a list of your strengths might include honesty and patience. Your weakness might be a tendency to put things off until the last minute.

After you gather your information, you might notice something you want to change. Then you can set a goal and make a plan to reach that goal. The next lesson will show you how.

Having a positive self-concept does not mean that you think you are perfect. It means that you feel confident about who you are. Remember, you don't have to be *the* best. You just have to do *your* best!

DRAW CONCLUSIONS Why is it easier to make changes in your life when you have a positive self-concept?

Every Day—

1. Do something that makes you happy.
2. Do something that makes someone else happy.
3. Exercise your mind.
4. Exercise your body.
5. Talk to a parent or another trusted adult about something important to you.
6. Do a task you have been avoiding. Being responsible increases your self-respect.

Lesson 1 Summary and Review

1 Summarize with Vocabulary

Use vocabulary and other terms from this lesson to complete the statements.

Your picture of yourself is called your _____. If you value yourself, you have _____. People who think that there is something wrong with how they look are concerned about their _____. To really know yourself, you must identify your _____ and weaknesses.

2 Critical Thinking Why is having a positive self-concept an important part of being healthy?

3 Why do you think many young people have a negative body image?

4 MAIN IDEA AND DETAILS Draw and complete this graphic organizer to show things that make up a positive self-concept.

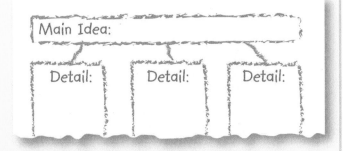

Main Idea:

Detail: | Detail: | Detail:

5 Informative Writing—How-To

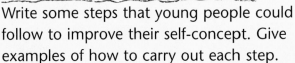

Write some steps that young people could follow to improve their self-concept. Give examples of how to carry out each step.

315

Setting Goals and Making Decisions

Setting Goals

What goals do you have for your life? A **goal** is something you want to achieve. Characters in television shows tend to reach their goals quickly and easily, but people in real life must plan ahead and work hard to achieve their goals.

Tamiko has a goal. Her brother Jiro will be eleven years old next month, and what he wants more than anything is a baseball glove. Tamiko plans to buy him one. The glove Jiro wants costs $25, so her goal is to earn $25 before her brother's birthday.

First, Tamiko thinks about her skills and identifies several that she could use to earn some money. For example, she is good with animals and enjoys working in her family's garden. Then Tamiko lists three neighbors who might pay her to walk their dogs and two neighbors who might hire her to weed their gardens.

◀ Goals should be realistic. Tamiko is confident that she can earn $25 before her brother's birthday.

Tamiko's next step is to visit the neighbors who are on her list. Before she knows it, she has a schedule for walking dogs and weeding gardens!

As Tamiko works toward her goal, she checks her progress. During one of the weeks, it rains every day, so she cannot do any weeding. To earn enough money for the glove, she walks three extra dogs that week—in the rain! Tamiko meets her goal and cannot wait for Jiro to open her gift to him.

Buying the glove was a *short-term goal*, or a goal that can be met in a month or less. A goal that is set for far in the future is a *long-term goal*. Graduating from high school is Tony's long-term goal. Tony has set several short-term goals as he works toward his long-term goal. For example, he has a short-term goal of raising his math grade from a *C* to a *B* this grading period because he knows that getting better grades will help him want to stay in school and graduate.

Having goals helps you get what you need and what you want. It gives you a sense that your life is going in the right direction. Your whole family might share a goal, such as saving money for a vacation. You might also share a goal with a friend, such as reading all the books written by a favorite author.

CAUSE AND EFFECT What could happen if you had no goals of your own?

Consumer Activity

Analyze Advertisements and Media Messages
Review the ads in several magazines. How many of them encourage consumers to plan carefully? How many encourage people to set realistic goals? Share with your class the messages you find.

Jiro's smile tells Tamiko that she successfully met her goal. ▶

317

Making Decisions to Reach Goals

You make many decisions every day. When you have goals, making decisions becomes much easier. Goals provide a framework to help you make these decisions.

Ivan has a goal of becoming a champion speed skater. This sport requires hours of practice on the ice plus workouts to improve his strength and endurance. When Ivan needs to decide how to spend his time, he thinks about his goal. He knows that watching too much television will not help him meet his goal.

To make a wise decision, you must first identify your choices and eliminate any that are against family or school rules. Next, you must consider the possible consequences of each choice. Having goals enables you to select choices that help you meet those goals.

One of La Tonya's goals is to be a more caring friend. When she hears her classmates gossiping about someone, La Tonya knows that she could gossip with them.

Having a goal can help you decide how to spend your time. ▶

318

However, doing so would not help her meet her goal. Instead, she changes the subject and asks, "Who's going to the basketball game this week?"

Choose your goals carefully. Make sure each one is realistic—something you can achieve by yourself or with a little help. Select a goal that's important to you—something you *really* want. State your goal in a positive way. Say, "I will get a *B* in math," not "I won't get any more *C*'s in math."

Talk with your parents or other trusted adults about the goals you have in mind. Think about what you are willing to give up to reach your goals. Setting and reaching goals is an excellent way to strengthen your self-concept because you will be proud of what you have achieved.

SUMMARIZE What are some reasons people might not reach their goals?

Setting and Reaching a Goal

1. Choose a realistic, important goal.

2. Make a plan and set a deadline for each step, giving yourself enough time. Determine whether you will need any help.

3. Follow your plan.

4. Check your progress. Make any needed changes in your plan or in your goal.

5. Celebrate when you reach your goal!

Quick Activity

Set a Goal Set your own goal, and write a plan that will help you meet it. Then follow your plan.

Lesson 2 Summary and Review

1 Summarize with Vocabulary

Use vocabulary and other terms from this lesson to complete the statements.

Something you want to achieve is a _____. Wanting to finish a report by Friday is a _____ goal. Wanting to score at least ten points a game all season is a _____ goal. Having goals can help you make wise _____.

2 Why is the ability to set goals for yourself a sign of maturity?

3 Critical Thinking How can having a goal help you make a choice that is different from those of your friends?

4 (Focus Skill) **MAIN IDEA AND DETAILS** Draw and complete this graphic organizer to show ways that goal-setting helps you.

Main Idea:

Detail: | Detail: | Detail:

5 Write to Entertain—Story

Write a story about someone who set and reached a goal. The main character could be your age or older. Show how this person made decisions that helped him or her reach this goal.

Dealing with Unpleasant Feelings

Lesson Focus

Knowing how to deal with uncomfortable feelings is part of learning how to take care of yourself.

Why Learn This?

When you understand your uncomfortable feelings and know how to deal with them, you feel more in control.

Vocabulary

aggression
self-control
stress
anxiety
relaxation
grief

Managing Anger

You have a right to get angry. Your anger might rise quickly and then disappear just as fast. It might stay inside you for a long time or explode into angry words, fights, or tears. You might feel anger toward others or even with yourself. Anger that is not controlled is dangerous. It can lead to **aggression** (uh·GREH·shuhn)—forceful words or actions that can harm others emotionally or physically.

Along with your right to get angry is your responsibility to have good self-control. **Self-control** is the ability to manage your actions appropriately. This can be difficult when you have unpleasant feelings. Having self-control enables you to manage your anger and avoid aggression.

Jumping rope can help release angry feelings. ▶

Quick Activity

Ask Questions Think about the last time you were angry. Ask yourself questions like these: "Why was I angry? With whom was I angry? On a scale of one to ten, how angry was I? How could I have better managed my anger?"

Everyone feels angry sometimes. Anger and other uncomfortable feelings can make you feel out of control. Having self-control gives you confidence.

How can you manage your anger? If you know that a situation makes you angry, try to avoid it. If you cannot avoid it, learn to use one or more techniques when you feel your anger building. You might take several deep breaths or count to ten. If possible, try exercising, doing something fun, or listening to soothing music. These actions will help you cool off and get your angry feelings under control.

You could use "I" messages to express your feelings. You might feel like shouting "You always make me wait for you!" Instead, you could say, "I feel angry when I have to wait because I don't feel as though I am respected." Then listen to what the other person has to say.

If you are still angry, talk to a parent or another trusted adult about your feelings. Expressing your feelings in art, music, or writing also helps. Try different ways to manage your anger until you find safe ways to control and express it. With practice, you can control anger in ways that will make you feel secure and confident.

SEQUENCE **What steps can you take to help get your angry feelings under control?**

Ask for Help If...

1. your anger affects you in or out of school.
2. the situation has continued for a long time.
3. you do not feel safe or in control.
4. more people have become involved in the conflict.
5. the situation might become violent.

Talking to a parent or another trusted adult can help you explore the reasons for your anger and find ways to manage it. ▼

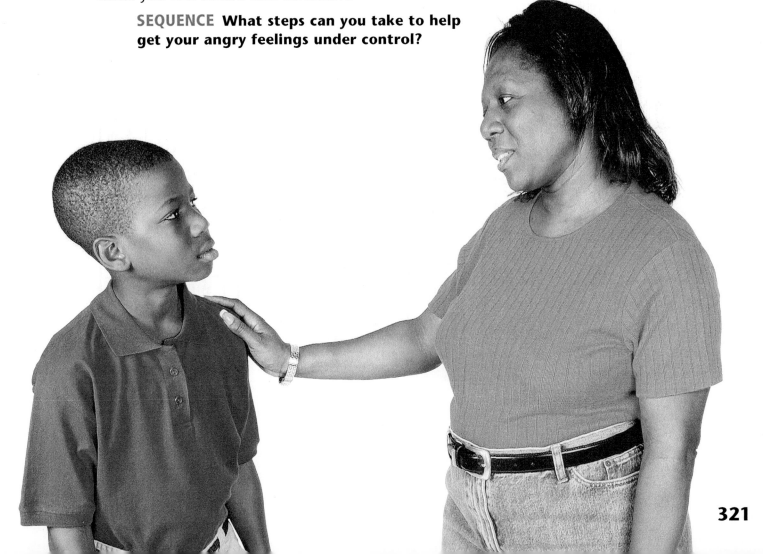

321

Coping with Stress

You have a big test this morning, and your body knows it. You have "butterflies" in your stomach and sweaty palms. This nervous feeling is called **stress**. Some stress is positive because a little bit of nervousness and excitement helps you do your best. A little stress can help you focus during a test, a sports competition, an oral presentation, or a similar challenge.

However, too much stress or stress that goes on for too long can lead to anxiety. **Anxiety** is an uneasiness or worry that you cannot connect to a specific cause. Anxiety can result in trouble sleeping or eating, poor concentration, tiredness, and headaches. If you feel anxious without knowing why, it might be time to ask for help.

To cope with stress, you must first identify its cause. Are you stressed because of an argument with a friend or family member? Are you having trouble getting your homework done because of soccer practice after school every day? Did your family recently move to a new town and you must face making new friends?

Tips for Coping with Stress

1. Set realistic goals.
2. Don't put things off. Make yourself do things that need to be done.
3. Get enough sleep.
4. Allow time for exercise, chores, and errands.
5. Leave time in your schedule for fun and relaxation.

Quick Activity

Evaluate a Graph
The graph identifies causes of stress in adults. Which of these also cause stress for young people? List what you think are the five main causes of stress for you and your classmates.

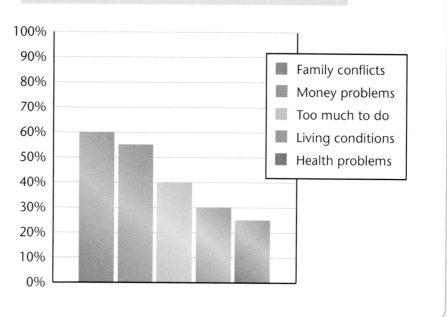

Leading Causes of Stress

- Family conflicts
- Money problems
- Too much to do
- Living conditions
- Health problems

▲ How do you cope with stress? Enjoying a waterfall or petting an animal helps relieve stress for many people.

Some people relax by putting together puzzles. ▼

Often you can reduce your stress by better managing your time or improving your study habits. Putting off a report until the last minute definitely causes stress. Instead, begin planning right after the report is assigned. Estimate how many hours the report will take, and divide that time over several days or weeks. Set up a schedule so that each day, you work on the report for the amount of time you had planned.

If managing your time better doesn't reduce your stress, find ways to relax. **Relaxation** can include resting, reading, listening to music, and anything else that's fun.

Stress is a fact of life, but it doesn't have to take over your life. When you manage your time well and know how to relax, you will feel more in control of yourself.

COMPARE AND CONTRAST Describe a healthful way and an unhealthful way of dealing with stress.

ACTIVITY

Building Good Character

Caring Erin's dog has been lost for two weeks, and it's beginning to look as if she might never find him. What can Erin's friends do to show that they care?

Coping with Grief

Everyone feels sad at times. Disappointments and changes in friendships are two of the things that can cause sadness. However, when someone you love dies, it's natural to experience grief. **Grief** is a painful sadness that lasts for a while. You can also feel grief when a best friend or family member moves far away or when a pet dies.

If you are sad or grieving, tell someone. It may help to write about your feelings. Exercise also helps you feel better physically and emotionally. At the same time, find someone whom you can help. Helping others makes you feel better about your own life.

If someone you know is grieving, here are some ways you can help:

- Suggest that the person tell a parent or another trusted adult about his or her feelings.
- Encourage the person to talk about the situation—and then be a good listener. Don't pretend that nothing has happened.
- Include the person in fun activities.
- Support the person's positive ideas. For example, if he or she wants to see a movie, go along.

Volunteering your time to assist others can help you cope with your own feelings. ▼

Be patient with yourself if you are grieving over a loss. No one can tell you how long grief should last. Talking about your feelings of loss will help you start to feel better. Some people even write poems or plant small gardens in memory of a lost loved one. Just as life continues to change, so will your feelings. In time, your pain will be replaced with happy memories.

Ask for Help If . . .

- your sadness has lasted for a long time.
- you cry frequently or for no reason.
- you don't enjoy doing the things you used to enjoy.
- you don't care about seeing your friends anymore.
- you are having trouble concentrating.
- you don't want to think about the future.

SUMMARIZE **What do you think is the best way to cope with grief?**

Did You Know?

Take a shower—you might feel better! Scientists have learned that breathing negatively charged air can help you feel better. This air is found near moving water, such as ocean waves, a rushing river, or even a shower. So, hop into the tub and breathe deeply!

Lesson 3 Summary and Review

❶ **Summarize with Vocabulary**

Use vocabulary from this lesson to complete the statements.

Handling strong feelings requires _____. If you do not manage your anger, you might use _____ to express your feelings. If you are having sadness over the death of someone, you are feeling _____. Having too much to do and other worries for a long time can lead to _____. Talking about your feelings can help, and so can _____, such as resting or just having fun.

❷ How can managing your time well cut down on your stress?

❸ Critical Thinking Why should people have several strategies ready to manage anger?

❹ (Focus Skill) MAIN IDEA AND DETAILS Draw and complete this graphic organizer to show strategies you can use to manage anger.

Main Idea: _____

Detail: _____ Detail: _____ Detail: _____

❺ **Write to Explain—Friendly Letter**

Pretend that a friend is having trouble with an unpleasant feeling. Make up a name for your friend, and write him or her a letter suggesting ways to handle the feeling. Remember to be respectful.

Manage Stress
at School

No one can avoid stress all of the time, but you can learn ways to manage it. Knowing how to handle stress is a skill that you can use during your entire life. Practicing the steps to **Manage Stress** will give you more control over your life. It will also help you feel good about yourself.

In his science class tomorrow, Rob has to give a presentation explaining how planets orbit the sun. His presentation is ready, but he still feels very nervous. What can Rob do to control his nervousness? What steps can he take to help control the stress he is feeling?

1 **Know what stress feels like.**

2 **Try to determine the cause of the stress.**

Rob realizes that he is feeling stress. His stomach is upset, and he has a headache. His heart beats faster, and he starts to sweat every time he thinks about his presentation.

Rob knows what is causing his stress. He is worried about standing in front of his class and speaking. What if he makes a mistake? Will everyone laugh at him?

3 Do something to relieve these feelings, such as preparing to handle the stressful situation.

4 Relax by listening to music or reading.

Rob decides to read more about the planets and finds a diagram that will help him explain why some planets have seasons. Now he feels better prepared for his presentation.

After Rob listens to his favorite CDs and reads a book by his favorite author, he feels much better!

 Problem Solving

A. Wen-Li is playing the piano in a recital this afternoon. She has practiced her piece many times, but the recital starts in an hour and she is making more mistakes than ever!
   • Use the steps to **Manage Stress** to help Wen-Li deal with her feelings and do her best.

B. Brian's coach expects him to show up at baseball practice in 15 minutes, but Brian really needs to study for tomorrow's science test. His stomach is so upset that he cannot eat the apple he saved for a snack.
   • Explain the responsible thing for Brian to do. Then describe how he can avoid getting into such a stressful situation in the future.

Choosing and Keeping Friends

Changing Friendships

Many things are probably changing in your life now, including your friendships. Friends often have many shared interests, but even best friends can grow apart as their interests change. This is normal and to be expected.

Friendships also change when students from the same elementary school are assigned to different middle schools or when families move to other towns. It's harder to stay friends when you don't see each other very often.

You might decide to stay away from a friend if he or she starts making choices that are against your values. On the other hand, people who value the same things, such as honesty and responsibility, might stay friends for a long time. They help each other work toward the same goals.

Many young people change friends often as they explore new interests and become adults. The end of a friendship will not be as upsetting if you know how to make new friends.

Friends enjoy and respect each other, do things together, and support each other when they try new things.

328

How can you find and make new friends? You might join a group or club to gain the attention of people who enjoy the same activities you do. Having shared interests and goals brings people together in a positive way and helps them become friends. In your search for friends, don't overlook your family members. A brother, sister, or cousin can be your best and most loyal friend.

If you are on a sports team, some of your teammates might become your friends. However, you might see these friends only at your games. In the same way, you might spend time with friends who live in your neighborhood but not see them anywhere else. If your parents' friends have children, those children might become your friends. People of all ages have different friends in different places.

Shared interests and values are equally important in groups that include both boys and girls. As you get older, you will begin to go places and attend events with mixed groups. Group activities enable you to have fun and feel safe as you begin to explore friendships with members of the opposite sex.

DRAW CONCLUSIONS Suppose that someone is trying to get you to do something that goes against your values. Why is this person not really your friend?

You might have some friends who like to play exciting games. ▼

PersoNaL HeaLth PLaN ▶

Real-Life Situation
You want to make new friends and gain attention from people your age.

Real-Life Plan
Make a list of acceptable ways to get attention and make friends. For example, instead of talking only about yourself, you can ask others to share their interests.

You might have other friends who would rather see the latest movie. ▼

329

ACTIVITY

Life Skills

Resist Negative Peer Pressure With a partner, list five situations that could result from giving in to negative peer pressure. Plan one or more ways you could resist the pressure in each situation. For example, you might say *no* several times, give a reason, suggest something else to do, make a joke about the request, ignore the person, or just leave.

Peers and Peer Pressure

Your **peers**, or people who are about your own age, often urge you to do things with them. They do this by using peer pressure. **Peer pressure**, or the influence peers bring to bear on someone, can make it difficult to think for yourself. Before you agree to participate in an activity, you should always consider the possible consequences.

Positive peer pressure leads people into healthful, safe activities such as trying out for a team or reading aloud to younger children. *Negative* peer pressure leads people into activities that are illegal or harmful to themselves or to others. Examples include cheating on a test and shoplifting.

Engaging in harmful activities in order to gain attention from your peers is unwise and unhealthful. If an activity will get you into trouble, you must resist it. Resisting your peers takes practice, courage, and self-respect, but you can do it. Remember that true friends do not try to get each other into trouble.

SEQUENCE **What should you do before you agree to take part in an activity?**

Lesson 4 Summary and Review

❶ Summarize with Vocabulary

Use vocabulary and other terms from this lesson to complete the statements.

Friends your own age are your _____. When they urge you to do something, they are using _____. A friend's request to help rake a neighbor's leaves is _____ peer pressure. A request that ends with "No one will find out" is probably _____ peer pressure.

❷ List three places where you might meet new friends.

❸ Critical Thinking Describe how you could use positive peer pressure to help a friend make a wise, healthful decision.

❹ (Focus Skill) MAIN IDEA AND DETAILS Draw and complete this graphic organizer to give reasons friendships can change.

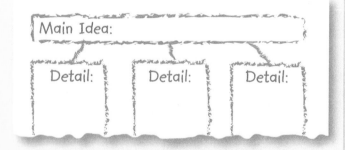

Main Idea:

Detail: | Detail: | Detail:

❺ Write to Inform—Explanation

Write a request that uses positive peer pressure and one that uses negative peer pressure. Explain how these requests are the same and different.

330

Trustworthiness

Being a Dependable Friend

A dependable friend shows up on time, is there when you need help, does what he or she promised to do, and can keep a secret. A dependable friend is also someone you can trust to do the right thing. If you are tempted to give in to negative peer pressure, a dependable friend says, "No, we don't do that" or "No, that wouldn't be right."

Here's how you can be a dependable friend:

- **Set a good example for your friends by following the school rules and your family's values and rules. If your friends do not share your values, such as being honest and a good sport, start looking for new friends.**

- **Do not give in to negative peer pressure. For example, a dependable friend does not try to gain attention by joining peers in making fun of someone.**

- **Support your friends' healthful decisions.**

- **Join friends in activities that provide exercise and fun. Find ways to adapt activities so that everyone can participate.**

- **Encourage friends to use their skills and talents and to learn new skills.**

Activity

List ways to show that you are dependable. These might include meeting your friends on time, doing your chores at home, and saying *no* when someone wants you to do something against your family rules. Then choose something that is hard for you to do, such as not joining in on gossip. Plan how you can become more dependable in that area.

Working Together

Lesson Focus

Working well with others requires skill in listening, cooperating, and respecting differences.

Why Learn This?

Learning how to work with others will help you throughout your lifetime.

Vocabulary

collaborate
stereotype
prejudice
diversity

Listening

Do you like to work with people who do not listen to you? Most people don't. People know when others are listening—or not listening—to them. Listening shows respect for others' opinions. It shows consideration for their feelings. Listening helps you better understand the other person's point of view.

Here are some ways to show others that you are listening:

- Look at the person who is speaking.
- Lean toward the speaker to show your interest.
- Nod to show that you want to hear more.
- Do not interrupt to tell your own stories.
- Ask questions and make comments to show that you are interested and want to hear more.

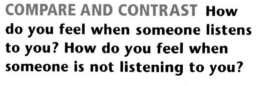

Then I heard a loud crash behind me!

What happened next?

ACTIVITY

Building Good Character

Respect A student who is blind has joined your class. How can you show respect by including the new student in a group activity? List ways you can adapt your classroom environment for this student.

COMPARE AND CONTRAST How do you feel when someone listens to you? How do you feel when someone is not listening to you?

Cooperating

To cooperate means "to collaborate." When you **collaborate** (kuh•LAB•uh•rayt), you work with other people toward a goal. For example, you might collaborate to complete a group science project or to plan a birthday party. Working with a group, however, takes patience and skill.

Group members often have different opinions. When the members respect each other, these ideas can help them solve problems and meet their goals. Without respect, different opinions can lead to arguments.

Some people are quick to judge those who are different from them. They make oversimplified judgments based on stereotypes. A **stereotype** (STAIR•ee•uh•typ) is the belief that everyone in a certain group has the same characteristics. For example, some people might think that everyone who lives in a big city is rude.

Stereotyping can lead to **prejudice** (PREJ•uh•dis), or an opinion or judgment of an entire group that is not based on fact. Prejudiced people might decide that since everyone who lives in a big city is rude, they do not like anyone who lives in a big city! Stereotyping and prejudice keep people from working together.

CAUSE AND EFFECT How could forming a stereotype about someone keep you from getting to know him or her?

Consumer Activity

Analyze Media Messages Read three newspaper articles and identify stereotypes. Use them to complete this sentence: "Everyone who _____ is _____." Then write a sentence or description that restates the same information without the stereotype.

◄ People look different on the outside, and they have different feelings on the inside.

333

Making a Difference in Your Community

Can people your age help others learn not to use stereotypes or be prejudiced? Can students your age help others work together with respect and consideration? The answer is *yes*!

You can start by finding out about volunteer opportunities in your community. You can volunteer wherever you see a need. Some students your age help organize recycling programs in their schools. Others read books to younger children or exercise dogs at animal shelters.

There are many other ways young people make a difference in their communities. They haul away tons of litter to turn trash-covered lots into parks. They clean up old hiking trails and help build new ones. They help at community dinners for the elderly and listen to their stories of long ago.

Attending festivals is a good way to learn about other cultures. People are different and alike in many ways. ▼

Joining in on community projects can help you learn about **diversity** (duh•VER•suh•tee), or the ways people differ from each other. When students help in their communities, they might work with people who speak other languages, eat different foods, wear different clothes, and celebrate different holidays. The more you find out about the differences between people, the more you will notice the likenesses!

Although people differ in many ways, we all have the same needs and many of the same wants. You can make a difference by helping others meet their needs or wants. For example, you can use your skill in being a good friend and a good listener. Don't wait until you are an adult to put your skills to work. You can make a difference now in the lives of others!

DRAW CONCLUSIONS How can volunteering help you make new friends?

Health & Technology

Collaborate Through the Internet Projects like iEarn (International Education and Resource Network) are helping young people in schools around the world work together online. About 1,000,000 students, ages five to nineteen, are carrying out 120 projects. For example, students from Suriname and the United States are working on a project called Medicine in Our Backyard. All the projects help young people in many nations learn more about each other and how to make a difference.

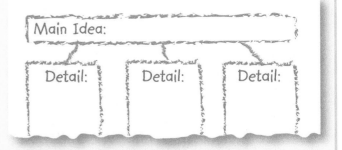

Lesson 5 Summary and Review

❶ Summarize with Vocabulary

Use vocabulary from this lesson to complete the statements.

A person who thinks that everyone who lives in a certain part of town is the same is using a _____. A person who dislikes others because they live in a certain part of town displays _____. Instead of seeing differences as obstacles, people should appreciate their _____.

❷ Name a stereotype some people have about a group, such as the elderly. Why is this stereotype incorrect?

❸ Critical Thinking What would your life be like if we all looked the same, spoke the same language, and ate the same foods?

❹ MAIN IDEA AND DETAILS Draw and complete this graphic organizer to show how prejudice is harmful.

Main Idea:

Detail: | Detail: | Detail:

❺ Write to Inform—Report

Choose a culture in your community that is different from yours, and write a short report about it. To gather information, you might talk to people from that culture, use library reference sources, or visit reliable Internet sites.

Resolving Conflict

Seeking Peaceful Solutions

A **conflict** is a dispute or strong disagreement. Conflicts happen all the time to people of all ages. Conflicts become problems when people cannot reach peaceful solutions. In some cases, a conflict that is not resolved may lead to anger or even violence. A serious conflict can end a friendship.

People choose how to resolve their conflicts. Some people choose to pretend there is no problem. Others choose to lose their tempers and call each other names. Wise people use conflict resolution to find a solution that everyone can accept. **Conflict resolution** is a process for solving problems peacefully.

Conflicts are bound to happen when people live and work together. Conflicts can happen at school or at home when people have different needs and expectations. ▶

336

Steps for Resolving Conflict

Use "I" messages to tell how you feel and to explain your point of view in a respectful way.

Listen to the other person, and consider his or her feelings and point of view.

Work together to brainstorm as many solutions as possible.

Choose a solution that enables both of you to "win." You each might have to *compromise*, or give something up.

One important part of conflict resolution is a process called brainstorming. **Brainstorming** means "thinking of as many solutions to a problem as possible." Everyone who is brainstorming shares any ideas that come to mind. No one evaluates the ideas until the brainstorming is finished. Then you can eliminate any ideas that will not work or that someone involved cannot accept.

If two people have trouble finding a solution they can both accept, they might ask a mediator to help. A *mediator* (MEE·dee·ay·ter) is someone trained to resolve conflicts.

DRAW CONCLUSIONS Why might students your age have trouble resolving conflicts on their own?

337

Conflicts in the Community

Adults sometimes need mediators to help them solve conflicts. Police departments and other government agencies often hire mediators. The most important thing these people do is listen and encourage the people having the conflict to listen to each other. Then the mediators help in brainstorming possible solutions. The goal is to solve the problems peacefully.

Knowing how to solve conflicts helps you feel confident. It also shows others that you are a good example to follow. Being able to solve your own conflicts is part of becoming responsible for yourself. It strengthens your self-concept and gives you skills that you can use throughout your life.

SEQUENCE In conflict resolution, what should you do before you begin brainstorming?

Lesson 6 Summary and Review

❶ Summarize with Vocabulary

Use vocabulary and other terms from this lesson to complete the statements.

Another term for *disagreement* is _____. You can use the process of _____ to find a solution that everyone can accept. When you try to think of many possible ways to solve a conflict, you are _____. If you cannot solve a conflict on your own, a _____ might help.

❷ If everyone in your school practiced conflict resolution, what do you think could change?

❸ Critical Thinking Why is ignoring a conflict a bad idea?

❹ **MAIN IDEA AND DETAILS** Draw and complete this graphic organizer to show why conflicts are normal.

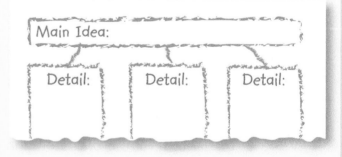

Main Idea:

Detail:　　Detail:　　Detail:

❺ Write to Entertain—Song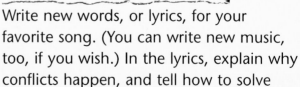

Write new words, or lyrics, for your favorite song. (You can write new music, too, if you wish.) In the lyrics, explain why conflicts happen, and tell how to solve them peacefully.

338

ACTIVITIES

Physical Education

Isometric Exercises Find a description of isometric exercises, in which you tense and then relax certain muscles. Try some of these exercises to see if you think they might help reduce stress or get rid of angry feelings.

Science

Setting Realistic Goals
Many people are working to protect our environment. You can do your part by setting a goal to improve your school or neighborhood. Choose a goal that you can reach by yourself. For example, you might decide to reuse paper or to buy only things made from recycled products. You might also walk whenever you can, instead of riding in a car. You might help in school or community beautification projects.

Technology Project

Communicate Online Use a computer to communicate with members of another sixth-grade class in a local school. Use e-mail to get to know students in that class. Perhaps you will become friends and—with your parents' and teachers' permission—meet each other.

GO **For more activities, visit**
ONLINE **The Learning Site.**
www.harcourtschool.com/health

Home & Community

Reducing Stress Talk with your family members about stress. What kinds of things help them to reduce their stress? What seems to work best?

Career Link

Psychiatrist Imagine that you are a psychiatrist. A young patient comes to you and says, "There must be something wrong with me because I am always having arguments with my friends. Help me!" Write what you would tell your young patient about conflicts and friendships.

Reading Skill

MAIN IDEA AND DETAILS

Draw and then use this graphic organizer to answer questions 1 and 2.

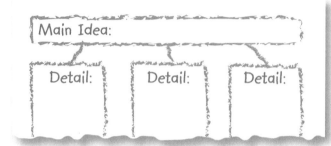

Main Idea:

Detail: Detail: Detail:

1 Complete the following main idea with the name of an uncomfortable or unpleasant feeling: Being responsible means knowing how to deal with _____.

2 In each Detail box, write a way to manage or deal with the feeling you named.

 Use Vocabulary

Match each term in Column B with its meaning in Column A.

Column A	Column B
3 Your opinion of how you look	**A** self-concept
4 Work together	**B** conflict
	C collaborate
5 People your own age	**D** goal
6 The way you think about yourself	**E** body image
	F peers
7 Something you want	
8 An argument or disagreement	

Check Understanding

Choose the letter of the correct answer.

9 When you think of as many solutions as possible, you are _____. (p. 337)
A collaborating
B brainstorming
C using peer pressure
D being aggressive

10 Thinking that all teenagers like loud music is an example of _____. (p. 333)
F diversity   H peer pressure
G self-control   J a stereotype

11 Riding bikes and listening to music are activities that provide _____. (p. 323)
A aggression   C relaxation
B diversity   D conflict resolution

12 Mohammed is from Saudi Arabia, and Colleen is from Ireland. They add to the _____ in their classroom. (p. 335)
F mediation   H self-respect
G diversity   J brainstorming

13 Learning to use "I" messages instead of shouting to express anger helps promote _____. (p. 321)
A anxiety   C self-confidence
B goal-setting   D peer pressure

14 Staring someone down is a form of _____. (pp. 320–321)
F collaboration   H aggression
G self-respect   J prejudice

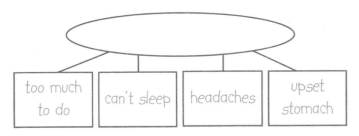

15 Which word belongs in the oval?
(pp. 322–323)

  A grief   **C** anger

  B conflict   **D** stress

16 In _____, two people try to solve a
problem in a way they both can accept.
(pp. 336–337)

  F conflict resolution

  G collaboration

  H peer pressure

  J goal-setting

17 What is this girl showing? (p. 312)

  A self-respect   **C** anxiety

  B aggression   **D** conflict
                            resolution

18 If you feel sad and no longer enjoy doing
things with your friends, you might be
feeling _____. (pp. 324–325)

  F peer pressure   **H** anxiety

  G grief   **J** anger

19 Someone who doesn't like people who
have red hair is showing _____. (p. 333)

  A diversity   **C** aggression

  B prejudice   **D** self-control

Think Critically

20 Charlene cannot decide whether to stay
home and finish her book report or go
to the movies with her friends. How can
having goals help her make this decision?

21 Describe three ways you could use positive
peer pressure in your life.

22 Paul is feeling stressed this afternoon
because he needs to learn his lines for the
school play, but he also needs to go to
basketball practice. How could his stress
turn into anxiety? How can he prevent this
from happening?

Apply Skills

23 **BUILDING GOOD CHARACTER**
Trustworthiness You and your best
friend sit beside each other in math class.
Tomorrow you are having a big test, and
your friend asks to be able to look at your
paper during the test. How can you be a
dependable friend?

24 **LIFE SKILLS**
Manage Stress A student at school
constantly teases and makes fun of you. It's
gotten so bad that you don't want to go
to school tomorrow morning. You consider
pretending to be sick so you can stay
home. What is a more healthful way to
cope with this situation?

Write About Health

25 **Write to Inform—Explanation**
Explain why it's important to know
yourself well.

341

11 Family
and
Responsibility

Reading Skill

DRAW CONCLUSIONS Sometimes, authors don't tell you everything directly. You have to use information from the passage plus what you already know to draw conclusions. Use the Reading in Health Handbook on pages 402–403 and this graphic organizer to help you read the health facts in this chapter.

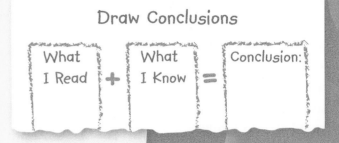

Draw Conclusions

What I Read + What I Know = Conclusion:

Health Graph

INTERPRET DATA Sixth graders are busy people with lots of obligations and responsibilities. According to this graph, what kinds of activities do sixth graders spend most of their time doing?

Percent of Sixth Graders Participating

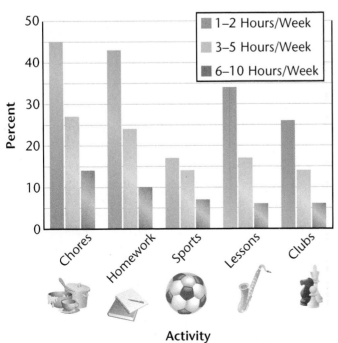

Legend:
- 1–2 Hours/Week
- 3–5 Hours/Week
- 6–10 Hours/Week

Y-axis: Percent (0, 10, 20, 30, 40, 50)

X-axis (Activity): Chores, Homework, Sports, Lessons, Clubs

Daily Physical Activity

Exercise should be an important part of your daily routine. Developing ways to exercise with family members will help you live a healthful lifestyle and help strengthen your family.

 Be Active!

Use the selection, Track 11, **Funky Flex**, to practice exercises you can share with your family.

Being a Responsible Family Member

Lesson Focus

Self-discipline and accepting responsibility are important skills that help build strong families.

Why Learn This?

Being a responsible family member makes you feel good about yourself. It is a part of becoming mature.

Vocabulary

responsible
self-discipline

Being Responsible

A family is a kind of team. Each member depends on the other members to do their part. A strong family is made up of responsible team members who care for each other.

Becoming a responsible person is an important part of growing up. Being **responsible** (rih•SPAHN•suh•buhl) means that other people can depend on you. It means that you keep your word. When you agree to clean your room every week, you do it without being asked. When you set a goal, you work hard to make it happen.

Being a responsible family member means that you follow family rules and respect family traditions. When there is a family activity, you join in. It also means that you try to resolve conflicts with your brothers, sisters, or friends by yourself. It means you are aware of times when family members need extra help or support, and you find ways to give it to them.

Responsible family members do their part. All of these people are showing responsibility in different ways.

Self-Discipline

Having **self-discipline** (self•DIS•uh•plin), the ability to control your own actions, is a big part of being responsible. Self-discipline means choosing to do what you know you should do. For example, if it is your job to take out the trash, you do it even if you don't like to, because that is your responsibility. Or if you have a book report to do, you spend less time playing games until the report is finished.

When you have self-discipline, you don't lose control when you feel hurt or angry. You can respectfully accept limits that your parents and teachers set. You follow family rules and respect family traditions.

When you watch over your own actions, your parents and other adults don't have to. You take charge of yourself. Your family can count on you. As with any skill, being more responsible takes practice. You can start practicing right away.

 DRAW CONCLUSIONS How are discipline and self-discipline related?

ACTIVITY
Building Good Character

Responsibility Ari is supposed to go straight home from school. On his way home, he sees some friends going into the community center. They ask him to come in and play a quick game of basketball. What is the responsible thing for Ari to do?

Quick Activity

Analyze Responsible Behaviors Look at the photographs on these two pages. How is each person showing responsibility? List things you can do to be a responsible family member.

345

Real-Life Situation

One sign of responsibility is taking care of yourself so that others do not have to.

Real-Life Plan

Write a list of ways you take care of yourself. What new ways could you learn and add to the list?

Responsible Family Members

Being a responsible family member—a team player—is an important role. A responsible family member

- practices self-discipline.
- is dependable.
- puts family plans first.
- respects family traditions.
- offers help when needed.

- follows family rules.
- participates in family events.
- tries to resolve conflicts.
- listens to others.

CAUSE AND EFFECT How can a family member's behavior help make the family strong?

Having self-discipline means putting responsibilities first. ▶

Lesson 1 Summary and Review

① Summarize with Vocabulary

Use vocabulary and other terms from this lesson to complete the statements.

A family is a kind of _____. Members count on each other. For that reason, each member needs to be _____. A responsible family member follows family _____ and respects family _____. The ability to control your own actions, called _____, is a big part of being responsible.

② How is being responsible a part of growing up?

③ Critical Thinking How can your responsible behaviors help your family?

④ DRAW CONCLUSIONS Why is it important for family members to be responsible?

What I Read	+	What I Know	=	Conclusion:

⑤ Write to Inform—Description

Describe how your family benefits from five responsible behaviors you practice.

Caring

Caring About Family Members

Caring is important in a strong, healthy family. When family members truly care about each other, they are happier, more self-confident, and better able to handle hard times.

Here are some ways you can show family members you care about them:

- **Be appreciative. Recognize others' talents and contributions. Say, "Thank you."**
- **Be considerate. Try to look at situations from the other person's point of view.**
- **Think of others' feelings. Be kind.**
- **Show respect.**
- **Give support. Be there to listen and to help.**
- **Learn to forgive. Learn to let bygones be bygones. Let go of hurt feelings.**

Activity

Play a game of appreciation and respect with your family. For each family member, write the person's name at the top of a sheet of paper. Pass the papers around. When you get each paper, write something you appreciate or admire about the person. When everyone is finished, read the papers aloud.

You can show caring by making a card for a family member who is ill. ▶

Communication and Cooperation in Families

Working as a Team

Honest, respectful communication and cooperation are important in a healthy, loving family. Communication determines how family members relate to each other. Respectful, honest communication allows family members to share their ideas, feelings, and needs. This benefits everyone.

Like any team, a family runs more smoothly when the members cooperate. That means working together toward shared goals.

For example, suppose everyone in your family wants to have a picnic at the lake on Saturday. There are some jobs that need to be done before you can go. How can all of you cooperate so you can have the picnic?

 DRAW CONCLUSIONS How might cooperation help in meeting a goal that benefits the entire family? Give an example that involves good communication.

Personal Health Plan

Real-Life Situation
Suppose your family needs to paint a room.
Real-Life Plan
Write a list of ways you can work as a team member to paint the room with your family.

How are the families on these pages practicing communication and cooperation? ▶

348

Abuse and Neglect

Sometimes family members act in ways that are not healthful. They may relate to each other in harmful and irresponsible ways. When that happens, the whole family suffers.

Abuse and neglect are unhealthful behaviors. Abuse is the harmful or hurtful treatment of another person. It can be physical or verbal. Neglect is the failure to take care of another person. Neglect can be a form of abuse.

When family members act in ways that are harmful to the family or to themselves, they still need your love and support. It's also important to know how to take care of yourself. Find ways to express your own feelings in nonthreatening ways. Talk to a parent, a relative, a trusted adult friend, or your school counselor. There are laws to protect children from abuse and neglect. Every child deserves a safe and loving home.

COMPARE AND CONTRAST Make a chart to show some of the differences between healthful and unhealthful communications and behaviors.

Health & Technology

Cell Phones and Pagers

Many families use cell phones and pagers to stay in touch. Some scientists think that cell phones might be dangerous to users' health. Here are some ways to protect yourself and others while you wait for this issue to be resolved:

- Use a regular phone whenever you can.
- If your cell phone has an antenna, pull it up while you're talking.
- Never use a cell phone inside a hospital.
- Always follow posted cell phone rules.

▲ You are being responsible when you let your family know where you are and what you're doing.

Consumer Activity

Analyze Media Messages Analyze a family conflict on a popular TV show. Did the family find a solution that was fair to everyone? How realistic was it?

Conflict Resolution

Even when family members work together, there sometimes are disagreements. All families have conflicts. Learning to compromise is part of resolving conflicts. When people **compromise** (KAHM•pruh•myz), they each get something they want by giving up part of what they want. Compromising takes patience and skill. To compromise, you must understand that other people's needs are important to them.

Compromising means you won't get your way at times. Sometimes you will be disappointed, but you'll find solutions everyone can live with. You'll be better able to solve problems in the future.

> **SUMMARIZE How can communication and cooperation help you avoid or resolve conflict?**

◀ All families have conflicts. Learning how to resolve them takes patience and skill. How is this girl helping her younger brother and sister resolve their conflict?

Ways to Resolve Conflicts

1. Talk over problems.

2. Express your feelings honestly and respectfully.

3. Listen closely to other people.

4. Get help from a third person who is not part of the conflict.

5. Use humor.

6. Accept responsibility for your actions.

7. Admit your mistakes. Apologize.

8. Be willing to compromise.

9. Follow family rules.

10. Take time out to cool down and think of solutions.

ACTIVITY

Life Skills

Resolve Conflicts

Stewart's younger brother, Jamie, is riding a tricycle. His sister, Lisa, wants a turn. Lisa and Jamie are yelling and pushing each other. How can Stewart help them resolve this conflict without simply telling them what to do?

Lesson 2 Summary and Review

1 Summarize with Vocabulary

Use vocabulary and other terms from this lesson to complete the statements.

Two important parts of family life are _____ and _____. When family members _____, or work together, everyone benefits. Still, _____ can come up. Sometimes family members have to _____ to resolve a conflict. _____ and _____ are unhealthful, harmful behaviors.

2 Critical Thinking List three situations in which it would be helpful for family members to cooperate.

3 What is a compromise?

4 DRAW CONCLUSIONS Why do responsible family members compromise and cooperate?

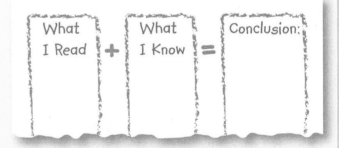

What I Read	+	What I Know	=	Conclusion:

5 Write to Entertain—Story

Write a story about a family conflict. Tell how two family members reach a compromise to solve their problem.

Resolve Conflicts
with Family Members

The needs and wishes of family members sometimes conflict with one another. Often, thinking through a situation can help you resolve a conflict.

Nara wants to get online to do her homework. Her sister, Alicia, has been on the phone for more than thirty minutes. Nara is getting impatient. She has already interrupted Alicia's call three times. Because of that, Alicia is tying up the line longer. Nara unplugs the phone and disconnects Alicia's call. Both girls are angry. How can they resolve this conflict?

1 **Use "I" messages to tell how you feel.**

I am tired of waiting.

At first, both girls want to blame each other. Then they start to calm down. They both realize that it will be better to tell how they feel by using sentences with "I" instead of "you".

2 **Listen to the other person. Consider the other person's point of view.**

I'm sorry I disconnected your call, but I was angry!

I get angry, too, when I feel rushed.

The girls keep talking in a respectful way. It's hard for them not to interrupt each other, but they both control themselves and listen.

352

3 Negotiate.

I need to get online to do my homework.

Give me five minutes to finish up my call, and then the line is yours.

Because they listened to each other, Nara and Alicia can see each other's point of view. They work out a fair system for using and sharing the phone line.

4 Compromise on a solution.

Alicia got the five minutes more that she wanted on the phone conversation. Nara was able to go online after that. The girls resolved their conflict by compromising.

Problem Solving

A. Wednesday is family night at Zane's house. Zane's friends have invited him to go to a movie this Wednesday night. Zane really wants to go to the movie, but his younger brother wants him to stay home.
- Use the steps for **Resolving Conflict** to help Zane with his problem.

B. Paula's older sister likes to tease. Paula feels that her sister is always picking on her, and she doesn't like it.
- Explain how Paula can show responsibility and self-control by using the steps for **Resolving Conflict** with her sister.

Dealing with Changes in Families

Families Change

Many different kinds of events affect families. When one of these events occurs, the family changes as a result. Any major change challenges family members to stay close. They need to talk about their feelings, respect the feelings of others, and find new ways to be together as a family.

Change can be good or bad. Either way, it is stressful. Some changes can seem good *and* bad. For example, a new baby brings joy to a family. The baby also brings added responsibilities. Family members need time to adjust.

When things change, old routines are interrupted. It takes time and attention to get used to new ways. The question to keep in mind is "How can I be responsible and help out during a time of adjustment?"

⭐ Focus Skill **DRAW CONCLUSIONS How might a family be affected by a major change such as having a new baby?**

◀ The adoption of a child is a happy change for a family.

▲ It's hard to say good-bye to friends, but telephones and e-mail make it easy to keep in touch. Think of moving as a great adventure.

Job Loss and Moving

Most parents try hard to provide for their families, but sometimes a parent loses his or her job. It can happen to anyone for many different reasons. Losing a job can be frightening for a parent, and it's hard for children to see their parents worried or unhappy. You may feel worried and sad, too. You might think it's up to you to make things better, but don't worry too much. Talk to your parents about your feelings. Help out by being a responsible family member and by thinking of small ways to show your parents that you care.

A move can involve a new house, neighborhood, school, or city—or all of these things. It can mean saying good-bye to people and places that are familiar to you. Your feelings may be a mixture of excitement, fear, sadness, and anticipation. You will make new friends and get used to your new school, but these adjustments take time. Be patient. You and your family can help each other by pulling together as a team.

SEQUENCE Give the order in which changes might occur when a family moves to a new location.

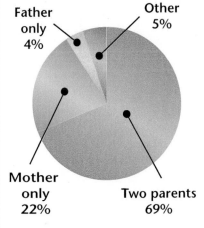

Family Living Arrangements

Father only 4%

Other 5%

Mother only 22%

Two parents 69%

Quick Activity

Interpret Data The circle graph shows the percent of children living in different family arrangements in the year 2000. In which family arrangement did the most children live? What percent of children lived in this kind of family?

Divorce, Marriage, and Remarriage

When a family member marries or divorces, the rest of the family changes, too. Sometimes these changes are very difficult. If a **sibling**—a brother or a sister—marries, he or she may be busy with the new family. If your parents divorce, you may feel angry, unhappy, unsure, and worried. If a parent remarries, you'll have to get used to a stepparent and maybe stepbrothers and stepsisters. Getting used to changes in the family takes patience and understanding. Remember:

- Give yourself and others time to adjust.
- Talk about your feelings with someone you trust.
- Be cooperative.
- Make an effort to find the positive aspects of the change.

MAIN IDEA AND DETAILS **How do divorce, marriage, and remarriage affect a family? Give examples of ways a family might change in each situation.**

When a sibling marries, you may feel happy, sad, left out, important, or all these things. ▶

◀ During stressful times, make time for things you enjoy.

Illness and Death

When a member of your family is seriously ill, it can be a scary and uncertain time. Everyone's responsibilities and schedules may change. You may feel worried, sad, and even angry. Although you want to help the family member who is ill, you may not know what to do.

A death in the family is perhaps the biggest change a family can experience. Even when it is expected, death comes as a shock. After a death occurs in a family, nothing is ever quite the same. It usually takes a long time to adjust.

The period during a serious illness or after a death is a hard time for everyone. It is a time for family members to pull together. Talk to each other. Be supportive and caring.

 DRAW CONCLUSIONS What kinds of changes in schedules and responsibilities might occur during a serious illness?

Quick Activity

Cope with Change
List six things you can do to help yourself or someone else cope with a big change. Which of these have you tried?

357

Consumer Activity

Accessing Valid Health Information There are organizations such as the American Red Cross that can help people deal with family problems. Ask your school counselor or media specialist to help you find the names of three organizations. List them and their contact information.

Other Serious Problems

Whenever a problem arises in a family, the first place to turn is to parents or other family members. Sometimes, however, the problems are too difficult for a family to deal with alone. It's important to know that there are other adults you and your family can turn to for help.

 DRAW CONCLUSIONS How can a change be good and bad at the same time?

Problems Families Seek Help For	Whom to Ask for Help
• Drugs	• Family members outside your home
• Alcohol	• School counselor or nurse
• Abuse	• Teacher
• Anger or grief	• Clergy member
• Ongoing conflicts that may become violent	• Trusted neighbor or family friend

Lesson 3 Summary and Review

1 Summarize with Vocabulary

Use vocabulary and other terms from this lesson to complete the statements.

All families go through _____. Major changes include the addition of a new _____, moving, losing a job, divorce, and marriage. Talking with someone you _____ can help you in times of change.

2 What types of changes might a family go through?

3 Critical Thinking Why is it important for family members to pull together in times of change?

4 **DRAW CONCLUSIONS How and why do family members react differently to change?**

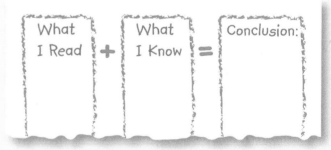

What I Read	+	What I Know	=	Conclusion:

5 Write to Express—Solution to a Problem

Write a "Dear Friend" letter about a family change. Then switch roles and answer the letter with advice about how to cope with the change.

ACTIVITIES

Art

Family Collage Using magazine pictures, drawings, and designs, make a collage of families in different situations. Show the things about family life that you learned in this chapter.

Physical Education

Family Favorites Make a collection of family members' favorite songs. You can make a family songbook of lyrics and sheet music and record favorites onto a cassette tape or CD. Then work with your parents to organize a family fitness night. Use the recording for dancing or exercising together.

Technology Project

Photo Album Use a computer to create a family photo album. Gather photographs from different years and situations. Scan the photographs into a computer. Use a software program to arrange the images in a computer album. Copy the album onto CD-ROMs so that each family member has a copy. If a computer or scanner is not available, place the photographs on pages of a real photo album.

GO ONLINE For more activities, visit The Learning Site.
www.harcourtschool.com/health

Home & Community

Communicating Make a special place in your home for notes and other messages from family members. You might make a bulletin board or use special magnets to hold messages on your refrigerator.

Career Link

Child-Care Worker Many families need help in caring for younger children while the parents work. Child-care workers offer a range of services. Some will care for infants and toddlers, while others care for older children. Suppose that you are a child-care worker. Write a letter to introduce yourself to parents. Tell them what your qualifications are and the services you offer.

359

Reading Skill

DRAW CONCLUSIONS

Draw and then use this graphic organizer to answer questions 1 and 2.

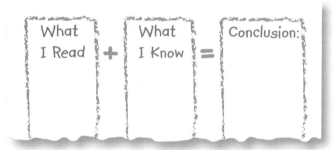

What I Read + What I Know = Conclusion:

1 How can doing your own laundry help you and your family?

2 How can you show a family member that you care about him or her?

 Use Vocabulary

Match each term in Column B with its meaning in Column A.

Column A	Column B
3 Brother or sister	**A** self-discipline
4 Ability to control your actions	**B** responsible
	C compromise
5 Harmful, hurtful treatment	**D** abuse
	E sibling
6 A group of people who care about each other	**F** family
	G cooperation
7 Working together	**H** neglect
8 Dependable, trustworthy	
9 Failure to take care of another person	
10 Settle a difference by giving up something	

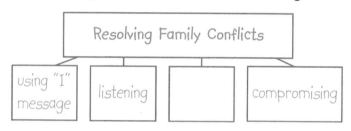 **Check Understanding**

Choose the letter of the correct answer.

11 How is a family like a team? (p. 344)
  A A family plays sports.
  B Family members work together.
  C Family members wear uniforms.
  D Family members act alone.

12 People your age help their families by spending a lot of time _____. (p. 344)
  F working   **H** singing
  G doing chores   **J** walking

Resolving Family Conflicts

using "I" message | listening | | compromising

13 Which of the following is missing from the graphic organizer? (pp. 352–353)
  A demanding your rights
  B leaving the room
  C negotiating
  D calling the family doctor

14 Being responsible includes _____. (p. 344)
  F being selfish   **H** being late
  G arguing   **J** setting goals

15 Which of these behaviors is responsible? (pp. 344–345)
  A cleaning your room
  B doing your homework on time
  C teaching your little brother to tie his shoes
  D all of these

16 Which of these is unhealthful? (p. 349)
 F verbally abusing a sibling
 G apologizing for something you did
 H keeping a promise
 J telling the truth

17 When family members cooperate, everyone _____. (p. 348)
 A gets tired
 B loses
 C misses out
 D benefits

18 Which of these situations requires a compromise? (p. 350)
 F borrowing a sweater
 G making a sandwich
 H having the flu
 J settling a disagreement

19 Which of the following is **NOT** a major change in a family's life? (p. 354)
 A a serious illness
 B a new baby
 C a birthday
 D a move to a new city

Think Critically

20 What is a strong family? Make a list of characteristics that all families share. Also make a list of characteristics that all strong families share.

21 Jake's sister Vanessa broke her arm one week before her basketball team was to play in a tournament. That same week, Jake's team played in a different tournament. Jake brought home a trophy. How might Jake and Vanessa feel about his award?

22 Both of Reese's parents have been working a lot of overtime lately. Reese volunteered to take on extra responsibilities around the house to help out. Now Reese is starting to realize that she's taken on too much. What can Reese do to solve her problem?

Apply Skills

23 **BUILDING GOOD CHARACTER**
 Caring Your mom has been sick in bed for the past two days. She's still not feeling well, but she thinks she needs to get out of bed to care for the family. Identify three ways you can be a loving, caring family member.

24 **LIFE SKILLS**
 Resolve Conflicts You borrowed a CD from your brother without asking, and you lost it. When you told your brother, he was very angry. How can you resolve this conflict?

Write About Health

25 **Write to Inform—Explanation** Explain how a strong family uses cooperation, communication, and compromise in daily activities.

Reading Skill

SEQUENCE You sequence things when you determine the order of events or steps in a process. Use the Reading in Health Handbook on pages 408–409 and this graphic organizer to help you read the health facts in this chapter.

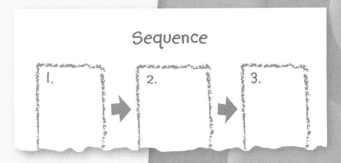

Sequence

1. → 2. → 3.

Health Graph

INTERPRET DATA Today, 28 percent of waste in the United States is recycled. This is almost twice the amount recycled 15 years ago. What is the percent difference between the least and the most recycled materials shown on the graph?

Percents of Materials That Are Recycled

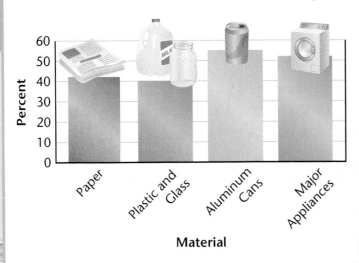

Daily Physical Activity

Be aware of community resources, such as parks and bicycle paths, that you can use for exercising. Using these resources can help you stay healthy.

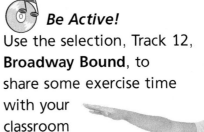 **Be Active!**
Use the selection, Track 12, **Broadway Bound**, to share some exercise time with your classroom community.

Preparing for Disasters

Lesson Focus

Local governments and volunteer groups plan ahead to help people cope with disasters.

Why Learn This?

You can use what you learn to make sure your community is prepared for all disasters.

Vocabulary

natural disaster

Health & Technology

Doppler Radar One way scientists monitor and predict tornadoes is by radar. Doppler radar can show forecasters the strength, structure, and movement of a storm. Air moving toward the radar device is shown in green and blue. Air moving away from the radar device is shown in red and yellow. Conditions that give rise to tornadoes are shown on the radar screen by areas where red and yellow touch green and blue. Objects caught up in a tornado may show up as white on the radar screen.

Natural Disasters

The whirling funnel cloud shown on page 365 means trouble. It shows a powerful storm, a tornado, approaching. Tornadoes are windstorms that roar across the land at speeds of up to 70 miles (about 112 km) per hour. Large objects such as railroad cars and airplanes have been lifted into the air by tornadoes. Tornadoes are usually less than a mile (about 1.6 km) in diameter. The damage they cause is local, but where they touch down, they can destroy everything in their paths.

Another destructive storm is a hurricane. Hurricanes are large swirling masses of clouds and rain pushed by strong winds. Hurricanes form over warm oceans. When hurricanes reach land, they demolish houses and uproot trees. Unlike tornadoes, hurricanes are hundreds of miles wide. The damage caused by a hurricane can cover thousands of square miles and affect thousands of people.

Just as tornadoes and hurricanes are natural disasters, so are blizzards, floods, and earthquakes. A **natural disaster** is an event that occurs in nature and causes great damage.

A blizzard is a type of natural disaster that occurs in cold weather. During blizzard conditions, snow falls rapidly or is blown by winds of 35 miles (about 55 km) or more per hour. As a result, whole cities may shut down because travel is dangerous.

When heavy rain or melting snow causes rivers, lakes, or streams to overflow their banks, floods occur. Floodwaters wash over fields, onto streets, and into buildings. They can destroy crops, homes, and businesses.

◄ Doppler radar images show storms that can lead to tornadoes.

United States Disasters

Type	Results
Hurricanes	In 2001 Tropical Storm Allison caused more than $6 billion in property and crop damage in Texas.
Tornadoes	In 2003 the United States experienced one of the worst and most costly tornado seasons on record.
Earthquakes	On November 3, 2002, Alaska experienced a major earthquake, registering a magnitude of 7.9.
Blizzards	In March 2003 a blizzard dropped more than 8 feet of snow in Colorado and caused $100 million in damage.
Floods	In 1993 the Mississippi River flooded, and 12,000 square miles of farmland became useless; damage amounted to $10–25 billion.

An earthquake may begin without warning, causing the ground to vibrate. These vibrations can cause landslides or rockslides in hilly or mountainous areas. Earthquakes that disturb large portions of the ocean floor may result in giant waves that can damage coastal areas. Cities directly affected by earthquakes may suffer damaged buildings and collapsed bridges. Fires caused by gas escaping from broken gas pipes can also cause damage. In homes, injuries may result as chimneys topple, furniture falls over, or walls weaken and collapse.

 SEQUENCE What are the events of hurricane development and movement?

The winds of a tornado can gust up to 300 miles (about 480 km) per hour. ▶

Local Governments Prepare

Surviving a dangerous storm or an earthquake requires the cooperation of many people. Local governments work with many other organizations to help communities prepare for and respond to natural disasters. To prepare for disasters, local governments

- teach people about disasters.
- set up emergency shelters.
- plan ways to warn communities.
- work with police, fire departments, and hospitals.
- plan routes for people to follow.
- buy and maintain material and equipment such as sandbags, sand, salt, dump trucks, and snowplows.

DRAW CONCLUSIONS **Why is it important for local governments to plan routes for people to follow in an emergency?**

Local Governments Respond

When a natural disaster occurs, plans that local governments have made are put to the test. For example, as a hurricane approaches, the local government directs efforts to close businesses and limit traffic as quickly as possible. During the storm, officials use radio and television stations to give continual updates on the storm's position, path, and strength and to give instructions to people in the path of the storm.

Similar steps are taken for other storms. For example, during a winter storm, local governments send out snowplows and sand or salt trucks to improve dangerous road conditions.

Once the storm or other natural disaster is over, local governments repair damaged roads and downed electrical and telephone lines and organize cleanup activities. If the damage is great, local officials may ask the governor or the President to declare the area a disaster area, so the community can get state or federal help.

Focus Skill **SEQUENCE** **How do local governments respond to natural disasters?**

▲ Cleanup after a hurricane includes removing the remains of homes and businesses.

Volunteers Prepare

Before a Disaster The American Red Cross is the largest and best known of the many volunteer groups that help communities during disasters. It has hundreds of local chapters throughout the United States and thousands of volunteers who are ready to go to work when a disaster strikes. Red Cross volunteers go through regular practice drills and exercises so that they will be able to respond effectively when they need to.

Volunteer organizations develop plans that describe what they will do during a disaster, what resources they will need, and how they will coordinate and use these resources. They work with local governments to identify places suitable for shelters and service centers. They arrange to get the supplies they need and also arrange to have vehicles and communications equipment ready to use.

Volunteers often provide support to disaster workers. ▼

During a Disaster When a disaster strikes, volunteer groups work to feed people affected by the disaster and to provide shelter. They also talk with concerned family members who are outside the disaster area. Counselors comfort people frightened by the possible loss of their homes and businesses.

After a Disaster After a disaster occurs, volunteer groups help people replace what they have lost. Volunteers pass out clothing and try to find ways to quickly replace items such as eyeglasses. They help people get loans to rebuild businesses and homes. Red Cross volunteers help out by making Friendship Boxes. These small containers, filled with items such as toothbrushes, toothpaste, crayons, paper, and puzzles, are sent to children in disaster shelters.

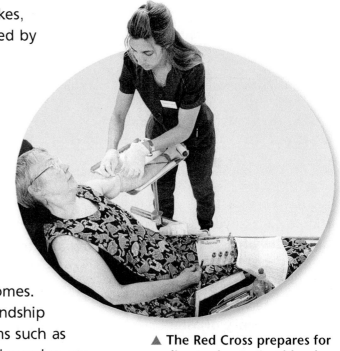

▲ The Red Cross prepares for disaster by storing blood given by volunteer donors.

SUMMARIZE **How do volunteers help before, during, and after a disaster?**

Lesson 1 Summary and Review

1 **Summarize with Vocabulary**

Use vocabulary and other terms from this lesson to complete the statements.

Tornadoes, hurricanes, and earthquakes are examples of _____. Local _____ make plans for such emergencies. Surviving a disaster requires the _____ of many people. Disaster relief often depends on the work of _____ before, during, and after a disaster.

2 Name three kinds of storms that can be natural disasters.

3 **Critical Thinking** Describe how a local government might prepare for something unpredictable, such as an earthquake.

4 **SEQUENCE** Draw and complete this graphic organizer to answer this question: What do volunteer groups do to prepare for and handle emergency situations?

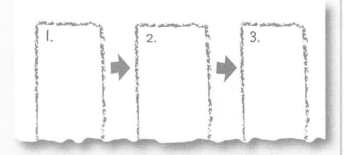

5 **Write to Inform—Personal Letter**

Suppose a classmate isn't paying attention during a tornado-alert drill. Write a letter to him or her explaining the importance of knowing what to do in an emergency.

Making Family Disaster Plans

Earthquake Safety

When making a disaster plan for an earthquake, think first about what happens during an earthquake. Earthquakes release tremendous amounts of energy. This energy rolls across the land in rippling waves. The waves shake buildings. If the waves are strong enough, parts of buildings and objects in them may fall.

If you live in an area where earthquakes happen frequently, you should take some precautions. For example, make sure that heavy objects such as mirrors, pictures, and tall pieces of furniture are firmly attached to walls. In your emergency safety plan, outline what each person in your family should do if an earthquake strikes. Make sure each room in your house has a flashlight that everyone can find easily. If an earthquake strikes at night and the electricity goes out, you don't want to stumble around in the darkness.

An earthquake can damage a house, but people can avoid injury if they stay out of the way of falling objects. ▼

Predictions of earthquake damage are based on where strong earthquakes are likely to occur and how many people live there. ▼

Predicted Damage Map

No Damage
Minimal Damage
Moderate Damage
Severe Damage

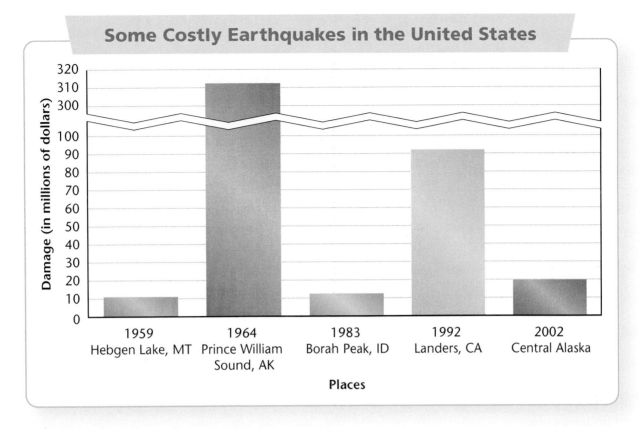

Some Costly Earthquakes in the United States

Damage (in millions of dollars)

| 1959 Hebgen Lake, MT | 1964 Prince William Sound, AK | 1983 Borah Peak, ID | 1992 Landers, CA | 2002 Central Alaska |

Places

▲ Property damage caused by earthquakes can run to many millions of dollars.

If an earthquake occurs, remember the following safety tips:

• If you are outdoors when an earthquake happens, head for an open area such as a large, grassy field or lawn where there are no trees or other objects that might fall on you.

• If you are indoors, seek cover under a sturdy table or in a doorway, or crouch against an inside wall.

• Stay far from objects such as bookcases, mirrors, or windows.

The danger from an earthquake doesn't end with the end of the shaking. Someone should check your home carefully for damage that could be dangerous. Here are a few things to keep in mind:

• Open closets and cupboards slowly. Objects inside may have shifted and could fall on you.

• Make sure water pipes and natural gas lines have not been damaged.

• Clean up all broken glass, and make sure all utensils are free of broken glass.

 SEQUENCE What should you do before and during an earthquake?

Preparing for Severe Weather

Did You Know?

In 1999, 46 people were killed by lightning in the United States. By contrast, in the same year, 21,000 people were killed in the United States in car crashes.

How can you prepare for severe weather? First, learn what to expect. Weather forecasters can help in two ways. They can issue a storm watch or a storm warning. A **storm watch** means that a storm *may* strike in your area. A **storm warning** means that a storm *is* on the way and your community is almost certain to get hit by it.

Severe storms usually bring strong winds. These winds can knock down power lines. For this reason, you should have candles and flashlights readily available. You should also store enough fresh water in your home to get you through a few days. To keep up with news about the storm, use a portable radio or television that operates on batteries. Make sure you have a supply of fresh batteries. Fully charge cell phones before the storm strikes.

You should also buy and store canned and dried foods, since roads and bridges may be impassable. Take in or tie down objects that might be blown around by the wind outside your home.

Storms such as hurricanes and severe thunderstorms can cause serious flooding. ▼

Storm Watches and Warnings

Type of Weather	Storm Watch	Storm Warning
Hurricane	A hurricane may strike within 24 to 36 hours. Flooding is possible.	A hurricane and flooding are likely within 24 hours.
Tornado	Conditions are right for the development of a tornado.	A tornado has been sighted.
Severe Thunderstorm	Severe thunderstorms may develop. Flooding is possible.	Heavy rain, strong winds, lightning, and possibly hail are coming. Flooding is likely.
Winter Storm	Snow with wind and cold temperatures may occur.	Snow with wind and cold temperatures is likely.

When a hurricane is predicted, many people who might be in its path board up windows. People who live along coastal areas may move inland temporarily.

If a blizzard is on the way, make sure you have shovels, sand, and de-icing salt on hand. Stay indoors during a blizzard.

A tornado warning should be the signal for your family to seek shelter in a storm cellar or on the lowest floor of a building. Thunderstorms bring a special threat—lightning. Lightning usually strikes the tallest objects in an area, so stay away from tall trees. If you are caught outdoors, crouch down, and stay away from water. The safest place to be is indoors. If you are in a car, roll up the windows, and don't touch any metal parts.

COMPARE AND CONTRAST How are a storm watch and a storm warning alike and different?

Myth and Fact

Myth: Windows should be open during a tornado to make the air pressure inside and outside your home equal.
Fact: Opening windows does nothing to reduce tornado damage. Stay away from windows to avoid flying glass.

Preparing a Disaster Kit

A natural disaster may isolate your family at home. It may force your family to leave your home. It may damage your home or injure family members. To cope with these possibilities, you should put together a disaster kit well before a natural disaster occurs in your area. The pictures on this page and the list on page 375 identify important items that you should put in your disaster kit.

Quick Activity

Analyze a Family Disaster Kit A disaster kit contains supplies you would need if a natural disaster resulted in loss of electricity and water. Choose one type of natural disaster. Describe how you would use the items given on these pages. Add any items you think are missing.

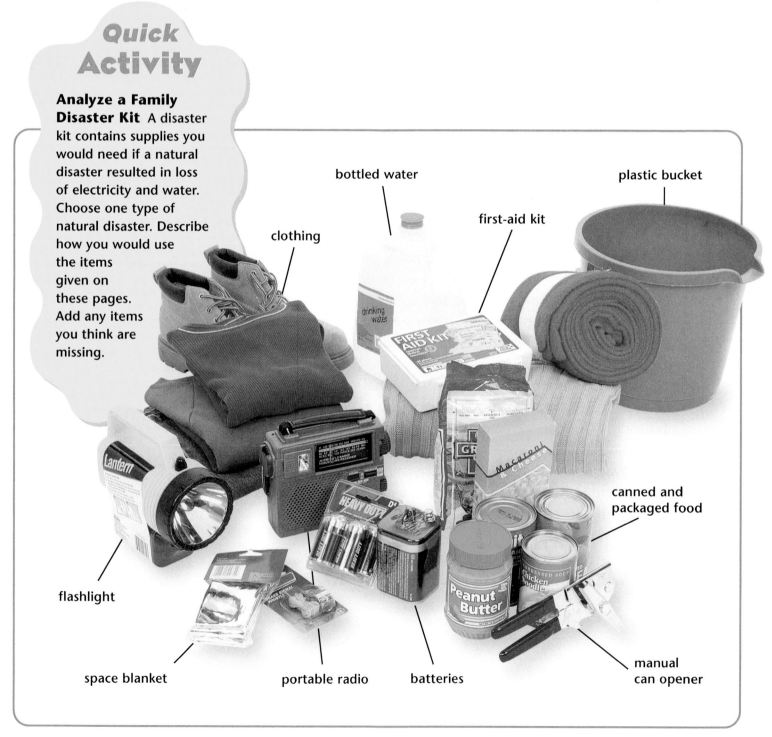

bottled water

plastic bucket

first-aid kit

clothing

canned and packaged food

flashlight

space blanket

portable radio

batteries

manual can opener

Be Prepared with

1. fully charged cell phone
2. battery-operated radio
3. two weeks' supply of packaged and canned food; bottled water (4 liters, about a gallon, per person per day)—at least a 3-day supply; a 7-day supply is recommended
4. first-aid kit
5. flashlight with extra batteries
6. blankets
7. changes of clothing for each person
8. manual can opener
9. soap and hygiene products
10. medicines needed by family members

SUMMARIZE What should all disaster kits include regardless of the type of disaster that may occur? Explain your answer.

Lesson 2 Summary and Review

1 Summarize with Vocabulary

Use vocabulary and other terms from this lesson to complete the statements.

Before a disaster occurs, it is good to know what to _____. A _____ tells you that a storm may be on the way. A _____ tells you that a storm is likely to strike. It is very important to prepare well for severe _____. To cope with possible emergencies, families should put together a _____.

2 Critical Thinking What do all natural disasters have in common?

3 About how much time do you have to prepare for a hurricane if a storm warning is issued?

4 **SEQUENCE** Give the sequence of things you should do before, during, and after an earthquake.

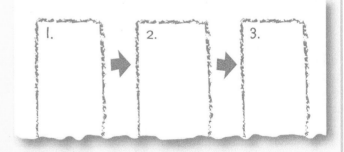

5 Write to Inform—Description

Describe a storm that struck where you were, and tell what you or your family did to prepare for it or what you did to stay safe during the storm.

Health Services and Safety

Lesson Focus

Health agencies, businesses, families, and individuals work to ensure food safety, water quality, and waste disposal.

Why Learn This?

You can use what you learn to tell who is responsible for the safety of your food and your drinking water, as well as for waste disposal.

Vocabulary

sanitary landfill
incineration

Ensuring Food Safety

Responsibility for food safety begins with the producers or catchers of the food. These include farmers, ranchers, and fishers. The next people who must keep food safe are those who prepare and ship the foods for market. Next, responsibility is taken by people who work in your local food shop or restaurant. Finally, your family needs to ensure the safe preparation of food at home.

The first three of these stages in food handling must follow safety rules set down by local, state, and federal government agencies. One of the most important of these agencies is the United States Food and Drug Administration (FDA). This agency not only sets national rules for food safety, it also employs inspectors to make sure that the rules are followed.

Food inspectors work for the FDA as well as for local and state health departments. They inspect farms, cattle ranches, food factories, food shops, and restaurants in the United States. They also check the safety of food from other countries.

 SEQUENCE List in order the people responsible for seeing that the food you buy is safe to eat.

Federal, state, and local health inspectors check foods to make sure they are safe for you to eat. ▶

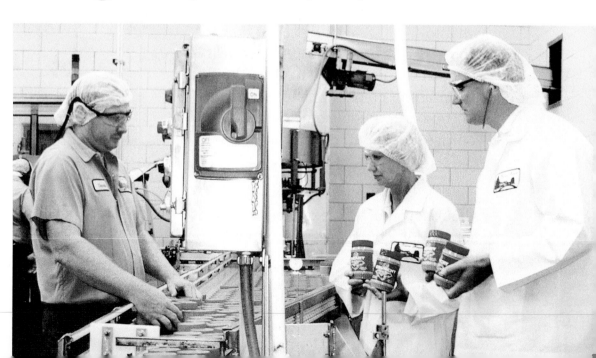

Sewage Treatment

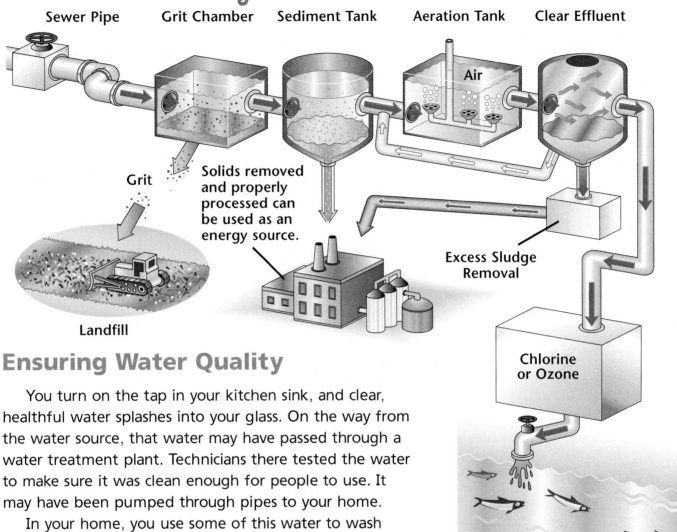

Sewer Pipe | Grit Chamber | Sediment Tank | Aeration Tank | Clear Effluent

Grit

Solids removed and properly processed can be used as an energy source.

Landfill

Air

Excess Sludge Removal

Chlorine or Ozone

Ensuring Water Quality

You turn on the tap in your kitchen sink, and clear, healthful water splashes into your glass. On the way from the water source, that water may have passed through a water treatment plant. Technicians there tested the water to make sure it was clean enough for people to use. It may have been pumped through pipes to your home.

In your home, you use some of this water to wash clothes, bathe, drink, and prepare food. Water that runs out through any of the drains in your house may flow through underground pipes to a sewage treatment plant. There the water passes through screens and tanks that remove solid material. Chemicals are added to the filtered water to kill germs. The water is tested before it is released into the environment.

Some people get their water from wells deep in the ground. Others get it from cisterns, or tanks that catch and store rainwater. Homes in areas where there is no sewage system usually have septic tanks that are buried in the ground. Wastewater flows into the septic tank. Bacteria in the septic tank break down solid wastes. Septic tanks must be located far away from wells so that drinking water is not polluted by wastewater.

COMPARE AND CONTRAST How are a cistern and a septic tank alike and different?

377

Personal Health Plan ▶

Real-Life Situation

Flooding after a storm can pollute well water.

Real-Life Plan

Write instructions about what you might do to avoid getting sick from drinking polluted water.

Disposing of Solid Waste

How would you like to turn trash into a park or an athletic field? Impossible? Maybe not. The trash you threw away last year may lie under a park picnic table today. It's done this way.

In many communities, trash collected from homes is taken by truck to a **sanitary landfill**, a large, lined hole in the ground where trash is disposed of safely. Bulldozers even out and flatten the trash. More trash is added, which bulldozers level and flatten again. To help reduce odors and keep animals away, at the end of each day the trash is covered with clay or soil.

When the location can't hold any more trash, bulldozers level the trash and seal it with soil. Landscapers may then be called in to plant trees, grass, and flowers. Construction workers may build paths and benches. Other workers may build a public ball field. The landfill becomes a place where families can relax and play.

Sanitary landfills are often smoothed out and covered to make recreation areas where people can relax and play. ▼

Landfills may be transformed into other useful structures. If you have ever flown into John F. Kennedy Airport in New York City, your plane landed on a sealed landfill.

Sometimes trash is turned into electricity. The trash is trucked to a building in which a furnace reduces solid wastes by **incineration**, or burning. There the trash is burned to ashes. The ashes take up less than half the volume of the original trash. This saves space in the landfill to which the ashes are hauled.

Burning trash produces heat energy and some harmful gases. Devices called scrubbers remove many of the harmful gases before they reach the air. Some community incinerators have been equipped with machinery that turns the heat energy of burning trash into usable electricity.

 SEQUENCE Describe in order the steps required to turn trash into a park.

▲ Some communities send their trash to energy plants, where the energy from burning wastes is used to produce electricity.

Lesson 3 Summary and Review

❶ Summarize with Vocabulary

Use vocabulary and other terms from this lesson to complete the statements.

Many groups and organizations are required to ensure the health of the community. Food inspectors work to ensure _____. Water treatment plants help ensure _____. Solid wastes are managed by _____, or burning, and by the use of _____, or places that have been properly prepared to receive solid waste.

❷ Critical Thinking Why might chemicals be added to water before it's sent through pipes to homes and businesses?

❸ When installing a septic tank, what should you be careful NOT to do?

❹ SEQUENCE Draw and complete this graphic organizer to show the main steps used to treat sewage.

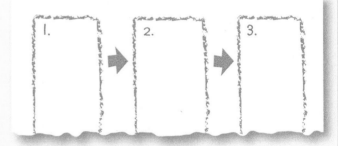

❺ Write to Inform—Explanation

Do research to find out how trash is processed in your community. Write a report describing the process. Trace what happens to a piece of trash throughout the entire process.

Using Resources Wisely

Lesson Focus

Conserving resources is important to your health and to the health of the planet.

Why Learn This?

You can use what you learn to conserve energy and other resources.

Vocabulary

resource
conserve
insulation

Using Energy Resources

When you hear the word *resource*, you might first think of building materials—such as iron, aluminum, and lumber. You would be partly right. A **resource** is any material that people obtain from the environment to use. Resources include materials used to construct buildings, cars, planes, and bridges.

But a few very important resources—such as oil, coal, and natural gas—are used to produce energy. As the circle graph shows, energy resources heat homes, allow steel mills and other industries to operate, light offices, and run airplanes. Industry is the greatest consumer of energy. Huge amounts of energy are used to run machines that make products.

Transportation 27%

Industrial 34%

Residential 21%

Commercial 18%

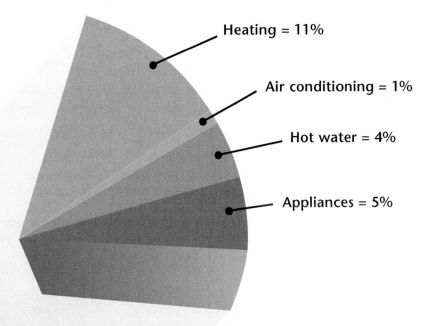

Heating = 11%

Air conditioning = 1%

Hot water = 4%

Appliances = 5%

◀ About half the energy used in homes goes into heating and cooling them.

Some energy resources, like wood, are renewable. If you cut down a tree to build a fire, you can plant another tree to take its place. Sunlight and wind are two other forms of renewable energy. However, most energy resources are nonrenewable. There is a limited amount of oil, coal, and gas on Earth, and it takes a long time for these resources to form. That is why it's important to **conserve**, or save, such resources.

Like most families, your family probably uses a lot of energy to run your home. A large amount of energy goes into heating. In many houses, the heat comes from burning natural gas or oil. In others, it comes from electricity. But most of the electricity in the United States is produced by burning coal, oil, and gas. So running a home reduces our supply of nonrenewable energy resources. Here are some ways you and your family can help conserve these resources:

- Wear warm clothing at home, and lower thermostat settings.
- Turn thermostat settings lower at night. Sleep under warm blankets.
- Make sure your home is well insulated. **Insulation** (in•suh•LAY•shuhn) is material that slows the loss of heat from inside your house to outside.
- If you can, substitute fluorescent bulbs for incandescent bulbs.
- Turn off the lights and television when you leave a room.

Did You Know?

If every home in the United States were kept 6°F (about 3°C) cooler in the winter, people in the United States would save the equivalent of 500,000 barrels of oil *every day*. One barrel holds 42 gallons of oil.

 SEQUENCE Trace the flow of energy from a resource to the heating of a home.

Water Needs

1. People need to drink about 2 liters (about 2 quarts) of water a day.

2. Cows need to drink 15 liters (4 gallons) of water to produce 4 liters of milk.

3. About 76,000 cubic feet of water is used for each person living in the United States each year. That would fill a tower 1 foot square and 76,000 feet tall.

People, farms, and industries all need fresh, clean water to function. ▼

Using Water Resources

No one can live for very long without clean, fresh water. You must drink water every day. The vegetables and fruits you eat must have water to grow. The cattle and poultry you eat cannot survive without fresh water. Farms and the industries that make products such as medicines, cars, and electricity use most of the water used in the United States.

COMPARE AND CONTRAST About how much more water is used for farm irrigation and livestock than for homes and businesses?

Water Used Each Day

Use	Billions of Gallons
Homes and businesses	46.5
Farm irrigation and livestock	139.5
Commercial, mining, industrial	26.2
Electrical power generation	132

◀ Electric buses conserve oil resources.

▲ Light bulbs run on electricity, much of which is produced by burning energy resources such as oil and coal. By using light bulbs that consume less electricity, you will save energy.

Conserving Resources

The natural resources available to us are limited. Everyone can help conserve our limited natural resources. You and your family can make a difference by following the tips below to conserve energy and water.

Energy

- Carpool when possible.
- Ride a bicycle or walk instead of riding in a car.
- Use public transportation as often as possible.
- When possible, buy a car that gets the most miles per gallon of gasoline.

Water

- Fix leaky faucets.
- Take short showers instead of baths.
- Install water-saving shower heads.
- Turn off water while brushing your teeth or washing dishes by hand.
- Install water-saving toilets.
- Water lawns early in the morning or late in the evening, when evaporation is lowest.
- Sweep driveways and sidewalks instead of hosing them down.

ACTIVITY

Life Skills

Communicate

Your cousin is visiting for the weekend. She doesn't turn off lights when she leaves a room. She also doesn't turn off the television when she goes outside. How could you explain to her the importance of saving resources?

By recycling used product containers, you can conserve the raw materials and energy used to make new ones. ▶

Raw materials, such as trees and metal, can also be conserved by you and your family. For example, you can save trees by recycling paper. Each year enough trees to fill a forest the size of the state of Maine are cut down to supply the United States with paper.

Aluminum is a nonrenewable resource. Every three months, people in the United States throw away enough aluminum to rebuild all the commercial planes in the country. Recycle your aluminum cans, and one day you might be flying in them.

CAUSE AND EFFECT What is likely to happen if people don't take steps to conserve resources?

Lesson 4 Summary and Review

❶ Summarize with Vocabulary

Use vocabulary and other terms from this lesson to complete the statements.

One way to slow heat loss is by improving the _____ in our homes. This also helps to _____, or save, energy. People need _____ to survive, so it is essential to conserve it at home. If we don't conserve resources, they will _____ more quickly.

❷ What is most of the energy in a family's home used for?

❸ Critical Thinking Identify one way you can conserve fresh water.

❹ (Focus Skill) SEQUENCE Draw and complete this graphic organizer to show how you can reduce your use of natural resources bit by bit.

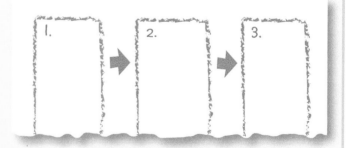

1. → 2. → 3.

❺ Write to Inform—How-To

Write a television or radio advertisement describing how people can conserve water.

Citizenship

Building Good Character

Caring for Your School

You and your friends spend many of your waking hours at school. During this time, your environment is your school and the land that surrounds it. There are many things you can do to help make this environment a pleasant place to spend your time.

- **Put trash in waste disposal containers.**
- **Encourage friends and classmates to pick up after themselves.**
- **Speak softly in classrooms and lunch rooms.**
- **Clean up tables after meals.**
- **Volunteer to work outdoors on plants and trees.**
- **Share play areas with other students, or take turns using play areas.**
- **Don't mark up sidewalks or other outdoor surfaces.**

Activity

When you're at home, discuss with your family how you can contribute to improving your home environment. Make a list of what you should and should not do. Think about how the things on the list will affect family members and your surroundings. Place a plus mark next to things that will have positive outcomes. Identify which of these things are related to what you can do to improve the school environment.

385

Pollution and Health

Lesson Focus

Pollution is a threat to your health and your environment.

Why Learn This?

You can do things to help reduce pollution and safeguard your health and the health of those around you.

Vocabulary

pollution
acid rain
toxic wastes
catalytic converters

Pollution Harms People

Pollution (puh•LOO•shuhn) is the presence of harmful materials in the environment. Contact with polluted air, water, or soil can make people ill.

In the United States most air pollution comes from the burning of fuels such as coal, oil, gasoline, and natural gas. Pollution comes from factories and the exhaust of cars, buses, and trucks. Some air pollution contains solids, such as bits of dust and soot. Air pollution also includes gases. Many of these gases are toxic, or poisonous. If the concentration of these gases in the air becomes great enough, the gases can cause irritation to people's eyes, noses, and other parts of their respiratory systems. Their blood may not be able to pick up enough oxygen from the lungs. This could put stress on the heart, which could trigger heart attacks in people who have heart disease. Some air pollutants may also cause cancer.

One common gas in polluted air is so toxic that it can kill. It's called carbon monoxide. It's a colorless, odorless gas produced when gasoline or other fuels don't burn completely. This happens in the engines of cars and other motor vehicles.

Every cell in your body needs oxygen to survive. Carbon monoxide escaping from the exhaust pipe of a car in a closed garage can be deadly. If a person breathes in this gas, it keeps the blood from carrying oxygen through his or her body. For this reason, people should never keep a car running in a closed garage. Also, carbon monoxide can build up in a home in which a gas furnace isn't working properly.

Focus Skill **SEQUENCE** **Describe how air pollution can lead to a heart attack.**

Gases and solid particles that escape from factories cause air pollution that can be harmful to living things. ▼

Acid Rain

Two other gases, sulfur dioxide and nitrogen oxide, are air pollutants. Sulfur dioxide gas comes mostly from industry. Nitrogen oxide gases come mostly from motor vehicle exhaust. In the air, these gases go through a number of chemical reactions. The resulting chemicals combine with water in the air to form two acids, sulfuric acid and nitric acid. **Acid rain** is a type of pollution formed when sulfuric and nitric acids form droplets that fall to Earth.

Winds may blow the gases and the acids far from where they were formed. Clouds may build up along the way, and precipitation may fall from them in the form of acid rain, snow, sleet, or hail.

Acid rain falls on trees, ponds, buildings, and statues. Over time, the trees die. Living things in the ponds die. The stone and metal of buildings and statues dissolve.

COMPARE AND CONTRAST How are acid rains made of sulfuric acid and nitric acid alike and different?

Acid rain harms living things, such as trees, and even the stone of buildings and statues. ▼

◀ Pollution that runs into ponds, lakes, rivers, and streams can poison fish and people who eat fish.

▲ Rain can wash oil leaking from cars into groundwater and surface water, such as rivers and streams, from which people get drinking water.

Water Pollution

Water may become polluted by chemicals or trash or by disease-causing organisms. Polluted drinking water can be harmful to your health. Some sources of chemical pollution are

- oil wells, oil refineries, and manufacturing plants
- factories that remove metals from ores
- fertilizers, pesticides, and weed killers
- paper mills
- runoff from parking lots and streets
- radioactive wastes
- acid rain

Septic tanks and wastewater treatment plants that don't work properly may cause contamination by pathogens. Animal waste from farms and human waste can contaminate groundwater.

Diseases transmitted by bacteria and viruses in polluted water include

- typhoid fever and cholera (bacterial), which can cause vomiting, diarrhea, and even death
- infectious hepatitis (viral), which causes fever, headache, and stomach pain and can lead to liver damage

CAUSE AND EFFECT How might acid rain affect water supplies?

389

Toxic Wastes Cause Pollution

Every year in the United States, factories, hospitals, businesses, and homes produce billions of tons of waste. Some of these wastes can poison living things, including people. Wastes that are poisonous are called **toxic wastes**.

If not handled properly, toxic wastes can pollute the air, the water, and the soil. People who breathe contaminated air, drink contaminated water, or eat products grown in contaminated soil can get sick.

Some toxic wastes are discarded from people's homes. These include weed killers, bug sprays, furniture polish, drain cleaners, and oil-based paints. These products serve a purpose, but if they are not stored and disposed of properly, both people and the environment may suffer.

For example, some chemicals that people might use to help grass and flowers grow can harm pets, other animals, and small children. Songbirds can be poisoned by tiny bits of solid lawn chemicals that they mistake for seeds.

MAIN IDEA AND DETAILS **What kinds of toxic wastes may be found in the home?**

If not properly packed and stowed away, nuclear waste from a storage place like this one could contaminate drinking water. ▼

Your home holds many toxic materials that could pollute your environment if they are not stored and then disposed of properly. ▼

390

What Can Be Done?

In the United States, laws restrict the amount of harmful gases that industry and cars release into the air. All new cars are also fitted with catalytic converters. **Catalytic converters** (kat·uh·LIT·ik kuhn·VER·terz) reduce the amount of nitrogen oxides that cars and trucks release into the air. What can you do to control pollution where you live? Here are some pointers.

- Don't dump toxic liquids on the ground.
- Don't overfertilize lawns and shrubs.
- Avoid using herbicides to kill weeds. Pull them out by the roots.
- Use biological controls instead of pesticides to kill insects.

DRAW CONCLUSIONS If you used biological controls to limit the growth of plant-eating insects, what toxic substances could you avoid using?

Workers who clean up toxic wastes must wear special safety suits. ▼

Lesson 5 Summary and Review

1 Summarize with Vocabulary

Use vocabulary and other terms from this lesson to complete the statements.

People can become ill from _____ of the air, water, or soil. Some gases are _____, or poisonous. When these combine with precipitation, the result is _____, which can harm people, animals, or things many miles from the source. Diseases like typhoid fever and cholera can be caused by polluted _____. Pollution from cars has been reduced by fitting _____ to their exhaust systems.

2 Which acids make rain acidic?

3 Critical Thinking Why would running a gas-powered generator in a closed garage be a bad idea?

4 (Focus Skill) **SEQUENCE** Draw and complete this graphic organizer to show how acid rain forms.

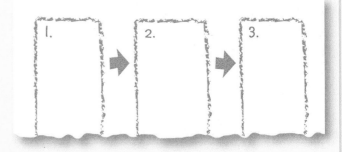

5 Write to Entertain—Poem

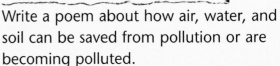

Write a poem about how air, water, and soil can be saved from pollution or are becoming polluted.

Set Goals
To Protect the Environment

Everyone can take actions that affect the environment. Setting goals helps in making plans and organizing actions. Using the steps for **Setting Goals** can ensure that your actions to protect the environment are effective.

Jim and Kay have noticed that a nearby vacant lot would be ideal for a small community park. The lot is overgrown and full of trash. What can Jim and Kay do?

1 **Choose a goal.**

Jim and Kay talk with their teacher. They show him the lot and explain what they would like to achieve.

2 **Plan steps to meet the goal.**

Jim and Kay list the things that must be done to clean up the lot and make it a good park.

3 Check your progress as you work toward your goal.

With help from their teacher, Jim and Kay take away the trash. Gradually they can see they are making real progress.

4 Evaluate your progress toward the goal.

Jim, Kay, and their teacher look at what they have achieved. The lot is now a pleasant park for the whole community.

Problem Solving

A. Janyce has noticed unsafe conditions at her school. She knows that other schools in her community have committees made up of teachers and students that address safety issues.
- Describe how Janyce can use the steps for **Setting Goals** to help her work with teachers and school officials to establish a safety committee.

B. Rosa and her family have just moved to a new community. Rosa's father says that recent storms may cause local floods. He asks the family to think about what to do if the area around their home is flooded. Rosa thinks setting goals will be useful.
- Explain what Rosa might say to help the family with their plan.

Lesson Focus

You can improve your environment by reducing, reusing, or recycling the resources you use.

Why Learn This?

You can use what you learn to help preserve your environment.

Vocabulary

reduce
reuse
recycle
noise pollution

Remember the Three *R*'s

You can do three things to improve your environment. First, you can **reduce** the number of things you use. Second, you can **reuse** old things instead of buying new ones. And, third, you can **recycle** things instead of throwing them in the trash. You can remember these actions by thinking of them as the three *R*'s: reduce, reuse, and recycle.

Reduce

Many products, such as plastic bags, are made from oil. You can reduce the rate at which oil is used up by cutting back on your use of products such as plastic bags.

Some forms of pollution can also be reduced. Your environment can be polluted by something that you can't see—noise pollution. **Noise pollution** is loud, disturbing, or harmful sounds made by human activities.

Don't throw away containers. Instead, reuse them in creative ways! ▼

Sound is measured in units called decibels (dB). The sound of a whisper is about 20 dB. The sound of a normal conversation is about 60 dB. A sound greater than 80 dB, such as that made by a chain saw, can damage your hearing.

Vacuum cleaners, power lawn mowers, portable stereos, and jackhammers are a few sources of noise pollution. To cut down on noise pollution, many communities regulate the times of day that devices like lawn mowers can be used.

Reuse

Don't throw away anything that can be reused. Old clothing can be given to younger children. So can the toys you have outgrown. Avoid buying disposable items like plastic cups and plates.

Write a list of ideas about how to reuse some common household items, such as milk containers and glass jars. Ask your parents to post it in the kitchen so that all family members can help follow the second of the three *R*'s.

Recycle

Many materials can be recycled. That is, the substances they are made of can be used to make new products. This conserves resources like trees and metals. Recycling paper products saves trees because paper is made from wood. Recycling metal cans made of aluminum conserves this metal.

When you buy a product, check for words like *Made from recycled materials.* And recycle the products you use. Most communities have recycling programs. Find out how they work and how you can contribute to them.

 SEQUENCE Identify one item in the house that you can reduce the use of, reuse, and eventually recycle. Describe the steps.

Quick Activity

Identify Reused Materials Look at the sculpture below. Make a list of the materials in the sculpture that you think were reused or recycled.

Other Things You Can Do

Your school can help improve the environment by starting a 3-R club. Invite an adult to sponsor the club. Ask friends to join. Choose a time and place to meet.

Choose a community environmental problem to solve. Learn as much as you can about the problem. Ask for advice from local officials who are in charge of the problem. Develop a workable plan to solve the problem.

Keep careful notes and records of what you've done. After you're finished, write a club report. It may be a model that other members of your community can imitate to improve your environment.

SUMMARIZE Write a statement explaining how a 3-R club can help your community.

Lesson 6 Summary and Review

❶ Summarize with Vocabulary

Use vocabulary from this lesson to complete the statements.

There are several things people can do to help the environment. By cutting back on use of products like plastic bags, we can _____ the rate at which resources are used up. We can _____ items instead of throwing them away. We conserve resources when we _____ items that can be used to make new products.

❷ Identify three sources of noise pollution.

❸ Critical Thinking Recycling aluminum cans also saves energy resources. Explain why that might happen.

❹ (Focus Skill) SEQUENCE Draw and complete this graphic organizer to show the first three steps a 3-R club can take to help improve its community's environment.

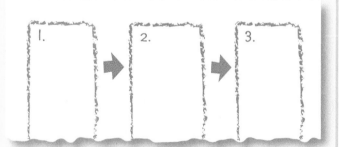

❺ Write to Express—Business Letter

Write a letter to a community official requesting permission to clean up a littered area. Use language designed to persuade the official to allow your group to do the cleanup.

ACTIVITIES

Art

Draw a Hurricane Scene Do research about recent hurricanes. Look at the photographs that go with the articles. Then make a painting or drawing of a scene in which you are in a hurricane. The scene can be on shore or at sea. Make your painting or drawing express how you might feel.

Science

Natural Disasters Presentation

Scientists have found evidence that a great natural disaster may have wiped out the dinosaurs that once roamed Earth. Do research to find out what that disaster might have been. Make notes on the evidence the scientists have gathered. Create a colorful illustrated poster to display what you have learned. Somewhere on your poster, ask and answer this question: "Could this kind of disaster happen again?"

Technology Project

Community Pollution Photograph some examples of pollution in your community. Display your photographs with a caption for each one. Use the display to help set goals to protect your environment.

GO ONLINE For more activities, visit The Learning Site. www.harcourtschool.com/health

Home & Community

Investigate Find out what kinds of natural disasters could strike your community. Find out whether such disasters can be predicted and, if so, how much time you would have to prepare for the disaster. If the disaster might cause you to leave your home in search of safety, draw a map of the route you should take. Make a checklist of things to do—and not do—before and during the disaster. Share your map and checklist with your family and friends.

Career Link

Environmental Technician Suppose that you are an environmental technician who assists home builders in construction projects. One home builder has decided to install septic tanks for houses that use well water. Write guidelines that help the builder decide how to position these tanks to ensure the safety of the well water.

Reading Skill

SEQUENCE

Draw and then use this graphic organizer to answer questions 1 and 2.

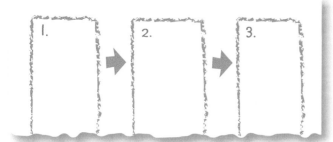

1 Responsibility for food safety passes from one group to another. What is the sequence from first to last?

2 Describe how burning fossil fuels can affect people's health.

Use Vocabulary

Match each term in Column B with its meaning in Column A.

Column A	Column B
3 A storm may strike in your area.	**A** sanitary landfill
	B insulation
4 A storm is almost sure to strike your area.	**C** natural disaster
	D conserve
5 A place where trash is disposed of safely	**E** storm watch
	F storm warning
6 An event that occurs in nature and causes great damage	
7 A material that slows heat loss	
8 To use less of a resource	

Check Understanding

Choose the letter of the correct answer.

9 Water draining from a washing machine is an example of _____. (p. 377)
- **A** purified water
- **C** wastewater
- **B** precipitation
- **D** treated water

10 A sanitary landfill is _____. (p. 378)
- **F** free of germs
- **H** odorless
- **G** full of trash
- **J** full of water

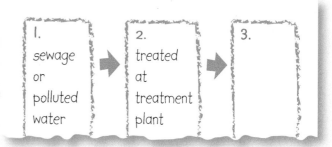

11 Which choice best completes the graphic organizer? (p. 377)
- **A** bottled in factory
- **B** returned to environment
- **C** becomes acid rain
- **D** infected with pathogens

12 A catalytic converter is used to _____. (p. 391)
- **F** clean water
- **G** clean exhaust gases
- **H** remove acids from rain
- **J** remove poisonous wastes from soil

13 Acid rain is harmful to _____. (p. 388)
- **A** people
- **C** buildings
- **B** animals and trees
- **D** all of the above

14 Which of the following is **NOT** a source of pollution? (p. 386)
- **F** car
- **H** tree
- **G** oil refinery
- **J** factory

15 The three *R*'s are reduce, recycle, and
_____.
(p. 394)

A retrain   **C** reuse
B reveal   **D** reclean

16 The loudness of a sound is measured
in _____. (p. 395)

F decibels   **H** grams
G meters   **J** bells

17 Burning trash to get rid of it is also
called _____. (p. 379)

A landfilling
B insulation
C incineration
D catalytic conversion

18 The safest place to be in the event of a
tornado is _____. (p. 373)

F outside   **H** the basement
G the top floor   **J** the roof

19 Carbon monoxide is a poison because it
_____. (p. 387)

A burns skin
B prevents bones from growing
C damages the brain
D prevents blood from carrying oxygen

Think Critically

20 The ingredients for acid rain enter the air
from industries and from motor vehicles.
Which of these two sources can people
more easily influence? Why?

21 Explain why pesticides and herbicides
are both good and bad for people.

22 Electric cars cannot travel very far before
they need recharging. They don't go as
fast as cars that run on gasoline. Yet many
people believe we should switch from
gasoline-powered cars to electric cars.
Why would we want to do this?

Apply Skills

23 **BUILDING GOOD CHARACTER**
Responsibility Your parents are
letting you have a party at your house.
Foods and soft drinks are laid out on large
picnic tables along with plastic plates,
cups, forks, spoons, and knives. After the
party is over, everyone starts to gather
plastic dishes and aluminum cans and
dump them in a garbage bag along with
discarded food. What is the responsible
thing for you to do? Why?

24 **LIFE SKILLS**
Make Responsible Decisions The
manager of your local recreation center
hears about an electric heater that is on
sale. She thinks it would be a good idea
to replace the oil-burning furnace with
an electric heater. What could you ask her
to consider before she decides whether
to buy the electric heater?

Write About Health

25 **Write to Inform—Explanation** Explain
how using resources wisely can benefit
your health. Give specific examples.

Compare and Contrast

Learning how to compare and contrast information can help you understand what you read. You can use a graphic organizer like this one to show information that you want to compare and contrast.

Topic: Name the topic—the two things you are comparing and contrasting.

Alike	Different
List ways the things are alike.	List ways the things are different.

Tips for Comparing and Contrasting

- To compare, ask—*How are people, places, objects, ideas, or events alike?*
- To contrast, ask—*How are people, places, objects, ideas, or events different?*
- When you compare, look for signal words and phrases such as *similar*, *both*, *the same as*, *too*, and *also*.
- When you contrast, look for signal words and phrases such as *on the other hand*, *unlike*, *different*, *however*, *yet*, and *but*.

Here is an example.

> Carl has been studying the likelihood of his mom or dad developing heart disease. Because this disease is present on both sides of the family, Carl knows there are hereditary risk factors for both of them. Carl's mom is overweight and smokes. His dad, on the other hand, exercises daily and does not smoke.

Compare

Contrast

Here is what you could record in the graphic organizer.

Topic: Parents' Risk Factors for Heart Disease

Alike	Different
Disease runs in both families.	Mom—overweight, smokes Dad—exercises, does not smoke

More About Compare and Contrast

Identifying how things are alike and how they are different can help you understand new information. Use the graphic organizer on page 400 to sort the following new information about Carl's mom and dad.

Mom:	Enjoys reading	Does not like fruits and vegetables	Enjoys crocheting	Loves to sing
Dad:	Likes fruits and vegetables	Enjoys running	Loves to sing	Enjoys golf

In the following paragraph, one topic of comparison is underlined. Find a second topic for comparison or contrast.

<u>Yolanda and her son Enrique look alike. They both have dark hair, dark eyes, and round faces. Even their smiles look the same.</u> Enrique and his father, Carlos, do not look very much alike. Carlos has blue eyes instead of brown. His face has a more oval shape than Enrique's does.

Skill Practice

Read the following paragraph. Use the Tips for Comparing and Contrasting to answer the questions.

Vitamins A and D are important to good nutrition. Sources of vitamin A include vegetables, liver, eggs, and milk. Vitamin D sources include saltwater fish, egg yolks, and fortified milk. Both vitamins A and D help keep teeth and bones strong. However, vitamin A keeps skin and eyes healthy, while vitamin D helps with calcium absorption. Because vitamins A and D are both stored in the body, it is important not to take in too much of either of them.

1 What are two ways that vitamins A and D are alike?

2 What are two differences between vitamins A and D?

3 What two signal words helped you identify likenesses and differences in this paragraph?

Draw Conclusions

You draw conclusions by using information from the text and your own experience. This can help you understand what you read. You can use a graphic organizer like this one to help you draw conclusions.

What I Read
List facts from the text to help you understand.

+

What I Know
List related ideas from your own experience.

=

Conclusion:
Combine facts from the text with your own experience.

Tips for Drawing Conclusions

- To draw conclusions, ask—*What text information do I need to think about?*
- To draw conclusions, ask—*What do I know from my own experience that could help me draw a conclusion?*
- Pay close attention to the information the author gives and to your own experience to be sure your conclusion is valid, or makes sense.

Here is an example.

> As soon as Phil fell off the horse, he could feel his arm throbbing. Soon after, he was sitting in a waiting room as his mom gave someone her insurance card. Finally, the nurse walked Phil back to the examining room and asked him to lie down on the table. The pain seemed to be getting worse instead of better.

Story information

Your own experience

Here is what you could record in the graphic organizer.

What I Read
Phil fell off a horse and had a throbbing arm. He was soon with a nurse.

+

What I Know
A throbbing arm could be a result of a serious injury. After an accident, people are often taken to the emergency room of a hospital. Nurses work in emergency rooms of hospitals.

=

Conclusion:
Phil broke his arm and was taken to the emergency room of a hospital.

More About Drawing Conclusions

Sensible conclusions based on the facts you read and your experience are valid. Suppose the paragraph on page 402 included a sentence that said a siren was blaring and Phil appeared to be unconscious. You might then come to a different conclusion about Phil's horseback-riding accident.

What I Read		What I Know		Conclusion:
Phil had an accident on a horse. He was knocked unconscious. A siren was blaring.	+	Being knocked unconscious could signal a serious condition. Sirens are on ambulances.	=	Phil was rushed to the hospital by ambulance after falling from a horse and losing consciousness.

Sometimes a paragraph might not contain enough information for you to draw a valid conclusion. Read the paragraph below. Think of one valid conclusion you could draw. Then think of a conclusion that would be invalid.

Jeff was worried about his grandmother. The doctor said that the operation would last about two hours, but it had been about three hours since it started. The double doors opened and through them walked the doctor. He looked exhausted.

Skill Practice

Read the following paragraph. Use the Tips for Drawing Conclusions to answer the questions.

Patti wanted to go to her friend's house to watch a movie. Her mom told her she could go after she cleaned her bedroom. Patti kicked some clothes under the bed and ran out the door. After Patti arrived at her friend's house, the phone rang. It was for Patti.

1 What conclusion did you draw about Patti's visit to her friend's house?

2 What information did you use from your personal experience to help you draw the conclusion?

3 What story information did you use to draw the conclusion?

Identify Cause and Effect

Learning how to identify cause and effect can help you understand what you read. You can use a graphic organizer like this one to show cause and effect.

Cause:
A cause is an action or event that makes something happen.

Effect:
An effect is what happens as a result of an action or event.

Tips for Identifying Cause and Effect

- To find an effect, ask—*What happened?*
- To find a cause, ask—*Why did this happen?*
- Remember that events can have more than one cause or effect.
- Look for signal words and phrases, such as *because* and *as a result*, to help you identify causes and effects.

Here is an example.

> Mallory enjoys working out. Three times a week, the main part of her workout focuses on aerobic exercise. As a result of this type of exercise, she is strengthening her heart and lungs and building cardiovascular fitness.

Cause

Effect

Here is what you could record in the graphic organizer.

Cause:
Mallory does aerobics three times a week.

Effect:
Mallory is strengthening her heart and lungs and building cardiovascular fitness.

More About Cause and Effect

Events can have more than one cause or effect. For example, suppose the paragraph on page 404 included a sentence that said Mallory eats a low-fat diet that is rich in fruits and vegetables. You could then identify two causes of Mallory's stronger heart and lungs.

Cause:
Low-fat diet rich in fruits and vegetables

Effect:
Mallory is strengthening her heart and lungs and building cardiovascular fitness.

Cause:
Aerobic exercise three times a week

In the following paragraph, one cause and its effect are underlined. Find a second cause and its effect.

Sophia did not enjoy running. After ten minutes she chose to sit down and wait for her teammates to finish. Sophia did not benefit from the aerobic exercise because she did not maintain her target heart rate for at least twenty minutes. <u>Sophia's coach ran past and gave Sophia a concerned look. Later, Sophia had to walk three laps after the rest of the team was finished.</u>

Skill Practice

Read the following paragraph. Use the Tips for Identifying Cause and Effect to help you answer the questions.

Tobacco and alcohol are both dangerous drugs. As a result of abusing alcohol, a person's brain, heart, liver, stomach, and even small intestine can become damaged. Because of a person's decision to smoke tobacco, respiratory disease or lung cancer can develop. Realizing the dangers of alcohol and tobacco makes some people choose not to use them.

1 What has been the cause of respiratory disease or lung cancer for some people?

2 What are three effects of using alcohol?

3 What signal words or phrases helped you identify the causes and effects?

Identify Main Idea and Details

Being able to identify the main idea and details can help you understand what you read. You can use a graphic organizer like this one to show the main idea and details.

Main Idea: The most important idea of a paragraph, *several paragraphs, or a selection*

Detail: Information that tells more about the main idea	Detail: Information that tells more about the main idea	Detail: Information that tells more about the main idea

Tips for Identifying the Main Idea and Details

- To identify the main idea, ask—*What is this mostly about?*
- Remember that the main idea is not always stated in the first sentence.
- Be sure to look for details that help you answer questions such as *who, what, where, when, why,* and *how.*
- Use pictures as clues to help you figure out the main idea.

Here is an example.

> Goal setting helps when you are making choices. When you have goals, you have a framework to help you make decisions. Your goals give you strong reasons for doing or not doing something. They can help you make wise choices.

Main Idea

Detail

Here is what you could record in the graphic organizer.

Main Idea: Goal setting helps you when you are making choices.

Detail: Goals provide a framework to help you make decisions.	Detail: Goals give you reasons for doing or not doing something.	Detail: Goals help you make wise choices.

More About Main Idea and Details

Sometimes the main idea of a passage is at the end instead of the beginning. The main idea may not even be stated. However, it can be understood from the details. Look at the following graphic organizer. What do you think the main idea is?

Main Idea: ?

Detail:	Detail:	Detail:
Ann told Nicky not to climb on the furniture.	Ann made Nicky a nutritious lunch.	Nicky's parents were scheduled to be home in two hours.

There are many types of details. In the following paragraph, identify whether the details give reasons, examples, facts, steps, or descriptions.

When electricity is not used safely, it can kill or injure someone. Always cover electrical outlets to prevent young children from poking things into them. Be sure to use plugs properly. Never put a three-pronged plug into an extension cord or adapter with a two-pronged plug. Remember, most electricity-related injuries are both predictable and preventable.

Skill Practice

Read the following paragraph. Use the Tips for Identifying the Main Idea and Details to answer the questions.

Fire safety is very important around stoves. Before cooking, be sure the stovetop is clean and free of grease. Roll up long sleeves. Keep pot handles pointed inward so that they do not catch on anything, causing spills. In addition, be sure to remove hanging tags from potholders so that they don't catch on fire.

1 What is the main idea of the paragraph?

2 What supporting details give more information about the main idea?

3 What details answer any of the questions *who, what, where, when, why,* or *how?*

Sequence

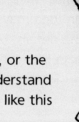

Paying attention to the sequence of events, or the order in which things happen, can help you understand what you read. You can use a graphic organizer like this one to show sequence.

1. The first thing that happened		2. The next thing that happened		3. The last thing that happened

Tips for Understanding Sequence

- Pay attention to the order in which events happen.
- Remember dates and times to help you understand the sequence.
- Look for time-order signal words such as *first*, *next*, *then*, *last*, and *finally*.
- Sometimes it is helpful to add your own time-order words to help you understand sequence.

Here is an example.

> The key to cell division is the duplication of material within the nucleus. First, the material inside the nucleus makes a copy of itself. Then, the membrane surrounding the nucleus disappears. The two sets of nuclear material move to opposite sides of the cell. Finally, the cell divides and forms two new cells.

Time-order Words

Here is what you could record in the graphic organizer.

1. Material in the nucleus makes a copy of itself.		2. Membrane surrounding the nucleus disappears. The two sets of nuclear material move to opposite sides of the cell.		3. The cell divides and forms two new cells.

More About Sequence

Sometimes information is sequenced by dates. For example, natural disasters are recorded by the dates of the events. Use a graphic organizer like the following to sequence any bad storms or disasters that have occurred in or near your community.

1.
September 26, 2000: Level 3 Tornado

2.
October 29, 2002: Flood that destroyed five homes

3.
January 15, 2003: Blizzard that knocked out power to 30,000 homes

When time-order words are not given, add your own words to help you understand the sequence. In the paragraph below, one time-order word has been included and underlined. How many more time-order words can you add to help you understand the paragraph's sequence?

Charlie noticed that his baby brother, Sam, was quickly learning to talk. <u>First</u>, Charlie noticed that Sam could say a couple of words. When Charlie was with Sam and pointed to things, Sam was saying more words. Charlie noticed that Sam was starting to put words together in simple phrases.

Skill Practice

Read the following paragraph. Use the Tips for Understanding Sequence to answer the questions.

Sara could tell that a terrible storm was brewing. First, she heard cracks of lightning that roused her from her sleep. Next, she could hear the house creak as the wind blew violently. Then, she was alarmed by the sound of hail pelting the roof. Finally, her family went to the safe room because a tornado warning had been issued.

1 What was the first thing Sara noticed about the coming storm?

2 If you were in Sara's situation, would you have done the last step of the sequence sooner than she and her family did?

3 What four signal words helped you identify the sequence of events in this paragraph?

Summarize

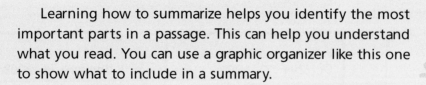

Learning how to summarize helps you identify the most important parts in a passage. This can help you understand what you read. You can use a graphic organizer like this one to show what to include in a summary.

Main Idea:	+	Details:	=	Summary:
Tell about the most important information you have read.		Give details that answer important questions such as <u>who</u>, <u>what</u>, <u>where</u>, <u>when</u>, <u>why</u>, and <u>how</u>.		Retell what you have just read, and include only the most important details.

Tips for Summarizing

- To write a summary, ask—*What is the most important information in the paragraph?*
- To include details with your summary, ask—*Who, what, when, where, why, and how?*
- Remember to use fewer words than the original has.
- Do not forget to summarize the information in your own words.

Here is an example.

> Main Idea

There are two ways to get medicines when you need to prevent, treat, or cure health problems. You can buy prescription medicines only after a doctor has written an order for them. You can buy over-the-counter medicines right off the shelf without a prescription.

> Detail

Main Idea:	+	Details:	=	Summary:
There are two ways to get medicines.		Prescription medicines require a doctor's order. Other medicines can be bought right off the shelf.		The two main ways to get medicines are by prescription and over the counter.

More About Summarizing

Sometimes a paragraph includes information that would not be included in a summary. For example, suppose the paragraph on page 410 included a sentence that told what the doctor is required to write in a prescription for a medicine. These details would not be included in the graphic organizer because they are not important to understanding the paragraph's main idea.

Main Idea:
There are two ways to get medicines.

+

Details:
You get some medicines by prescription only. Others are purchased without prescriptions.

=

Summary:
If you cannot get a medication as an over-the-counter medicine, you have to get a doctor's prescription.

Sometimes the main idea of a paragraph is not in the first sentence. In the following paragraph, two important details are underlined. What is the main idea?

Conner had a terrible headache. He went into his mother's medicine cabinet and found a bottle of pills. Conner did not ask his mother before taking two of the pills from the bottle. Conner ended up in the emergency room. He learned that he should never decide on his own to take medicine.

Skill Practice

Read the following paragraph. Use the Tips for Summarizing to answer the questions.

Tyler saw blood spurting from Ben's wrist. He saw the sharp badge—which Ben had tried to catch—fall to the floor. Tyler quickly put on protective gloves and applied pressure to Ben's wound. He elevated Ben's wrist so that it rested above the level of the heart. Tyler was relieved that the bleeding stopped. Ben's mom quickly took Ben to the emergency room.

1 If a friend asked you what this paragraph is about, what information would you include? What would you leave out?

2 What is the main idea of the paragraph?

3 What two details would you include in a summary of the paragraph?

First Aid

412

Health and Safety

For Bleeding–Universal Precautions

You can get some diseases from a person's blood. Avoid touching anyone's blood. Wear protective gloves if possible. To treat an injury, follow the steps.

If someone else is bleeding

1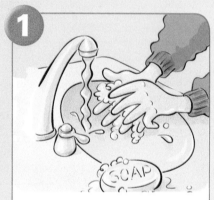

Wash your hands with soap if possible.

2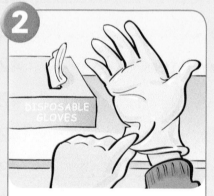

Put on protective gloves, if available.

3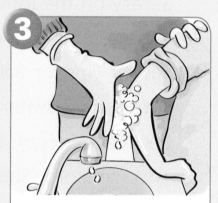

Wash small wounds with soap and water. Do not wash serious wounds.

4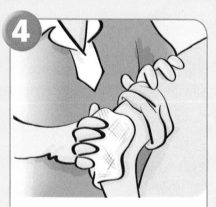

Place a clean gauze pad or cloth over the wound. Press firmly for ten minutes. Don't lift the gauze during this time.

5

If you don't have gloves, have the injured person hold the gauze or cloth in place with his or her hand for ten minutes.

6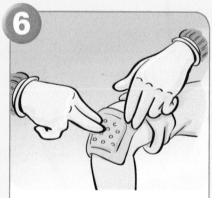

If after ten minutes the bleeding has stopped, bandage the wound. If the bleeding has not stopped, continue pressing on the wound and get help.

If you are bleeding

Follow the steps above. You do not need to avoid touching your own blood.

For Choking

If someone else is choking

1

Recognize the Universal Choking Sign—grasping the throat with both hands. This sign means a person is choking and needs help.

2

Stand behind the person, and put your arms around his or her waist. Place your fist above the person's belly button.

3

Grab your fist with your other hand. Pull your hands toward yourself, and give five quick, hard, upward thrusts on the person's stomach.

If you are choking when alone

1 Make a fist, and place it above your belly button. Grab your fist with your other hand. Pull your hands up with a quick, hard thrust.

2 Or keep your hands on your belly, lean your body over the back of a chair or over a counter, and shove your fist in and up.

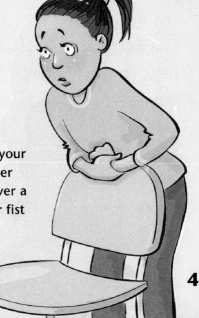

415

For Burns

- Minor burns are called first-degree burns and involve only the top layer of skin. The skin is red and dry, and the burn is painful.

- Second-degree burns cause deeper damage. The burns cause blisters, redness, swelling, and pain.

- Third-degree burns are the most serious because they damage all layers of the skin. The skin is usually white or charred black. The area may feel numb because the nerve endings have been destroyed.

All burns need immediate first aid.

Minor Burns

- Run cool water over the burn, or soak it for at least five minutes.

- Cover the burn with a clean, dry bandage.

- Do not put lotion or ointment on the burn.

More Serious Burns

- Cover the burn with a cool, wet bandage or clean cloth. Do not break any blisters.

- Do not put lotion or ointment on the burn.

- Get help from an adult right away.

For Nosebleeds

- Sit down, and tilt your head forward. Pinch your nostrils together for at least ten minutes.

- You can also put a cloth-covered cold pack on the bridge of your nose.

- If your nose continues to bleed, get help from an adult.

For Insect Bites and Stings

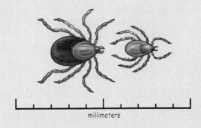

millimeters

- Always tell an adult about bites and stings.

- Scrape out the stinger with your fingernail.

- Wash the area with soap and water.

- A wrapped ice cube or cold pack will usually take away the pain from insect bites. A paste made from baking soda and water also helps.

- If the bite or sting is more serious and is on an arm or leg, keep the leg or arm dangling down. Apply a cold, wet cloth. Get help immediately.

- If you find a tick on your skin, remove it. Protect your fingers with a tissue or cloth to prevent contact with infectious tick fluids. If you must touch the tick with your bare hands, wash your hands right away.

- If the tick has already bitten you, ask an adult to remove it. Using tweezers, an adult should grab the tick as close to your skin as possible and pull the tick out in one steady motion. Do not use petroleum jelly or oil of any kind because it may cause the tick to struggle, releasing its infectious fluids. Thoroughly wash the area of the bite.

For Skin Rashes from Plants

Many poisonous plants have three leaves. Remember, "Leaves of three, let them be." If you touch a poisonous plant, wash the area and your hands. Change clothes, and wash the ones the plant touched. If a rash develops, follow these tips.

- Apply calamine lotion or a paste of baking soda and water. Try not to scratch. Tell an adult.

- If you get blisters, do not pop them. If they burst, keep the area clean and dry. Cover the area with a bandage.

- If your rash does not go away in two weeks or if the rash is on your face or in your eyes, see your doctor.

For Dental Emergencies

Dental emergencies occur less often than other health emergencies, but it is wise to know how to handle them.

Broken Tooth

• Rinse your mouth with warm water. Wrap a cloth around a cold pack, and place it on the injured area. Save any parts of the broken tooth. Call your dentist immediately.

Bitten Tongue or Lip

• Apply direct pressure to the bleeding area with a cloth. Use a wrapped cold pack to stop swelling. If the bleeding doesn't stop within fifteen minutes, go to a hospital emergency room.

Knocked-Out Permanent Tooth

• Find the tooth, and clean it gently and carefully. Handle it by the top (crown), not the root. Put it back into the socket if you can. Hold it in place by biting on a piece of clean cloth. If the tooth cannot be put back in, place it in a cup with milk or water. See a dentist immediately because time is very important in saving the tooth.

Food or Object Caught Between Teeth

• Use dental floss to gently take out the food or object. Never use anything sharp to remove what is stuck between your teeth. If it cannot be removed, call your dentist.

Remember that many dental injuries can be prevented if you

• wear a mouth guard while playing sports.

• wear a safety belt while riding in a car.

• inspect your home and get rid of hazards that might cause falls and injuries.

• see your dentist regularly for preventive care.

Food Safety Tips

Tips for Preparing Food

- Wash your hands thoroughly before preparing food. Also wash your hands after preparing each dish.

- Defrost meat in a microwave or the refrigerator. Do NOT defrost meat on the kitchen counter.

- Keep raw meat, poultry, and fish and their juices away from other foods.

- Wash cutting boards, knives, and countertops immediately after cutting up meat, poultry, or fish. Never use the same cutting board for meats and vegetables without thoroughly washing the board first.

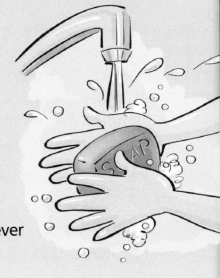

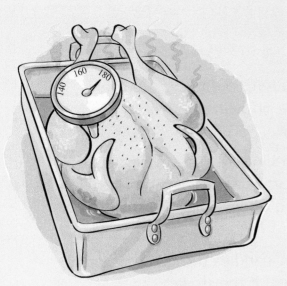

Tips for Cooking

- Cook all food thoroughly, especially meat. This will kill bacteria that can make you ill.

- Red meats should be cooked to a temperature of 160°F. Poultry should be cooked to 180°F. When fish is safely cooked, it flakes easily with a fork.

- Eggs should be cooked until the yolks are firm. Never eat foods or drink anything containing raw eggs. Never eat uncooked cookie dough made with raw eggs.

Tips for Cleaning Up the Kitchen

- Wash all dishes, utensils, and countertops with hot, soapy water.

- Store leftovers in small containers that will cool quickly in the refrigerator. Don't leave leftovers on the counter to cool.

- Your refrigerator should be 40°F or colder.

- Write the date on leftovers. Don't store them for more than five days.

Kitchen Safety

Sometimes you may cook a meal or prepare a snack for yourself. Be careful—kitchens can be dangerous. You need to follow safety rules to avoid burns, cuts, and other accidental injuries. You should be especially careful if you're home by yourself.

General Rules

- Follow rules for preparing and storing food safely (page 419).

- Be sure a responsible adult knows what you plan to cook and which kitchen tools you will use.

- Learn fire safety rules for the home.

- To avoid the risk of burns and fires, use the stove or oven as little as possible.

- Clean up after yourself. Turn off all appliances before you leave the kitchen.

Stoves and Ovens

- Get an adult's permission to use the stove or oven. If possible, use a microwave.

- Keep clothing away from burners. Avoid clothes with sleeves or laces that hang down. They could catch fire.

- Keep pot handles turned in toward the center of the stove.

- Use an oven mitt to handle hot trays or metal pot handles. A mitt covers your whole hand.

- Be sure you have a firm grip before you lift a container of hot food.

Microwaves

Always follow the directions on the food labels. Remember these rules:

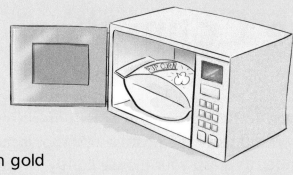

- Be careful when you take food out of a microwave. Even if the container isn't hot, steam can burn you.

- Never use metal containers, dishes with gold or silver decoration, or aluminum foil in a microwave. The metal can cause sparks or even start a fire.

- Never use a microwave to heat only water. When heating water, always place a non-metal object such as a wooden stirrer in the container.

Appliances and Kitchen Tools

- Check with an adult to find out which appliances you are allowed to use.

- Never turn an appliance off or on while your hands are wet.

- Kitchen knives are sharp and very dangerous. You should use knives and other sharp kitchen tools only with an adult's permission.

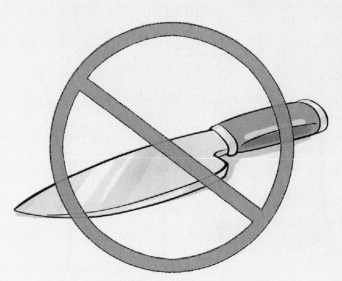

Good Posture at the Computer

Good posture is very important when using the computer. To help prevent eyestrain, muscle fatigue, and injuries, follow the posture tips shown below. Remember to grasp your mouse lightly, keep your back straight, avoid facing your monitor toward a window, and take frequent breaks for stretching.

top of screen at or just below eye level

shoulders in line with ears and hips

neck and shoulders relaxed

arms at sides bent as shown

wrists straight

feet flat on floor

Safety on the Internet

The Internet is a remarkable tool. You can use it for fun, education, research, and more. However, like anything else, it has some downsides. Some people compare the Internet to a city—not all the people there are people you want to meet, and not all the places you can go are places you want to be. On the Internet, as in a real city, you have to use common sense and follow safety guidelines to protect yourself. Below are some easy rules you can follow to stay safe online.

Rules for Online Safety

- Talk with an adult family member to set up rules for going online. Decide when you can go online, how long you can be online, and what kinds of places you can visit. Do not break the rules you agree to follow.

- Don't give out personal information such as your name, address, and telephone number or information about your family. Don't give the name or location of your school.

- If you find anything online that makes you uncomfortable, tell an adult family member right away.

- Never agree to meet with anyone in person. If you want to get together with someone you have met online, check with an adult family member first. If a meeting is approved, arrange to meet in a public place, and bring an adult with you.

- Don't send your picture or anything else to a person you meet online without first checking with an adult.

- Don't respond to any messages that are mean or make you uncomfortable. If you receive a message like that, tell an adult right away.

423

When Home Alone

Everyone stays home alone sometimes. When you stay home alone, it's important to know how to take care of yourself. Here are some easy rules to follow that will help keep you safe when you are home by yourself.

Do These Things

- Lock all the doors and windows. Be sure you know how to lock and unlock all the locks.

- If someone who is nasty or mean calls, say nothing and hang up immediately. Tell an adult about the call when he or she gets home. Your parents may not want you to answer the phone at all.

- If you have an emergency, call 911. Be prepared to describe the problem and to give your full name, address, and telephone number. Follow all instructions given to you. Do not hang up the phone until you are told to do so.

- If you see anyone hanging around outside your home, call a neighbor or the police.

- If you see or smell smoke, go outside right away. If you live in an apartment, do not take the elevator. Go to a neighbor's house, and call 911 immediately.

- Entertain yourself. Time will pass more quickly if you are not bored. Work on a hobby, read a book or magazine, do your homework, or clean your room. Before you know it, an adult will be home.

Do NOT Do These Things

- Do NOT use the stove, microwave, or oven unless an adult family member has given you permission and you know how to use these appliances.

- Do NOT open the door to anyone you don't know or to anyone who is not supposed to be in your home.

- Do NOT talk to strangers on the telephone. Do not tell anyone that you are home alone. If the call is for an adult family member, say that he or she can't come to the phone right now and take a message.

- Do NOT have friends over unless an adult family member has given you permission to do so.

A caller ID display can help you decide whether to answer the phone.

Safety Tips for Babysitters

Being a babysitter is a very important job. As a sitter you are responsible for the safety of the children in your care. Adults depend on you to make good decisions. Here are some tips to help you be a successful and safe babysitter.

When you accept a job as a babysitter, ask

- what time you should arrive.

- how long the adults will be away.

- what your responsibilities will be.

- the amount of pay you will receive.

- what arrangements will be made for your transportation to and from the home.

When you arrive to start a job, you should

- arrive several minutes early so that the adults have time to give you information about caring for the child.

- write down the name and phone number of the place the adults are going and what time they will be home.

- find out where emergency phone numbers are listed. The list should have numbers for the police, the fire department, and the children's doctor.

- find out where first-aid supplies are kept. You should be prepared to give first aid in an emergency.

- ask what and when the children should eat.

- ask what activities the children may do.

- ask when the children should go to bed and what their bedtime routine is.

While you are caring for children, you should

- never leave a baby alone on a changing table, sofa, or bed.
- never leave a child alone, even for a short time.
- check children often when they are sleeping.
- never leave a child alone near a pool or in the bathtub.
- never let a child play with a plastic bag.
- keep dangerous items out of a child's reach.

- know where all the doors are, and keep them locked. Do not let anyone in without permission from the adults.
- take a message if the phone rings. Do not tell the caller that you are the babysitter or that the adults are out.
- call the adults if there is an injury or illness. If you can't reach them, call the emergency numbers on the list.

Never leave children playing alone.

Never leave a child to eat alone.

Never leave children alone near a pool or in the bathtub.

Safety near Water

Water can be dangerous—a person can drown in five minutes or less. The best way to be safe near water is to learn how to swim. You should also follow these rules:

- Never swim without a lifeguard or a responsible adult present.

- If you can't swim, stay in shallow water. Don't rely on an inflatable raft.

- Know the rules for the beach or pool, and obey them. Don't run or play roughly near water.

- Do not dive in head-first until you know the water is deep enough. Jump in feet-first the first time.

- Watch the weather. Get out of the water at once if you see lightning or hear thunder.

- Protect your skin with sunscreen and your eyes with sunglasses.

- Wear a Coast Guard-approved life jacket anytime you are in a boat.

- Know what to do in an emergency.

Backpack Safety

Carrying a backpack that is too heavy can injure your back. Carrying one incorrectly also can hurt you.

Safe Use

- Choose a backpack with wide, padded shoulder straps and a padded back.

- Lighten your load. Leave unnecessary items at home.

- Pack heavier items so that they will be closest to your back.

- Always use both shoulder straps to carry the backpack.

- Never wear a backpack while riding a bicycle. The weight makes it harder to stay balanced. Use the bicycle's basket or saddlebags instead.

This is the right way to carry a backpack.

This is the wrong way to carry a backpack.

Safe Weight

A full backpack should weigh no more than 10 to 15 percent of your body weight. Less is better. To find 10 percent, divide your body weight by 10. Here are some examples:

Your Weight (pounds)	Maximum Backpack Weight (pounds)
70	7
80	8
90	9

429

Thunderstorm Safety

Thunderstorms are severe storms. Lightning can injure or kill people, cause fires, and damage property. Here are thunderstorm safety tips.

- **If you are inside, stay there.** The safest place to be is inside a building.

- **If you are outside, try to take shelter.** If possible, get into a closed car or truck. If you can't take shelter, get into a ditch or another low area.

- **If you are outside, stay away from tall objects.** Don't stand in an open field, on a beach, on a hilltop, or near a lone tree. Find a low place and crouch down, with only your feet touching the ground.

- **Stay away from water.** Lightning is attracted to water, and water conducts electricity.

- **Listen for weather bulletins.** Storms that produce lightning may also produce tornadoes. Be ready to take shelter in a basement or in a hallway or other room without windows.

Earthquake Safety

An earthquake is a strong shaking of the ground. The tips below, many for adults, can help you and your family stay safe.

Before an Earthquake
- Bolt tall, heavy furniture, such as bookcases, to the wall. Store the heaviest items on the lowest shelves.
- To prevent fires, bolt down gas appliances and use flexible hose and connections for both gas and water lines.
- Firmly anchor overhead light fixtures to the ceiling to keep them from falling.

During an Earthquake
- If you are outdoors, stay there. Move away from buildings and electric wires.
- If you are indoors, stay under heavy furniture or in a doorway. Stay away from glass doors and windows and heavy objects that might fall.
- If you are in a car, go to an open area away from buildings and overpasses.

After an Earthquake
- Continue to watch for falling objects as aftershocks shake the area.
- Have the building checked for hidden structural problems.
- Check for broken gas, electric, and water lines. If you smell gas, shut off the gas main and leave the area. Report the leak.

430

Blizzard Safety

A blizzard is a dangerous snowstorm with strong winds and heavy snowfall. It may last for 12 to 36 hours, with snowfall greater than 6 inches in 24 hours and winds gusting higher than 35 miles per hour. Visibility may be less than $\frac{1}{4}$ mile. The following tips can help you and your family stay safe during a blizzard.

Your home should have

- a working flashlight with extra batteries.
- a battery-powered NOAA weather radio, radio, or TV.
- extra food and water, plus medicines and baby items if needed.
- first-aid supplies.
- heating fuel such as propane, kerosene, or fuel oil.
- an emergency heating source.
- a smoke detector and a fire extinguisher.

If traveling by car or truck, your family should

- keep the gas tank nearly full. The vehicle should be fully checked and properly prepared for winter use.
- always let a friend or relative know the family's travel plans.
- keep a blizzard survival kit in the vehicle. It should contain blankets; a flashlight with extra batteries; a can and waterproof matches to melt snow for drinking; and high-calorie, nonperishable food.
- remain in the vehicle in a blizzard, and tie something bright to the antenna. Run the motor for short times for heat. Use the inside light only while running the motor.

431

Glossary

Numbers in parentheses indicate the pages
on which the words are defined in context.

PRONUNCIATION RESPELLING KEY

Sound	As in	Phonetic Respelling	Sound	As in	Phonetic Respelling	Sound	As in	Phonetic Respelling
a	bat	(BAT)	eye	idea	(eye•DEE•uh)	th	thin	(THIN)
ah	lock	(LAHK)	i	bit	(BIT)	u	pull	(PUL)
air	rare	(RAIR)	ing	going	(GOH•ing)	uh	medal	(MED•uhl)
ar	argue	(AR•gyoo)	k	card	(KARD)		talent	(TAL•uhnt)
aw	law	(LAW)		kite	(KYT)		pencil	(PEN•suhl)
ay	face	(FAYS)	ngk	bank	(BANGK)		onion	(UHN•yuhn)
ch	chapel	(CHAP•uhl)	oh	over	(OH•ver)		playful	(play•fuhl)
e	test	(TEST)	oo	pool	(POOL)		dull	(DUHL)
	metric	(MEH•trik)	ow	out	(OWT)	y	yes	(YES)
ee	eat	(EET)	oy	foil	(FOYL)		ripe	(RYP)
	feet	(FEET)	s	cell	(SEL)	z	bags	(BAGZ)
	ski	(SKEE)		sit	(SIT)	zh	treasure	(TREZH•er)
er	paper	(PAY•per)	sh	sheep	(SHEEP)			
	fern	(FERN)	th	that	(THAT)			

A

abdominal thrusts (ab•DAHM•uh•nuhl THRUHSTS)
A first-aid technique for treating choking when the trachea is blocked and a person
cannot breathe *(195)*

abstinence (AB•stuh•nuhns)
Avoiding behavior that puts your health at risk *(34, 220)*

acid rain (AS•id RAYN)
A type of pollution that results when sulfuric acid and nitric acid form droplets that fall
to the earth *(388)*

acne (AK•nee)
A common skin disorder caused when oil plugs the pores of the skin, resulting in pimples
and blackheads *(44)*

Activity Pyramid (ak•TIV•uh•tee PIR•uh•mid)
A diagram that shows types of activities and how often people should do them *(122)*

addiction (uh•DIK•shuhn)
A condition in which people believe they need a drug the way they need food or sleep *(252)*

additives (AD•uh•tivz)
Substances added to food to keep them fresh or improve their color or flavor *(102)*

adolescence (ad•uh•LES•uhns)
The period in which puberty takes place and a person changes from a child to an adult *(21)*

advertising (AD•ver•ty•zing)
Giving people information and ideas to encourage them to buy something *(48)*

aerobic exercise (air•OH•bik EK•ser•syz)
Activity that strengthens your heart and lungs by making them work harder *(132)*

aggression (uh•GREH•shuhn)
Forceful words or actions that can harm others emotionally or physically *(320)*

alcohol (AL•kuh•hawl)
A drug found in drinks such as beer, wine, and liquor *(288)*

alcoholic (al•kuh•HAWL•ik)
A person who needs to drink to feel normal *(291)*

alcoholism (AL•kuh•hawl•ihz•uhm)
A disease in which people cannot control their use of alcohol *(291)*

amphetamines (am•FET•uh•meenz)
Powerful stimulants that greatly increase the brain's activity *(258)*

anaerobic exercise (an•air•OH•bik EK•ser•syz)
Short, intense activities that build muscle strength *(133)*

anorexia (an•uh•REK•see•uh)
An eating disorder involving dieting nearly to the point of starvation *(96)*

antibiotic (an•ty•by•AHT•ik)
A medicine that kills pathogens, such as bacteria *(226)*

antibodies (AN•tih•bahd•eez)
Substances produced in the blood to fight disease *(223)*

anxiety (ang•ZY•uh•tee)
Uneasiness or worry that a person cannot connect to a specific cause *(322)*

astigmatism (uh•STIG•muh•tih•zuhm)
A condition in which the cornea or lens of the eye is unevenly curved, causing blurred vision *(61)*

balanced diet (BA•luhnst DY•uht)
A diet in which a variety of foods are eaten daily to provide the nutrients the body needs *(86)*

behavioral risk factors (bee•HAYV•yer•uhl RISK FAK•terz)
Harmful behaviors that increase the chances of becoming ill or being injured *(209)*

blizzard (BLIH•zerd)
A dangerous snowstorm with strong winds and heavy snowfall *(182)*

blood alcohol level (BLUHD AL•kuh•hawl LEH•vuhl)
The amount of alcohol in a person's blood *(288)*

body image (BAHD•ee IM•ij)
Your opinion about your physical appearance *(314)*

booster (BOO•ster)
A later dose of a vaccine; needed to keep up immunity *(225)*

brainstorming (BRAYN•stawrm•ing)
A process used to suggest as many ideas about a topic as possible *(337)*

bulimia (byoo•LEE•mee•uh)
An eating disorder in which a person eats a lot and then uses vomiting and laxatives to get rid of the food *(97)*

calories (KAL•uh•reez)
Units used to measure the amount of energy the body is able to get from food *(80)*

carbohydrates (kar•boh•HY•drayts)
Sugars and starches that supply the body with energy; there are two kinds of carbohydrates, simple and complex *(80)*

carbon monoxide (KAR•buhn muh•NAHKS•yd)
A poisonous gas found in tobacco smoke; it fills the spaces that normally carry oxygen in red blood cells *(281)*

carcinogens (kar•SIN•uh•juhnz)
Substances that cause cancer *(230)*

cardiovascular diseases (kar•dee•oh•VAS•kyuh•ler dih•ZEEZ•uhz)
Diseases of the heart and blood vessels *(228)*

cardiovascular fitness (kar•dee•oh•VAS•kyuh•ler FIT•nuhs)
A measure of how well your heart, lungs, and circulatory system work *(121)*

carpal tunnel syndrome (or CTS) (KAR•puhl TUH•nuhl SIN•drohm)
A repetitive strain injury to the wrists that causes shooting pains and numbness in the hands *(66)*

catalytic converter (kat•uh•LIT•ik kuhn•VER•ter)
A device that reduces the amount of nitrogen oxide that a car or truck releases into the air *(391)*

cholesterol (kuh•LES•ter•awl)
A substance, found in animal fat, that can clog the arteries over time and reduce the flow of blood to the heart *(81)*

chromosome (KROH•muh•sohm)
A long strand of genetic material made up of DNA and other chemicals; it carries genes that determine heredity *(16)*

circulatory system (SER•kyoo•luh•tawr•ee SIS•tuhm)
The body system made up of your heart, blood vessels, and blood *(6)*

cirrhosis (suh•ROH•suhs)
A disease that makes the liver unable to keep the blood free of toxins *(293)*

cocaine (koh•KAYN)
A strong stimulant made from the leaves of the coca plant *(267)*

collaborate (kuh•LAB•uh•rayt)
To work with other people toward a goal *(333)*

communicable disease (kuh•MYOO•nih•kuh•buhl dih•ZEEZ) A disease that can be spread from one person to another *(214)*

compromise (KAHM•pruh•myz)
An agreement made to resolve a conflict; it involves both sides giving up part of what they want *(350)*

conflict (KAHN•flikt)
A situation in which people strongly disagree with each other *(336)*

conflict resolution (KAHN•flikt reh•zuh•LOO•shuhn)
The solving of problems peacefully *(336)*

conjunctivitis (kuhn•juhngk•tih•VY•tuhs)
Pinkeye; a highly contagious infection of the tissues on the outside of the eye and under the eyelid *(61)*

conserve (kuhn•SERV)
To save; to use a resource carefully to make it last *(381)*

consumer (kuhn•SOO•mer)
A person who buys and uses a product or service *(48)*

contamination (kuhn•tam•uh•NAY•shuhn)
Damage to foods caused by the addition of harmful substances to them *(110)*

convenience foods (kuhn•VEEN•yuhns FOODZ)
Foods that are partly or completely prepared when you buy them *(102)*

cool-down (KOOL•down)
In a workout, the part at the end, in which easier activity lets your breathing and heart rate slowly return to normal *(131)*

crack (KRAK)
A rocklike form of cocaine that is highly addictive *(267)*

cuticle (KYOO•tih•kuhl)
The skin that grows around each fingernail *(45)*

decibels (DEH•suh•belz)
Units used to measure the loudness of sounds *(64)*

dental appliances (DENT•uhl uh•PLY•uhns•uhz)
Devices such as braces and retainers that help straighten teeth to improve their appearance *(59)*

dental sealant (DENT•uhl SEEL•uhnt)
A clear coating that helps protect teeth against cavities *(58)*

depressant (dee•PRES•uhnt)
A drug that slows the activity of the brain, slows the heart, and relaxes the muscles *(259)*

dermis (DER•muhs)
The thick skin layer below the epidermis; it contains the sweat glands, oil glands, and hair follicles *(43)*

digestive system (dih•JES•tiv SIS•tuhm)
The body system that breaks down food so the body can use its nutrients *(8)*

disaster (dih•ZAS•ter)
An event that causes great damage and affects many people *(182)*

disease (dih•ZEEZ)
An illness or condition that damages or weakens the body *(214)*

distraction (dih•STRAK•shuhn)
Something that takes your attention away from your surroundings *(68)*

diversity (duh•VER•suh•tee)
The variety in people and the ways people differ from one another *(335)*

DNA
A long molecule found in a cell's nucleus; it carries codes for inherited traits *(16)*

dominant gene (DAHM•uh•nuhnt JEEN)
A gene that results in a displayed trait even when another gene carries a different code for the trait, such as eye color *(17)*

dosage (DOH•sij)
The amount of medicine a patient should take *(249)*

drug (DRUHG)
A substance, other than food, that causes a change in the way the body or mind works *(246)*

drug abuse (DRUHG uh•BYOOS)
Use of any illegal drug or improper use of any medicine *(252)*

drug dependence (DRUHG dih•PEN•duhns)
A condition in which people need to keep using drugs to feel normal *(252)*

earthquake (ERTH•kwayk)
A strong rolling, shaking, or sliding of the ground *(182)*

electric shock (ee•LEK•trik SHAHK)
Direct contact with electricity, causing a painful jolt, severe injury, or death *(146)*

embryo (EM•bree•oh)
A human being in the stage of development from about the second week through the eighth week after conception *(12)*

emergency (ih•MER•juhn•see)
An unexpected situation that calls for quick action to save people from harm *(178)*

emphysema (em•fuh•SEE•muh)
A disease that makes breathing difficult due to damage to the air sacs in the lungs *(282)*

endocrine system (EN•doh•krihn SIS•tuhm)
The body system made up of glands that produce hormones, some of which regulate development and growth *(22)*

environmental risk factors (in•vy•ruhn•MENT•uhl RISK FAK•terz)
Harmful substances and other dangers in the environment that increase the chance of becoming ill *(207)*

environmental tobacco smoke (or ETS) (in•vy•ruhn•MENT•uhl tuh•BAK•oh SMOHK)
Tobacco smoke in the air; it can harm nonsmokers *(284)*

epidermis (eh•puh•DER•muhs)
The outer layer of the skin; it protects the body by keeping germs out and body fluids in *(43)*

excretory system (EKS•kruh•tawr•ee SIS•tuhm)
One of the body systems; it removes wastes from the blood as urine or sweat *(9)*

expiration date (ek•spuh•RAY•shuhn DAYT)
The date after which a medicine should not be used *(249)*

farsighted (FAR•syt•uhd)
Able to see faraway objects clearly while nearby objects appear blurry *(61)*

fats (FATS)
The nutrients that have the most calories per gram of food *(81)*

fetus (FEE•tuhs)
A human being in the stage of development from about the ninth week after conception until birth *(13)*

fiber (FY•ber)
The chewy or gritty material in some foods that helps move food through the digestive system *(81)*

fire extinguisher (FYR ek•STING•gwish•er)
A metal tank filled with water or chemicals for putting out a fire *(181)*

fire hazard (FYR HA•zerd)
A dangerous situation that might result in a fire *(148)*

first aid (FERST AYD)
Immediate care that is given to someone who is injured or who suddenly becomes ill *(186)*

flammable (FLAM•uh•buhl)
Easily set on fire *(148)*

flexibility (fleks•uh•BIL•uh•tee)
The ability to move the body easily from one position to another; the ability to bend, stretch, and twist *(121)*

floss (FLAWS)
A special thread used to clean between teeth *(57)*

fluoride (FLOHR•yd)
A mineral that strengthens tooth enamel *(58)*

food guide pyramid (FOOD GYD PIR•uh•mid)
A diagram that helps people choose foods for a balanced diet *(86)*

fracture (FRAK•cher)
A break or crack in a bone *(186)*

frostbite (FRAWST•byt)
A condition in which body tissue freezes *(192)*

gang (GANG)
A group of people who have an informal but close relationship, often with strict rules; most gangs engage in crimes and violence, often involving drugs and weapons *(168)*

genes (JEENZ)
Chemical codes of DNA that provide the instructions needed to build and run the body *(16)*

goal (GOHL)
Something a person wants to achieve *(316)*

grief (GREEF)
A painful sadness that lasts for some time *(324)*

growth spurt (GROHTH SPERT)
A period of rapid growth *(24)*

hair follicles (HAIR FAH•lih•kuhlz)
Tiny sacs from which hair grows *(43)*

hallucinogens (huh•LOO•sih•nuh•jenz)
Illegal drugs that affect the brain and distort senses *(267)*

health risk factor (HELTH RISK FAK•ter)
A condition that increases the chances of becoming ill *(206)*

hereditary risk factors (huh•RED•ih•ter•ee RISK FAK•terz)
Inherited traits that increase the chances of becoming ill *(206)*

heredity (huh•RED•ih•tee)
The passing of traits from parents to their children *(16)*

hormones (HAWR•mohnz)
Chemicals, produced by glands, that regulate many body functions *(22)*

hurricane (HER•uh•kayn)
A violent storm with strong winds and heavy rain; it forms over warm oceans *(182)*

hygiene (HY•jeen)
Habits that keep a person clean *(25)*

hyperthermia (hy•per•THER•mee•uh)
A condition in which the body's internal temperature gets too high *(140, 191)*

hypothermia (hy•poh•THER•mee•uh)
A condition in which the body's internal temperature becomes too low *(140, 192)*

immune system (ih•MYOON SIS•tuhm)
The body system that recognizes and destroys invading pathogens *(223)*

immunity (ih•MYOON•uh•tee)
Protection against a specific disease due to the body's memory of how to make antibodies to a specific pathogen *(223)*

immunization (ih•myuh•nuh•ZAY•shuhn)
The giving of a vaccine to make a person immune to a disease *(225)*

incineration (in•sin•er•AY•shuhn)
A way to dispose of solid waste by burning it *(379)*

infection (in•FEK•shuhn)
The result of a pathogen's multiplying in the body *(214)*

ingredients (in•GREE•dee•uhnts)
Substances used in a product *(50)*

inhalants (in•HAY•luhnts)
Products that some people abuse by breathing in their fumes *(266)*

inherited traits (in•HAIR•it•uhd TRAYTS)
Characteristics passed on from parents to their children *(16)*

insulation (in•suh•LAY•shuhn)
Material that slows the loss of heat—for example, from the inside of a home *(381)*

insulin (IN•suh•luhn)
A substance that helps move sugar from the blood into the cells *(231)*

intoxicated (in•TAHK•sih•kay•tuhd)
Drunk *(289)*

marijuana (mair•uh•WAH•nuh)
A drug that comes from the leaves and flowers of a type of hemp plant *(262)*

maturity (muh•TUR•uh•tee)
The adult stage of development of a plant or an animal, including a human *(29)*

mediator (MEE•dee•ay•ter)
A person who helps others resolve their conflicts *(337)*

medicines (MED•uh•suhnz)
Drugs that can prevent, treat, or cure health problems *(246)*

minerals (MIN•uhr•uhlz)
Nutrients that help the body grow and work *(82)*

muscular endurance (MUHS•kyuh•ler in•DUR•uhnts)
The ability to use one's muscles for a long time without getting tired *(120)*

muscular strength (MUHS•kyuh•ler STRENGKTH)
The ability to use one's muscles to lift, push, or pull heavy objects *(120)*

muscular system (MUHS•kyuh•ler SIS•tuhm)
The body system made up of muscles that act to move bones; muscles work in pairs to move the bones *(10)*

narcotics (nar•KAH•tiks)
Powerful depressant drugs that slow down the nervous system and relieve pain *(260)*

natural disaster (NACH•er•uhl dih•ZAS•ter)
An event that occurs in nature and causes great damage *(364)*

nearsighted (NIR•syt•uhd)
Able to see nearby objects clearly while faraway objects appear blurry *(60)*

nervous system (NER•vuhs SIS•tuhm)
The body system made up of the brain, spinal cord, and nerves; it controls the body's activities *(4)*

nicotine (NIK•uh•teen)
An addictive poison found in tobacco *(280)*

noise pollution (NOYZ puh•LOO•shuhn)
Loud, disturbing, or harmful sounds made by human activities *(394)*

noncommunicable disease (nahn•kuh•MYOO•nih•kuh•buhl dih•ZEEZ)
An illness or condition that is not caused by pathogens and does not spread from person to person *(228)*

nucleus (NOO•klee•uhs)
The control center of a cell *(14)*

nutritional deficiency (noo•TRISH•uhn•uhl dee•FISH•uhn•see)
The lack of a certain nutrient in the diet *(97)*

over-the-counter medicines
(oh•ver•thuh•KOWN•ter MED•uh•suhnz)
Medicines that can be bought without a prescription *(249)*

ovum (OH•vuhm)
An egg cell, supplied by the mother in human reproduction *(12)*

pathogen (PATH•uh•juhn)
An organism or a virus that can cause illness *(207)*

peer pressure (PIR PRESH•er)
The influence that other people your age have on your actions and decisions
(330, 254)

peers (PIRZ)
People who are about your own age *(330)*

perspiration (per•spuh•RAY•shuhn)
Sweat, produced by the sweat glands *(25)*

pituitary gland (pih•TOO•uh•tair•ee GLAND)
The "master gland"; it produces growth hormone and other hormones that control the
actions of the other endocrine glands *(23)*

plaque (PLAK)
A sticky substance that coats your teeth *(56)*

poison (POY•zuhn)
A substance that can harm or even kill a person if it is inhaled, swallowed, or absorbed
through the skin *(152)*

pollution (puh•LOO•shuhn)
The presence of harmful materials in the environment *(386)*

prejudice (PREJ•uh•dis)
A judgment about an entire group of people that is not based in fact *(333)*

prescription medicines (pree•SKRIP•shuhn MED•uh•suhnz)
Medicines that can be bought only with an order written by a doctor *(249)*

preservatives (pree•ZERV•uh•tivz)
Chemicals added to foods to prevent them from spoiling *(102)*

proteins (PROH•teenz)
Nutrients that build and repair cells; they also provide energy *(81)*

puberty (PYOO•ber•tee)
A physical process in which the body begins to develop reproductive cells *(20)*

reach and throw (REECH AND THROH)
Lifesaving techniques used to help people who are at risk of drowning *(162)*

recessive gene (rih•SEHS•iv JEEN)
A gene that does not result in a displayed trait when another gene carries a different
code for the trait, such as eye color *(17)*

recovery programs (rih•KUHV•er•ee PROH•gramz)
Programs developed to help people who are learning to live without alcohol *(305)*

recycle (ree•SY•kuhl)
To collect used things so they can be made into new things *(394)*

reduce (ree•DOOS)
To use fewer things in order to make less trash to pollute the environment *(394)*

relaxation (ree•lak•SAY•shuhn)
Resting by doing something enjoyable *(323)*

repetitive strain injury (or RSI) (rih•PEH•tuh•tiv STRAYN IN•juh•ree)
An injury that results from making the same motion again and again for long periods *(66)*

rescue breathing (RES•kyoo BREE•thing)
A first-aid technique in which a rescuer breathes into the lungs of a person who has stopped breathing, to keep the person alive *(196)*

resistance (rih•ZIS•tuhnts)
The body's natural ability to fight off pathogens *(222)*

resource (REE•sawrs)
Any material that is from the environment and that people can use *(380)*

respiratory system (RES•per•uh•tawr•ee SIS•tuhm)
The body system that moves oxygen into the body and takes out carbon dioxide *(7)*

responsible (rih•SPAHN•suh•buhl)
Dependable because you keep your word, you don't need others to remind you to do things, and you can resolve conflicts by yourself *(344)*

reuse (ree•YOOZ)
To use something again *(394)*

S

sanitary landfill (SAN•uh•tair•ee LAND•fil)
A large, lined hole in the ground for disposing of trash safely *(378)*

seizure (SEE•zher)
A sudden loss of consciousness, caused by unusual nerve activity in the brain; it may also result in muscle spasms or jerky movements *(190)*

self-concept (self•KAHN•sept)
The way you think about yourself *(312)*

self-control (self•kuhn•TROHL)
Your ability to manage your actions and emotions *(320)*

self-discipline (self•DIS•uh•plin)
Your ability to control your actions *(345)*

self-respect (self•rih•SPEKT)
Your recognition of your value as a person *(295, 312)*

serving (SERV•ing)
The measured amount of a food recommended for a meal or as a snack *(86)*

sexually transmitted disease (or STD) (SEK•shoo•uh•lee trans•MIT•uhd dih•ZEEZ)
A communicable disease spread by sexual contact *(220)*

shock (SHAHK)
A condition in which the circulatory system slows down *(198)*

sibling (SIB•ling)
A brother or a sister *(356)*

side effects (SYD ih•FEKTS)
Unwanted reactions to medicines *(248)*

skeletal system (SKEL•uh•tuhl SIS•tuhm)
The system of bones that support the soft tissues of the body and protect the most important organs *(10)*

smokeless tobacco (SMOHK•les tuh•BAK•oh)
Tobacco that is chewed or sucked rather than smoked *(285)*

sperm (SPERM)
The cell supplied by the father in human reproduction *(12)*

SPF (Sun Protection Factor)
A rating that indicates about how many times longer a sunscreen will protect you from sunburn than no protection will *(46)*

splint (SPLINT)
Something straight and stiff, such as a board, that is used to hold a bone or joint in place *(187)*

sprain (SPRAYN)
An injury caused by twisting a joint *(187)*

stamina (STAM•uh•nuh)
The ability to work or exercise for a long time without getting tired *(36)*

staple (STAY•puhl)
A main food in a diet *(90)*

stereotype (STAIR•ee•uh•typ)
The belief that everyone in a certain group has the same characteristics *(333)*

steroids (STAIR•oydz)
Hormone drugs that doctors prescribe to treat many diseases *(261)*

stimulant (STIM•yoo•luhnt)
A drug that speeds up the brain's activity *(258)*

storm warning (STAWRM WAWRN•ing)
A term used by weather forecasters to indicate that a storm is actually on the way *(372)*

storm watch (STAWRM WAHCH)
A term used by weather forecasters to indicate that weather conditions are right for a storm to form *(372)*

stress (STRES)
A nervous feeling in the body and the mind *(322)*

sty (STY)
An infection of an oil gland in the eyelid *(61)*

sunscreen (SUHN•skreen)
A cream, lotion, or oil containing chemicals that help protect you from ultraviolet rays *(46)*

survival floating (ser•VY•vuhl FLOHT•ing)
A technique for conserving energy while waiting for rescue from deep water if you
are not wearing a life jacket *(163)*

symptoms (SIMP•tuhmz)
Signs of a disease *(216)*

target heart rate (TAR•guht HART RAYT)
The heartbeat rate at which your heart and lungs become stronger *(133)*

tars (TARZ)
Sticky substances left by the smoke from burning certain substances, including tobacco *(281)*

terrorism (TAIR•er•iz•uhm)
The use of violence to achieve a social or political goal *(171)*

thunderstorm (THUHN•der•STAWRM)
A storm with strong winds, heavy rain, lightning, and possibly hail *(182)*

tobacco (tuh•BAK•oh)
A substance made from the dried leaves of a plant—used for smoking or chewing *(280)*

tolerance (TAH•luh•ruhns)
The need for larger or more frequent doses of a drug to get the same effect *(253)*

tornado (tawr•NAY•doh)
An extremely strong windstorm that forms a funnel shape *(182)*

toxic wastes (TAHK•sik WAYSTS)
Wastes that are poisonous *(390)*

toxins (TAHK•suhnz)
Substances that damage the body's cells; for example, wastes produced by some bacteria *(215)*

transmitted (trahns•MIHT•uhd)
Spread *(220)*

tumor (TOO•mer)
An abnormal mass of cells *(230)*

vaccine (vak•SEEN)
A medicine that contains dead or weakened pathogens that cause the immune system to
form antibodies; this results in immunity to a disease without actually producing the disease *(225)*

vegetarian (veh•juh•TAIR•ee•uhn)
A person who has chosen to eat no meat or, in some cases, no foods that come from animals *(88)*

vitamins (VYT•uh•minz)
Nutrients that help important chemical reactions to take place in the body *(83)*

warm-up (WARWM•uhp)
First part of a physical workout; it prepares the body for exercise by gradually increasing heart rate and blood flow *(131)*

weapon (WEH•puhn)
An object, such as a gun or knife, that can be used to injure or kill an animal or a person *(153)*

withdrawal (with•DRAW•uhl)
The body's physical reaction to not getting a drug it has become used to having *(253)*

workout (WERK•owt)
An exercise session *(131)*

Index

Boldfaced numbers refer to illustrations.

AA. *See* Alcoholics Anonymous (AA)

Abdominals, 10

Abdominal thrusts, 195, **195**

Abstinence, 34, 220

Abuse, by family members, 349

Acid rain, 388, **388**

Acne, 26, **44**
defined, 44
medicated products for, 51
myth and fact about, 26, 44

Activity Pyramid, 122–123, **122–123**

Addiction. *See also* Alcohol; Tobacco
defined, 252
to drugs, 252
to heroin, 264
to opiates, 260

Additives, 102

Adolescence
acne in, 26
attraction in, 31
communicating about changes in, 32–33, **32–33**
defined, 21
growth in, 15, **15**, 21, **21**
mood swings in, **28**, 28–29, **29**
puberty and, 20–21
weight of teenage girls and, 96

Adoption, of child, **354**

Adrenal glands, 22

Advertising
of alcohol and tobacco, **296**, 296–297, **297**
analyzing, 49, **49**, 50, **50**, 98, 250, 296, 317
bargains and, 49
defined, 48
evaluating, 53

by famous people, 48, **48**
understanding jargon of, 104
ways of selling products and, 48–49

Aerobic exercise, 122, 132–133, **133**

Aggression, 320

AIDS (Acquired Immune Deficiency Syndrome), 220–221

Air passages, clear and narrow, **232**

Air pollution, 386–388
from insecticides, **207**
laws restricting, 391

Al-Anon, 306

Alateen, 306

Alcohol
activities without, **294,** 295, **295**
advertising of, **296,** 296–297
choosing not to use, 294–299
dangers of, 288–293
defined, 288
driving and, 288, **288, 289**
effects on body systems, **4,** 292–293, **292**
help with, 302–306
myth and fact about, 289, 295
quitting use of, 302
reaction times and, 290
reasons for choosing not to use, 298, **298**
refusing, 295, 300–301, **300–301**
safety and, 290, **290**

Alcoholic
defined, 291
help for, **302,** 302–306, **303**
new treatments for, **305**

Alcoholics Anonymous (AA), 306

Alcoholism, 291
defined, 291
epilepsy and drugs for, 306
help from community groups, 304, **304**
recovery programs for, 305

Allergies
to alcohol ingredients, 298
to pollen, **233**
respiratory, 233
shock and, **198**
treatment of, 233

Aluminum, conserving, 384

Alveoli, 7, **7**

American Dental Association (ADA) seal, 58, **58**

American Heart Association, information from, 71

American Lung Association, information from, 71

American National Standards Institute (ANSI) sunglasses, 62

Amphetamines
defined, 258
effects on body systems, **259**
short-term effects of use, 258, **259**

Anabolic steroids, 261
effects of, **271**

Anaerobic exercise, 133

Anemia, 97

Anger, mood swings and, **28,** 29

Anger management, 320–321
activities for releasing feelings, **320**
help with, 321, **321**
techniques for, 321

Animals, pathogens from, **236**

Anorexia, 96

ANSI. *See* American National Standards Institute (ANSI) sunglasses

Antibacterial soap, 52

Antibiotics, 226–227, **246**
pathogen resistance to, 227

Antibodies, 223, **223, 224**

Antiperspirants, 51

Anxiety, 322

Appliances
electric, 147

CREDITS

Cover Design: Bill Smith Studio

Photographs:

KEY: (t) top, (b) bottom, (l) left, (r) right, (c) center, (bg) background, (fg) foreground

Cover Photographer: Brian Fraunfelter

11 (tl) Sercomi/Photo Researchers; 11 (tc) Science Photo Library/Photo Researchers; 11 (tr) Custom Medical Stock Photo; 14 Carolina Biological Supply Company/Phototake; 18 Science Photo Library/Photo Researchers; 37 F. Carter Smith/Corbis Sygma; 59 (br) Barbara Penoyar/Photodisc/PictureQuest; 61 (t) Dennis MacDonald/PhotoEdit; 61 (b) Dennis MacDonald/PhotoEdit; 72 (c) National Institutes of Health; 90 Burke/Triolo Productions/FoodPix; 92 (t) Joy Skipper- Food Styling & Recipe Development/StockFood; 115 Eric Futran/FoodPix; 120 (b) Simpson's Nature Photography; 122 (t) Dennis MacDonald/PhotoEdit; 122 (tl) Index Stock Imagery; 122 (cl) Getty Images; 122 (bl) Creatas Royalty Free Stock Resources; 122 (br) Cindy Charles/PhotoEdit; 123 (b) Mary Kate Denny/PhotoEdit; 132 (r) Macduff Everton/Corbis; 133 (c) David Madison; 141 LWA-Dann Tardif/Corbis; 149 (tl) Charles O'Rear/Corbis; 149 (cr) Philip James Corwin/Corbis; 153 (t) Royalty-Free/Corbis; 160 (inset) AP/Wide World Photos; 160 (inset) Mark E. Gibson Photography; 160 (b) Wallace Garrison/Index Stock Imagery; 161 Jeff Greenberg/eStock Photography/PictureQuest; 171 (t) Kim D. Johnson/AP/Wide World Photos; 171 (b) David Zalubowski/AP/Wide World Photos; 173 Getty Images; 179 Walter Hodges/Corbis; 182 (l) Getty Images; 182 (r) Roger Ressmeyer/Corbis; 183 (t) David Pollack/Corbis; 183 (b) Getty Images; 186 (l) Collection CNRI/Phototake; 186 (r) Science Photo Library/Photo Researchers; 198 (t) Kim Taylor/Bruce Coleman, Inc.; 201 Michael Newman/PhotoEdit; 207 John Marshall/AGStock USA; 208 (inset) Visuals Unlimited; 208 (t) Carl Purcell/Words & Pictures/PictureQuest; 210 (t) Jean Miele/Corbis; 210 (b) Richard T. Nowitz/Science Source/Photo Researchers; 215 (tl) Microfield Scientific Ltd.; 215 (tc) Collection CNRI/Phototake; 215 (tr) Science VU/CDC/Visuals Unlimited; 215 (bl) Dr. Gary Gaugler/Visuals Unlimited; 215 (bc) Kwangshin Kim/Photo Researchers; 215 (br) CNRI/Science Photo Library/Photo Researchers; 219 (l) Science Photo Library/Photo Researchers; 219 (r) Custom Medical Stock Photo; 220 (t) Alfred Pasieka/Science Photo Library/Photo Researchers; 220 (b) Custom Medical Stock Photo; 222 (r) Visuals Unlimited; 224 (r) Custom Medical Stock Photo; 225 Tim Boyle/Newsmakers/Getty Images; 226 (t) Visuals Unlimited; 226 (b) Science Photo Library/Photo Researchers; 228 (t) Collection CNRI/Phototake; 228 (bl) Custom Medical Stock Photo; 228 (br) Cavallini James/Photo Researchers; 230 (t) Custom Medical Stock Photo; 230 (b) Scott Camazine and Sue Trainor/Photo Researchers; 231 Visuals Unlimited; 232 (l) Custom Medical Stock Photo; 232 (c) Custom Medical Stock Photo; 233 (t) Dr. Stanley Flegler/Visuals Unlimited; 233 (b) D. Lovegrove/Photo Researchers; 236 (t) Joe McDonald/Corbis; 236 (b) Getty Images; 237 (t) Tony Freeman/PhotoEdit; 237 (c) RubberBall Productions/PictureQuest; 238 (bl) Steve Skjold/PhotoEdit; 238 (br) Richard Hamilton Smith/Corbis; 241 James King-Holmes/Science Photo Library/Photo Researchers; 246 (t) Barts Medical Library/Phototake; 246 (br) James King-Holmes/Science Photo Library/Photo Researchers; 247 (tl) Heather Angel/Naturalvisions; 247 (c) University of Hawaii/Botany Dept.; 247 (bl) TH Foto-Werbung/Science Photo Library/Photo Researchers; 247 (br) Hans Dieter Brandl/Frank Lane Picture Agency/Corbis; 248 (b) Greg Leary/Harcourt; 256 Tony Freeman/PhotoEdit; 260 (t) Custom Medical Stock Photo; 260 (bl) Ken Graham/Accent Alaska; 260 (br) Fred Loney/Index Stock Imagery/PictureQuest; 262 (l) Getty Images; 262 (r) Scott Camazine/Photo Researchers; 264 (l) Michael Newman/PhotoEdit; 264 (c) Dr. Jeremy Burgess/Science Photo Library/Photo Researchers; 264 (r) E. R. Degginger/Photo Researchers; 270 Kwame Zikomo/Superstock; 274 Myrleen Ferguson Cate/PhotoEdit; 275 John Madere/Corbis; 281 (l) Clark Overton/Phototake; 281 (r) Martin Rotker/Phototake; 285 Science Photo Library/Photo Researchers; 288 Tom Carter/PhotoEdit; 290 Bob Daemmrich Photography; 291 Mark Reinstein/The Image Works; 293 (t) Science Photo Library/Photo Researchers; 293 (b) Custom Medical Stock Photo; 294 David Young-Wolff/PhotoEdit; 295 Alaska Stock Images; 296 (l) Getty Images; 296 (inset) Erik Aeder/Pacific Stock; 296 (r) Alamy Images; 297 (inset) Brad Wrobleski/Masterfile; 297 (r) Custom Medical Stock Photo; 298 Jim West/The Image Works; 303 Mary Kate Denny/PhotoEdit; 304 Dennis MacDonald/PhotoEdit; 307 AP/Wide World Photos/The Argus, Jane Tyska; 312 (inset) Ronnie Kaufman/Corbis; 312 (b) Tom McCarthy/PhotoEdit; 313 (l) Paul Conklin/PhotoEdit; 323 (t) Mark E. Gibson Photography; 329 (b) Rudi Von Briel/PhotoEdit; 334 (t) Jeff Greenberg/PhotoEdit; 334 (c) Lawrence Migdale; 334 (bl) Jeff Greenberg/PhotoEdit; 334 (br) Kelly Parris/Unicorn Stock Photos; 349 (c) Myrleen Ferguson Cate/PhotoEdit; 357 Terry Wild Studio; 359 Getty Images; 364 Phil Degginger/Bruce Coleman, Inc.; 365 (bg) E. R. Degginger/Bruce Coleman, Inc.; 366 (t) Royalty-Free/Corbis; 367 (tr) Tony Savino/The Image Works; 368 AP/Wide World Photos; 369 Kathy McLaughlin/The Image Works; 370 Joseph Sohm/ChromoSohm/Corbis; 372 Adam Jones/Photo Researchers; 376 AP/Wide World Photos; 378 (inset) David R. Frazier Photolibrary; 378 (b) PhotoEdit; 379 (t) Roger Ressmeyer/Corbis; 380 (tl) Royalty Free/Corbis; 380 (bl) Paul Almasy/Corbis; 380 (br) Mark E. Gibson Photography; 382 (bl) Jack W. Dykinga/Bruce Coleman, Inc.; 382 (br) James L. Amos/Corbis; 383 (l) David R. Frazier; 386 (b) Dennis MacDonald/PhotoEdit; 388 (bg) Will & Deni McIntyre/Corbis; 388 (inset) Chinch Gryniewicz/Ecoscene/Corbis; 389 (l) Jean Laucon/Publiphoto/Photo Researchers; 389 (r) Jeremy Walker/Science Photo Library/Photo Researchers; 390 (t) Roger Ressmeyer/Corbis; 391 David R. Frazier; 392 (l) Tony Freeman/PhotoEdit; 395 (t) Hubert Stadler/Corbis; 397 (t) NOAA; 397 (b) David M. Jennings/The Image Works.

All other photos © Harcourt School Publishers. Harcourt photos provided by the Harcourt Index, Harcourt IPR, and Harcourt photographers; Weronica Ankarorn, Victoria Bowen, Eric Camden, Annette Coolidge, Doug Dukane, Ken Kinzie, Brian Minnich, and Steve Williams.

Illustrations:

Michelle Barbera 134; Jill and Ken Batelman 3, 28, 29, 46, 72, 79, 119, 136, 343, 363; David Brooks 400, 402, 404, 406, 408, 410; Patrick Gnan 72, 143, 201, 224, 227, 281, 294–295, 308, 398; Joe LeMonnier 90, 92, 94, 370; Scott MacNeil 72, 117, 148, 177, 180, 240, 249, 266, 271, 311, 377; Mick McGinty 50, 163, 164, 178, 285, 289; Larry Ross 15, 27, 35, 37, 44, 46, 58, 75, 84, 85, 93, 97, 112, 114, 115, 124, 129, 130, 140, 141, 148, 150, 155, 173, 180, 189, 190, 197, 221, 223, 240, 241, 242, 247, 258, 263, 275, 281, 283, 285, 289, 295, 307, 325, 335, 339, 341, 356, 359, 366, 368, 372, 373, 381; Fran Milner 414–431; Remy Simard x–xi, 33, 34, 54, 55, 96, 98, 104, 106, 109, 113, 126, 169, 212, 250, 252–253, 254, 255, 268, 300, 301, 314, 318, 326, 332, 337, 394; Bart Vallecoccia 4, 5, 6, 7, 8, 9, 10, 12–13, 14, 17, 22, 23, 39, 42, 44, 47, 56, 60, 63, 214, 220, 223, 224, 229, 259, 263, 282, 292; Sally Vitsky 90, 93, 95.

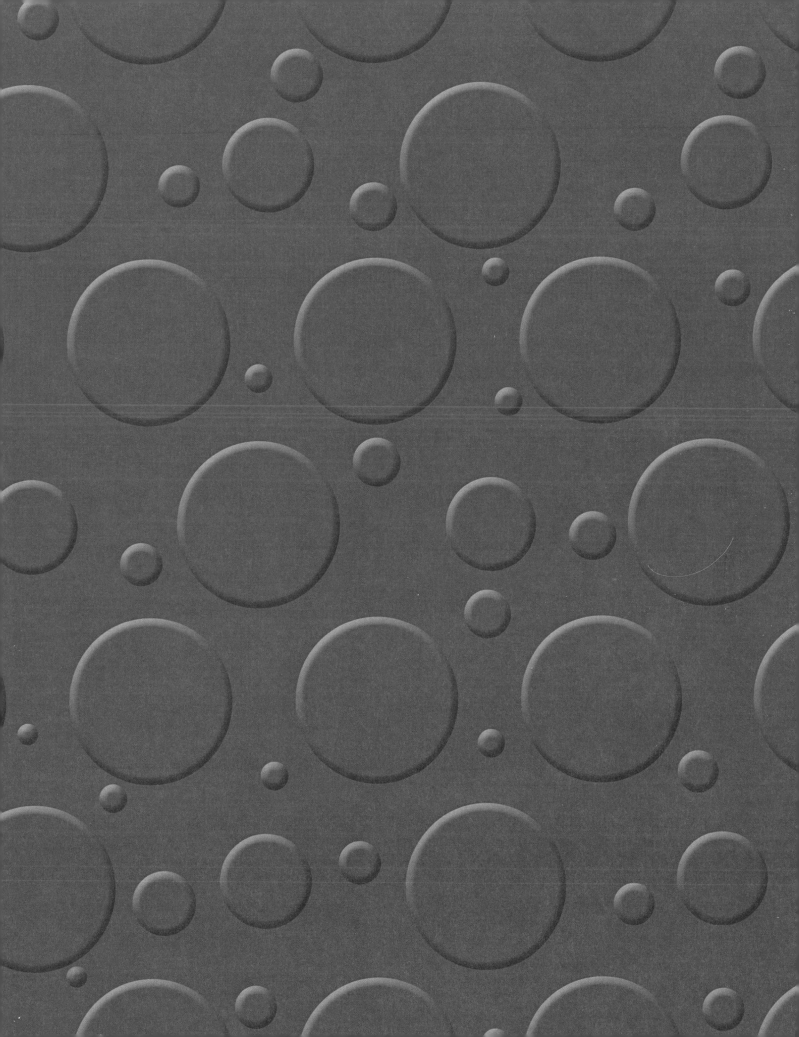

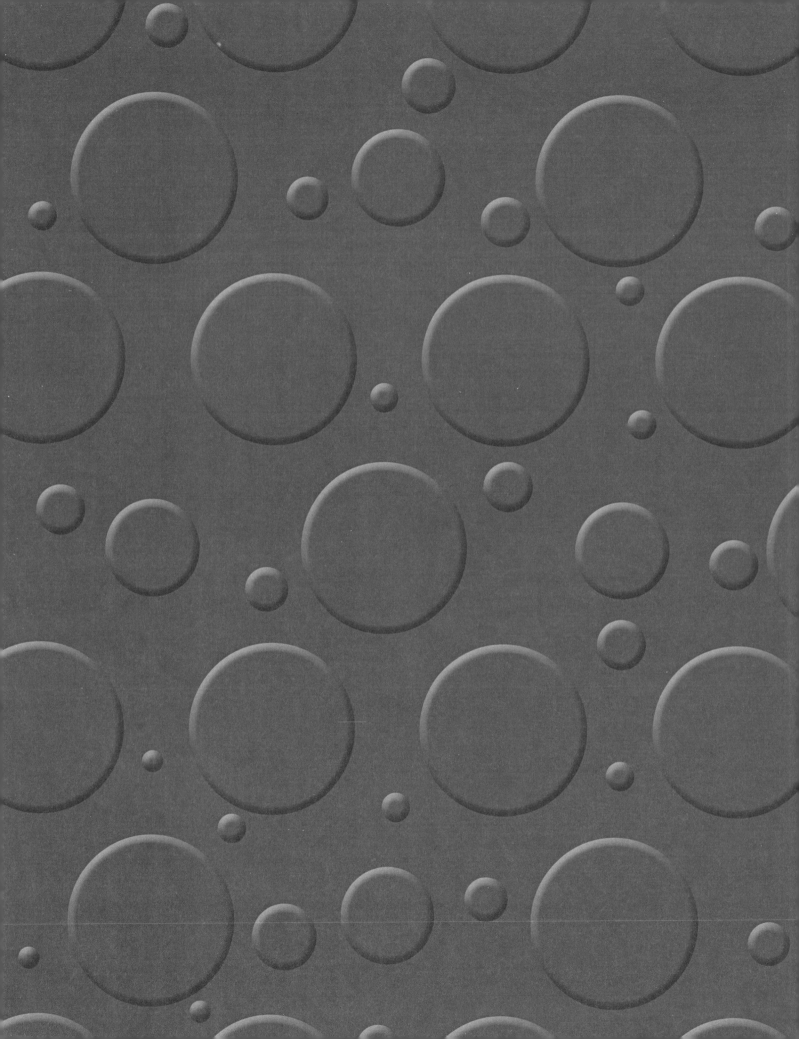